2/1/12
$85.00

CRITICAL
INSIGHTS

Mrs. Dalloway

by Virginia Woolf

CRITICAL INSIGHTS

Mrs. Dalloway

by Virginia Woolf

Editor
Dorothy Dodge Robbins
Louisiana Tech University

Salem Press
Pasadena, California   Hackensack, New Jersey

Cover photo: The Granger Collection, New York

Copyright © 2012 by Salem Press,
a Division of EBSCO Publishing, Inc.

Editor's text © 2012 by Dorothy Dodge Robbins
"The *Paris Review* Perspective" © 2012 by Thessaly La Force for *The Paris Review*

∞ The paper used in these volumes conforms to the American National Standard for Permanence of Paper for Printed Library Materials, Z39.48-1992 (R1997).

Library of Congress Cataloging-in-Publication Data
Mrs. Dalloway, by Virginia Woolf / editor, Dorothy Dodge Robbins.
    p. cm. — (Critical insights)
Includes bibliographical references and index.
    ISBN 978-1-58765-841-9 (alk. paper) — ISBN 978-1-58765-821-1 (set, Critical insights : alk. paper)
    1. Woolf, Virginia, 1882-1941. Mrs. Dalloway. 2. Psychological fiction, English—History and criticism. 3. Stream of consciousness fiction, English—History and criticism. 4. Married women in literature. I. Robbins, Dorothy Dodge.
    PR6045.O72M737 2012
    823'.912—dc22
                                                    2011019118

PRINTED IN CANADA

Contents

"The sane & the insane, side by side": The Object-Relations of
Self-Management in *Mrs. Dalloway*, Thomas C. Caramagno

Resources_____

About This Volume

Dorothy Dodge Robbins

Readers can envision Clarissa Dalloway living in the fashionable Westminster district of London, near Big Ben and the Houses of Parliament, preparing for her party in one of the stately brick buildings that tower over narrow Barton Street. In 1923 Virginia Woolf found an attractive house for let on that very street, but the exorbitant rent precluded her move into the neighborhood. It is likely, however, that on her stroll down Barton Street, Woolf found the perfect residence for her memorable character, the social maven Mrs. Dalloway, whose story was, at that very moment, incubating in her creator's mind.

There are many rooms in the house of *Mrs. Dalloway*, sufficient in number to accommodate the varied critical responses elicited over the years by readings of Virginia Woolf's fourth novel. *Mrs. Dalloway* is so rich in subject matter, form, character, and style that nearly every critical approach in practice has been employed in response to this substantial work. There is room enough to house biographical, cultural, historical, psychological, formalist, gender, and comparative studies, among others. Frequently two or more of these approaches converge to further illuminate the novel. This volume serves as a depository for a representative range of scholarly interpretations about *Mrs. Dalloway*.

The purpose behind this volume is three-fold: to enhance readers' understanding of this work; to facilitate research and new writing about *Mrs. Dalloway*; and to foster greater appreciation of Woolf's acclaimed novel. To that end, six original chapters plus *The Paris Review* have been prepared exclusively for this work. In addition, ten previously published works, journal articles or chapters from books, have been selected for inclusion based on the merits of their contributions to Woolf studies in this area. Finally, a detailed bibliography of recent *Mrs. Dalloway* scholarship is provided to direct readers to additional sources of study. Students, teachers, and lay readers alike may find this volume a useful resource for informing their own responses to *Mrs. Dalloway*.

Works Original to This Volume

An appropriate place to begin a study of *Mrs. Dalloway* is with its author, Virginia Woolf. Thomas C. Caramagno's "Biography of Virginia Woolf" provides essential information about the novelist's life and offers a backdrop for the study of her extensive oeuvre. Caramagno presents factors relevant to Woolf's emergence and achievements as a modern writer. As major influences upon her work, he cites Woolf's Victorian upbringing, her happy childhood marred by tragedy, her affiliation with the Bloomsbury Group, her partnership with her husband Leonard (including their operation of the Hogarth Press), her lifelong condition as a manic-depressive, and her intimate relationships with other women. In contrast to biographers who classify Woolf as a secluded intellectual who wrote largely independent of world events, Caramagno depicts Woolf as a writer vitally in touch with the historical and political times that informed her writings and to which her writings responded.

"On *Mrs. Dalloway*" presents an overview of Woolf's 1925 novel and includes information about the work's origins and composition. In this chapter, I discuss James Joyce's *Ulysses* and T. S. Eliot's "The Waste Land" as acknowledged influences upon Woolf's novel. I consider Woolf's rejection of Victorian realism and the novelist's efforts to create a new form for the novel appropriate for a new age. But while Woolf's *Mrs. Dalloway* breaks with Victorian realism, it pays homage to an earlier group of writers, the Romantics. Poet John Keats and his aesthetics are discussed as an important, but often neglected, influence upon *Mrs. Dalloway*. Finally, the novel's legacy is evaluated in terms of its numerous offspring.

Vereen M. Bell elucidates the turbulent historical era that inspired Woolf to create *Mrs. Dalloway*. In "The 'Death of the Soul' in *Mrs. Dalloway*," Bell analyzes world events and social conditions that provide context for the novel, chief among them World War I and the industrialized military power of modern European nations. Bell reveals how—despite the best efforts of members of the privileged classes in

London to isolate themselves from reminders of that devastation—the aftermath of war intrudes upon Clarissa Dalloway's social gathering, creating a necessary disquiet. Nationalism, class division, and women's suffrage also are examined to provide additional context for the novel's numerous characters, events, and themes.

Whereas Bell's assessment of Woolf's novel includes a broad spectrum of contextual material, Justyna Kostkowska narrows the critical lens in "'All Taken Together': Ecological Form in *Mrs. Dalloway.*" In her chapter, she focuses upon environmental issues vital to the novel. Offering an eco-critical interpretation, Kostkowska discerns the form and style of *Mrs. Dalloway*, in particular the author's use of free indirect discourse, to be representative of Woolf's larger vision of the world: one composed of varied but interrelated elements. As Kostkowska observes in her chapter, "Woolf's novel models a web of relationships in a diverse ecosystem and shows how overtly dissimilar beings are inherently connected and interdependent."

In "A Dialogue in Books: Virginia Woolf's *Mrs. Dalloway* and Michael Cunningham's *The Hours*," Yelena Furman examines the intertextual relationship that exists between these companion works. She posits that Cunningham's 1998 novel is irrevocably bound to Woolf's 1925 novel, *Mrs. Dalloway*, while simultaneously *The Hours* exists independent of its source story. Furman identifies a shared feature of these works in their respective authors' abilities to create thematic links between characters. Cunningham, in his homage to Woolf's novel, adds another dimension to this connection as he links his characters back to Woolf's. But Furman likewise highlights where these two works diverge, noting for instance that Cunningham breaks with Woolf's more experimental literary "devices to produce a more stylistically straightforward work."

Pam Fox Kuhlken provides both a summary and an assessment of responses to Woolf's novel in her chapter, "*Mrs. Dalloway* and the Critics." Kuhlken begins with Woolf's contemporaries, including novelist E. M. Forster, who were among the first to voice their opinions about their, in many cases, friend and competitor's novel. Progressing decade by decade, Kuhlken examines scholarly publications that reflect not only diverse reactions to *Mrs. Dalloway* but also developments in methods of literary inquiry. From New Criticism to Deconstruction, practitioners have found something decisive to say about *Mrs. Dalloway*. A separate section on feminist criticism is provided that substantiates the popularity of that particular approach to Woolf's novel. Furthermore, Kuhlken considers the ongoing appeal of this novel to scholars and suggests that the critical inquiry is likely to continue.

In her *Paris Review* piece, Thessaly La Force asks, "Who is Mrs. Dalloway?" Drawing upon competing and often contradictory images provided in the novel, La Force offers a multifaceted answer to this essential question. A portrait appears of a middle-aged woman who is simultaneously confident and insecure; young and old; outgoing and withdrawn; selfish and selfless; in short, a complex character who evades easy categorization. La Force considers as well the novel's response to World War I in its depiction of the shell-shocked war veteran, Septimus Warren Smith, who acts as Mrs. Dalloway's counterpoint and who is an equally enigmatic character. Finally, La Force reminds readers that at the time of its publication, *Mrs. Dalloway* was truly a radical work of literature, the likes of which had not been seen.

Works Reprinted in This Volume

The largest category of reprinted works contained in this volume is, not surprisingly, in the field of comparative literature. *Mrs. Dalloway* is by its very nature dialogic, engaged effectively in an ongoing conversation with other stories. This dialogism is present in the novel's numerous literary allusions to works by other authors, including William Shakespeare. Thus Woolf's novel invites comparison with other works of literature, both those that influenced its composition, like Homer's *Odyssey* (eighth century B.C.E.), and those that it has in turn influenced, like Toni Morrison's *Sula* (1973). Molly Hoff's "The Pseudo-Homeric World of *Mrs. Dalloway*" (1999) examines how "Virginia Woolf paraphrases, parodies, and burlesques a chrestomathy of texts, Homer included, as part of the novel's encyclopedic repertoire." Hoff defends Woolf against charges she appropriated James Joyce's Homeric update, *Ulysses* (1922), to gather material for *Mrs. Dalloway.* Instead, Hoff identifies Woolf's more subtle incorporation of Homeric elements. Lorie Watkins Fulton's "'A Direction of One's Own': Alienation in *Mrs. Dalloway* and *Sula*" (2006) identifies connections between Woolf's and Morrison's characters and themes. Fulton posits that Morrison—whose graduate thesis explored alienation in Woolf's oeuvre—borrows from her literary predecessor to develop similar themes, though updated, for a different cultural-historical place and time: Morrison's racially divided town in Ohio during the years between the world wars.

Scholars often compare *Mrs. Dalloway* to Woolf's next novel, the equally acclaimed and popular *To the Lighthouse* (1927). Susan Bennett Smith's "Reinventing Grief Work: Virginia Woolf's Feminist Representations of Mourning in *Mrs. Dalloway* and *To the Lighthouse*" (1995) evaluates these novels' dissimilar approaches to bereavement. Smith observes that *Mrs. Dalloway* cautions against anaesthetizing sorrow, while *To the Lighthouse* "provides a positive model for grief work" as characters express and thus expiate their loss through physical and creative labors. Smith concludes that in *Mrs. Dalloway* grief is problematically feminized, while in *To the Lighthouse* the emotion appears more effectively gender-neutral. In Kathryn Stelmach Artuso's "From Text to Tableau: Ekphrastic Enchantment in *Mrs. Dalloway* and *To the Lighthouse*" (2006), the focus is on Woolf's adaptation of visual and auditory art forms for literary purposes. Stelmach Artuso proposes that Woolf transcends time and space limitations in these two novels, thus avoiding artistic stasis, through the "imaginative motion of memory."

Cultural and historical studies consider how the beliefs, practices, and shared experiences of a group of people provide context for a work of literature. In Woolf studies, this focus frequently includes an examination of Victorian and modern points of view. Christopher Herbert's "*Mrs. Dalloway*, the Dictator, and the Relativity Paradox" (2001) proposes that Woolf's intent in *Mrs. Dalloway* was to espouse relativism, a philosophy often associated with the moderns, chiefly as a deterrent to the violence inherent in absolutist thought and practice, typically associated with the Victorians. This absolutism would soon become associated with the rise of fascism in Europe. Herbert believes Woolf warns against the tyranny of dictatorship throughout her novel, most vividly in her portrayal of Sir William Bradshaw, the specialist whose insistence on committing Septimus Warren Smith to a rest home contributes to the veteran's suicide. George A. Panichas's "Virginia Woolf's *Mrs. Dalloway:* 'A Well of Tears'" (2004) focuses on the historical situation that informed Woolf's novel. He perceives *Mrs. Dalloway* to be expressive of the malaise that afflicted both individuals and their societies following the devastation of World War I.

Formalist studies examine the literary elements that compose a work of literature, excluding any consideration of the author's life and times. Since *Mrs. Dalloway's* publication in 1925, many critics have responded to the novel's experimental structure through formalist inquiry. Nathalia Wright's "*Mrs. Dalloway*: A Study in Composition" (1944) deems *Mrs. Dalloway* a "thematic study, juxtaposing certain patterns for purely aesthetic ends." Wright identifies these patterns as reflective of character, psychology, time (as expressed through sound), and color. She further notes that together these patterns function as a kaleidoscope to project images of human consciousness and memory throughout the novel. Interest in the novel's innovations with temporal and spatial elements has not waned. Teresa Prudente explores nonlinear representations of time in *Mrs. Dalloway* in "A-linear Time and Stream of Consciousness," a chapter from her Woolf study, *A Specially Tender Piece of Eternity* (2008). Prudente discusses the fluid timeframe evoked in the novel through Woolf's use of stream-of-consciousness techniques. In particular, Prudente notes how Septimus Warren Smith, the young mentally ill war veteran, experiences a-linear time as a separation rather than an escape from reality.

Gender studies focus on portrayals of men and women in fiction, and consider how these depictions reinforce or dismantle culturally acquired stereotypes of male and female identities and social roles. Jacob Littleton's "*Mrs. Dalloway*: Portrait of the Artist as a Middle-Aged Woman" (1995) offers such a study. Littleton argues that Mrs. Dalloway's artistry is essential to an understanding of her character. Clarissa's art, which he believes to be expressed through the creation of her party, is muted by the patriarchal ideology of her day that did not acknowledge the existence of artistry in the realm of women.

Psychological studies probe human consciousness and behavior as portrayed in works of literature, frequently, though not necessarily, through the application of theories made prominent by Sigmund Freud and Carl Jung. Thomas C. Caramagno's "'The sane & the insane, side by side': The Object-Relations of Self-Management in *Mrs. Dalloway*," a chapter from his psychobiography *The Flight of the Mind: Virginia Woolf's Art and Manic-Depressive Illness* (1992), breaks with traditional studies by considering Woolf's novel in light of her own experience with manic-depressive illness. Caramagno notes how bipolar symptoms are exhibited by certain characters to varying degrees, including Clarissa Dalloway, Peter Walsh, and Septimus Warren Smith. He further demonstrates the manner in which Woolf's knowledge of her illness influenced other facets of *Mrs. Dalloway*, including structure, style, and theme.

Obviously, thoughtful analytical attention to *Mrs. Dalloway* is far from complete. Additional insights and considerations will continue to emerge even as this volume is being read.

THE BOOK
AND
AUTHOR

On *Mrs. Dalloway*
Dorothy Dodge Robbins

"Life, London, this moment in June" (4): with these six words Virginia Woolf situates her novel about Clarissa Dalloway, seeker of society and of solitude, upon a scale that both encompasses the enormous—"life, London"—and the miniscule—"this moment in June." It is a novel that is simultaneously overtly public and intimately private. As readers, we are privy to the thoughts of Clarissa Dalloway and other characters, both major and minor, and we follow events, both climactic and mundane, throughout this single June day in 1923 London. The scope of *Mrs. Dalloway* (1925) is vast and exceeds the parameters of time and space, as Woolf intended, through her deliberate experiments with form and style. *Mrs. Dalloway* is monumental as well in terms of its reception by readers and critics. *Mrs. Dalloway* is Woolf's fourth of nine novels and for sheer literary acclaim and popularity vies only with her fifth novel, *To the Lighthouse* (1927), another work that features a day in the life of a middle-aged woman, a day that ends with a dinner party hosted by its heroine. But that day occupies only the first section of *To the Lighthouse*; its story line traverses a decade in section two and returns to a second single day ten years later in section three. The matriarch, Mrs. Ramsey, unlike the socialite Mrs. Dalloway, dies early; only memories of her permeate the rest of the work. In *Mrs. Dalloway*, Clarissa remains a living presence from the first line that opens upon a June morning until the last line that brings the evening and the novel to a close, from "Mrs. Dalloway said she would buy the flowers herself" (3) to "there she was" (194). Mrs. Dalloway never leaves her novel; even in those scenes where she is not tangibly present, her presence is felt. For though we may travel through the thoughts of other characters and their alternate perceptions, we know that it is back to her thoughts and perceptions that we shall return. Virginia Woolf, who considered a number of titles in the process of completing her manuscript for *Mrs. Dalloway*, among them *A Lady of Fashion* and

The Life of a Lady (Hussey 172), chose with exactness in the end: for it is one specific lady, Clarissa Dalloway, that forms the novel's heart.

Origins

As a character Mrs. Dalloway lives an earlier life, one that precedes the famous novel that bears her name. She debuts in Woolf's first novel, *The Voyage Out* (1916), in which Mrs. Dalloway and her politician husband Richard, both minor characters, appear as passengers aboard a ship where they befriend the novel's heroine, Rachel Vinrace. Though underdeveloped as a character in her inaugural appearance, Clarissa Dalloway's interest in parties, her love of British literature, and her upper-class pretensions are present, and these traits are enhanced in *Mrs. Dalloway* (1925). The character also features in several of Woolf's short stories, including "Mrs. Dalloway in Bond Street," published in the collection *Mrs. Dalloway's Party* (1973), along with other sketches. To suggest that Woolf was obsessed with Mrs. Dalloway is an overstatement; but, obviously, Clarissa was a character that Woolf felt a need to explore more fully in a longer and more complex work. The genesis of Mrs. Dalloway's male double, the shell-shocked Septimus Warren Smith, likewise is traceable to a preliminary piece, "The Prime Minister" (1922), a story in which a disturbed war veteran plans to assassinate the title character. While trace elements of these two stories survive into the novel—"Mrs. Dalloway in Bond Street" narrates Clarissa's famous walk through London, for example—*Mrs. Dalloway* is an independent work and not a continuation of either story. In the course of writing *Mrs. Dalloway*, Woolf herself changed directions. Initially she intended to kill Clarissa, either as a suicide or from natural causes, but the novel's climactic death scene, a fatal leap from a window onto a spiked fence, was reserved for Septimus. Mrs. Dalloway is spared to ponder his fate and its relevance to her life in a quiet moment in the midst of her noisome party.

Woolf began writing *Mrs. Dalloway* in 1922; she would establish the timeframe of the novel's events as a June day in 1923. During the novel's gestation, Woolf herself grappled with the problem of breaking with the certitude of her literary predecessors, eminent Victorian authors such as Charles Dickens (1812-1870) and William Makepeace Thackeray (1811-1863), and their authoritative and unambiguous accounts of men and women and their respective lives. While Woolf's first two novels, *The Voyage Out* (1916) and *Night and Day* (1919), were largely grounded in such Victorian realism, her third, *Jacob's Room* (1922), cast off such practices by recounting the life and death of soldier Jacob Flanders, a victim of the Great War, with the title character chiefly absent from his own story. With her fourth novel, Woolf hoped to improve upon her earlier experimentation with character, form, and style. She mused about *Jacob's Room* and its potential critics, "If they say all this is clever experiment, I shall produce Mrs. Dalloway in Bond Street as the finished product" (*Diary 2* 178). In her diary entries from the time, Woolf described her efforts to compose *The Hours*, one of the working titles of the novel that would become *Mrs. Dalloway:* "I foresee, to return to The Hours, that this is going to be the devil of a struggle. The design is so queer & so masterful. I'm always having to wrench my substance to fit it" (249). She also expressed her desire for the structure of the new work: "It is to be a most complicated spirited solid piece, knitting together everything & ending on three notes . . . each saying something to sum up Clarissa" (*Diary 2* 312). The final "note" of the novel offers just such a summation in three words, when Peter Walsh, Clarissa's first suitor whom she abandoned in her youth in order to marry Richard Dalloway, observes "It is Clarissa," and the narrator echoes in affirmation "For there she was" (194), and the novel ends.

Even as Woolf broke free of Victorian constraints through her efforts to create a new form and style for the modern novel, she embraced their immediate predecessors, the Romantics, whose influence upon her writing, and upon *Mrs. Dalloway*, is evident. One poet in particular was much admired by Virginia Woolf, who observed of John

Keats (1795-1821) that "no one would wish to sacrifice a line that Keats ever wrote" (*Collected Essays* 2: 229). Keats is mentioned directly in *Mrs. Dalloway* when the narration shifts from Septimus Warren Smith's memories of his prewar education to the thoughts of his instructor at the time, Isabel Pole: "Was he not like Keats? she asked; and reflected how she might give him a taste of *Antony and Cleopatra* and the rest" (85). But the poet's aesthetic theory is a more palpable influence upon Woolf's novel. Keats explored in his poetry the "tangle of inseparable, but irreconcilable opposites" (Greenblatt 1821) that comprised human experience in his Romantic world. *Mrs. Dalloway*, Woolf's magnum opus, is a work that not only examines but also manages to integrate the inseparable but irreconcilable opposites of her own modern life and times. In *Mrs. Dalloway*, Woolf presents various dichotomous pairs and explores the fluidity of their supposed boundaries, marking not so much their intersections but the points at which they blur. Youth and age, men and women, heterosexual and homosexual, lower class and upper class, the foreign and the familiar, town and country, war and peace, public and private, past and present, the sane and the insane, interiors and exteriors, the natural and the artificial, land and water, clock time and psychological time, life and death: these and other pairings are contrasted and blended in this novel about a single day in the life of Clarissa Dalloway during which she anticipates and then enacts her famous party. While tensions between these binaries are exhibited throughout this June day—a chronology pronounced by the chiming of various clocks throughout London but obscured by their echoes—the evening hours of the social gathering engender a momentary, if necessarily impermanent, resolution to their oppositions.

Contemporary Influences

In the experimental structure and style of *Mrs. Dalloway*, Woolf also was influenced by her contemporaries, in particular James Joyce

(1882-1941), the Irish author of *Ulysses* (1922), a novel that explores one day in the life of Leopold Bloom, a Jewish businessman self-consciously residing in staunchly Catholic Dublin, Ireland. Woolf's response to Joyce's masterpiece was ambivalent; she recorded in her diary that she felt at intervals "amused, stimulated, charmed interested . . . then puzzled, bored, irritated, & disillusioned" (*Diary 2* 188). The structure of Joyce's novel follows Bloom's perambulations, both mental and physical, throughout the city. Like Joyce, Woolf centers the action of her novel within her characters' minds in a style termed stream of consciousness, in which the thoughts, feelings, and memories of various characters are presented directly to the reader without the assistance or interpretation of a traditional narrator. And like Joyce's homage to Dublin, Woolf pays tribute to the great city of her birth, London, and its environs. Both Joyce and Woolf draw from classical literature, Homer's *Odyssey* (which Woolf reread in 1922) in particular, for subject matter for their respective novels. While Joyce consciously parallels events from Homer, including encounters with modern-day sirens and a Cyclops, Woolf's allusions to the epic are more subtle than Joyce's.

Homer's *Odyssey* recounts Ulysses's journey home to Ithaca by boat following the Trojan wars. He and his crew of soldiers encounter many sea dangers en route, so it is appropriate that water imagery, often suggestive of drowning, be prevalent in Woolf's novel. Both Clarissa and Septimus express sensations of engulfment at various points in the novel; only Clarissa will rise to the surface, while Septimus dives to his death. Furthermore, while Woolf's doubles, Clarissa and Septimus, maintain separate paths throughout London, never meeting face to face, the journeys of Joyce's doubles, the businessman Leopold Bloom and the young teacher Stephen Dedalus, eventually converge and the duo spend a significant portion of the novel together in the "Circe" chapter, which recounts their visit to a brothel where the timid Bloom emerges as the drunken Stephen's protector. Clarissa and Septimus cannot meet; their separate stations in life, mental conditions, and chosen goals for the day—Clarissa to host a party and Septimus to terminate his life—preclude such a meeting. Though their observations on life at times reflect the other's perspective, they remain isolated from each other physically, and neither one will prove to be the other's protector.

Woolf also was influenced by the ideas of modern poet T. S. Eliot (1888-1965). During the period when she began to write *Mrs. Dalloway*, she also typeset—a laborious process involving letter-by-letter insertion into a template—Eliot's poem *The Waste Land* (1922) for publication through the Hogarth Press, a literary press founded and operated by Virginia and her husband, Leonard. Like *Mrs. Dalloway*, the poem is set in postwar London and highlights extreme oppositions, including birth and death, barrenness and fecundity, drought and downpour, and Woolf may have been influenced by Eliot's own water imagery as she composed *Mrs. Dalloway*. In Part I of Eliot's poem, a tarot reader reveals a card bearing the image of the drowned Phoenician Sailor and warns her client to "fear death by water" (55); Part IV returns to that prediction with its assignation "DEATH BY DROWNING." Eliot's narrator, one of multiple voices in *The Waste Land*, acknowledges society's stagnation and its need for renewal, a topic also under examination in *Mrs. Dalloway*. He queries, "What are the roots that clutch, what branches grow/ Out of this stony rubbish? Son of man,/ You cannot say, or guess, for you know only/ A heap of broken images" (19-22).

Eliot's interwoven themes of alienation and fragmentation are present as well in *Mrs. Dalloway*, particularly in the character and circumstances of Septimus Warren Smith, whose shell shock has caused him to withdraw into a broken world of his own mental projection. But other characters suffer alienation as well, including the title character whose recent illness has forced her to withdraw from society, a situation she hopes to remedy by throwing her party. The marginalization of historian Miss Kilman, tutor to Mrs. Dalloway's daughter Elizabeth, is ensured by her German ancestry, lesbian orientation, outsider's view of historical events, and reduced economic circumstances. Peter Walsh, who just that day has returned from years in civil service in India to petition the courts for a divorce for his lover, Daisy, feels the changes in the city to be so disorienting he experiences a hallucinatory dream while resting on a bench in Regents Park. Novelist E. M. Forster, a friend of Woolf's and a fellow member of the Bloomsbury Group, coined a mantra for what ailed members of modern society, "simply connect," and used it as the epigram for *Howards End* (1910), his novel about divisions between social classes. Such connection between people proves difficult in an alienating world. Shortly before he commits suicide, a skeptical Septimus parrots medical platitudes, "Communication is health; communication is happiness" (93), advice he knows to be insufficient to engender his recovery, while Clarissa acknowledges the distance that exists between all people: "And there is a dignity in people; a solitude; even between husband and wife a gulf; and that one must respect" (120). In their works written during this time period, both Eliot and Woolf grappled with the changes wrought by the First World War and its alienating effects upon men and women.

Inseparable, but Irreconcilable Opposites

Although in length the novel is less than two hundred pages and in setting limited to a single day in a single city, *Mrs. Dalloway* is nevertheless epic in its scope, covering a vast expanse of experience through its presentation of numerous themes, emotions, and ideas central to humanity. That Woolf is able to present such a broad picture of life on a relatively small scale is due largely to her use of inseparable, but irreconcilable opposites, which are juxtaposed throughout the novel. These binaries are useful in revealing the human condition in postwar London as one that is not only uncertain but also in flux. Frequently, Woolf blurs the boundaries that ostensibly separate one from the other in these sets, men from women, the sane from the insane, the private self from its public persona, but tensions between these oppositions are never fully resolved. They are like magnetic impulses, alternately attracted and repelled depending on their alignment.

A binary essential to the theme and plot of *Mrs. Dalloway* is sanity and insanity. Woolf records her intent to present "a study of insanity & suicide: the world seen by the sane & the insane side by side" (*Diary 2* 207). Clearly Septimus Warren Smith suffers from mental illness; the world he envisions is grossly distorted through his altered perception, a remnant of his horrific war experiences. In one scene, peaceful Regents Park becomes a psychological battle field as the traumatized veteran projects fantastic visions onto its manicured lawns and orderly paths: before his eyes a terrier threatens to mutate into a man; his dead friend Evans brings messages from the next world; and birds in the tree branches sing to him in Greek, their notes decoding the secrets of the universe. Seated next to him, literally side by side on a park bench, is the sane Rezia, his war bride. Her husband's suffering enhances her own rational comprehension of isolation and loneliness. She is an Italian residing in a foreign city where her British husband is the most foreign to her of all London's inhabitants. Rezia recognizes how close she is to crossing over to his despair and perhaps sharing in his madness, "Septimus let himself think about horrible things, as she could too, if she tried" (66), but she resists. Woolf locates the source of Septimus's break with reality as the repression of his feelings following his friend's combat death: "far from showing any emotion or recognizing that here was the end of a friendship, [he] congratulated himself upon feeling very little and very reasonably. The War had taught him. It was sublime" (86). Septimus transforms the horrific into the sublime, a dog into a man, and ultimately life into death. Ironically, it is at the point of suicide that he appears most clearheaded: "He did not want to die. Life was good. The sun was hot. Only human beings—what did they want? . . . 'I'll give it to you!'" (149). While he questions what people want, he quickly decides it is his life, but when he gives his life by plunging from the ledge onto the spiked fence, it is not to the plural and anonymous "them" he gives it, but to the more personal second person "you," the final word he utters. He gives it—his life— to Dr. Holmes, who has been arranging Septimus's removal to, and subsequent incarceration in, an asylum; he gives it to the old man who observes events from a staircase across the street and with whom Septimus makes brief eye contact prior to jumping; and he gives it to the "you" that is the reader, a moment of communication that at last allows him to break from the confines of his story. Clarissa, hearing of his death at her party, concludes that the young man's "Death was defiance . . . an attempt to communicate" (184). She is another "you" to whom his death is offered. Septimus becomes the sacrificial lamb as well for a society that has masked the insanity of war behind personal respectability and national honor.

Not even the title character in *Mrs. Dalloway* is allowed an unambiguous presentation. The two men in her life, Richard Dalloway and Peter Walsh, cannot agree on the nature of Clarissa's interest in social gatherings:

> They thought, or Peter at any rate thought, that she enjoyed imposing herself; liked to have famous people about her; great names; was simply a snob in short. Well, Peter might think so. Richard merely thought it foolish of her to like excitement when she knew it was bad for her heart. It was childish, he thought. And both were quite wrong. What she liked was simply life. (121)

But all three perspectives—Peter's, Richard's, and the narrator's— are incomplete. Clarissa is both a public and a private person. Her own thoughts vacillate from one extreme to the other, from a desire to withdraw "like a nun" (31) to the solitude of her room to an equally strong impulse to rejoin her party after contemplating the relevance of Septimus's death: "But she must go back. She must assemble. She must find Sally and Peter. And she came in from the little room" (186). Critics still differ about whether Clarissa is compassionate or indifferent to the suffering of the world, satisfied with her marriage to Richard or still pining after Peter, heterosexual or lesbian in her sexual orientation, accepting or defiant of her own aging process, for or against the disintegration of class society, Victorian or modern in her world views. Woolf suggests in her presentation of differing images of Clarissa Dalloway that she may possess all of these attributes, feelings, and views, may be shifting from one to another or, at times, embracing contradictory positions. That is why it is difficult for readers and critics to offer a definitive assessment of the character Clarissa Dalloway or of the novel as a whole. Like many works in the modern tradition, *Mrs. Dalloway* allows little resolution and the novel ends ambiguously with the line "For there she was" (194), a reference to Clarissa that offers no summative account or judgment of Woolf's character, no description of her attire or manner, no clue to her next action, and no revelation of what she might be feeling at this moment in time. She is there, a presence, and no more. At this point, readers must accept this vague narrative proclamation or define Mrs. Dalloway for themselves. Readers seeking closure must bring it to the novel, and they may do so in error, because *Mrs. Dalloway* is a novel that resists closure.

Legacy

The enduring relevance of *Mrs. Dalloway* is apparent in its thriving literary presence and cultural manifestations. The novel is not only required reading for most college and university English curricula, but a popular selection for book clubs as well as the solitary reader. Woolf's story about a day in the life of a middle-aged woman hosting a party in an affluent neighborhood of 1923 London, and its correlative account of events leading up to the suicide of a mentally ill war veteran, has generated numerous offspring. *Mrs. Dalloway's* heirs include the Pulitzer Prize-winning *The Hours* by Michael Cunningham (1998), a novel with multiple and interwoven storylines. Cunningham's characters include a mid-twentieth-century reader of Woolf's classic novel as well as late-century characters modeled after those in *Mrs. Dalloway*, and even a fictional portrayal of Woolf herself in the process of writing her work. Rather than limiting himself to a single day, the author of *The Hours* allows his story to span decades and to cross the ocean to America as it pays homage to its predecessor, *Mrs. Dalloway*, and its source of inspiration, Virginia Woolf. Robin Lippincott's *Mr. Dalloway* (1999) and John Lanchester's *Mr. Phillips* (2000) also draw upon or allude to characters first introduced in Woolf's novel. Lippincott borrows subject matter from Woolf's novel, including homosexuality, as he narrates a story about a gay love affair involving his title character, Richard Dalloway. Lanchester switches Clarissa's gender and updates the time period in which she lives in his novel, *Mr. Phillips*, as he portrays one day in the life of a middle-aged man as he experiences downward economic and emotional spirals.

Likewise the medium of film has introduced *Mrs. Dalloway* to new generations of viewers and potential readers. A successful film version adapted from Woolf's novel was produced in 1997, and featured Vanessa Redgrave as Mrs. Dalloway and Rupert Graves as Septimus Warren Smith. More recently the 2002 award-winning film version of Cunningham's *The Hours*, starring Nicole Kidman as Virginia Woolf and Meryl Streep as a modern-day Clarissa, garnered both critical and popular acclaim, and induced many of its viewers to explore works by (or about) Virginia Woolf for themselves. There have been musical adaptations as well, including the chamber opera *Mrs. Dalloway* (1993) by Libby Larsen and Bonnie Grice. Likely more *Mrs. Dalloway* descendents are in development, but the book itself still trumps all works that claim it as their inspiration. Frequently these literary, film, and musical tributes guide readers, viewers, and listeners alike back to their font: Woolf's remarkable 1925 novel, *Mrs. Dalloway*, in which a woman gathers the living in her home to celebrate their social connections, while blocks away a war veteran has taken his life to assert his permanent disconnection from all society.

That the novel endures is evident, but how can one explain its continuing appeal? How account for the fact that *Mrs. Dalloway* remains a widely read and frequently reread classic? At the time of its publication in 1925, the novel was received by readers and, in particular, by literary critics, as wholly original in style, concept, and characterization. Woolf had envisioned, and succeeded, in producing a new novel for a new era, one that had been utterly changed by recent global events. That *Mrs. Dalloway* should still read as fresh today as it did then is testimony to Woolf's genius, and assures the novel's status as not only one of the great works of British literature, but of the world. Certainly Virginia Woolf has created one of the most memorable female characters in literature. "Remember my party tonight!" (48) Clarissa Dalloway cries out to Peter Walsh as he departs her home following their afternoon visit, and like Peter, we do. And perhaps, like Peter, we are "unable to get away from the thought of her" (76) and so we return to Woolf's novel and to Clarissa Dalloway.

Works Cited

Eliot, T. S. "The Waste Land." *T. S. Eliot: The Complete Poems and Plays 1909-1950*. New York: Harcourt, 1980. 37-55.

Forster, E. M. *Howards End*. New York: Penguin, 2000.

Hussey, Mark. *Virginia Woolf A-Z*. New York: Oxford UP, 1995.

"John Keats." *The Norton Anthology of English Literature* 8th ed. Ed. Stephen Greenblatt. New York: Norton, 2006. 1820-22.

Woolf, Virginia. *Collected Essays*. 4 vols. New York: Harcourt, 1967.

_____. *The Diary of Virginia Woolf*. Vol 2. Eds. Anne Olivier Bell and Andrew McNeillie. New York: Harcourt, 1978.

_____. *Mrs. Dalloway*. New York: Harcourt, 1981.

_____. *Mrs. Dalloway's Party: A Short Story Sequence*. Ed. Stella McNichol. New York: Harvest/Harcourt, 1973.

Biography of Virginia Woolf _____

Thomas C. Caramagno

Virginia Woolf was born Adeline Virginia Stephen on January 25, 1882, to Julia Stephen and Sir Leslie Stephen at the family house, No. 22 Hyde Park Gate, London. The family was large and rife with tragic losses: Leslie's first wife, Harriet Thackeray, died suddenly during her second pregnancy. Their first child, Laura, was institutionalized all of her adult life for an unspecified mental illness. Woolf's mother, Julia, had three children, George, Stella, and Gerald, by her first husband, Herbert Duckworth (who died suddenly of an aneurysm). With chronic mourning in common, widower and widow married and had four more children: Vanessa, who became a painter; Thoby, who died of typhoid fever; Virginia; and Adrian, who became a psychoanalyst.

Nevertheless, Woolf remembered her childhood as one of unparalleled happiness. As a child, Woolf showed a precocious talent for narrative. She was the family storyteller and would create elaborate fantasies nightly. Her thirst for knowledge quickly outgrew the usual education a Victorian girl could receive. Only the sons were sent to school. When Thoby came home from Cambridge University, Woolf would quiz him on what he had learned. When he studied Greek at school, she studied it at home. She also had free run of her father's large library. The nine-year-old Woolf wrote her own newspaper accounts of family life, *The Hyde Park Gate News*, and she showed a flair for style, parodying famous writers of the day, some of whom she met. During this time Leslie served as the first editor of the *Dictionary of National Biography*, and so the family often was visited by eminent figures of Victorian literature—George Meredith, Henry James, Alfred Lord Tennyson—as well as scholars from Oxford and Cambridge.

But when Woolf's mother died of influenza in 1895, Woolf suffered her first manic-depressive breakdown, which lasted several months. Then Stella died of peritonitis at age twenty-eight. Then Leslie died of a protracted battle with intestinal cancer. The physical and emotional strains of caring for her father triggered another breakdown, this one so severe it was marked by delusions, auditory and visual hallucinations, and an attempted suicide. But manic depression is a periodic disorder, it comes and it goes, and within six months Woolf was well again. The Stephen children left the gloomy Hyde Park Gate house, moved to the lively and bohemian district of Bloomsbury. They invited friends over, nascent modernists who would talk about art and literature, sex and love, without Victorian prudery or convention. Informal Thursday night gatherings included young men such as the future art critics Clive Bell and Roger Fry, the historian Lytton Strachey, the philosopher G. E. Moore, the artist Desmond MacCarthy, the poet T. S. Eliot, the economist Maynard Keynes, and Leonard Woolf, who eventually became the principal political writer for the Liberal Party in England. They came to be known as the Bloomsbury Group, a first-rate dissident think tank that discussed socialism, feminism, homosexuality, and free love. No other group was asking such impertinent questions of British culture or living such unconventional lives. In 1912 Woolf married Leonard, sharing his passion for literature, politics and ideas, but not for sex. Instead, she had passionate love affairs with women: Violet Dickinson in her youth, Ethyl Smyth in her fifties; and in between there was the famous affair with novelist Vita Sackville-West.

With this Bloomsbury background, Woolf became a subversive writer, and that most dangerous kind of subversive, because she wrote about seemingly conventional subjects—family life, relationships, parties—but used them to question our most basic assumptions about how we make meaning. As *Mrs. Dalloway* shows, nothing threatens us so much as to suspect that our way of making interpretations does not differ essentially from the way an insane person does. Or a lesbian. Or a feminist. Use what category you want. We like it when the Other remains other, recognizably different, so that we can keep a safe distance. Woolf does not allow us this comfort zone.

To destabilize our reading, Woolf re-created the novel as a form in revolutionary ways. She did not write plots in the traditional sense;

summarizing the action in her novels is frustrating because its significance does not reside exactly in *what* happens but to *whom* it happens, *how* that character perceives it, and *what* meaning or lack of meaning was gained. She did not create characters readers can easily describe to non-readers. She resists easy formulas, dramatizing consciousness as a constantly shifting borderland between individuals and their environment, so permeable that nothing certain can be proved about either the individual or the environment because each is implicated in the construction/perception of the other. Certainty is a convenient illusion that is often self-serving, a form of paranoia fed by cultural logic. When Dr. Holmes wants to "convert" the psychotic war veteran Septimus Warren Smith in *Mrs. Dalloway*, one kind of paranoia elicits another. One is conventional, the other is not; the former is authorized, the latter pathologized.

Not surprisingly, there are many Woolfs to choose from when we read her critics. The Freudians see a neurotic woman who wrote about herself, but the Self they describe is in such denial that she doesn't seem worth reading. They assume that an ill author produces ill works, full of gaps and evasions, incomplete—until the critic fills in the missing pieces, altering meaning through posthumous editing. Since she fell in love with women, some critics slide sex and illness together, reading any desire that isn't directed toward men as evidence of frigidity or maladjustment. Aesthetes describe Woolf as an avant-garde experimentalist who hybridized literary genres, aiming for abstract form—but one removed from the real world of politics and history. Why, then, are *A Room of One's Own* and *Three Guineas* regarded today as groundbreaking feminist texts, rethinking the cultural and material conditions under which women are raised and oppressed? Can one read her 3,750 letters or the five volumes of her diary or the hundreds of her book reviews without recognizing that she clearly did not live in a vacuum? Woolf saw the political in everyday life.

Life's Work

In 1907 Woolf began writing her first novel, *The Voyage Out* (1915). Seemingly a conventional tale of a young woman who ventures out into the world to discover love and loss, in fact it is disturbing because the heroine's death by fever leaves an inexplicable gap at the end of the novel, a shapeless catastrophe that neither uplifts nor depresses. The reader struggles to make sense of it. The second novel, *Night and Day* (1919), was better received, but Woolf still used conventional techniques.

Then Woolf's creativity blossomed. With Leonard she founded the Hogarth Press, which not only allowed her to write what she wanted without the interference of editors, but to publish new and controversial writers, such as W. H. Auden, T. S. Eliot, Roger Fry, Rainer Maria Rilke, Rebecca West, Katherine Mansfield, and Sigmund Freud. Hogarth published Woolf's highly experimental short stories. Using stream-of-consciousness narrative techniques, complex psychological portraits of characters, and hybrids of literary genres (fiction-essay, fiction-drama, fiction-poetry, fiction-history), she redrew the boundaries of literature, leaving readers either puzzled or intoxicated or both.

In 1919 she published her manifesto, "Modern Fiction," rejecting Victorian and Edwardian realism, embracing modernism as a liberating rebellion against authority, rationalism, and objectivity in fiction:

> Life is not a series of gig lamps symmetrically arranged; but a luminous halo, a semi-transparent envelope surrounding us from the beginning of consciousness to the end. Is it not the task of the novelist to convey this varying, this unknown and uncircumscribed spirit, whatever aberration or complexity it may display, with as little mixture of the alien and external as possible? (*Common Reader* 154)

Modern characters, she believed, should only be "splinters & mosaics; not, as they used to hold, immaculate, monolithic, consistent wholes"

(*Diary 2* 314). In other words, to tell a new story, it must be told in a new way.

Jacob's Room (1922) put this theory to the test. A mock-*Bildungs-roman* ("coming-of-age" novel), the narrative's rapid transitions, shifting perspectives, and dream-like disconnectedness frustrate readers looking for guidance, predictability and truth. Jacob Flanders is impossible to pin down, his essential Self obscured by jingoistic British attitudes he learned at Cambridge that eventually lead to his senseless death in the First World War. Although his room is full of clues, we cannot hope to understand them. We are left with the narrator's own musings on how limited our knowledge of others—and even of ourselves—is. *Jacob's Room* may not seem like an antiwar novel, but it shakes the epistemological ground upon which patriotic gore stands.

Mrs. Dalloway (1925) brings the war home. The reader is led by a narrator who verbalizes the most intimate thoughts of various characters, one of whom is psychotic. But the descriptive style does not change from one character to another; the indirect interior monologues sound curiously alike, blending thoughts together. Like Jacob, Septimus is the victim of his own patriarchal upbringing, but unlike *Jacob's Room*, *Mrs. Dalloway* does not leave us dazed and hurt with an inexplicable loss. Instead, she offers us a vision of a profound unity of consciousness that heals the wound of loss.

To the Lighthouse (1927), seemingly an elegy to Woolf's childhood, subverts cultural assumptions about gender and parenting. Conventional readings see Mrs. Ramsay as "feminine" (intuitive, sensual, empathetic), while Mr. Ramsay is "masculine" (rational, objective, and repressive). But Woolf anticipated such interpretations and designed the text to subvert them, deconstructing Victorian verities about men and women in a way that foreshadows postmodernism. Still, Woolf was a modernist; in the end, she offers us a vision of unity that poetically fuses opposites. Lily Briscoe creates a satisfying solution in her painting of the Ramsays that reconciles without reducing the complexity of her subjects.

Adventurous and prolific, Woolf wrote three more masterpieces in the next five years: *Orlando: A Biography* (1928), *A Room of One's Own* (1929), and *The Waves* (1931). In *Orlando* Woolf combines biography, feminist theory, and history in such an irreverent way that imagination triumphs joyously over dull fact. The protagonist, born male in the Elizabethan age, is transformed into a woman in modern times, a transition that unveils the cultural construction of gender.

Published in 1928, one year after women got the vote in Britain, *A Room of One's Own* is a lecture that subverts traditional lecturing as a form of masculine domination. Woolf invites the audience to share in the construction of the lecture's meaning, which reveals the material conditions in which women are raised and taught that their subjugation is natural and good. Contemplating the privileged, well-fed, all-male students of Cambridge University, "I thought how unpleasant it is to be locked out; and I thought how it is worse perhaps to be locked in" (*Room* 24). Thinking outside the box is perhaps impossible if one has spent all of one's life comfortably inside the box.

In her next novel, *The Waves*, Woolf combined the genres of fiction, poetry, and drama.

Aiming for "an abstract mystical eyeless book: a playpoem" (*Diary 3* 203), she dramatizes a mind thinking by dividing it into six personas delivering "dramatic soliloquies" running "homogeneously in & out, in the rhythm of the waves" (*Diary 3* 312), sometimes sharing thoughts, images, and linguistic style, but each interprets perceptions differently. There are few external references and no narrator. Readers are treated as eavesdroppers, listening to voices that may only be the diverse thoughts of one mind, suggesting that consciousness requires more flexibility than a single narrative voice can provide.

The 1930s saw a gradual weakening of liberalism and modernism as the fascist threat loomed, and younger writers saw Bloomsbury aesthetics as naïvely pacifist, elitist, or irrelevant. Woolf's last two novels, *The Years* (1937) and *Between the Acts* (1941), were not calls to action but reflective, elegiac. Woolf's childhood dominates the former; her vision of healing art informs the latter. Neither excited the audience response she desired. Modernism by its very nature is ever questioning, exploratory, attempting the impossible: to represent the unrepresentable. By the end of Woolf's life, war had put an end to speculation as an unaffordable luxury.

Through most of Woolf's adult life, she suffered several major and many minor depressions, in which she found inspiration to explore consciousness. But in 1941 a very severe depression began, from which she did not think she would recover. She was afraid of being a burden to her Jewish husband at a time when Germany seemed on the verge of invading England, and, at age fifty-nine, she felt she did not have the strength to endure institutionalization. On March 28 she put stones into her jacket pockets and drowned herself in the River Ouse near her house in Sussex.

Bibliography

Barrett, Eileen, ed. *Virginia Woolf: Lesbian Readings*. New York: New York UP, 1997. The first book devoted entirely to Woolf's lesbianism, this collection of essays focuses on how Woolf's private and public experience and knowledge of same-sex love influenced her fiction.

Briggs, Julia. *Virginia Woolf: An Inner Life*. New York: Mariner, 2006. An intellectual biography that moves from Woolf's works to her mind—a lively, progressive, passionately engaged mind.

Dubino, Jeanne, ed. *Virginia Woolf and the Literary Marketplace*. New York: Palgrave Macmillan, 2010. This collection of essays examines the nearly six hundred essays and reviews that clearly express Woolf's brand of modernism.

Ellis, Steve. *Virginia Woolf and the Victorians*. New York: Cambridge UP, 2007. Did Woolf totally reject Victorian values? Ellis finds her work more complex a mixture of past and present than most readers give her credit for.

Froula, Christine. *Virginia Woolf and the Bloomsbury Avant-Garde: War, Civilization, and Modernity (Gender and Culture Series)*. New York: Columbia UP, 2005. Good medicine for anyone who thinks modernism is too abstract or artsy to be inherently political.

Goldman, Jane. *The Cambridge Introduction to Virginia Woolf*. New York: Cambridge UP, 2006. An informative introduction to Woolf's life, works, and cultural and critical contexts, useful for any student new to Woolf.

_____. *The Feminist Aesthetics of Virginia Woolf: Modernism, Post-*

Impressionism, and the Politics of the Visual. New York: Cambridge UP, 2001. An informative book, lavishly illustrated, especially well-suited for students of modernism, art history, and women's studies.

Lee, Hermione. *Virginia Woolf*. New York: Vintage, 1999. A massive, well-researched volume considered by many to be the best biography of Virginia Woolf.

Reynier, Christine. *Virginia Woolf's Ethics of the Short Story*. New York: Palgrave Macmillan, 2009. This book shines new light on Woolf's highly experimental short stories.

Sellers, Susan, ed. *The Cambridge Companion to Virginia Woolf (Cambridge Companions to Literature)*. New York: Cambridge UP, 2010. A collection of critical essays intended to introduce students to Woolf's life and work.

Woolf, Virginia. *The Common Reader*. New York: Harcourt, 1953.

_____. *The Diary of Virginia Woolf*. Vol. 2. Ed. Anne Oliver Bell. New York: Harcourt, 1978.

_____. *A Room of One's Own*. New York: Harcourt, 1957.

The *Paris Review* Perspective_____

Thessaly La Force for *The Paris Review*

Who is Mrs. Dalloway? It is seductive to search for clues about the woman while reading one of Virginia Woolf's most beloved novels. She is Clarissa, wife of Richard Dalloway, mother of Elizabeth Dalloway, doyenne of London society. She is kind to her servants; socially gifted, and socially conscious, "If you put her in a room with some one, up went her back like a cat's; or she purred"; an indelible presence with unremarkable looks, "Not that she was striking; not beautiful at all; there was nothing picturesque about her; she never said anything specially clever; there she was, however; there she was." But Mrs. Dalloway also is a contradiction—a woman of fifty-two years who feels "unspeakably young; at the same time unspeakably old," and whose actions provoke a self-loathing that hints at something deeper beneath the surface of her life, "half the time she did things not simply, not for themselves; but to make people think this or that; pure idiocy she knew."

Mrs. Dalloway centers on a single day, and though Woolf gives us little time with her enigmatic protagonist, Woolf is swift in her movements and clear with her diction, "What a lark! What a plunge!" says Mrs. Dalloway at the start of the novel and the start of her day. We begin briskly in the morning, right before Big Ben strikes, as Clarissa prepares for the party she is to give that evening: "Mrs. Dalloway said she would buy the flowers herself." As she moves through the streets of London—picking up her roses, brushing past an acquaintance—we move steadily into her mind, where memories of her past replay uninterrupted. We learn of a turbulent love with Peter Walsh, a man she would eventually choose *not* to marry; of a stolen kiss shared with the wild and handsome Sally Seton. But finally, it is in her innermost thoughts, where we discover something altogether startling about Mrs. Dalloway:

> But often now this body she wore . . . this body, with all its capacities, seemed nothing—nothing at all. She had the oddest sense of being herself invisible, unseen; unknown; there being no more marrying no more having of children now, but only this astonishing and rather solemn progress with the rest of them, up Bond Street, this being Mrs. Dalloway; not even Clarissa any more; this being Mrs. Richard Dalloway.

What dissonance! How isolating it must be for Mrs. Dalloway. While on the surface she concerns herself with the chatter and glamour of London society, darkness lurks underneath. Woolf created the character of Septimus Smith, whom she saw as a counterpoint to the frivolity and comfort in Clarissa's life (as Woolf states in her original introduction). While the tragedy of the First World War only touches the fringes of Clarissa's world, Smith is a shell-shocked veteran who is now unhappily wed to his wartime Italian sweetheart. He is suicidal and incoherent and, Woolf implies, mentally ill. Though he and Clarissa never meet, his death makes an entrance at Clarissa's party, when a prominent psychiatrist who was treating Septimus, mentions the suicide. At first: "Oh! thought Clarissa, in the middle of my party, here's death she thought." But then:

> She felt somehow very like him—the young man who had killed himself. She felt glad that he had done it; thrown it away. The clock was striking. The leaden circles dissolved in the air. He made her feel the beauty; made her feel the fun. But she must go back. She must assemble.

When *Mrs. Dalloway* was published in 1925, World War I had just ended, and civilians and soldiers were forced to adjust to the shock of their experiences and losses. "The War was over," Mrs. Dalloway thinks to herself as she runs her errand, "Except for some one like . . . Lady Bexborough . . . with the telegram in her hand, John, her favorite, killed." Woolf understood the need to talk about the war in its own peculiar way. In *The Common Reader,* which was published the same year as *Mrs. Dalloway,* she wrote: "In the vast catastrophe of the European war our emotions had to be broken up for us, and put at an angle from us, before we could allow ourselves to feel them in poetry or fiction."

It is easy to forget—given the fluidity of Woolf's prose, and the magical way she weaves between the narratives of her many characters—how radical *Mrs. Dalloway* was from the other novels published in the early 1900s. It was an experiment in structure and form. There were no chapters. The entire story takes place within less than twelve hours, juxtaposing the minutia of shopping for flowers with deeper, existential thoughts. Woolf was married, firmly established within the Bloomsbury Group, and had already published three novels to much critical acclaim: *The Voyage Out, Night and Day,* and *Jacob's Room.* But it was *Mrs. Dalloway* that was heralded as a truly modern novel, a classic—it would become one of the most popular works of fiction in the twentieth century. As Woolf wrote in her diary:

> So I have to create the whole thing afresh for myself each time. Probably all writers now are in the same boat. It is the penalty we pay for breaking with tradition, and the solitude makes the writing more exciting though the being read less so. One ought to sink to the bottom of the sea, probably, and live alone with ones words.

Sixteen years later, in 1941, Woolf would end her life under water. She battled mental illness for years, and finally drowned herself near her home, in the River Ouse, her overcoat weighed down with stones. Woolf was a prodigious writer, but it is impossible not to wonder what more she would have written had she lived. It would be another twelve years before the first *Paris Review* was published. The inaugural issue included an interview with E. M. Forster—a friend of Woolf's and one of the original members of the Bloomsbury Group. It is easy to imagine that the magazine would have extended a similar honor to the author of *Mrs. Dalloway.* Perhaps George Plimpton would have been bold enough to ask Virginia Woolf herself: Who is Mrs. Dalloway?

Works Cited

Woolf, Virginia. *The Common Reader.* New York: Harcourt, 1925.
_____. *Mrs. Dalloway.* New York: Harcourt, 1925.
_____. *A Writer's Diary.* New York: Harcourt, 1953.

CRITICAL
CONTEXTS

"All Taken Together":
Ecological Form in *Mrs. Dalloway*_____

Justyna Kostkowska

> Leaves were alive; trees were alive. And the leaves being connected by millions of fibers with his own body, there on the seat, fanned it up and down; when the branch stretched he, too, made that statement. The sparrows fluttering, rising, and falling in jagged fountains were part of the pattern. . . . Sounds made harmonies with premeditation; the spaces between them were as significant as the sounds. A child cried. Rightly far away a horn sounded. All taken together meant the birth of a new religion.
>
> —Virginia Woolf, *Mrs. Dalloway*

> For technological breakthroughs, legislative reforms, and paper covenants about environmental welfare to take effect, or even to be generated in the first place, requires a climate of transformed environmental values, perception, and will. To that end, the power of story, image, and artistic performance and the resources of aesthetics, ethics, and cultural theory are crucial.
>
> —Lawrence Buell, *The Future of Environmental Imagination*

The highly interconnected form of *Mrs. Dalloway* can be read as a model of a larger ecological interconnectedness that Woolf was aware of and often referred to. Woolf's early vision of the world as one whole finds its expression through characters desiring universal empathy and unity, which includes nonhuman beings. Not only this theme, but also the form of the novel supports an ecological reading. Woolf uses free indirect discourse to create a revolutionary narrator that remains in an active relationship with her various textual, intertextual, and extratextual environments. *Mrs. Dalloway* is a text that, as Lawrence Buell contends, can contribute to transforming environmental values through its "power of story, image . . . and aesthetics" (Buell vi). Seen from an ecological perspective, Woolf's novel models a web of relationships in a diverse ecosystem and shows how overtly dissimilar beings are inherently connected and interdependent.

Woolf's early vision of a flower in the garden at St. Ives was formative of what I call her ecological consciousness. She recalls in a passage from "A Sketch of the Past": "I was looking at the flower bed by the front door: 'That is the whole', I said. I was looking at a plant with a spread of leaves; and it seemed suddenly plain that the flower itself was part of the earth; that a ring enclosed what was the flower; and that was the real flower; part earth; part flower. It was a thought I put away as being likely to be very useful to me later" (*Moments* 71). A few paragraphs later she talks about the pleasure of making connections in writing as "the strongest pleasure known to me. It is the rapture I get when in writing I seem to be discovering what belongs to what. . . . From this I reach what I might call a philosophy; at any rate it is a constant idea of mine; that behind the cotton wool is hidden a pattern; that we—I mean all human beings—are connected with this; that the whole world is a work of art" (72). She is aware that the environmental wholeness that she observed in nature also pervades humanity. A work of art reveals the hidden pattern, shows the connections to the rest of the world. "The pattern behind the cotton wool" is a concept that can be said to diagram the structure of *Mrs. Dalloway*.

While conceiving the novel, Woolf writes in her diary about the new book as an inclusive environment: "[to] get closer & yet keep form and speed and enclose everything, everything" (*Diary 2* 13); "I feel I had loosed the bonds pretty completely and could pour everything in" (*Diary 2* 302); "I feel I can use up everything I have ever thought" (*Diary 2* 272). The characters have behind them "caves that shall connect" (*Diary 2* 263) by "tunneling" (*Diary 2* 272). She imagines the new novel as a space that has been opened and is now capable of enclosing all things. Her two main characters and their stories remain overtly unrelated until the end of the book, yet Woolf casts a net of thematic and formal connections that brings them together. The text functions as an ecosystem that binds overtly dissimilar beings in an inherently interdependent relationship. As in nature, their interdependence is not immediately obvious but is gradually discovered and appreciated by the observer.

The two protagonists of *Mrs. Dalloway*, Clarissa Dalloway and Septimus Smith, are visionary characters who proclaim a belief in the world's deeply imbedded interconnectedness. In the epigraphic passage, Septimus Smith's socially dysfunctional yet environmentally harmonious madness allows him a unique perspective, whereby he perceives trees as "alive" and connected to him.[1] Septimus feels their fibers in his body and moves when they move. He is acutely aware of his environment, which includes sparrows and sounds interspersed with silence. The description of sparrows "falling in . . . fountains" underscores the world's unity, integrating the traditionally separate natural realms. Septimus notes that silences are equally as important as sounds, and relishes in the harmony they create. Again, Woolf's ecologically laden word "spaces" (instead of "pauses" or "silences") between sounds makes us aware of the environment in which sounds travel, and brings in air as their vehicle. None of the members of this environment is more important than any other, and the human child and the cars' horns complete this environmental system, adding their voices to the sparrows'. Septimus concludes that "all [that] taken together" has a significance of a "new religion" (22-23). This grand term could signify a new attitude that would treat the world's beings as equal, with no hierarchy that privileges humans above nonhumans.

The vision of universal unity that Septimus calls a "new religion," Clarissa Dalloway describes as her "transcendental theory":

> She felt herself everywhere; not "here here here" . . . but everywhere. She waved her hand, going up Shaftesbury Avenue. She was all that. So that to know her, or any one, one must seek out the people who completed them; even the places. Odd affinities she had with people she had never spoken to, some woman in the street, some man behind a counter—even trees or barns. (152-53)

Clarissa feels physically connected and present in other people and places, experiencing empathy and sharing their experience. She believes all beings and environments share that transcendental unity on a deep level, where the "unseen part . . . spreads wide" (153). Clarissa expresses this vision several times during the novel, first very early, thinking of Bourton: "she being part, she was positive, of the trees at home; of the house there . . . part of people she had never met; being laid out like a mist between the people she knew best, who lifted her on their branches as she had seen the trees lift the mist, but it spread ever so far, her life, herself" (9). Here she does not simply feel "an affinity," but a *part* of other humans, nonhumans, and environments. Appropriately for Clarissa's vision, Woolf uses natural metaphors and similes here, portraying humans as trees and mist, part of the nonhuman environment. Later Clarissa explains a similar sentiment in her need to throw her party as a desire to "combine": "Here was So-and-so in South Kensington; some one up in Bayswater; and somebody else, say, in Mayfair. And she felt quite continuously a sense of their existence; and she felt what a waste; and she felt what a pity; and she felt if only they could be brought together; so she did it. And it was an offering: to combine, to create" (122). To connect and combine also is Septimus's dream; both are willing to make an offering, hers being the party, his being the ultimate: his life. Here Clarissa also draws a sketch of the whole novel: the narrator connecting the characters in various parts of the city, relating one continuous day in their lives. Importantly, she calls their separation, and lack of connection "a waste," "a pity," and she tries to remedy it with her party and her sympathy for Septimus.

But Clarissa's sympathetic reaction to Septimus is an exception in the novel. Most of the time in the novel, the characters do not have a deeper knowledge of each other; they walk around, observing each other from the outside as strangers do. We as readers see them as related only because of how Woolf's narrator—the connecting thread—shows them. She extends the connections she places between the characters to other texts, and ultimately to the reader, to enclose them together in a meaningful web of relationships, creating "the pattern behind the cotton wool." Septimus's "new religion" and Clarissa's "transcendental theory" of connectedness find their embodiment in the novel's narrative form, fulfilling the characters' vision on the textual level. The narrator is a revolutionary figure hitherto unprecedented in the history of the novel. The narrator is an expression of Woolf's project of decentering the patriarchal "I," the omniscient speaking subject.[2] In *Mrs. Dalloway*, Woolf replaces the single master perspective with an inclusive voice that frequently steps aside to allow multiple character voices through: "Instead of the narrator delivering impressions of Clarissa, we receive the 'support of innumerable other characters'" (Mezei 84-86). Christopher Herbert notes that in creating such a narrative, Woolf takes a stand against absolutism and for relativity: "no one point of view prevails" (Herbert 121); they interact and communicate. "The general axiom of relativity: that nothing is one thing just by itself and that a thing cut off from communication with other things . . . would simply cease to exist" (Herbert 120) also is an axiom of ecology. The narrator's voice is a link that reveals the underlying connections between the characters and between the characters and their milieu.

The elaborate multiplicity of perspectives that the free indirect discourse narrator creates is one of the qualities that prompt a reading of the novel as a dialogic, polyphonic, and therefore ecological, text. Free indirect discourse is a complex method where "the narrator substitutes his words for a character's speech, thought, or sensory perception" (Hernadi 35). Such a narrator is an underlying presence shared by all characters' voices, no matter how diverse. Although some critics argue that she dominates and "interrupts" (Hoff 254) the others, in my ecological reading, this quality emphasizes the unity of the characters through their common DNA, the cellular base all natural beings share. Myriad personas, most diligently named and surnamed, often appear once only to offer a glimpse of Clarissa or others in their environment, as in this early instance: "She stiffened on the kerb, waiting for

Durtnall's van to pass. A charming woman, Scrope Purvis thought her (knowing her as one does know people who live next door to one in Westminster), a touch of a bird about her. . . . There she perched, never seeing him, waiting to cross, very upright" (4). Woolf's method here disperses the singleness of vision and portrays a multiplicity of perspectives. In one short paragraph, we experience two viewpoints on the same moment of Clarissa's walk: first the narrator's, placing Clarissa in a specific place and an exact moment of a car passing, and then the neighbor's catching a glimpse of her from a different direction. As Clarissa looks, she is looked at. Hers is not the only gaze; "life; London; this moment in June" (4) has many participants, and we are made aware of them because Scrope Purvis's presence intimates the existence of others. By quickly shifting to Scrope's viewpoint and back, the narrator makes us aware of a complete environmental ecosystem surrounding Clarissa.

Another particularly ecological quality of Woolf's narrator is that she establishes connections between characters through the physical environment. The environment is the glue that connects characters who don't know each other, such as Clarissa and Septimus (who both look at the passing car), and Peter and Rezia (who see each other in the park). It is the physical environment that makes them part of one system. All of the participants live within the larger space of the city of London, and their different locations are traversed by the famous method of the walk: most centrally Clarissa's, Peter's, Hugh's, and Richard's.[3] The narrator also connects the different persons by her manipulation of their surroundings, including the other characters (the nurse, the beggar woman, the little girl running into Rezia), airplanes writing in the sky, cars passing by (the Prime Minister's and the ambulance carrying Septimus), and buses (connecting Elizabeth and Septimus). In the following instance, by placing an airplane in the sky the narrator creates a common space between two complete strangers, Mrs. Dempster and Mr. Bentley, whose thoughts are revealed to us:

There is a fine young feller aboard of it [the plane], Mrs. Dempster wag-
ered, and away and away it went . . . over the little island of grey churches . . .
on either side of London, fields spread out and dark brown woods where
adventurous thrushes hopping boldly, glancing quickly, snatched the snail
and tapped him on a stone, once, twice, thrice. Away and away the airplane
shot . . . an inspiration, a concentration, a symbol (so it seemed to Mr.
Bentley, vigorously rolling his strip of turf at Greenwich) of a man's soul;
of his determination, thought Mr. Bentley, sweeping around the cedar tree,
to get outside of his body. (28)

As a characteristic of free indirect discourse, it is unclear where the
thoughts of the characters end and the narrator's comments begin. The
narrator's voice ties together two very different human figures that
would normally appear as unrelated. What is also important from the
ecological point of view is that this inclusive space contains, in its
sweep of points of view, nonhuman subjects as well as human. The
thrushes are the third subject perspective inhabiting the space of the
plane's flight. The birds are shown in surprising detail, busy getting
their meal in distant woods, complete with personality traits ("adventurous," "boldly"). They express themselves through discrete taps,
their body language resembling the vigorous body language of the
sweeping man. Through the eyes of the free indirect discourse narrator,
diverse human and nonhuman perspectives are shown as similar,
equal, and coexisting within one ecosystem.

Of the environmental elements that the narrator uses as connectors,
sounds—especially those of the chiming clocks—assume a prominent
place. The narrator describes their sound as a living thing, permeating
the environment:

It was precisely twelve o'clock; twelve by Big Ben; whose stroke was
wafted over the northern part of London; blent with that of other clocks,
mixed in a thin ethereal way with the clouds and wisps of smoke, and died
up there among the seagulls—twelve o'clock struck as Clarissa Dalloway

laid her green dress on her bed, and the Warren Smiths walked down Haley Street. (94)

The sound of the bells connects the passage about the Smiths to the passage about Clarissa in her room and back to the Smiths who are walking from Dr. Bradshaw's office. The verb "mixed" repeats the meaning of "blent" to underscore the sound's active merging with its surroundings, which include other clocks, clouds, smoke, and the seagulls, becoming a part of a diverse ecosystem. As Septimus stresses in his opening quote, sounds and spaces between them are parts of the environment as much as sights. In fact, they have a political significance of destabilizing the primacy of vision, of the masterly, traditionally male "gaze." Sound has a unifying quality: it creates a community of listeners rather than objectifying the perceived and isolating the perceiver, which are the attributes of vision, as Angela Frattarola observes (136). Melba Kuddy-Keane sees "acts of listening [as] the bridge between the individual and the world; and the fragmented, discontinuous, polytextual music conveys a wholeness, a comprehensiveness, that embraces the communal life of the universe. Although sounds never are completely harmonized for Woolf, they do connect her characters to the world" (qtd. in Frattarola 139). Such a reliance on sound rather than vision is important in terms of ecological theory as it has the potential of changing the way we perceive ourselves and the surrounding world: "because the ear does not as easily perceive the world as 'separate things, commodities,' auditory perception may allow for a different way of being in the world as well as a novel conception of the self" (Frattarola 136). Woolf's narrator uses sound—as she does with the rest of the physical environment—to alter the traditional view of individual beings as separate. She creates a common space that unites diverse listeners within its reach and points to their invisible but existing connection.

Stuart Rosenberg's early analysis calls Woolf's technique, specifically her "interest in language as language . . . an obtrusive art: Virginia

Woolf continually calls attention to what she is doing" (219). Through her awareness of the reality of the text, the narrator points to the existence of a space on its outside. This consciousness is what makes this narrative figure environmentally aware and therefore ecological. The narrator shows her awareness of the textual space around her through multiple allusions to artistic or literary creativity, and to the form of the book itself. Through Peter's thoughts, she points to the book's intricate design: "there was design, art everywhere; a change of some sort had undoubtedly taken place" (71). And later: "Odd, unexpected people turned up, an artist sometimes; sometimes a writer, queer fish in that atmosphere. And behind it all was a network of visiting . . . running about with bunches of flowers" (77). Here Peter names some characteristic elements of the novel. The narrator alludes to the text's connecting "thread" on several occasions: "the invincible thread of sound" (82-93), the "thread" extending between Lady Bruton and her lunch guests (112), Richard's mind like a "spider's thread"(115); sound described as "that string" (127). Septimus's writings, which are fragmented and incoherent, bring to mind the overt fragmentation of the novel's own plot in the chasm between Septimus and Clarissa. But the book is so masterfully interwoven that even the comments about chaos ironically imply the narrator's awareness and her integrating function in this system. By being aware that she is a part of a text, the narrator intimates the existence of a larger reality beyond it.

The narrator extends her relationship with the extratextual environment to other texts through numerous literary allusions. William Shakespeare's plays are a haunting presence, especially *Cymbeline* in the recurring quote "Fear no more the heat o' the sun/ Nor the furious winter's rages" (9, 139); *Richard II* is present in Lady Bruton's celebration of England's past (Wyatt 441), and *The Tempest* is present through the references to the "drowned sailor" (104). As Joan Wyatt points out, the drowned sailor reference (*MD* 93) also brings to mind Eliot's *The Waste Land*, spanning four centuries in a whirlwind motion (444). Imagery of Dante's *Inferno* is present in Septimus's description of Rezia as a "flowering tree" (*MD* 148) and the myth of Ishtar and Aphrodite in the beggar's song (Wyatt 440). Peter's musings about his vision of the girl in the street "smashed to atoms" (*MD* 81) can be related to Eliot's fragments and ruins in *The Waste Land*, and to William Butler Yeats's imagery of chaos (Garvey 61). The novel's structure can be linked to literary history as well as to some contemporary works Woolf had read. Molly Hoff compares Woolf's "labyrinthine" method to that of Homer and Plato: "The labyrinthine structure in the dialogues, constructed as playlets, a structure that we also see in the *Odyssey*, is continued in the textual labyrinths of Virgil (*The Aeneid*), Ovid (*Metamorphoses*), Dante (*The Inferno*), Proust (*À la recherche du temps perdu*), Joyce (*Ulysses*)" (2). Hoff also notes that "As in the *Odyssey* where female characters contribute to a portrait of Penelope, the female characters in *Mrs. Dalloway* contribute to the portrait of Clarissa" (248). Closer to home, Peter refrains from imagining the people inside the passing ambulance, commenting that sentimentality is "fatal to art, fatal to friendship," echoing Woolf's own opinion on the subject recorded in her diary: "I go in dread of 'sentimentality'" (*Diary 3* 110).

The ultimate reality outside of the text that the novel's narrator senses is that of the reader. *Mrs. Dalloway*'s narrator impersonates Woolf's own philosophy of the reader-author relationship: that of equality, communication and cooperation. She talks about her effort to find a new narrative voice to suit modern times in "Mr. Bennett and Mrs. Brown" a year before *Mrs. Dalloway* is published. Woolf visualizes finding a "common ground" between the writer and the reader, "a convention which would not seem to you too old, unreal, and farfetched to believe in" (*CE* I 332). It is evident that she imagines this space when we read *Mrs. Dalloway*: the narrator seems aware of the reader's presence and trusts in his/her ability to create meaning. As Johanna Garvey observes, "In a sense, the whole novel partakes in gossip, between the narrator and the reader, quoting not only characters' spoken words but their inner thoughts as well as depicting sensations and emotions with vivid images" (73).

As I have mentioned before, the free indirect discourse narrator engages the reader by not identifying relationships between characters but by portraying them as overtly isolated individuals. Irena Ksiezopolska notes that the figure of the nurse connects Peter, Rezia, Septimus, and Clarissa "though they remain unaware of the connection. . . . Neither of them realizes that they form one plot; this knowledge is only shared by the narrator and the reader" (23-24). During his walk, Richard runs into the beggar woman, whom we have met before independently of his perspective. Similarly, Peter observes Rezia and Septimus. We receive his thoughts about them, a clean slate of someone who sees them for the first time, from a different angle:

> And that is being young, Peter Walsh thought as he passed them. To be having an awful scene—the poor girl looked absolutely desperate—in the middle of the morning. But what was it about, he wondered, what had the young man in the overcoat been saying to her to make her look like that; what awful fix had they got themselves into, both to look so desperate as that on a fine summer morning? (71)

Woolf's characters function towards each other as observing strangers; the narrator leaves it to the reader to make the connections from the outside. Through such passages, she sends "winks" to the reader, who is privy to the information she has hidden from the characters. She shows an awareness of the reader's existence, of the physical space that extends beyond the book. Thankfully, she stops short of addressing us as "dear reader," but throws us ball after ball confident we will catch them. As Donna Reed observes, "By allowing an insider's view of overlapping minds . . . [Woolf] involve[s] the reader in a communion of understanding but without labeling it as such. This narrative style tacitly embraces the reader" (127).[4]

Another important way the narrator communicates with the reader is through significant repetition. Characters repeat each others' thoughts, often using similar wording. Richard foreshadows Sally's view that "it is a thousand pities never to say what one feels" (112, 116). Clarissa's thought on "friends attached to one's body" resonates in Lady Bruton's mind (112). Richard and Lady Bruton both ponder the concept of the spider's thread that creates ties between people (112). Recurring phrases are also noticeable structural ties: Peter's twice repeated "There she was," "The leaden circles dissolved in the air" connecting Rezia and Clarissa (94, 186), and the Shakespearian "Fear no more" shared by Clarissa and Septimus. Even within paragraphs repetition creates coherence, a connectedness of a system. Woolf often builds paragraphs in a frame structure, starting with an image or action that is later returned to or completed towards the paragraph's end. Lady Bruton picking up carnations to lay them down on the table at the end of her musings about her lunch guests is an example (105). Similarly, a Spanish necklace punctuates Richard's thoughts at the jeweler's (113).

Recurring images foreshadow events to the reader and integrate the plot, haunting our reading and keeping us on the lookout for possible connections. These include Clarissa standing at the top of the stairs, Clarissa and Septimus standing in their respective open windows, an old woman seen in the house opposite—mirrored in Septimus's life as an "old man coming down an opposite staircase"(149). Images of birds are used repeatedly for Clarissa and Rezia, and those of hyacinths for Clarissa and Elizabeth. All these significant recurrences make the reader alert to the text's unity and design; through them the narrator establishes communication with the reader, leaving it for the reader to discover her design. She thereby extends her environment to include us. Reed rightly describes this method as fulfilling "the 'boundless' wishes of their protagonists to find realization through the narrative that embraces characters and readers together" (125).

Planning *Mrs. Dalloway*, Woolf wanted it to be a different book. Woolf conceived of it as a space to be filled with "everything." While writing, she stressed the need for all the elements to be closely knit, "screwed . . . tighter" (*Diary 2* 210) than in the preceding *Jacob's*

Room. In a letter to C. P. Sanger, she confessed: "the reason I inflict these experiments upon you is that I can't lie down in peace until I have found some way of liberating my sympathies, instead of giving effect to my analytic brain" (*Letters 3* 184). She wants the new form to do more than boast a cerebral structure; she wants it to have an emotional effect. I have argued that this effect is of an ecological nature, and that the book provides the reader with a model of environmental coexistence. Woolf creates a new narrative voice that acknowledges and interacts with the characters, and connects them through their physical environment. Her awareness extends beyond her text to other texts, and to the reader. The book's theme of empathy and unity is embodied by this elaborate net of connections. Multiple subject perspectives told in the pervasive voice of the free indirect discourse narrator weave a network of relationships within a shared space. *Mrs. Dalloway* transforms the hegemonic narrative space it had inherited into a democratic, multi-voiced, interconnected environment. Woolf's book is a model of an ecosystem functioning in accordance with the main tenets of modern ecology: environmental connectedness and interdependence, a model for the transformation of our own environmental values.

Notes

1. Gregory A. Wilson interprets this passage as "a vision of mankind's wholeness and triumph over division after the war's devastating effects" (37). I extend this wholeness to the environmental dimension, to include the nonhuman as well.

2. Frustrated with the omniscient convention, Woolf criticizes Arnold Bennett's narration in *Hilda Lessways*: "But we cannot hear her mother's voice, or Hilda's voice; we can only hear Mr. Bennett's voice telling us about rents and freeholds and copyholds and fines" (*Collected Essays* I 330).

3. Andelys Wood discusses the relationship of the walk and clock time in the novel.

4. Reed further writes: "Since the characters do not see into one another as fully as readers perceive them, ideal communion lies beyond the boundaries of the novel. The union of voices in the reader's mind realizes Clarissa's theory of immortality" (129). Mark Hussey comments on the text's relationship to the reader: "Peter Walsh and Clarissa . . . strive through the novel to complete a circle, joining past and present in the hope of achieving unity. The party at the end does not solve the problem . . . because the characters are no longer the people that came together at Bourton. This 'incom-

plete circle'. . . is the form of the novel; it involves the reader by placing him or her in the memories of the characters (and vice versa). For the reader, then, the circle can be completed in that the whole timescale is not in the actual world of time and death, but in the virtual space between reader and text" (*Singing* 123).

Works Cited

Buell, Lawrence. *The Future of Environmental Imagination*. Malden, MA: Blackwell, 2005.

Dixon, Peter, and Marisa Bortolussi. "Literary Communication: Effects of Reader-Narrator Cooperation." *Poetics* 23 (1996): 405-430.

Frattarola, Angela. "Developing an Ear for the Modernist Novel: Virginia Woolf, Dorothy Richardson and James Joyce." *Journal of Modern Literature* 136 (Fall 2009): 132-153.

Gardiner, Michael. "Ecology and Carnival: Traces of a 'Green' Social Theory in the Writings of M. M. Bakhtin." *Theory and Society* 22.6 (1993): 765-812.

Garvey, Johanna X. K. "Difference and Continuity: The Voices of *Mrs. Dalloway*." *College English* 53.1 (Jan. 1991): 59-76.

Herbert, Christopher. "*Mrs. Dalloway*, the Dictator, and the Relativity Paradox." *Novel: A Forum on Fiction* 35.1 (Fall 2001): 104-24.

Hernadi, Paul. "Dual Perspective: Free Indirect Discourse and Related Techniques." *Comparative Literature* 24.1 (Winter 1972): 32-43.

Hoff, Molly. *Invisible Presences*. Clemson, SC: Clemson U Digital P, 2009.

Hussey, Mark. *The Singing of the Real World: The Philosophy of Virginia Woolf's Fiction*. Columbus: Ohio State UP, 1986.

Kostkowska, Justyna. "'Scissors and Silks,' 'Flowers and Trees,' and 'Geraniums Ruined by the War': Virginia Woolf's Ecological Critique of Science in *Mrs. Dalloway*." *Women's Studies* 33 (2004): 183-199.

Ksiezopolska, Irena. "Props and Personages: The Significance of the Secondary Characters in *Mrs. Dalloway*." *Virginia Woolf Miscellany* 66 (Sept. 2004): 23-25.

Mezei, Kathy. "Who Is Speaking Here? Free Indirect Discourse, Gender, and Authority in *Emma*, *Howards End*, and *Mrs. Dalloway*." *Ambiguous Discourse: Feminist Narratology and British Women Writers*. Ed. Kathy Mezei. Chapel Hill: U of North Carolina P, 1996. 66-92.

Reed, Donna. "Merging Voices: *Mrs. Dalloway* and *No Place on Earth*." *Comparative Literature* 47.2 (1 Mar. 1995): 118-135.

Rosenberg, Stuart. "'The Match in the Crocus': Virginia Woolf's Obtrusive Art in *Mrs. Dalloway*." *Modern Fiction Studies* 13.2 (Summer 1967): 211-220.

Waller, L. Elizabeth. "Writing the Real: Virginia Woolf and an Ecology of Language." *The Bucknell Review* 44.1 (2000): 137-156.

Wilson, Gregory A. "'This Insatiable Hunger for Sympathy': Virginia Woolf's Vision of Unity in *Mrs. Dalloway*." *The CEA Critic* 66.1 (Fall 2003): 32-42.

Wood, Andelys. "Walking the Web in the Lost London of *Mrs. Dalloway*." *Mosaic: A Journal for the Interdisciplinary Study of Literature* 36.2 (June 2003): 19-32.

Woolf, Virginia. *Collected Essays*. Vols. 1-4. New York: Harcourt Brace, 1967.

_____. *The Diary of Virginia Woolf*. Vols. 1-4. San Diego: Harcourt Brace, 1978.

_____. *Moments of Being*. New York: Harcourt Brace, 1976.

_____. *Mrs. Dalloway*. New York: Harcourt Brace, 1981.

Wyatt, Jean M. "*Mrs. Dalloway*: Literary Allusion as Structural Metaphor." *PMLA* 88.3 (May 1973): 440-451.

The "Death of the Soul" in *Mrs. Dalloway*_____

Vereen M. Bell

As readers, we experience *Mrs. Dalloway* as a novel of parts. Its story is conveyed to us primarily through the most intimate thoughts of its several main characters. They construct on their own terms the reality they pass through, and even these constructions waver and re-form from one minute to the next. In its very design *Mrs. Dalloway* describes a human reality within a certain privileged social class that, however stable and coherent it pretends to be on the outside, is fluid, incoherent, and fragmented underneath. The novel is set in London on one June day in 1923. It is not yet five years since the world had suffered through the most devastating four years of war (1914-1918) in human history. Thanks to the industrial might of the European nations and the modernization of warfare, more than sixteen million people had been killed and more than twenty-one million wounded. Yet in *Mrs. Dalloway* even such absurdity and carnage as this seems to be fading in the collective memory of the British establishment. The governing classes collude to sustain an ordered way of life, understood to be ordained by nature: men in men's proper roles, women in women's, servants in the wings, and poor people out of sight. Woolf wrote in her diary: "I want to criticize the social system, & to show it at work, at its most intense" (*Diary 2* 248). By "at its most intense" she may have meant to imply "under extreme pressure" in a period in which British culture's cherished, sustaining shibboleths and fictions were slowly disintegrating.

The society that Clarissa Dalloway and her peers inhabit exhibits little interest in the lives or pain of other people. Its members hardly seem aware of the shadowed historical moment they are living in. The mental isolation chamber in which they circulate seems impenetrable. So, in a sense, for them there is no context. They have dedicated their lives to holding context at bay. Clarissa's husband, Richard, is an exception, for he is a member of Parliament and a leader of his party, and he is at least aware of the injustices of the social system. Clarissa's old friends of thirty years ago, Sally Seton and Peter Walsh, are exceptions as well, or, at least, are more reflective and observant. Richard's and Clarissa's daughter, Elizabeth, seems about to escape the confines of her social class, ironically because of the influence of her lesbian history tutor, whom Clarissa despises; but this is far from a foregone conclusion. The rest of the friends who attend Clarissa's party have pretty much "gone under," in the novel's memorable phrase, having long since fitted their living selves to the templates of the social order.

Clarissa herself is on the verge of "going under." She is self-absorbed and unfocused. She has an oddly uncertain perspective on the realities of the modern world. On the one hand she is reading Jean Baptiste Marbot's romantic memoirs of the Napoleonic Wars. On the other hand she is scarcely conscious of who the Armenians are. To her they are a problem that Richard is engaged with in Parliament. To most of the world, by 1923, the Christian Armenians would have been recognized to be the horrific victims of ethnic cleansing during the war (and before and after) by Germany's ally, the Ottoman Empire. The Armenians were, in a sense, the Jews of the First World War. In August 1939, issuing his order for the total destruction of the Poles, Adolf Hitler would say, "Only thus shall we gain the living space that we need. Who, after all, speaks today of the annihilation of the Armenians?" (qtd. in Lochner 4). Shamefully, Clarissa confuses the Turks with the Armenians, the oppressors with their victims, and decides that "She cared much more for her roses than for the Armenians. Hunted out of existence, maimed, frozen, the victims of cruelty and injustice (she had heard Richard say so over and over again)—no, she could feel nothing for the Albanians, or was it the Armenians? but she loved her roses (didn't that help the Armenians?)" (Woolf 120). Unexamined disconnects like these show that although Clarissa knows that there is something missing from her life, she is also powerless to understand or act upon it. She is both gratified and depressed by the life she has chosen. Thirty years before she could have married Peter Walsh, who loved her and still does, but she married the more manly Richard instead because he was less emotional and invasive and had more to offer, social standing and luxury—and, as it would turn out, idleness, loneliness, and ennui.

Clarissa is confined literally and symbolically to a world comprising the London districts of Westminster, St. James's, Mayfair, Piccadilly, and Kensington, where the wealth and power of London are congregated. She and Richard live within a ten-minute walk from St. James Park, Westminster Abbey, and the Houses of Parliament. When she sets out to buy the flowers herself on the day of her party rather than sending the servants for them, she is exhilarated to have wandered as far as Bond Street. Later in the novel, her daughter, Elizabeth, sets out on a similar journey, but hers takes a different direction and she rides an omnibus, along with the common people. On a lark, Elizabeth heads East, along the Strand, where the animated professional life of the city flourishes, where the city's business is done—the law courts, the barristers' chambers, the journalists of Fleet Street, the Bank of England, St. Paul's, the City, where finance capitalism and the un-landed gentry prevail. Elizabeth is inspired by all this vitality to consider taking charge of her own future. She disembarks at Chancery Lane and walks, she thinks, like a Dalloway "pioneer" towards St. Paul's: "The feet of those people busy about their activities, hands putting stone to stone, minds eternally occupied . . . with thoughts of ships, of business, of law, of administrations, and with it all so stately (she was in the Temple), gay (there was the river), pious (there was the Church), made her quite determined, whatever her mother might say, to become either a farmer or a doctor" (137).

These two spatial contexts map contrasting journeys of the spirit. Elizabeth may yet escape her own beauty and the admiration of others, though here she ends a little disconcerted by the boldness of her fantasies, and she is not very enterprising. Clarissa has remained, even venturing forth, in her own comfort zone, where she appears to have been briefly in the presence of the Queen in a motor car, stalled in traffic:

"Greatness was passing, hidden, down Bond Street, removed only by a hair's-breadth from ordinary people who might now, for the first and last time, be within speaking distance of the majesty of England, of the enduring symbol of the state" (16). Enduring is the key term here; the fact of the monarchy creates the illusion of the absence of change. Clarissa reflects upon death, upon the enduring Empire, upon the past, upon her inconsequential life. There is an old lady who lives in a flat across from the Dalloways whom Clarissa occasionally sees watching from her window, often in the dark. The old lady seems to be looking at Clarissa, who wordlessly looks back. She is Clarissa's doppelganger: alone, in darkness, inside looking out. Clarissa sleeps alone in her small attic room in a single bed that is said to be like a coffin.

Woolf's treatment of beautiful young Elizabeth is gently satiric: she is a daddy's girl who is not ready to break free. But there is a line drawn between her life and its possibilities and her mother's. After the Treaty of Versailles, David Lloyd George's National Liberal coalition pressed through Parliament a bill which became the Sex Disqualification (Removal) Act of 1919 (Whitworth 43, 51). The Act prohibited British women from being disqualified from entering the professions or enrolling in universities. Such a change in the legal status of women meant that the opportunities Elizabeth dreams of in her journey up the Strand could be possible for her. At the time, this was the most radical victory for feminists in the history of the movement. A partial victory had been achieved the year before when women had been granted the right to vote by the Representation of the People Act of 1918. Both of these acts were the result of a long struggle by suffragists but, most immediately, the result of women having successfully populated the work force in the absence of men during the war. Full suffrage for women would not come until 1928. Psychological emancipation for women would take longer, as Woolf knew. Cultures do not change as fast as laws.

Clarissa and her friend Sally Seton had dreamed of being rebels thirty years before at Clarissa's childhood country home at Bourton.

They read socialist writers and Plato and discussed ideas. Sally ostentatiously smoked cigars. They loved each other and wanted to change the world, but being women they were trapped in their historical moment. They had no chance of being among the movers and shakers of the world. Elizabeth has that chance, if she chooses to take it. The novelist Barbara Cartland, who was raised in circumstances similar to Clarissa's roughly a decade later, said of her own upbringing: "We lived in manless homes. We were brought up by women, and Edwardian women at that. We were fenced round with narrow restrictive social customs, nurtured on snobbery and isolated from any contact with, or knowledge of, people outside our own accepted class" (qtd. in Nicolson 4). Clarissa had been raised in isolation at Bourton by her Aunt Helena, "who never liked discussion of anything" (Woolf 33). Sally's transgressive influence still resides in Clarissa's brain and, for better or worse, disturbs her tranquility.

One of the uninvited intrusions into Clarissa's insular existence is Doris Kilman. Hired by Richard Dalloway, Miss Kilman tutors Elizabeth in modern history. She brings an outsider's version of history into the Dalloway household, and although it is not stated openly, this fact alone could explain why Clarissa despises and fears her. Miss Kilman also is a modern woman, or struggling to be, and she takes Elizabeth to lectures about important ideas. Miss Kilman is marginalized in the English public sector because she is from an emigrant German family, one that changed its name from Kiehlman in order to expedite assimilation. The loathing of all things German was virulent in England both during and after the war. Before the war, there had been upward of fifty-five thousand Germans living in England. After the war, only twenty-two thousand remained. Miss Kilman lost her job as a teacher because, once the war started, she was deemed "not suitable." She does not help her cause by claiming, truthfully, that all Germans are not villains and that the English are not always right. She is a Christian convert, poor and graceless and badly dressed, all of which cause her to be abhorrent to Clarissa, who loves roses and fine gloves and giving parties and fears Miss Kilman's influence upon Elizabeth. Miss Kilman has set herself to the task of winning Elizabeth away from the vacuousness of her social class. "There were books. There were meetings. There were other points of view. . . . Law, medicine, politics, all professions are open to women of your generation, said Miss Kilman" (130), alluding obliquely to the Sex Disqualification (Removal) Act. Miss Kilman is an alien in this culture, and she is incapable of concealing her own feelings. When she clumsily professes her love to Elizabeth at tea in the Army and Navy Stores, vendor to the military and to emissaries of the empire, Elizabeth, being English and reticent, is horrified and bolts away. Ironically, when we last see Miss Kilman, this imposing, graceless German woman, she is grieving and shamed, kneeling in prayer, with her parcels from the stores beside her, in Westminster Abbey—the oldest symbol of the majesty of English history in London and the coronation site of all of England's monarchs since the fourteenth century.

Both Doris Kilman and Septimus Smith are links that carry us to a representation of the cruel realities of the class system in England and to the war's relationship to it. Doris Kilman despises the privileged class and does not seek admittance. Septimus, on the other hand, aspires to improve his station. He reads William Shakespeare, Charles Darwin, Will Durant's *History of Civilization* (the eleven-volume Bible of self-improvers), and George Bernard Shaw for the modern ideas. He writes poems for Miss Isabel Pole, who corrects his grammar. He works as a clerk at an auctioneer's house, where he is expected to rise to the top. If it were not for the war he might have advanced briskly through the social orders by mimicking his betters. But the war comes, and Septimus, wholly self-educated, is among the first to volunteer "to save an England which consisted almost entirely of Shakespeare's plays" (86). The war destroys his mind and his life. Once demobilized, he sinks deeper into madness, fearing and hating authority and despising humanity. He suffers from shell shock, a traumatic stress disorder peculiar to the Great War because of the heavy artillery bombardments of troops pinned down in their trenches. Shell shock was physiologically damaging to the brain, like a series of concussions, and in the mind the terrifying effects of fear produced a madness of its own. The Germans had one cannon called Big Bertha that was so massive, with a range of fifteen kilometers, that its fusillades at the Battle of Verdun in northeastern France were said to be audible as far away as London.

Septimus's two doctors, knowing little about the terrible emotional damage of combat, treat him impatiently as if he were a malingerer who should just pull himself together like a man and stop frightening his wife. He is said by Dr. Holmes to be "a little out of sorts" (21). When Septimus is finally compelled to take his own life, Dr. Holmes, who has arrived just in time to witness his plunge from the window, cries out, "The coward!"—as if Septimus because of a character flaw were betraying some cherished heroic ideal (149). Had the two doctors known that Septimus had formed an intimate relationship at the front with his friend Evans, who had been killed days before the Armistice, the truce agreement that ended the war, they would no doubt have submitted him to the courts for prosecution. Homosexual acts were illegal both under civilian and military law. But because of the restraints imposed upon male desire by the conditions of battle, homosexual relations between soldiers were not uncommon: "Two hundred and seventy soldiers and twenty officers were court-martialled for 'acts of gross indecency with another male person according the Guidance notes in the Manual of Military Law'" (Nicolson 25). The phrase "gross indecency" must have seemed ironic to men who had had to retrieve bits and pieces of the flesh of their friends "no larger than a Sunday roast" for burial in the mud of the killing fields (Nicholson 17).

After the First Battle of the Marne, the Great War rapidly became simply a brutal war of attrition. The field commanders and the high command on both sides concluded early on that no significant territorial gains could be made by either side, at least on the Western Front. The unspoken objective became to inflict as many casualties as possible until one side simply ran out of soldiers. The result of this murderous strategy was that in a little more than four years nearly ten million combatants on both sides were killed. In addition, 885,000 British soldiers, sailors, and airmen were killed, more than one million wounded. The original phrase "the Lost Generation" referred to these young men, who were indeed lost. The category of "wounded" did not count the thousands who suffered the aftereffects of shell shock. "Wounded" meant mutilated, lost arms and legs. A pension of sixteen shillings a week was granted for loss of a full arm, less for half an arm or for a leg (Nicholson 48). The faces of many soldiers had been mangled so badly that they had to be fitted with hammered metal masks, painted to match natural skin tones, so as not to horrify onlookers at home—or wives and sweethearts. The bodies of the dead were not shipped home. Identification and recovery (and reassembly) had become an insurmountable task. In the military cemeteries that sprang up after the war, like the famous one at Flanders Field, many of the crosses are memorials, not grave markers. Without funerals at home there could be no closure.

These appalling realities are not discussed in Clarissa's circle. Mutilated veterans would have been visible daily on the streets of London. Virginia Woolf certainly saw them: "with 'stiff legs, single legs, sticks shod with rubber, & empty sleeves' as well as the 'dreadful looking spiders propelling themselves along the platform—men all body—limbs trimmed off close to the body'"(qtd. in Zwerdling 283). Hundreds of thousands were jobless when they returned or disabled and unable to work. The actual dead were comfortably out of sight, and in a world like Clarissa Dalloway's, out of sight means out of mind. The war is present in the novel by its absence. Its physical horrors are repressed and not discussed because they disturb the normative idea of England, with its reassuringly scripted class structure, which in turn represents an idea of existence itself. If one crumbles, so does the other, and there is no longer the sealed off, vaguely literary, irreality to inhabit—as the enthusiastic young men who volunteered, like Septimus, deluded by their culture, perhaps expecting *Henry V* and a rousing St. Crispin's Day speech from their sovereign, were soon to discover. Instead, the most famous literary utterance of this war came from the poet Wilfred Owen, a bitter diatribe in verse describing the horrors of a mustard gas attack and sarcastically titled, "DULCE ET DECORUM EST." The title is a line fragment from an ode by the Latin poet Horace extolling courage in battle: "Dulce et decorum est pro patria mori," which translates "It is sweet and right to die for your country." Owen himself was killed a week before the Armistice was signed and his parents received the telegram the day the Armistice was being celebrated in the streets.

Among Clarissa's friends, the collective need for restabilization causes normalness to become fetishized. Lady Bexborough, for instance, Clarissa's role model, receives the news of the death of her favorite son in battle without batting an eye as she is about to open a bazaar. She remains the unemotional Englishwoman, and like her peers, she achieves stoicism "even if the price . . . is petrifaction" (Zwerdling 122). Or when the darkened motor car with (perhaps) the Queen inside passes down St. James Street, citizens stare in awe and "stand even straighter . . . ready to attend their Sovereign, if need be, to the cannon's mouth, as their ancestors had done before them" (Woolf 18). This invocation of ancestors is absurd, considering that only five years earlier more than half a million of England's young men had been blown to pieces charging into the cannon's mouth. *That* memory has been erased: too real. Later in the day, at lunch with Richard and Hugh Whitbread to discuss a plan of hers to emigrate suitable young people to Canada, the imposing Lady Bruton abruptly exclaims, "Ah, the news from India!" That news from India, the crown jewel of the Empire, concerns Mahatma Gandhi, who has recently assumed leadership of the Indian National Congress and will soon lead India into the modern world and eventually into complete independence from Britain. The normality of the Empire itself, which Lady Bruton's male forebears have served with distinction, is slowly disintegrating. Instability is setting in. On his stroll through Regent's Park, Peter Walsh ruminates on the changes that have taken place in the city since he was in

India. He marvels that the phrase "water closet" (itself a euphemism for toilet) is now openly used in the weekly papers (71). These two little words in the newspaper represent a huge change in the nature of public discourse—and a change therefore in what people will eventually come to think about themselves. (James Joyce's scandalously frank *Ulysses* had been published the year before.) At home, Elizabeth worries vaguely that because of her oriental eyes and her skin coloring, some dormant mutation has racially contaminated her genes, that she is possibly not all English (122-123). At Elizabeth's party, Aunt Helena Parry, past eighty, still dreams of collecting orchids in Burma "carried on the backs of coolies . . . over solitary peaks" (178). Also at the party is the Dalloways' old friend, Sir Harry, who paints cows for collectors who dream of a pastoral England that no longer exists. Clarissa, in her own moments of estrangement and anxiety, gladly finds reassurance in Richard's presence, normal Richard sitting there reading his paper as he normally does.

Sir William Bradshaw is normality's chief enforcer. "Once you fall," Septimus thinks at one point, "human nature is on you" (98). Abnormality can get out of hand. Proportion, therefore, has become Sir William's goddess: "Worshipping proportion, Sir William not only prospered himself but made England prosper, secluded her lunatics, forbade childbirth, penalized despair, made it impossible for the unfit to propagate their views until they too shared his sense of proportion" (99). Those who do not share this doctrine with the Sir Williams of the world must undergo therapeutic intervention by Proportion's more proactive sister, Conversion, "who feasts on the wills of the weakly" (100). Lady Bradshaw herself had been set upon by Conversion, and fifteen years ago had "gone under. It was nothing you could put your finger on; there had been no scene, no snap; only the slow sinking water-logged, of her will into his" (100). The truly horrifying aspect of this process, Woolf makes clear, is that it is normal. It is what societies do.

Existentialism as a philosophical construct, or even as a word, had not yet come into being in 1925, but *Mrs. Dalloway* is striated from be-ginning to end with existential issues. According to classic existential-ism, in a world without God (or, in some theological versions, without a knowable God) and where an assumed template of something called human nature has been discredited, human beings are charged with the responsibility for their own freedom. Within the limits of the circum-stances one is born into, in a world which is otherwise without mean-ing, one must choose the course of one's own life and one's identity and be responsible for that choice, regardless of rules or social or cul-tural conventions (whose influences are very strong: the twin god-desses of Proportion and Conversion are the sworn enemies of this idea). "Bad faith" is a repudiation of the challenge of existential free-dom in exchange for an inauthentic life, for the security of becoming what is expected. In *Mrs. Dalloway* the war has made a great tear in the fabric of established truth, if not ripped it to shreds, and, at one level or another, every thinking person has to come to terms with a new reality and his or her place in it. The irrational has prevailed. Supernatural agency or supervision has been exposed as a myth (at the very least, God is no longer an Englishman). Clarissa has come to despise religion as an assault upon the integrity of the self. The mystique of nationhood and Empire has begun to disperse. The wisdom of Authority has proved to be a lie. Even at this level of the caste system, people seem to be clinging precariously to a form of "bad faith." The equivalent terms in *Mrs. Dalloway* are having "gone under" and "the death of the soul." All five of the original Bourton group—Hugh Whitbread, Richard, Pe-ter, Sally Seton, and Clarissa—have reached a point in life where there is no turning back from the choices they have made. Sir Hugh seems perfectly happy with his choice, blind to everything "except self-esteem and comfort" (189). Peter and, surprisingly, even Richard re-flect during the day upon the meaninglessness of things. Unsinkable Sally Seton, now Lady Rosseter, married to a prosperous self-made man and living in the suburbs of Manchester with their five enormous boys, seems of all the group to be the most comfortable in her own skin, but even she, in the end, acknowledges humanity's essential lone-liness: "[For] what can one know even of the people one lives with ev-ery day? she asked. Are we not all prisoners? She had read a wonderful play about a man who scratched on the wall of his cell, and she had felt that was true of life—one scratched on the wall. Despairing of human relationships (people were so difficult), she often went into her garden and got from her flowers a peace which men and women never gave her" (193). She and Peter agree that it is only "the power of feeling" (193) that can save people from despair.

It is Clarissa, however, whose existential grief—the lost sense of purpose and meaning—gathers in that of all the others and gives it fo-cus: "Much rather would she have been one of those people like Rich-ard who did things for themselves, whereas, she thought, . . . half the time she did things not simply, not for themselves; but to make people think this or that. . . . Oh if she could have had her life over again! she thought, stepping on to the pavement, could have looked even differ-ently!" (10). This sad desire to be like someone else, Richard, for in-stance, or simply to *look* different, to be dark and imposing like Lady Bexborough, and interested in politics, suggests that Clarissa's respon-sibility for her own freedom can only be delegated to some other fan-tasy life. As Clarissa, she feels she is helpless to be anything different from what she is. She feels "invisible, unseen . . . not even Clarissa any more" (10-11), but Mrs. Richard Dalloway. She has a passion for gloves and shoes, and she wonders why Elizabeth—tellingly—does not. Her life is all form and artifice, inauthentic. She is therefore empty on the inside, unable to override her cultural programming. The choice between two men, Peter and Richard, has determined what kind of woman she would become. As it turns out, she thinks, much later, she has "lost herself in the process of living" (185) only to find it sporadi-cally in rare, but unsustaining, moments of delight. As a young woman of rank, born at the wrong time, the choice she did *not* have was not to marry.

We are given to understand that Clarissa would have been happiest living with Sally Seton the rest of her life, such was their girlish and animated love for each other during the idyll at Bourton; their solemn contempt at the time for the very notion of being married was prescient. But, of course, that life with Sally was not a real option either, only a fantasy version of what life could be like rather than what it is (or was then). That passion she had felt with and for Sally, it appears, was the last passion in her life. She lacks a desire for men, and this stranded condition has immobilized her in yet another way. At the end of the novel, Peter and Sally agree that, as *they* have grown older, feeling and passion are what they cherish most. It is what makes them feel real to themselves, authentic in an inauthentic world.

Clarissa broods upon death, which is made to seem continuous with her own life. She reads in Hatchards' bookshop window the first lines of the moving funeral song in Shakespeare's *Cymbeline*, commending death as a release from suffering, and displayed in the shop window as a silent memorial for the fallen: "Fear no more the heat of the sun/ Nor the furious winter's rages." She thinks, "This late age of the world's experience had bred in them, all men and all women, a well of tears" (9). After so much death and carnage, sorrow cannot be overcome by the living and transformed into hope once again, so there is no help for Clarissa's spirits from the world.

When Clarissa hears from Sir William of the suicide of this young man whose name she will not even know, she is affronted, at first, that death has been brought to her party. Then in the fluctuation of responses in her head, in the disturbed stream of her consciousness, she imagines—for this may or may not be true—that the young man has flung his life away as a gesture, paradoxically, that affirmed his existence:

A thing there was that mattered; a thing wreathed about with chatter, defaced, obscured in her own life, let drop every day in corruption, lies, chatter. This he had preserved. Death was defiance. Death was an attempt to communicate; people feeling the impossibility of reaching the centre which, mystically, evaded them; closeness drew apart; rapture faded, one was alone. There was an embrace in death. (184)

She is imagining a renunciation of her *own* life as a gesture of freedom. The revelation also has caused a momentary overcoming of bad faith, an understanding of her life as all periphery and no center, mystical or otherwise: "Somehow it was her disaster—her disgrace. It was her punishment to see sink and disappear here a man, there a woman, in this profound darkness, and she forced to stand here in her evening dress" (185). Encompassed by the ultimate context which is death, this judgment that Clarissa passes upon herself and her own life is breathtakingly clear and right. Tragic as the epiphany is, it is an act of dignity and courage beyond the means of any other character in the novel. Nothing will change as a consequence of it. She thinks graciously that, in truth, by taking his life the young man has simply ended his own suffering. He will "Fear no more the heat of the sun." Then she goes back to the party. A creature of fragments until now, she has become whole, momentarily, for however long it lasts, by facing the truth. In naming what is wrong with her self, she has also named what is wrong with her culture and has therefore stood apart from it.

There is no sense of an ending in *Mrs. Dalloway.* When the narrative simply stops, we are left with the feeling that things are going to continue as they are. We are not gratified by a formal resolution or reassured that everyone has now seen the light. The governing classes will continue to govern and to police disproportion and irregularity. Bold choices—collective or individual—will continue to go unmade. The war will become a dimmer and dimmer memory. But things continuing as they are means that the governing classes will remain in denial and unready for change, that drift and erosion and bad faith will persist, unacknowledged until it is too late. Already, during Richard's tenure in office, the Labour Party—with its interrogation of the status quo and its socialist economic agenda—is about to ascend to power and to become a dominant force in British politics from this point on. All but written in invisible ink on every page of Woolf's text is the still un-heeded observation of George Santayana: "Those who cannot remember the past are condemned to repeat it" (284). While this performance of the British governing classes is going on, outside, in another part of the world, Benito Mussolini and his *Fascisti* seize power in Rome. A year later, Adolf Hitler and his Nazi party attempt a similar *coup d'etat* in Munich, which fails. Two years later, while in prison, Hitler publishes the first volume of his memoirs, called *Mein Kampf*. *Mrs. Dalloway* and *Mein Kampf* are published in the same year.

Works Cited

Lochner, Louis P. *What About Germany?* New York: Dodd, Meade & Company, 1942.

Nicolson, Juliet. *The Great Silence*. New York: Grove Press, 2009.

Santayana, George. *The Life of Reason*. New York: Charles Scribner's Sons, 1917.

Whitworth, Michael H. *Virginia Woolf*. New York: Oxford UP, 2005.

Woolf, Virginia. *The Diary of Virginia Woolf*. Vol. 2. Ed. Anne Olivier Bell. New York: Harcourt, 1978.

_____. *Mrs. Dalloway*. New York: Harcourt, 1981.

Zwerdling, Alex. *Virginia Woolf and the Real World*. Berkeley: U of California P, 1986.

A Dialogue in Books:
Virginia Woolf's *Mrs. Dalloway* and
Michael Cunningham's *The Hours*_____

Yelena Furman

Virginia Woolf's *Mrs. Dalloway* (1925) recounts in parallel plot lines
the thoughts and actions in a single day of the upper-class Clarissa
Dalloway, who prepares to throw a party, and the shell-shocked war
veteran Septimus Smith, who commits suicide. One of the writers
greatly influenced by Woolf's novel was the contemporary American
writer Michael Cunningham, who referred to it as "the first great book
I ever read" ("First Love"). Cunningham's Pulitzer Prize-winning *The
Hours* (1998), which takes its title from the one Woolf originally intended to use for her novel, is both a tribute to Woolf's text and a reworking of its characters, themes, and narrative techniques.[1] In parallel
story lines, *The Hours* details a day in the lives of its three protagonists:
literary editor Clarissa Vaughan, who is throwing a party in 1990s New
York for her friend and former lover, Richard, who nicknames her
"Mrs. Dalloway"; Laura Brown, a suburban wife and mother in 1949
Los Angeles, engaged in the act of reading *Mrs. Dalloway* to escape
her confining existence; and (the fictional) Virginia Woolf, resident at
Hogarth House in Richmond, England, in 1923, engaged in the process
of writing *Mrs. Dalloway* and fighting off an impending bout of mental
illness.[2] In this way, "each strand remains focused throughout on the
literal text of *Mrs. Dalloway:* 'Mrs. Woolf' depicts its writing or production; 'Mrs. Brown' explores its reading or reception; and 'Mrs.
Dalloway' serves as a literal updating or retelling" (Schiff 367).

Mrs. Dalloway and *The Hours* thus exist in an intertextual relationship. Simply defined, intertextuality is the process of one text being in
dialogue with other texts by referencing them either overtly or implicitly. The degree to which *The Hours* references *Mrs. Dalloway* is so
great that not only is it in dialogue with Woolf's text, but rather its very
existence is dependent on it. This dependence is similar to, for example,

the way Jean Rhys's *Wide Sargasso Sea* (1966) depends on Charlotte Brontë's *Jane Eyre* (1847). *The Hours* is thus an example of a text that always functions in, and derives sustenance from, an inextricable relationship with its antecedent. This dependence means that, for readers, the fullest and most informed engagement with *The Hours* requires prior knowledge of *Mrs. Dalloway*. At the same time, although *The Hours* may not have been able to come into being without *Mrs. Dalloway*, it is still very much its own work, written by a completely different writer at a time and place far removed from Woolf's. As such, it manifests its own fictional universe and sensibilities that do not merely replicate those of her novel: "What becomes apparent in *The Hours* is that almost every technique, trope, motif, and theme derives from Woolf. . . . However, Cunningham employs these Woolfian elements to create something . . . that is his own" (Schiff 370). On the most basic level, this can be seen in the way Cunningham retains many of Woolf's character names but reworks the characters themselves. Thus, Woolf's high-society married couple Clarissa and Richard Dalloway become Clarissa and Richard, literary editor and writer, former lovers and now best friends, with Richard being gay; while Woolf's Sally Seton and Peter Walsh, Clarissa's lovers from her youth, turn into Sally, Clarissa's present-day live-in lover and television producer, and Louis, college instructor and Richard's ex-lover, respectively.

The tension between similarity and difference, between repetition and reinvention, is key to the intertextual relationship between *Mrs. Dalloway* and *The Hours*. This push-pull aspect is evident both in terms of the narrative techniques that Woolf and Cunningham employ and the major themes—love, including same-sex love; insanity and suicide; and artistic creation—that they explore in their respective texts.

Narrative Techniques

Mrs. Dalloway is structured on the principle of thematic links between the characters. In a diary entry—an excerpt of which Cunningham uses as one of his epigraphs to *The Hours*—Woolf described her newly discovered technique for writing what would eventually become *Mrs. Dalloway:* "I dig out beautiful caves behind my characters. . . . The idea is that the caves shall connect, & each comes to daylight at the present moment" (Woolf *Diary* 263). In digging out caves behind her characters, Woolf sought to go below the surface to explore their interior depths. The related idea that "the caves shall connect" reflects the structuring principle of thematic linkages that anchors *Mrs. Dalloway.* While Clarissa's and Septimus's plot lines do not intersect and the characters never meet, their parallel story lines produce several implicit linkages between the two. These range from objects that they both see or hear—"an 'official car' backfiring . . . the clocks strik[ing]" (Dick 53-54)—to similarities in their lives, such as both being trapped by their respective surroundings: Septimus by the medical establishment that seeks to confine him to an asylum and Clarissa by her male-dominated, upper-class world in which she is "not even Clarissa any more [but] Mrs. Richard Dalloway" (*Mrs. Dalloway* 14). While linked implicitly throughout the work, Clarissa's and Septimus's storylines intersect only once at the end of the novel, when Clarissa hears at her party that Septimus has died.

The thematic linking of the protagonists is arguably the most crucial structural device that Cunningham imports from Woolf, but whereas her linkages are largely implicit and readers must work to decipher them, he makes them much more overt. Among the multitude of objects and themes, the most prominent link between his protagonists is the novel *Mrs. Dalloway* itself, as each woman is connected to this text in various ways. The prominence of this text as a connecting principle underscores that in *The Hours*, the characters are simultaneously linked to each other and to Woolf's novel. Thus, the party thrown by Clarissa Dalloway is replicated through Clarissa Vaughan's attempt to throw a party in honor of Richard's winning a literary prize and through Laura Brown's preparing a much smaller family party in honor of her husband's birthday. Buying flowers, the centrality of which is highlighted in Woolf's famous opening line "Mrs. Dalloway said she would buy the flowers herself" (3), appears in Cunningham when Virginia pens this line, Clarissa purchases flowers for her party, and Laura attempts to make frosted roses on her husband's birthday cake. As in *Mrs. Dalloway*, the protagonists' storylines in *The Hours* directly intersect once, at the end of the novel in a reworking of Clarissa's and Septimus's encounter. Whereas Clarissa Dalloway hears about Septimus's death at her party, Clarissa Vaughan actually meets Laura Brown, who turns out to be Richard's mother, at what was supposed to be Clarissa's party for Richard, who has just killed himself. In a more figurative way, both Clarissa and Laura meet Virginia through their reading of her.

While both novels share the principle of thematic linkages, they notably differ in terms of other narrative strategies, which is to say in their degree of literary experimentation. *Mrs. Dalloway* was Woolf's modernist experiment with form and style as she strove to create a new direction for the English novel. This experimentation is evident in the stream-of-consciousness narration, the double narrative structure, a nonchronological unfolding of events that shifts between past and present, and—in what was arguably Woolf's main goal in breaking away from her literary predecessors—the turn away from external description and action toward a focus on the protagonists' inner worlds. In *Mrs. Dalloway*, the workings of the characters' interior lives—their perceptions and recollections, their consciousness—become the novel's central events. *Mrs. Dalloway* proceeds via the detailed revelations of Clarissa's and Septimus's thoughts and memories, further crystallized by the condensed time frame of a single day. In the novel's two-layer narrative, Septimus functions as Clarissa's double, or foil, with their consciousnesses reflected in and juxtaposed to each other, allowing consciousness as such to be represented from different vantage points. Although these exist to a lesser extent, additional points of view in the novel are those of Peter Walsh, Clarissa's former lover, and Rezia Smith, Septimus's wife. These characters' thoughts and memories flow into one another, without chapter breaks, through the stream-of-consciousness narration.

By the late twentieth century when Cunningham wrote *The Hours*, a focus on the interior self had essentially become the norm in literature. This focus is evident in his novel, which, like Woolf's, delves into its protagonists' thoughts and desires during a single day of their lives. From Woolf, too, he retains the focus on multiple points of view. *The Hours* has three protagonists, from whose varied perspectives the narrative unfolds. Yet *The Hours* is much less experimental than *Mrs. Dalloway*. Unlike Woolf's stream of consciousness, and despite an abundance of beautiful imagery, Cunningham's style is very straightforward. Whereas Woolf's narrative flows in one uninterrupted whole, Cunningham's is divided into chapters named after each of the protagonists—"Mrs. Dalloway," "Mrs. Woolf," and "Mrs. Brown"—and thus the storylines, although connected, are much more distinct, with switches in points of view much more clearly signaled.

Another difference between *Mrs. Dalloway* and *The Hours* lies in the relation between the protagonists' past and present, which is linked to narrative chronology. Woolf's experiments with a non-chronological structure are manifest in *Mrs. Dalloway*, which while proceeding linearly through the single day, simultaneously undercuts this linearity by shifting between the characters' present and their past, whereby the past is brought in via the present. This is particularly evident in terms of Clarissa, whose memories of her youth in Bourton, of her love for Peter Walsh, and of the single but unforgettable kiss with Sally Seton constitute a significant part of her day and consequently of the narrative. Thus, her thoughts and actions during the day as she prepares for her party continually alternate with her recollections about the past: "She could remember scene after scene at Bourton" (8). In a somewhat more muted fashion, the past is also highly significant for Septimus, whose memories of meeting Rezia in Italy and especially of his friend Evans, killed in the war, make up a significant part of his day. Given the novel's concern with the internal self, one's past—or more precisely, the interaction between one's past and present—forms an integral part of that self.

In contrast, the characters' past becomes less significant in *The Hours*. To be sure, Cunningham's protagonists recollect and reflect on their past. This is especially true for Clarissa Vaughan, whose recollections of her involvement with Richard at age eighteen are crucial for her self-definition and, consequently, form a major part of the novel. Yet the past is not a particular focus either for Laura Brown, whose thoughts revolve around her untenable existence as wife and mother, or for (the fictional) Virginia Woolf, focused on writing her novel while fighting off impending mental illness. Largely remaining in the present, Cunningham's novel—which is also narrated in the present tense—thus progresses more linearly than Woolf's.

Textual Themes

Love is a prominent theme in both *Mrs. Dalloway* and *The Hours*. Underscoring the complexity of human relations, both novels feature love triangles, suggesting that people can love their partners yet continue to have feelings for former or potential loves. In her youth, while in love with Peter Walsh, Clarissa also was in love with Sally Seton, and both Peter and Richard Dalloway rivaled to be her husband. She continues to care for the less successful but more exciting Peter even after she marries the kind but solidly conventional Richard. In *The Hours*, the young Clarissa rivals Louis for Richard's affections, whereas the adult Clarissa, while genuinely loving Sally, is haunted by the question of what would have been had she remained with Richard; and Laura, while married to Dan, has intense feelings for her neighbor, Kitty.

Mrs. Dalloway and *The Hours* thus feature a mixture of heterosexual and homosexual relationships. For both Woolf and Cunningham, the emphasis on same-sex love has an autobiographical aspect. Despite her marriage to Leonard Woolf, Virginia Woolf preferred women, the most well-known of these relationships being with the writer Vita Sackville-West. Although in the England of her time, she could not publish an openly lesbian text, the theme of lesbian desire was a distinct feature of Woolf's work. In *Mrs. Dalloway*, while Clarissa loved Peter and marries Richard, her most memorable experience has been with a woman. In Bourton, she kisses Sally Seton, a kiss that was "the most exquisite moment of her whole life. . . . Sally stopped; picked a flower; kissed her on the lips. The whole world might have turned upside down!" (52). Her memory of that kiss follows her through adulthood, and while she no longer has physical contact with women, "she could not resist sometimes yielding to the charm of a woman . . . she did undoubtedly then feel what men felt" (46-7). Clarissa's desire for other women renders her marriage a sexless endeavor, as she and Richard are not sexually intimate: "lying there reading . . . she could not dispel a virginity preserved through childbirth which clung to her like a sheet" (46). Yet despite her feelings for women, Clarissa's lesbianism largely remains latent. The path she takes in life is the socially sanctioned one of heterosexual marriage. Clarissa marries a man of high social standing, which provides her with position and wealth, which are extremely important to her. Maintaining this privilege requires suppressing her lesbian desires (Allan 107-10).

If the representation of homosexuality is muted in Woolf, it is amplified full force in Cunningham. Cunningham, who is openly gay, benefits from a change in times: at the end of the twentieth century, being gay or lesbian and/or portraying homosexuality in literature is no longer taboo. As such, characters in *The Hours* are not only openly gay or lesbian, but actually seem beyond viewing this as any sort of issue; for them, it is simply a given. Clarissa's latent lesbianism in *Mrs. Dalloway* is reworked in *The Hours* into one of the major love relationships: Clarissa and Sally live together and not only kiss, but make love. In one instance, however, Cunningham transports the notion of repressed lesbianism from *Mrs. Dalloway* to *The Hours*. Like Clarissa Dalloway, Laura Brown exhibits lesbian desire within a heterosexual marriage. Although unlike Clarissa, Laura enjoys sex with her husband, she also desires Kitty. The exquisiteness Clarissa feels when kissing Sally is replicated in Laura's passionate experience of kissing her neighbor: "Kitty snakes her arms around Laura's waist. Laura is flooded with feeling. . . . Kitty lifts her face, and their lips touch" (Cunningham *The Hours* 109-110). Further underscoring the link to Woolf, Cunningham adopts similar language for Laura's feelings. Her thought that "This is how a man feels, holding a woman" (109) echoes Clarissa's sentiment that "she did undoubtedly then feel what men felt." Yet as in 1920s British high society, lesbianism is taboo in 1940s suburban California, and Laura's desire cannot be given free expression and must be contained within one discrete moment.

In addition to love, another major theme in both works is madness and its frequent attendant consequence, suicide. For Woolf, these themes were not merely literary, but a stark aspect of her real-life experience. Woolf suffered from mental illness and attempted suicide; in creating the shell-shocked Septimus, she "was drawing on her own intermittent states of madness" (Lee 95). Although Woolf ultimately titled her novel *Mrs. Dalloway*, Septimus Smith figures as an equally significant character, a key part of her structural and thematic design. Referring to *Mrs. Dalloway*, Woolf wrote in her diary, "I adumbrate here a study of insanity & suicide: the world seen by the sane & the insane side by side—something like that. Septimus Smith?—is that a good name?" (Woolf *Diary* 207). Septimus's importance for Woolf resided both in enabling a new form for the novel, one with the double narrative structure, and in terms of content in that it allowed her to show the profound psychological effects of war on those who survive its physical atrocities. Septimus suffers from shell shock, a severe trauma that precipitates stark breaks with reality and causes continual slips into a world of his own making. He experiences terrifying hallucinations, seeing "an old woman's head in the middle of a fern" (*Mrs. Dalloway* 100) and himself "drowned . . . and lying on a cliff with the gulls screaming over him" (213). The doctors' attempts to heal him—

namely Sir William Bradshaw's decision to confine him to an asylum for a rest cure—prove not only utterly futile in dealing with war trauma but actively exacerbate his suicide attempt. When Dr. Holmes, working with Sir William Bradshaw, enters the room and Septimus sees no possibility of escape, he jumps out of a window.

In a very real sense, *The Hours* likewise becomes "a study of insanity and suicide." Cunningham's creation of the fictional character Virginia Woolf highlights that his engagement with these themes is not only an engagement with *Mrs. Dalloway*, but also with Woolf's biography, which becomes part of the narrative fabric of *The Hours*. Signaling the centrality of madness and suicide from the very beginning, the novel opens with a Prologue, set in 1941, that depicts Virginia's suicide by drowning, an act she undertakes because, as she says in her note to Leonard, "*I feel certain that I am going mad again*" (6; italics in the original). If the Prologue depicts the actual act of suicide, the "Mrs. Woolf" chapters, set nearly twenty years prior, chronicle her battle against recurring mental illness. The chapters are set in Hogarth House, the Woolfs' residence in the suburb of Richmond, to which Virginia has been confined as the excitement of London has proven harmful to her mental state. The monotony of life in Richmond is designed to protect her from the awful episodes in which "the voices start. . . . A flock of sparrows outside her window once sang, unmistakably, in Greek" (Cunningham *The Hours* 71).[3] Although she feels well enough to write, she is continuously haunted by the possibility of her disease's return: "She works, always, against the fear of relapse" (70).

Madness and suicide also plague Richard, an amalgam of Septimus and the real-life Woolf and linked to the fictional Virginia. Whereas Septimus suffers from shell shock and Virginia from mental illness, Richard is dying of AIDS, which has destroyed him both physically and mentally. In addition to having failing organs and emaciated limbs, Richard hears voices, like both the real and fictional Virginias; as he tells Clarissa, "They were singing, just now, in a foreign language. I believe it may have been Greek" (59). Richard's hearing voices also harks back to Septimus, who sees things that are not there. The manner of Richard's suicide follows Septimus's while creatively reworking the Clarissa-Septimus relation. In *Mrs. Dalloway*, the single instance of Septimus and Clarissa coming together is through news of his death at her party; in *The Hours*, a horrified Clarissa watches as Richard, in a manner similar to Septimus, throws himself out of his apartment window.

However, Septimus, Richard, and Virginia are not merely mad; in all three cases, this madness is linked with artistic creation. Virginia and Richard are brilliant writers; while Septimus is not a writer per se, his madness is simultaneously a debilitating disease and the poetic sensibility of an artist, providing a unique angle of vision that sets him apart from the conventional mentality of members of Clarissa's circle. Septimus's imaginative view of the world allows him to see it as full of divine possibility, if only temporarily. In Regent's Park, he watches a plane advertise toffee by writing the brand name in the sky, a prosaic act that in his perception becomes a sign of the world's splendor: "So, thought Septimus, looking up, they are signaling to me . . . it was plain enough, this beauty, this exquisite beauty, and tears filled his eyes as he looked at the smoke words languishing and melting in the sky" (Woolf *Mrs. Dalloway* 31). His visions reveal to him the potential to radically transform the war-ravaged world into one of peace and harmony, a world magnificently reborn.

Depicting a character with poetic sensibilities that is nevertheless not an artist reflects Woolf's ideas about art. Despite being very much concerned with the highly literary questions of artistic form and technique, Woolf strove to expand the definition of what is considered art, a theme also picked up by Cunningham: "Both Cunningham and Woolf depict 'the common' as a worthy content of fiction and try to close the gap between art and 'ordinary' experiences'" (Spengler 74). For example, some critics have pointed to Clarissa Dalloway as one of Woolf's examples of "artists in life" (Spengler 59), whose artistry consists of orchestrating a magnificent party that unites people in celebration on which the novel ends. Like her namesake, Clarissa Vaughan puts together a lavish party for Richard, complete with beautiful flowers and food; while it is thwarted by his suicide immediately prior, it nevertheless succeeds in bringing people together, being the moment that Clarissa and Sally meet Laura, who has come to pay tribute to her son. Arguably, it is Laura herself who constitutes Cunningham's most marked example of an "artist in life" through her attempt to bake a cake for her husband's birthday. Although the cake is ultimately a failure, Laura feels the process of making it to be similar to that required to produce a work of art, like her favorite novel: "This, she thinks, is how artists or architects must feel (it's an awfully grand comparison, she knows, maybe even a little foolish, but still), faced with canvas, with stone, with oil or wet cement. Wasn't a book like *Mrs. Dalloway* once just empty paper and a pot of ink?" (76). In associating such ordinary experiences as throwing parties and baking cakes with artistic inclinations, Woolf and Cunningham both allow the definition of art to be more inclusive and endow these daily actions with more fundamental significance.

Where Cunningham departs from Woolf is in his focus on not only everyday artists, but on those such as Virginia and Richard, who are actual writers. While Cunningham remains faithful to most of Woolf's themes in his novel, the instance of his greatest departure from her is arguably this focus on literature and literary endeavors. *The Hours* is, fundamentally, "a novel about reading and writing and how those activities fit within the larger context of a single day" (Schiff 367). The significance of reading and writing is evident everywhere in the novel, from its thoroughly intertextual form to the fact that several characters are engaged in literary occupations: Clarissa, whose circle of friends includes many literary types, edits books, as does Leonard Woolf; Laura Brown, an avid reader from a young age, becomes a librarian after leaving her family. Richard engages in the most literary of endeavors: like the real-life Woolf, he is an established and tremendously gifted writer, who has just received a prestigious literary prize, the reason for Clarissa's throwing a party. Echoing the way in which Woolf's literary efforts fundamentally transformed the direction of English literature, Richard's prodigious talents make him one of a select group of writers whose work determines the direction of writing in general: "literature itself (the future of which is being shaped right now) seems to feel a need for Richard's particular contribution" (Cunningham *The Hours* 64). His degenerate physical and mental state does not take away from his talents, and his works will live on even though he himself does not.

The most significant literary undertaking in *The Hours* is Virginia's efforts to write *Mrs. Dalloway*. The "Mrs. Woolf" chapters continuously highlight Virginia's writing process, filled with both chronic self-doubt and the simultaneous sense that she is capable of achieving something remarkable: "This morning she may penetrate the obfuscation, the clogged pipes, to reach the gold. She can feel it inside her. . . . It is an inner faculty that recognizes the animating mysteries of the world because it is made of the same substance, and when she is very fortunate she is able to write directly through that faculty" (*The Hours* 34-35). Reaching the gold, she is able to give voice to her text and her growing artistic vision, as Cunningham depicts her working out key problems in her novel. Whereas she starts out thinking that Clarissa should commit suicide, she ultimately realizes that this is not the right ending; rather, she decides that "Clarissa, sane Clarissa—exultant, ordinary Clarissa—will go on, loving London, loving her life of ordinary pleasures, and someone else, a deranged poet, a visionary, will be the one to die" (211). Cunningham's inclusion of this particular idea highlights how crucial this realization is: it is at this moment that Virginia begins envisioning Septimus and the new type of novel he makes possible. While Virginia, and Richard, may struggle with madness and commit suicide, they possess the unique ability to produce works of exquisite beauty and lasting import.

If the "Mrs. Dalloway" and especially "Mrs. Woolf" sections focus on writing, the "Mrs. Brown" sections focus on its complement: reading. Whereas Virginia is shown in the process of producing *Mrs. Dalloway*, Laura is shown in the process of consuming it. Cunningham cites several extensive passages from *Mrs. Dalloway* in the "Mrs. Brown" sections, thus incorporating his beloved novel into his own text and making his readers (re)read the novel along with his character. That a novel by a 1920s British writer resonates so profoundly with a 1949 American housewife suggests that "*The Hours* describes and celebrates a community constituted by (a work of) literature beyond the bounds of time and place" (Spengler 74).

For Laura, reading is a manifest necessity to counteract her domestic confinement. Relegated to the sole roles of wife and mother in 1949, she is stifled by an existence in which she must constantly pretend to be someone she does not wish to be: "A spasm of fury rises unexpectedly, catches in her throat. . . . She herself is trapped here forever, posing as a wife" (*The Hours* 205). While she does not actually kill herself, she continually thinks of suicide as a way out, thoughts connected to the fact that Virginia Woolf, whose novel she loves, died in this fashion. Reading is her only escape from this confinement, transporting her to a place outside the boundaries of her own life: "Laura occupies a twilight zone of sorts. . . . She is herself and not herself. She is a woman in London, an aristocrat, pale and charming, a little false; she is Virginia Woolf; and she is this other, the inchoate, tumbling thing known as herself" (*The Hours* 187). In a novel that stresses love, Laura's love of reading is a variation on that theme. Her act of stealing away for some uninterrupted reading time away from son and home is presented in highly charged, sexualized terms: she illicitly checks into a hotel room for the afternoon, where "[w]ith a sensation of deep and buoyant release, she begins reading" (150). Laura may sleep with her husband and desire Kitty, but it is to Virginia Woolf and *Mrs. Dalloway* that she gives herself most fully.

While Cunningham's *The Hours* exists in its own right, Woolf's *Mrs. Dalloway* is what makes that existence possible. A sustained engagement with *Mrs. Dalloway* lies at the core of *The Hours*, as Woolf's devices and themes become the basic narrative materials that reappear in altered form in Cunningham. In terms of narrative techniques, both writers are concerned with structure and form and both build their novels on the principle of thematic links between characters. Yet whereas Woolf uses experimental literary techniques such as stream-of-consciousness narration and plays with chronology, Cunningham foregoes several of her devices to produce a more stylistically straightforward work. In terms of major themes, both writers focus on love, including same-sex love; insanity and suicide; and artistic creation. However, the depiction of lesbianism in *Mrs. Dalloway* is muted, while it is markedly manifest in *The Hours*. While madness and suicide plague characters in both novels, they are especially reserved in *The Hours* for the creative geniuses. Finally, whereas both novels argue that the definition of artistry should be expanded to include everyday acts, *The Hours* simultaneously asserts the significance of specifically literary creation and demonstrates the import writers have for their readers. Doing so, Cunningham underscores the way *Mrs. Dalloway* has been instrumental to his own life and literary endeavors. Beyond the links established between its characters, *Mrs. Dalloway* thus connects with its readers. Long after its publication, Woolf's novel continues to speak to them and, as in *The Hours*, inspires some to talk back.

Notes

1. In 2002, *The Hours* was released as a film (dir. Stephen Daldry). This article, however, deals only with Cunningham's novel.

2. As critics have pointed out, Laura's last name derives from Woolf's essay "Mr. Bennett and Mrs. Brown," and "emphasizes links to Woolf's essayistic work, in particular to her concepts of fiction and her ideas about women" (Spengler 54).

3. This was one of Woolf's real-life symptoms of the disease. As her nephew and biographer, Quentin Bell, writes, "she lay in bed, listening to the birds singing in Greek" (90) during an episode of her illness.

Works Cited

Allan, Tuzyline Jita. "The Death of Sex and the Soul in *Mrs. Dalloway* and Nella Larsen's *Passing*." *Virginia Woolf: Lesbian Readings*. Ed. Eileen Barrett and Patricia Cramer. New York: New York UP, 1997. 95-113.

Bell, Quentin. *Virginia Woolf: A Biography*. Vol. 1. London: The Hogarth Press, 1990.

Cunningham, Michael. "First Love." *PEN American Center*. n.d. http://www.pen.org/viewmedia.php/prmMID/1114/prmID/547

_____. *The Hours*. New York: Picador, 1998.

Dick, Susan. "Literary Realism in *Mrs Dalloway*, *To the Lighthouse*, *Orlando* and *The Waves*." *The Cambridge Companion to Virginia Woolf*. Ed. Sue Roe and Susan Sellers. New York: Cambridge UP, 2000. 50-71.

Lee, Hermione. *The Novels of Virginia Woolf*. London: Methuen & Co., 1977.

Schiff, James. "Rewriting Woolf's *Mrs. Dalloway*: Homage, Sexual Identity, and the Single-Day Novel by Cunningham, Lippincott, and Lanchester." *Critique* 45.4 (2004): 363-82.

Spengler, Birgit. "Michael Cunningham Rewriting Virginia Woolf: Pragmatist vs. Modernist Aesthetics." *Woolf Studies Annual* 10 (2004): 51-79.

Woolf, Virginia. *The Diary of Virginia Woolf*. Vol. 2. Ed. Anne Olivier Bell. New York: Harcourt, 1978.

_____. *Mrs. Dalloway*. San Diego: Harcourt, 1985.

Mrs. Dalloway and the Critics _____

Pam Fox Kuhlken

Virginia Woolf and *Mrs. Dalloway* (1925) clearly have a library of their own in the twenty-first century to shelve the prodigious amount of criticism the novel has inspired and likely will continue to inspire. The first issue of F. R. Leavis's conservative literary journal, *Scrutiny* (1932), included a critical attack on *Mrs. Dalloway* as a portrait of a privileged woman written by a privileged woman who existed in an intellectual vacuum of no relevance (Bradbrook 36-37). In contrast, Hilary Thompson's 2008 incisive essay confronts a Clarissa who stares Darwinian society in the face with her opening line: "Virginia Woolf didn't always want the party to end, but she had no illusions that the people there didn't often want to die or kill each other" (86).

Writing in 1925, E. M. Forster, a member of Woolf's Bloomsbury salon, described Clarissa as "elderly, kind, graceful, rather hard and superficial, and a terrible snob. How she loves London!" ("The Early Novels" 110). In a different tone, O. P. Sharma recalls the monumental victory of the novel's publication in her 1975 essay "Feminism as Aesthetic Vision: A Study of Virginia Woolf's *Mrs. Dalloway*":

> A new peak of feminist achievement in fiction was thus reached in 1925 with the simultaneous publication of Woolf's *Mrs. Dalloway* and May Sinclair's *Three Sisters* in England and Edith Wharton's *The Mother's Recompense* and Ellen Glasgow's *Barren Ground* in America. . . . It was the first phase of the fulfillment of a new feminist impulse that had its gestation during the years of the First World War. (63-64)

By 1983 Clarissa is an emergent lesbian, according to second-wave feminist critics in Jane Marcus's *New Feminist Essays on Virginia Woolf*. And by the 1990s, she is a thwarted lesbian.

Remarkably, the text of *Mrs. Dalloway* remains fixed as published, whereas its meaning is in continual flux. Through the decades, aesthetics, feminist impulses, political realities, and cultural contexts evolve with the Zeitgeist ("Spirit of the Age") and inform critical responses to the novel. Since 1925, criticism of Woolf's most popular experimental modern novel has been proliferating, with renewed passion after a film adaptation or the publication of a Woolfian diary, memoir, biography, or another author's literary homage. Some critical views are favorable, calling the novel a triumph, but critics also write out of distemper, prejudice, personal wounds, disappointment, or simply different literary tastes and training.

Early critics with Victorian sensibilities were preoccupied with Woolf's innovations in narrative style as they used textual criticism to trace the evolution of the manuscript, and comparative criticism to appreciate its unique contribution to literature both within and without Woolf's canon. Some of these early critics found her characters and poetic narration artificial and one-dimensional, interrogating the reality of persona and place. They questioned the legitimacy of the concept of androgyny, and minimized innovations in gender roles, preferring to use the text for a historical understanding of modernism or of London after the Great War.

Overwhelmingly, critics write as admirers of *Mrs. Dalloway*'s intricate structure, shifting streams of consciousness, multiple personae, social equanimity, true-to-life characters, and often breathtaking prose. In the twenty-first century, prolific *Dalloway* criticism reflects the novel's popularity with eclectic, political, poetic, and innovative readings. *Mrs. Dalloway* appeals broadly since it lends itself to contemporary concerns, especially gender roles and identity; space, time, memory, and stream of consciousness; trauma and recovery; nihilism and suicide. *Mrs. Dalloway*'s critics are still being rewarded with new insights, and this seems to guarantee that readers will continue to find pleasure in Woolf's modern classic about a day in the life of its title character, an easily distracted London socialite, who unexpectedly confronts a veteran's suicide in her otherwise protected haven. Despite Clarissa's best efforts, the party does not go as planned. Similarly, outstanding criticism may follow trends, but the reader can also anticipate pleasurable shocks.

Early Critics: 1925-1949

An appropriate launch into the earliest criticism on *Mrs. Dalloway* predates the novel's publication. In 1924, Woolf published the essay "Mr. Bennett and Mrs. Brown," in which she sets forth the purpose of all novels: to deal with character, to realize and steep oneself in their atmosphere (102). For Woolf, a character is eternal, representing all of human nature that changes only on the surface. Woolf's characters will not function according to artificial conventions. The novelist admits that in order to accomplish her new way of telling the truth, she is prepared for a season of failures and fragments, and warns that stories may arrive in an exhausted and chaotic condition ("Mr. Bennett" 117).

Woolf treats readers to a rare gift in *A Writer's Diary* (1954): her responses to reviews. In a 1925 entry, Woolf feared that "Mrs. D" may be "a flawed stone," recalling how she found Clarissa "tinselly" until she invented her memories, and recognized the novel's form was ornate despite ordinary events. Woolf accepted a reader's comment that the book was "genius," but "coming when, one never can tell" (Woolf *Diary* 32). She restrained herself to a day, knowing that if she took a more fantastic framework she would lose touch with emotions (*Diary* 32). She dared to hope it was full of more genius than her previous work.

So the confident forty-three-year-old novelist was disappointed by *The Times Literary Supplement*'s 1925 criticism that the novel was "experimental" when Woolf intentionally expressed her meaning more fully than usual, with every scene supporting the idea of a character named for lucidity: "Clarissa." Woolf made an exception for the 1928 Modern Library edition of *Mrs. Dalloway* that she never made for another novel: she wrote a special preface that justified her intentions to critics who had been interrogating her ever since its publication three years earlier. Woolf explained the dual narration of Clarissa and

Septimus who should be seen as dependents, and identified which characters should be admired or disliked as representative social types. Woolf's Bloomsbury associate, E. M. Forster, in an assessment of her early novels including *Mrs. Dalloway*, noted that Woolf had set out to solve a problem that would "inaugurate a new literature . . . to retain her own wonderful new method and form, and yet allow her readers to inhabit each character with Victorian thoroughness" (114).

William Troy's "Virginia Woolf: The Novel of Sensibility" (1937), reprinted in Sprague's *Virginia Woolf* (1971), offers the last of the staunch Victorian responses. Troy considers Woolf to be a "novelist of sensibility" who champions "superior Bohemia" (29), and faults her literary style for being poetic and therefore highly artificial (35). Troy considers Woolf within her contemporary milieu to show that her fundamental view of reality reflects the ideology of an entire generation rather than of one individual.

David Daiches's classic *Virginia Woolf* (1942) argues that Woolf departs from her earlier novels in *Mrs. Dalloway*. She abandons traditional forms and masters a new technique that represents "the flux of experience, a style that was flexible, impressionistic, meditative" (53). The chapter opens with a lucid and convincing comparison between *Mrs. Dalloway* and *Ulysses* (53-54). Daiches contends:

> In *Mrs. Dalloway* a deliberate attempt is made both to bring all the tracts of experience explored into a single focus and to effect all transitions from one part to another in such a way that the unity of the work is emphasized rather than . . . weakened by the continual shifts. (62)

Daiches admires Woolf's genius for escaping the limitations of chronology through "monologue intérieur" and creating transitions by alternating time and space (63). He explains that Woolf records streams of consciousness indirectly, in contrast to Joyce's verbatim transcription. In Woolf, "We are either moving freely in time within the consciousness of an individual, or moving from person to person at a single moment in time" (65). The result is "a dialectical opposition between the flux of time and the moment" (xv) in an assertion of individuality and otherness within society. In this sophisticated novel that clearly breaks with nineteenth century models, Woolf's real accomplishment is "the dissolution of experience into tenuous insights" (78).

Nathalia Wright's structuralist essay, "A Study in Composition" (1944), statistically proves four themes: that Clarissa is primary; that Peter Walsh is secondary; that Septimus and Mrs. Dalloway are doubles; and that the English national character is represented by 116 named minor characters (351-52). Wright calculates that of the novel's seventeen-hour day, eleven are spent with Clarissa; ten with Peter; six with the English national character; and three with Septimus (355). Wright concedes, "*Mrs. Dalloway*, indeed, is an easier novel to diagram than to summarize" (358). But if it must be summarized, it would be that every British subject owns consciousness and memory, and will lose them both at death.

In *Virginia Woolf: Her Art as Novelist* (1945), Joan Bennett defends Woolf's art from critics who find her characters limited and narrow. Bennett appreciates Woolf's characters; they "are either sensitive or intelligent or both" (49) and considers the tightly interwoven connection between Clarissa and Septimus. She explores Mrs. Dalloway's pathological behavior as representative of her social class within a universe that juxtaposes order and chaos as reflected in contrasting images of luxury and poverty, war and peace, isolation and mass. Woolf wrestles with the modernists' dilemma of maintaining integrity in the face of the miseries of the world while nestled in the lap of luxury (103).

1950s

In the 1950s, critics generally covered formalist topics like manuscript revisions that privileged the composition over cultural or political implications. Reuben Brower's "Something Central Which Permeated: Virginia Woolf and *Mrs. Dalloway*" (1951) examines the novel as a complex web of symbolic relationships that become meaningful through their relationships. Brower analyzes how the interconnecting web of metaphors indicates and proves the "vision of experience it implies" (51). Brower conceives of two poles in tension with each other: one pole represents the process of life, and the second pole represents the imminent threat of death. All characters struggle with these poles and in this struggle are linked to one another in meaningful ways, whether Clarissa and Peter or Clarissa and Septimus. Sir William Bradshaw is the "allegorical destroyer" when he brings news of death to Clarissa's party at a point in the narrative when all the life metaphors converge (60).

Irma Rantavaara's *Virginia Woolf and Bloomsbury* (1953) is a study of Bloomsbury's counter-cultural aesthetics that features one of Woolf's novels in each chapter. Her discussion of *Mrs. Dalloway* focuses upon the fear of death. Without the advantage of a religious framework, Rantavaara contends, Woolf remains "in a state of suspense, full of anticipation and query, but none of her metaphysical questions ever got an answer, none reached a stage of strong positive conviction" (105-06). Her novels, then, are essentially amoral riddles. She considers the theme of the novel as being biographical (108), and sees Woolf's atheism as the root of Mrs. Dalloway's and Septimus's preoccupations with death and hopelessness.

1960s

Mrs. Dalloway scholarship waned in the 1960s, later to revive in the 1970s. Critics of this decade argued for the work's unity of theme and structure, and focused on subjects of sacrament, love, and time. In 1962, A. D. Moody revived the class-based objections from the 1930s, treating Clarissa as a shallow representative of her elitist social class distinguished by "non-life" (68). Moody aligns Clarissa with Dr. Bradshaw in their disgust and prejudice against the lower classes and "exaltation of the symbols and appearances of honour, achievement, civilization" (73).

In the wake of postmodernism, the last time a critic may have attempted to espouse "the meaning" of *Mrs. Dalloway* was Anna S. Benjamin's 1965 essay, "Towards an Understanding of the Meaning of Virginia Woolf's *Mrs. Dalloway.*" Benjamin finds in *Mrs. Dalloway* "a reassertion of the value of living life in its fullest as part of the universe" where we would least expect it: "among the restricted privileged class in London" (223). Simply living life transcends the question of its meaning or whether or not it is good, and brings moments of insight about tragedy, loneliness, and beauty.

Jean Guiguet's *Virginia Woolf and Her Works* (1965) is a harbinger of later postmodern criticism. Guiguet revisits the milestones of criticism on *Mrs. Dalloway*, such as the origin of the novel and the influence of Proust and Joyce. The result is a collection of bold and exciting interpretations through a linguistic paradigm that is best experienced rather than summarized. Guiguet infers how Woolf fused biographical remarks from her diaries together and began writing until she could not write another line (230-31). Her literary form was an achievement in opposition to—and not in imitation of—James Joyce's method in *Ulysses*, and a style greatly improved by her reading of Marcel Proust (244, 247). Woolf's intention for this novel, according to Guiguet, is to define how life moves through time, confronting love and loss, comedy and tragedy.

1970s

Burgeoning feminist criticism of the 1970s was fueled by Elaine Showalter's *A Literature of Their Own: British Women Novelists from Brontë to Lessing* (1977). In addition to feminist perspectives, critics of the 1970s addressed topics as diverse as archetypal patterns and radical sexual politics in an attempt to isolate the meaning of the novel. The monumental *Virginia Woolf: The Critical Heritage* (1975) presents reviews, longer articles, and book-length studies, and emphasizes the views of literary figures until Woolf's death in 1941.

Other critics invented their own paradigms for analyzing the novel. Alice van Buren Kelley looked at the paradox between the worlds of fact and of vision in *The Novels of Virginia Woolf: Fact and Vision* (1973), and Nancy Topping Bazin applied social definitions of masculine versus feminine to interpret order and chaos in *Virginia Woolf and the Androgynous Vision* (1973). Jean O. Love contributed two volumes often cited by Woolf scholars, *Worlds in Consciousness: Mythopoetic Thought in the Novels of Virginia Woolf* (1970), and *Virginia Woolf: Sources of Madness and Art* (1977). Love's project was a "two-part study of the more personal side of the artist's life" (*Worlds* 379). The first volume offers a substantial psychological assessment of Woolf's early years. Love's mythopoetic approach reveals how actions are unified by and through the deified Clarissa, whose party forms "a true community" and whose love for women models a "statement of unity" (156).

Shalom Rachman assesses the novel's critical historiography in "Clarissa's Attic: Virginia Woolf's *Mrs. Dalloway* Reconsidered" (1972), by pronouncing how critics have succeeded or failed to reach a valid conclusion. Rachman advises future critics to treat the form of interior monologue in *Mrs. Dalloway* as different from that used by Joyce in *Ulysses* and to focus on the real detestable objects in Woolf's novel: love and religion (Rachman 15). Waging a fight with his critical forerunners, Rachman delivers the "reconsideration" he promised in his essay's title. A less reactionary assessment is Mitchell Leaska's *The Novels of Virginia Woolf: From Beginning to End* (1977). Leaska urges readers to connect with the text by following Woolf's example and "tunneling" into the realm of the unconscious.

Mark Spilka's 1979 biographical criticism, "On Mrs. Dalloway's Absent Grief: A Psycholiterary Speculation," found evidence in Woolf's memoir, *Moments of Being* (1976), for the absence of romantic love in Clarissa's world. Spilka links this absence to Woolf's childhood sexual abuse and inability to mourn the death of her mother, Julia Stephen (335). Spilka finds Clarissa's portrait to be an unrealized psycho-literary evasion because Woolf could not kill the male opponent, the "Tyrant in the House" (336).

1980s

Among essential reading is Maria DiBattista's "Virginia Woolf's Memento Mori" (1980), which describes the novel as having an empty center that mystically evades people. Characters find it impossible to reach "the thing that mattered," whether it is the soul or the sovereign "I" (24). DiBattista contrasts the doomed spirit of the British Empire with scenes of inspiration in which Clarissa transcends time and place.

While not entirely devoted to *Mrs. Dalloway*, Pamela Transue's *Virginia Woolf and the Politics of Style* (1986) launches into a bold feminist reading of *Mrs. Dalloway* as a work that shows a decidedly female mode of perception, scrutinizing Clarissa's internal and external conflicts as a Victorian woman defined by a patriarchal sphere. Transue's analysis considers biographical factors that led Woolf to survive by means of creating literature; similarly her protagonist creates social havens as another form of survival against life's cruelties and constraints.

An often referenced chapter on Woolf's narrative is J. Hillis Miller's "*Mrs. Dalloway:* Repetition as the Raising of the Dead" (1982). Miller articulates the relevance of linguistic and temporal strategies (like repetition) that translate into thematic outcomes. Miller notes how Woolf organizes the novel through the characters' and the narrator's memories, extending the role of the traditional narrator. Lucio Ruotolo's overview text, *The Interrupted Moment: A View of Virginia Woolf's Novels* (1986), relies on Miller's work. Ruotolo proposes that Woolf has Clarissa host a party in order to utilize dramatic language in the denouement and to allow her character to take a stand against modern culture and society as she embraces a world of unpredictability and uncertainty (101). Alex Zwerdling's *Virginia Woolf and the Real World*

(1986) continues an ongoing interest in historical forces and social institutions that shaped Woolf's characters, a trend evident from the earliest critics who considered London to be a city in shell shock after World War I.

1990s

Laura A. Smith responds to seventy years of *Mrs. Dalloway* criticism by reporting that "the 1990s have not brought consensus" (219). The critics agree to disagree, and to generate new readings. Comparative readings with *Mrs. Dalloway* include texts by George Eliot, Emily Brontë, Charlotte Perkins Gilman, Doris Lessing, James Joyce, Joseph Conrad, T. S. Eliot, Dorothy Richardson, Zora Neale Hurston, and Toni Morrison. Theoretical favorites of the decade include Mikhail Bakhtin's theory of dialogism, Henri Bergson's theories of *temps* (mechanical, chronological time) and *durée* (fluid, emotional, experienced time), and Sigmund Freud's theories of human behavior.

David Dowling's *Mrs. Dalloway: Mapping Streams of Consciousness* (1991) explores the historical and sociological process of reading the novel as one of fragmentation and dislocation. Dowling appreciates how the novel theorizes and enacts the political implication of social change at the personal level (127). He challenges readers to take Clarissa's insights of completion and fulfillment from her party into their own busy social world. Harold Bloom's critical edition, *Clarissa Dalloway* (1990), features eleven essays and eighteen critical extracts attesting that although Clarissa may be confounding, she is not to be overlooked. Bloom's introduction lauds Woolf's achievement in creating a character who represents the Age of Freud, whose self—like ours—is reduced to drives and defenses; a naïve, repressed woman who has no name for the will except "a thing" (3).

In the 1990s, postmodern approaches predominate. Pamela Caughie's *Woolf and Postmodernism: Literature* (1991) acknowledges the limitations of unifying systems even as *Mrs. Dalloway* brings this desire to the surface. The sane doctors and the insane Septimus alike attempt to impose coherence on random life. Johanna Garvey's "Difference and Continuity: The Voices of *Mrs. Dalloway*" (1991) analyzes how Woolf uses voices for the seemingly antagonistic effect of both unifying and fragmenting urban time and space. She notes how fragmentation complements marginalization as part of Woolf's feminist vision of London. Deborah Guth's "Rituals of Self-Deception: Clarissa Dalloway's Final Moment of Vision" (1990) reconsiders the final moment at the party. Here Clarissa's vision serves as imaginative self-invention according to three schemata: the romantic, the pagan, and the Christian. In the final appraisal, Clarissa becomes a mater dolorosa who grieves and rejoices at a death that she is not called to follow, but to behold as a ritual celebration and sacrifice of the scapegoat.

2000-2010

Topics of interest from 2000-2010 generally involve four main areas: 1) aesthetic textual comparisons both inside and outside the Woolfian canon, and especially with Michael Cunningham's fictional homage to *Mrs. Dalloway, The Hours* (1998); 2) historical and cultural approaches that consider how various aspects of Modernism are treated in the novel; 3) psychoanalytical approaches involving memory, trauma, madness, and suicide; and 4) issues of gender, including feminism, queer theory, desire, and identity. Subcategories range from dialectical materialism to fairy tales and relativity, satire, phallic suppression, ecology, Bloomsbury, the ancients, and performative theory.

Michael Cunningham's popular Pulitzer Prize-winning novel, *The Hours* (1998) is a contemporary adaptation of *Mrs. Dalloway* set variously in 1980s Greenwich Village, 1940s Los Angeles, and Woolf's contemporary post-World War I London. Critics focus on issues such as self-identification, Woolf's modernism compared to Cunningham's pragmatism, and the temporal structures of the two works. Overall, critics admire the two novels as independent literary classics in their own rights: Woolf's modern and Cunningham's postmodern classics. James Schiff considers three retellings of *Mrs. Dalloway* in his essay "Rewriting Woolf's *Mrs. Dalloway*: Homage, Sexual Identity, and the Single-Day Novel by Cunningham, Lippincott, and Lanchester" (2004). Robin Lippincott's *Mr. Dalloway* (1999), in which Richard's male lover, Robbie, presses him toward madness out of jealousy, is the most conventional of the three, imitating Woolf's style and feel. John Lanchester's *Mr. Phillips* (2000) is less interested in talking back to Woolf. The novel offers an account of a single day in the life of a fifty-year-old middle-class, unemployed accountant from a London suburb who has a sexual obsession and a need to quantify everything as he grasps at control in a world hovering above a rotting superstructure of sewage. Other multimedia articles include Birgit Spengler's "Michael Cunningham Rewriting Virginia Woolf: Pragmatist vs. Modernist Aesthetics" (2004) and Mary Joe Hughes's "Michael Cunningham's *The Hours* and Postmodern Artistic Re-Presentation" (2004). Both Brenda Silver's *Virginia Woolf: Icon* (1999) and Hermione Lee's *Virginia Woolf's Nose* (2005) examine images of Woolf in popular culture.

Studies of the uniquely unified structure of *Mrs. Dalloway* include Pam Fox Kuhlken's "Clarissa and Cléo (En)durée Suicidal Time in Virginia Woolf's *Mrs. Dalloway* and Agnès Varda's *Cléo de 5 à 7*" (2008), an interdisciplinary look at Henri Bergson's conception of *temps* (masculine time) and *durée* (feminine time) as they play out in the London novel and a Parisian film. Henry Alley's "*Mrs. Dalloway* and Three of Its Contemporary Children" (2006) examines Cunningham's *The Hours* (1998), David Hare's *The Hours: A Screenplay* (2002), and Robin Lippincott's *Mr. Dalloway* (1999). Elisabeta Zelinka's "The Woolf-Cunningham Literary Trajectory: Feminization of Time" (2009) uses the theories of feminist giants like Hélène Cixous, Elaine Showalter, Julia Kristeva, Gloria Steinem, and Luce Irigary to explore feminine symbols in the significant shift from a Wednesday in *Mrs. Dalloway* (1925) to a Saturday in Cunningham's *The Hours* (1998).

Jo Alyson Parker's chapter on *Mrs. Dalloway* in *Narrative Form and Chaos Theory in Sterne, Proust, Woolf, and Faulkner* considers the novel's spiraling narrative trajectory—which she calls "the roving trajectory of focalization" (91)—as it topples gravity, clock time, and linearity as a direct descendant of *Tristram Shandy* and *In Search of Lost Time*. Parker argues that Woolf's version of bounded randomness is uniquely her own as she breaks the traditional male-authorized sentence and highlights women's concerns (89). Thus Woolf's novel answers two problems that merge aesthetic and ideological concerns: "to encapsulate the infinite with the finite, to convey the boundlessness and connectedness of all things—what she saw as a female way of knowing the world," and to address "constricting gender roles and same-sex love" with enough ambiguity to avoid arousing hostility (110).

Mrs. Dalloway and Feminism

Reviewers in the 1920s looked in vain for a hero in Woolf's novel about a heroine. Since the 1970s, one of the most prominent theoretical approaches to fiction by the author of *A Room of One's Own* (1929) is feminism. Indeed, rare among women authors, Virginia Woolf has remained in print for over a century, becoming Shakespeare's modern sister. The controversy surrounding Woolf's feminism began with E. M. Forster's 1941 Rede Lecture, "Virginia Woolf," that lauded her singleness of vision and her receptivity to sensual stimuli, but claimed she neglected to focus on human issues surrounding the work itself, and failed to imbue her characters with "life eternal" (21). Writing in 1956, Dorothy Bevis explained Clarissa Dalloway's "one moment when she knew for Sally Seton the feeling that a man would have" as "androgyny" (12), avoiding the word "lesbian" unlike bolder feminist critics of the 1970s.

The 1977 publication of Elaine Showalter's *A Literature of Their Own: British Women Novelists from Brontë to Lessing* was a catalyst for feminist studies in Woolf. As Showalter notes in her introduction:

In 1965, when I began to do research for my PhD dissertation on Victorian women writers, feminist criticism did not exist. Virginia Woolf's letters and diaries were scattered and unpublished. . . . No one edited women's studies journals or compiled bibliographies of women's writing. (xi)

Showalter's work helped define how women writers write, and how women write about themselves. In the chapter that addresses *Mrs. Dalloway*, "Flight Into Androgyny," Showalter writes: "Androgyny was the myth that helped [Woolf] evade confrontation with her own painful femaleness and enabled her to choke and repress her anger and ambition" (263-64). Showalter offers three worthy considerations. First, Showalter calls for critics to stop using Leslie Stephen, Woolf's father, as a scapegoat and patriarchal villain who instigated her suicide. Second, Showalter draws a parallel between Woolf's sexual identity and her various breakdowns, in view of contemporary psychologists who acknowledge relationships between hormones, the body, and personality. Third, Showalter correlates Woolf's breakdown in 1913 and her prescribed rest cure with the same cure that led to Septimus's suicide. Showalter's final pessimistic statement reflects the feminist outlook of the 1970s: "The ultimate room of one's own is the grave" (297).

O. P. Sharma's "Feminism as Aesthetic Vision: A Study of Virginia Woolf's *Mrs. Dalloway*" (1975) scrutinizes the novel's "triumphant aesthetic feminism" (71). The subtle character of Clarissa is the dominant force, ushering readers "into the fiery core of the new feminism, that is neither harsh nor grating, but the serene act of assimilation into the highest art" (63). Sharma spends most of the article praising Woolf's artistic achievement, arguing that man-woman relationships are frigid and apathetic, whereas woman-woman relationships are fertile and hypnotic. Sharma closes her discussion by analyzing the figure of the "battered woman" who appears in three pages of text, singing of a million-year love and a dead lover. Sharma argues that this woman embodies the timeless essence of the victorious life-force, and exudes a joy of living that offsets the men's world of boredom, sordidness, and insensibility (67). Like the beggar woman, Clarissa's aesthetic and imaginative endeavors ward off the numbing effect of her husband, Richard, described by the narrator as a politician and philistine with a second-class brain who loves horses and dogs.

Makiko Minow-Pinkney's chapter, "*Mrs. Dalloway*," in *Virginia Woolf and the Problem of the Subject: Feminine Writing in the Major Novels* (1987) applies the psychoanalytic theories of Julia Kristeva to Woolf's canon. Minow-Pinkney describes the novel as a dialectic between stasis and rupture, dissemination and reconstruction, in which women struggle to voice their consciousness while maintaining the original bond with and love for the mother—repressed by the patriarchal social and rational order—without being "mad." Clarissa can only negotiate (and ultimately oscillate) between two obvious options for feminists: to deny a woman's difference and become a token man or to refuse the symbolic realm altogether and risk being an outcast. No wonder she finds it "very, very dangerous to live even one day" (*Mrs. Dalloway* 9). Rachel Bowlby's *Virginia Woolf, Feminist Destinations* (1988) explores Woolf's changing and unfinished investigations of feminism. Bowlby discusses *Mrs. Dalloway* as "a more complex feminine or feminist temporality" (79), seeing Woolf's characters as realistic representations of the uncertain roles available to women in 1920s London. Bowlby contests Elizabeth Abel's 1983 psychoanalytic reading in which Clarissa abandons her own feminine sexuality to conform to heterosexual marriage; instead, Bowlby's Clarissa is a fluid feminine consciousness.

Laura A. Smith called the 1990s "the decade of Clarissa as lesbian," and is quick to note that even "lesbian" is a contested label with multiple variations. Smith summarizes the debate by asking whether Woolf represents Suzette Henke's celebratory lesbianism ("*Mrs. Dalloway*: The Communion of Saints" 1981) or Emily Jensen's denied lesbianism ("Clarissa Dalloway's Respectable Suicide" 1983) (Smith 219). In Julia Briggs's chapter on *Mrs. Dalloway* in *Virginia Woolf: An Inner*

Life (2005), the heart of the novel is the intimacy between Clarissa and Sally Seton, derived from Virginia's friendship—full of possibilities and secret pleasures—with Vita Sackville-West. Eileen Barrett's "Unmasking Lesbian Passion: The Inverted World of *Mrs. Dalloway*" in her edited volume *Virginia Woolf: Lesbian Readings* (1997) represents significant queer theory that argues "Woolf's lesbianism is inseparable from her feminism" and exposes how "the scathing depictions of heterosexuality in marriage demonstrate Woolf's lesbian-feminist critique of this institution" (147). Barrett explores how Woolf modeled the "subtle and sensitive" lesbian relationship between Clarissa and Sally Seton on her own intellectual, erotic, personal, and political love for her "feminist friendship" with Madge Symonds Vaughan (147, 151). Barrett concludes that Septimus's acceptance of the prevailing homophobia in his suicide protects Clarissa's private lesbian passion, whereas "Doris's [Kilman] lesbian existence enables Clarissa to release the lesbian trapped within her soul" (162).

Conclusion

Virginia Woolf's most famous character, Mrs. Dalloway, has not been lying in wait since 1925 for the birth of her true critic, an ideal reader who understands what Woolf was really saying. Such an arrogant piece of criticism would be intolerable in light of Woolf's enthusiastic openness to exploring relativity, the unknown, and change itself. Nor is Clarissa lying impotent in her grave. Indeed, the critics have never let her rest. Perhaps it is not unreasonable to propose that the verb "Dalloway-ing" be added to the lexicon as a decidedly engaging and illuminating—and potentially obsessive, frustrating, and time-consuming—pastime of literary critics? Critics do not easily forget Clarissa Dalloway and will continue to read between the lines to discuss her significance, meaning, gender, and politics. Readers may even become conscious of their own inner monologue as they reflect on the novel, like Clarissa muses in London: "For heaven only knows why one loves it so, how one sees it so, making it up, building it round one, tumbling it, creating it every moment afresh" (*Mrs. Dalloway* 5).

Works Cited

Abel, Elizabeth. "Narrative Structure(s) and Female Development: The Case of *Mrs. Dalloway*." *The Voyage In: Fictions of Female Development*. Eds. Elizabeth Abel, Marianne Hirsch, and Elizabeth Langland. Hanover, NH: UP of New England for Dartmouth College, 1983. 161-185.

Alley, Henry. "*Mrs. Dalloway* and Three of Its Contemporary Children." *Papers on Language and Literature: A Journal for Scholars and Critics of Language and Literature* 42.4 (Fall 2006): 401-19.

Barrett, Eileen. "Unmasking Lesbian Passion: The Inverted World of Mrs. Dalloway." *Virginia Woolf: Lesbian Readings*. Eds. Eileen Barrett and Patricia Cramer. New York: New York UP, 1997. 146-164.

Bazin, Nancy Topping. *Virginia Woolf and the Androgynous Vision*. New Brunswick, CT: Rutgers UP, 1973.

Benjamin, Anna S. "Towards an Understanding of the Meaning of Virginia Woolf's *Mrs. Dalloway*." *Wisconsin Studies in Contemporary Literature* 6.2 (Summer 1965): 214-27.

Bennett, Joan. *Virginia Woolf: Her Art as Novelist* (1945). New York: Cambridge UP, 1964.

Bevis, Dorothy. "*The Waves*: A Fusion of Symbol, Style and Thought in Virginia Woolf." *Twentieth Century Literature* 2 (1956): 5-20.

Bloom, Harold, ed. *Major Literary Characters: Clarissa Dalloway*. New York: Chelsea House, 1990.

Bowlby, Rachel. *Virginia Woolf, Feminist Destinations*. New York: Oxford UP, 1988.

Bradbrook, M. C. "Notes on the Style of Mrs. Woolf." *Scrutiny* 1.1 (1932): 33-38.

Briggs, Julia. *Virginia Woolf: An Inner Life*. Orlando, FL: Harcourt, 2005.

Brower, Reuben. "Something Central Which Permeated: Virginia Woolf and *Mrs. Dalloway*." 1951. *Virginia Woolf: A Collection of Critical Essays*. Ed. Claire Sprague. Englewood Cliffs, NJ: Prentice-Hall, 1971. 51-62.

Caughie, Pamela L. *Virginia Woolf and Postmodernism: Literature in Quest & Question of Itself*. Urbana and Chicago: U of Illinois P, 1991.

Daiches, David. *Virginia Woolf*. 1942. New York: New Directions, 1962.

DiBattista, Maria. "*Mrs. Dalloway* as Virginia Woolf's Memento Mori." *Virginia Woolf's Major Novels*. New Haven, CT: Yale UP, 1980. 22-63.

Dowling, David. *Mrs. Dalloway: Mapping Streams of Consciousness*. Boston: Twayne, 1991.

Forster, E. M. "The Early Novels of Virginia Woolf." 1925. *Abinger Harvest*. New York: Harcourt, 1936. 106-15.

_____. "Virginia Woolf." New York: Harcourt, 1942.

Garvey, Johanna X. K. "Difference and Continuity: The Voices of *Mrs. Dalloway.*" *College English* 53.1 (Jan. 1991): 59-76.

Guiguet, Jean. *Virginia Woolf and Her Works*. Trans. Jean Stewart. London: Hogarth Press, 1965.

Guth, Deborah. "Rituals of Self-Deception: Clarissa Dalloway's Final Moment of Vision." *Twentieth Century Literature* 36.1 (Spring 1990): 35-42.

Henke, Suzette. "Mrs. Dalloway: The Communion of Saints." *New Feminist Essays on Virginia Woolf*. Ed. Jane Marcus. Lincoln: U of Nebraska P, 1981. 125-47.

Hughes, Mary Joe. "Michael Cunningham's *The Hours* and Postmodern Artistic Re-Presentation." *Critique: Studies in Contemporary Fiction* 45.4 (Summer 2004): 349-61.

Jensen, Emily. "Mrs. Dalloway's Respectable Suicide." *Virginia Woolf: A Feminist Slant*. Ed. Jane Marcus. Lincoln: U of Lincoln P, 1983. 162-79.

Kelley, Alice van Buren. *The Novels of Virginia Woolf: Fact and Vision*. Chicago: U of Chicago P, 1973.

Kuhlken, Pam Fox. "Clarissa and Cléo (En)durée Suicidal Time in Virginia Woolf's *Mrs. Dalloway* and Agnes Varda's *Cléo de 5 à 7.*" *Comparative Literature Studies* 45.3 (2008): 341-69.

Leaska, Mitchell A. *The Novels of Virginia Woolf from Beginning to End*. New York: John Jay Press, 1977.

Lee, Hermione. *Virginia Woolf's Nose: Essays on Biography*. Princeton, NJ: Princeton UP, 2005.

Love, Jean O. *Virginia Woolf: Sources of Madness and Art*. Berkeley: U of California P, 1977.

_____. *Worlds in Consciousness: Mythopoetic Thought in the Novels of Virginia Woolf*. Berkeley: U of California P, 1970.

Majumdar, Robin, and Allen McLaurin, eds. *Virginia Woolf: The Critical Heritage*. Boston: Routledge, 1975.

Marcus, Jane, ed. *New Feminist Essays on Virginia Woolf*. Lincoln: U of Nebraska P, 1983.

Miller, J. Hillis. "*Mrs. Dalloway*: Repetition as the Raising of the Dead." *Fiction and Repetition: Seven English Novels*. Cambridge: Harvard UP, 1982. 176-202.

Minow-Pinkney, Makiko. "Mrs. Dalloway." *Virginia Woolf and the Problem of the Subject: Feminine Writing in the Major Novels*. Brighton, UK: Harvester, 1987. 70-81.

Moody, A. D. "The Unmasking of Clarissa Dalloway." *A Review of English Literature* 3.1 (1962): 67-79.

Parker, Jo Alyson. *Narrative Form and Chaos Theory in Sterne, Proust, Woolf, and Faulkner*. New York: Palgrave Macmillan, 2007.

Rachman, Shalom. "Clarissa's Attic: Virginia Woolf's *Mrs. Dalloway* Reconsidered." *Twentieth Century Literature* 18.1 (1972): 3-18.

Rantavaara, Irma. *Virginia Woolf and Bloomsbury*. 1953. Folcroft, PA: Folcroft Library Editions, 1978.

Ruotolo, Lucio. *The Interrupted Moment: A View of Virginia Woolf's Novels*. Stanford, CA: Stanford UP, 1986.

Schiff, James. "Rewriting Woolf's *Mrs. Dalloway*: Homage, Sexual Identity, and the Single-Day Novel by Cunningham, Lippincott, and Lanchester." *Critique* 45.4 (Summer 2004): 363-82.

Sharma, O. P. "Feminism as Aesthetic Vision: A Study of Virginia Woolf's *Mrs. Dalloway*." *Women's Studies: An Interdisciplinary Journal* 3 (1975): 61-73.

Showalter, Elaine. *A Literature of Their Own: British Women Novelists from Brontë to Lessing*. Princeton, NJ: Princeton UP, 1977.

Silver, Brenda R. *Virginia Woolf: Icon*. Chicago: U of Chicago P, 1999.

Smith, Laura A. "Who Do We Think Clarissa Dalloway Is Anyway? Re-Search into Seventy Years of Woolf Criticism." *Re: Reading, Re: Writing, Re: Teaching Virginia Woolf*. Eds. Eileen Barrett and Patricia Cramer. New York: Pace UP, 1995. 215-21.

Spengler, Birgit. "Michael Cunningham Rewriting Virginia Woolf: Pragmatist vs. Modernist Aesthetics." *Woolf Studies Annual* 10 (2004): 51-79.

Spilka, Mark. "On Mrs. Dalloway's Absent Grief: A Psycholiterary Speculation." *Contemporary Literature* 20.3 (1979): 316-38.

Sprague, Claire. *Virginia Woolf: A Collection of Critical Essays*. Englewood Cliffs, NJ: Prentice-Hall, 1971.

Thompson, Hilary. "Time and Its Countermeasures: Modern Messianism in Woolf, Benjamin, and Agamben." *Modernism and Theory: A Critical Debate*. London: Routledge, 2008. 86-98.

Transue, Pamela. *Virginia Woolf and the Politics of Style*. Albany: State U of New York P, 1986.

Troy, William. "Virginia Woolf: The Novel of Sensibility." 1937. *Virginia Woolf: A Collection of Critical Essays*. Ed. Claire Sprague. Englewood Cliffs, NJ: Prentice-Hall, 1971. 26-39.

Woolf, Virginia. "Mr. Bennett and Mrs. Brown." 1924. *The Captain's Death Bed and Other Essays*. New York: Harcourt, 1950.

_____. *Mrs. Dalloway*. 1925. New York: Harcourt, 1953.

_____. *A Writer's Diary*. 1954. San Diego: Harcourt, 1981.

Wright, Nathalia. "Mrs. Dalloway: A Study in Composition." *College English* 5.7 (1944): 351-59.

Zelinka, Elisabeta. "The Woolf-Cunningham Literary Trajectory: Feminization of Time." *Gender Studies* 1.8 (2009): 55-74.

Zwerdling, Alex. *Virginia Woolf and the Real World*. Berkeley: U of California P, 1986.

CRITICAL READINGS

The Pseudo-Homeric World of *Mrs. Dalloway*_____

Molly Hoff

A big book is a big bore.

—Callimachus, fragment 465

Never did any book [*Ulysses*] so bore me.

—Virginia Woolf, *Letters* 3: 80

The relationship between *Mrs. Dalloway* and Joyce's *Ulysses* has been construed by critics as adversarial almost from the beginning, partly because of the vitriolic attack on *Mrs. Dalloway* by Wyndham Lewis in 1934. But Lewis's cheap shot was merely a squib. The *ad ignorantiam* arguments by which he claimed that the scenes in Woolf's novel are "exact and puerile copies of the scenes in [*Ulysses*]" (138) launched a line of successors who swallowed his model whole.[1]

Lewis's claim that the sound of the smoke-writing airplane "*boring* into the ears of the crowd" (*MD* 29-30; emphasis added) is "a pathetic 'crib' of the fireworks display and the rocket that is the culmination of Mr. Bloom's beach ecstasy" (138-39) apparently relies on the sky that serves as a background in both instances. No doubt Lewis's interest in the pseudo-Homeric image of Bloom impersonating Odysseus among the Phaiakians admiring Nausicaa leaves Lewis dazzled; yet he doesn't mention the airplane that appears and reappears like a portentous bird in Proust's *Remembrance of Things Past*, an indebtedness that Woolf explicitly acknowledges (*Diary* 234, 322). Clearly excluding most contemporary novels, Lewis feels that *Ulysses* is or ought to be the cynosure of the literate world. As for *Mrs. Dalloway*, Odysseus, Nausicaa, and her Scherian family (suitably obscure) will appear elsewhere.

We need a more careful explication.[2] The fact is that Woolf's airplane is a writing instrument inscribing Homer's "winged words" with "white smoke from behind," quite unlike Joyce's fountain-pen-like fireworks (*MD* 29, 42). The aerial display follows the backfiring automobile (19), both of which are aurally related to Aristophanic crepitation from *boredom* (Henderson 196), a sequence of scatological commentary. Another serious oversight is the statue of a "canine" Gordon "with one leg raised" (*MD* 77). Doubtless those aware of the techniques of parody and satire, associating the raised leg with the smoke from behind, might also associate them (in spite of the chiastic arrangement)[3] with Joyce's *Ulysses*, which as Woolf expressed it includes "a dog that p's" and "a man that forths" (*Letters* 2: 234). Appropriately, Margaret Rose reminds us, "discrepancy between the parodied text and its new context is one of the chief sources of the comic effect" (23) and its criticism of society as well (Levin 248). Woolf herself says parodies should be amusing,

> do the work of the critic with greater daring than the critic can usually display. . . . First they make us laugh, and then they make us think . . . [giving] a little model of the work in question [with a] sense of the defects of that work by a few deft pinches and twists which bring out the absurdity without destroying the likeness. (*Essays* 89)

Rose addresses the problems associated with recognizing parody in literature—which as Jonathan Culler explains "requires a somewhat different mode of reading" (152)—the first concerning the naïve reader who is unable to recognize that parody exists at all. The second, also highly relevant to Lewis's situation, concerns the reader who recognizes the quotation "but does not comprehend the intention"; this reader may believe that the author is "unintentionally misquoting . . . because his sympathy for the parodied text is so strong that his assumptions about it have not been affected by the parody" (Rose 27). Lewis and others miss the actual parody and introduce irrelevancies that inspire accusations of plagiarism. Another reader might feel "both the parodied text and its author to be the targets of satire." Finally, Rose offers the "ideal reader reaction" as one in which the reader of the parodied effect "enjoys the recognition of the hidden irony and satire" (27). As a parody of *Ulysses*, a device that replaces "authorial intrusion" (Oettli 68) and that frees us from the "demands of poetic seriousness" (Culler 152), *Mrs. Dalloway* attacks Joyce's methods by appropriating his arcane sources. But beyond its considerable polemic value, it also dismantles Joyce's rigidly restrictive Homeric "narrow room" (Woolf, *CR* 151) and provides space in which readers may stretch out a bit.

Those who address the problem of whether or not Woolf plagiarizes Joyce without referring to the rather large body of scholarship on the subject of plagiarism ask questions that never seem to get answered.[4] Was *Ulysses* for her an occluded free lunch? Answer: yes and no, considering *Mrs. Dalloway*'s self-avowed potential for disregarding private property (49). Here, Virginia Woolf paraphrases, parodies, and burlesques a chrestomathy of texts, Homer included, as part of the novel's encyclopedic repertoire that punctures the illusory self-containment of realistic representation (Iser, *Act* 82); and if she had omitted Joyce, his fans would have been among the first to protest. There are at least 600 paraphrases and parodies that share the rhetoric of dismembering and re-membering. A restructuring so complete taken from a selection so broad suggests that, technically speaking, literature is one of the things that *Mrs. Dalloway* is about. By exploiting a unique point of view, Virginia Woolf, "always hesitating on the edge of caricature" (Eliot, *Prose* 93), shamelessly cannibalizes multitudes. As at a Quaker meeting, everyone participates. Meanwhile, Woolf's protean manipulations lie undiscovered while the accusations of Wyndham Lewis fester.[5]

Using Homer's *Odyssey*—using a "grand manner for trifling themes" (Worcester 47)—is prominent among these manipulations. *Mrs. Dalloway* tracks Homer across London—the most primitive literary track— a fact revealing that, for some, Homeric expertise may be limited to Joyce's novel. Virgil, Shakespeare, and Dickens (who like Dante "knew how to pillage right and left" [Eliot, *Wood* 63]) are a few who follow the same routes in this cento that makes something new out of what already exists. The working title, "The Hours," strongly suggests Homer's *Odyssey* (Woolf, *Diary* 2.242). It may disclose a hint of the original inspiration of *Mrs. Dalloway* in which timing is featured. "The whole *Odyssey* is a revelation in hexameters of the moral, physical, social, and cosmic dimensions of *hora* [timeliness]," which is the motivating impulse of the poem (Austin 266n7). "*Hora* can be applied to specific conjunctions such as spring," as well as the conjunction of many discrete events such as "lengthening days, shorter nights, the sun moving northwards, animals mating, plants in flower, the return of migratory birds" (Austin 88).

Horae, sometimes translated as "the Seasons" in Hesiod's *Theogony* (c. line 900) and the title of a lost Aristophanic comedy, adequately translates as the London season, the party world of summer, and Clarissa's Wednesday in June. This moment in June prominently features an erotically sensitive marriage text that rehearses amorosity in every social station, attesting to a universal erotic instinct. As the Preacher says, to everything there is a season and a time to every purpose under the heaven (Eccles. 3.1). Judicious timing in *Mrs. Dalloway* is facilitated by the ringing clocks that mark the passage of the hours.

Still, for the Dalloways as for Homeric humanity, "the sun is [a] great measuring rod whose course measures time and divides space" (Austin 91). Solar symbolism in the Homeric poem preoccupies many characters.[6] In *Mrs. Dalloway*, the heat of the sun marks the arrival of another day and its subtraction from the total allotment each person can expect. The heat of the sun is a reminder of the finiteness of human life. Tides in the body as well (*MD* 170-71) mark the *hora*. When Clarissa thinks "no more having of children now" (14), she is sympathetic with Sappho's sidereal calendar in the fragment attributed to her: "The Pleiades has set" (fragment 168b, Voigt). Both sleep alone.

When Homer's *Odyssey* is incorporated into *Mrs. Dalloway*, several things are accomplished. One is the blending of Homer's narrative with "the style, character and values appropriate to Roman elegy"

(Benediktson "Propertius" 26).[7] The novel thus exhibits an "attitude toward Homer . . . probably drawn from Callimachus, whose disinclination toward Homeric poetics"—that it was to be admired, not imitated—"was well known by the Augustan poets, and which could be used only if it underwent a transformation to conform with the needs of elegy" (Dalzell in Benediktson "Propertius" 17). Benediktson calls this the "elegiacization of Homer" (22), and it gives *Mrs. Dalloway* its character typical of Latin elegy, the erotic poems of Propertius in this case.[8]

Propertius's versions of Homer depart drastically from the familiar Greek epic, in size (elegies are small), values (the elegiac way of life is superior—make love, not war), and character (the entire epic code of behavior is satirized) (Benediktson "Propertius" 21). For example, Propertius (4.8) imitates Odysseus routing the suitors from Ithaca. The "hero" of the poem, the *persona loquens*, is discovered by Cynthia who returns unexpectedly from a trip and finds him "entertaining." She attacks the girls and afterwards fumigates the house, mops the threshold, and changes the oil in the lamps and the sheets on the bed. Cynthia, here, is the indignant "Odysseus" violently reclaiming her territory from a bevy of "suitors." Finally they end up in bed together like Odysseus and Penelope, a cozy loving pair. Here Propertius "consciously echoes Homer to call attention to his departure from Homer's version" (Benediktson "Propertius" 21). Role reversal is one technique by which this is accomplished, Homer's epic virtues being male *arete* (in Latin elegy meaning manliness and sexual standing) and female chastity. The male hero's role is performed by the promiscuous Cynthia, and the faithful "Penelope" is the unfaithful hero. The tricky demands of elegy are, says Peter Walsh in concert with Callimachus, potentially the readers' undoing, "not weeping at the right time, or laughing either" (*MD* 230; see Callimachus *Palatine Anthology* 7.415). In elegy the epic bed of Odysseus becomes the narrow bed of Propertius (*MD* 45-46; "Propertius" 1.8, 2.1; that is, the "narrow bed" is the love nest, the poem, and the elegiac genre itself). "Propertius consciously criticizes Homeric plot, character, and ethical ideals; and consequently, while writing poetry, also engages in what today would be called 'literary criticism'" (Benediktson "Propertius" 17).[9]

Virginia Woolf, too, draws on Homeric narrative, eroticizes it, and at the same time makes repeated allusion to Joyce's *Ulysses* (Richter) to show that she is departing from his "big hard book" (Pearce 60) while criticizing him as well. Moreover she treats Homeric tradition very differently from Joyce, and her only references, "nobody" and "useless" (*MD* 77, 90, 279), are negligible beside Joyce's copious extratextual clues. Peter Walsh carefully mimics Homer's hero, born to suffer, but Peter's version is elegiac: "It was impossible that he should ever suffer again as Clarissa had made him suffer" (for "suffering," see *MD* 63, 93, 120, 241).

Like Propertius she disperses many of the non-erotic roles, both monstrous and marvelous, among the minor characters. For example, her novel makes a fairly patent allusion to the *Odyssey* when in comes "little Mr. Bowley" who is "sealed with wax" like Odysseus's crew "over the deeper sources of life" (*MD* 28) and unlikely to respond erotically to the beautiful voices of the Sirens or anything else unless he comes unsealed. Similarly, the nondescript man on the steps of St. Paul's Cathedral carries a leather bag stuffed not with the winds of Aeolus but pamphlets that may be very much like hot air (41). In fact, flatus such as that emitted by the skywriter is only one aspect of contrary winds that blow from time to time. The image of the leather bag also suggests *Mrs. Dalloway* as a work stuffed with preformed discourse that escapes only if the bag is opened. *Mrs. Dalloway*, like the elegies of Propertius, "often resembles . . . a 'meta-literature,' or a literature about literature" (Benediktson "Propertius" 26). Storms and the winds of Aeolus often impede the Homeric hero's progress; here they are minor components inserted to suggest a Homeric context.

Miss Kilman is illustrative of the manipulation the Homeric epic undergoes in the making of the elegiac *Mrs. Dalloway*; her macintosh actually applies equally well to Proust's Albertine (Proust 2: 894; peace to Jenkins). Miss Kilman is characterized as a thoroughly unpleasant person whose grasping nature is exceeded only by her propensity for oral consumption. This pair of qualities suggests her relationship to the Odyssean pair, Scylla and Charybdis. Unfortunately, Odysseus must sail through the strait where on one side Scylla grabs and devours six of his crew while he is warily watching Charybdis, fearing destruction from her quarter. Eventually he must return to the strait where Charybdis swallows the ship and remaining members of the crew (*Odyssey* 12.80-126, 234-50, 430-44).[10] Although Miss Kilman does not have 12 feet or 6 heads, her grasping and controlling nature regarding Elizabeth Dalloway is definitive: "Miss Kilman could not let her go! this youth that was so beautiful, this girl, whom she genuinely loved! Her large hand opened and shut on the table" (199). She is characterized as a prehistoric monster (190), yet not one that will kill the girl; her nature is in tune with the elegiacization that Propertius perpetrates in his Homeric allusions. Kilman's motivation is love: "If she could grasp her, if she could clasp her, if she could make her hers absolutely and forever and then die; that was all she wanted" (199-200).

Kilman's "turbulent feelings" (*thumos*) (188) correspond to the surging turbulence that twice characterizes the maelstrom Charybdis (*Odyssey* 12.238, 241) that swallows Odysseus's entire ship.[11] Miss Kilman's voracious appetite, her greed for sugared cakes on the adjacent table ("the pleasure of eating was almost the only pure pleasure left her"), and her care for the last two inches of the chocolate éclair, is followed by the little whirlpool she makes in washing the tea "round in her cup" (197, 199).[12] The *thumos*, typically gratified by food and drink and suggested by Kilman's turbulent emotions, far from merely stimulating appetite, is also "the receptor, the governor, the organizer of sensory data" (Austin 108). When Septimus Smith returns from the war, it seems he has no *thumos*, no feeling, no taste for food. His *noos* works fine—"he could add up his bill" (132-33). What Kilman has in excess, Septimus lacks altogether. He simulates Achilles who, mourning his dead companion, denies the belly, contrary to Odysseus's advice (*Iliad* 9.225 ff.)—thus his disordered perceptions, his inability to organize sensory data accurately. If he is to be healed, the treatment should focus on his *thumos*. Porridge and milk are contraindicated.[13]

As for Charybdis, the vortex that swallows and regurgitates, the ebb and flow of water, simulates a boiling cauldron, recalling Miss Kilman's "boiling feelings" (188). Both images echo the predominant theme of both the *Odyssey* and *Mrs. Dalloway*—rising and falling, death and rebirth from the womblike cauldron.[14] Kilman's hidden thoughts that Elizabeth does not hear, the dialogue with her *thumos* taking the same form as speech, "embedded focalization" (de Jong 43), incorporates the send-off convention of ancient literature, the *propempticon*, with the pleas (don't go / don't forget me) that often characterize it: "Ah!, but she must not go! . . . Don't quite forget me" (199, 201).[15]

Elizabeth insists that she would like to go. As a maid of all work, she fulfills several Homeric requirements: her asking "'May I go now?' like a child of four" is reminiscent of the leave taking that Telemachus diplomatically demands of Menelaus (a conventional *syntacticon*), to which the host responds, "It is equally bad when one speeds on the guest unwilling to go, and when he holds back one who is hastening. Rather one should befriend the guest who is there, but speed him when he wishes" (*Odyssey* 15.64-74; trans. Lattimore), which in the voice of St. Margaret's the hostess becomes "Some grief for the past holds it back; some concern for the present" (74) and is like Mme. Swann's "sailing in without the least hurry, and imagining she's in heaps of time." Like a bee going from flower to flower "she knew her power of pollination" (Proust 1: 556, 568). Peter also indicates that the girl is "round-eyed" and "grown big" (84, 119), reminiscent of the Cyclops, in one of the longest episodes in Homer that gets only brief treatment here. Significantly, Miss Kilman is characterized as an "unwieldy battleship," "rocking slightly from side to side" (196, 201).

There is more here to suggest that Woolf made a more careful reading of Joyce than the nautical metaphor implies. One of Joyce's arcane sources, Maurice Clare, shows the Elizabethans Jonson and Shakespeare having a verbal joust after supper at the Mermaid until Shakespeare is "seized by a great distaste for the stale *odors* of wine and ale" and wishes for "anything that was out in the clean pure air"; and so, "making a hasty and inadequate excuse, he escaped into the street" (Clare 42-43; emphasis added). Elizabeth Dalloway's escape is comparable: "It was so nice to be out of doors. . . . It was so nice to be out in the air. . . . The fresh air was so delicious," an opinion shared with Beaumarchais in the *Barber of Seville* (*MD* 204-05; Hoff 162), injecting the deflating indication that the overfed and "windy" Miss Kilman smells of the stable (Henderson 196, par. 425; 197, par. 430). Miss Kilman's musical entrails serve as her bum-fiddle: "the sound was excruciating" (for her violin and gut strings, see *MD* 188, 201).

As in other instances, the discrepancy between the arcane original and its present use is too great to be anything other than burlesque. Soon thereafter, Elizabeth (a pirate) negotiates the Roving Rocks as only the Argos has been able to do, merely by "squeezing eellike and arrogant in between, and then rushing insolently all sails spread up Whitehall" (*Odyssey* 12:66-69)—as Peter's foil (205). Miss Kilman, "domineering, jealous" as Ben Jonson, a man said to be of *great size*, is characterized, like him, as a great galleon, "solid, but slow in his performance," and Elizabeth ("bored" [205]) like Shakespeare, a man of war "lesser in bulk, but lighter in sailing, [that] could turn with all sides, tack about, and take advantage of all winds" (Clare 41).[16]

The world of Clarissa Dalloway is characterized otherwise by Peter Walsh. Peter prefers the company of society women, "their faithfulness and audacity and greatness in loving" (241). By acknowledging his bondage to women, Peter makes a virtue of a narrative necessity. Yet in his self-dramatization as a man desired by many women, even though he is eminently unlucky in love, he claims a respect he does not merit. After all, Clarissa—conspicuously taking refuge in the typical complaint, headaches—refused *him*. As an island-hopping buccaneer, however, he shares with Elizabeth and others their fondness for nautical and equestrian metaphors popular in comedy for encoding sexual congress (Henderson 161 ff.; *MD* 269).

The allusions to the *Odyssey* in *Mrs. Dalloway* often concern the Mediterranean elite culture of semidivine seductresses, suggesting to some more comfortable with Joyce than with Homer a "snobbish" Virginia Woolf (Redfield 238-42, 244). Certainly some of Odysseus's greatest difficulties issue from the erotic goddesses who offer material resources and the other comforts of rampant heterosexuality. In the elegiac *Odyssey*, the problem is not so much the cultural impact of affluence (Redfield 246) as the cultural impact of idleness, the *otium* of Latin elegy. Although there is savagery latent in luxury (Redfield 244), there is also trouble of various kinds latent in the "seductive woman." Just as the Homeric hero, according to Athena, is in trouble with Calypso at the very beginning (*Odyssey* 1.13-15), Lady Bruton announces that Peter Walsh is back and "is in trouble with some woman" (161-63).

Peter has erroneously thought that *nobody* yet knew he was in London when clearly Lady Bruton knows, and this fairly obvious aporetic contradiction suggests the Homeric convention that assumes that what the reader knows, the characters may be assumed to know as well (Bassett 132-40).[17] Lady Bruton, having a vine as prominent as Calypso's and sharing her consciousness of ancestry as well, inclines to knowledge of this type (*Odyssey* 5.69; *MD* 159). Peter's pseudo-Homeric odyssey from one bed to the next parodies Odysseus's journey among erotic island nymphs. This much should be known if a qualified response is to be made by a readership sufficiently aware of which text is being burlesqued and which one is not. Lady Bruton, an omniscient, androgynous Athena, makes a prediction, clearly a reference to the text we have been reading: "We shall hear the whole story from Peter himself" (163). This suggests his major problem: no matter how agreeable a sinner, he is like those sinners in the Underworld, Sisyphus and Tantalus, who couldn't keep their mouths shut (*MD*

273; Harrison, *Prolegomena* 608-09). Peter talks too much and even expresses his concern about being overheard (120).

After Lady Bruton's luncheon, Richard Dalloway and Hugh Whitbread experience a close encounter with Odysseus. Hugh is interested in buying a necklace for his wife, Evelyn. He asks to see Mr. Dubonnet, who not only knows the dimensions of Evelyn's neck but also "the extent of her possessions in that line." Mr. Dubonnet is out, and Hugh pompously rejects the young clerk who doesn't know his business and postpones the purchase until "Mr. Dubonnet chose to be in" (171-73; compare Clare 39: "I would have a word with Mr. Shakespeare: is he within?"). The inconsequentiality of this episode suggests some dissonance between the denotative and the connotative levels of signification.

Mrs. Hugh's neck measurements are the most curious feature here. Surely there is some latitude involved in fitting necks to necklaces, except in the most extreme instances. As it happens, in antiquity there was a "popular belief that the neck (*collum*) of a virgin increased in circumference after intercourse" (Catullus 64.376; commentary from Adams 108n3). Thus if her neck measurements require such expert scrutiny, we can wonder if Evelyn's neck size varies with her sexual activity. Mr. Dubonnet, the absent jeweler, simulates Odysseus, a career womanizer who disguised himself as a peddler of jewelry in order to catch Achilles (a draft dodger) disguised as a woman (Ovid *Metamorphoses* 13.162 ff.; Frazer 73-75, 74n1). The necklace is also reminiscent of the husband aware of his wife's extramarital activities (Aristophanes *Lysistrata* 408 ff.) who says that the bolt has fallen out of its hole in the necklace the jeweler made, requiring him to visit and replace it sometime (Henderson 41). The connotative levels suggest that unbeknown to Hugh, his wife has been sleeping around. Hugh is unlikely to confront her lover, but the absent jeweler seems to think so.

Homer's Odysseus, the often-shipwrecked sailor, endures trials geared to retard his return to Ithaca while events are shaped as ritual actions and motifs that express his spiritual voyage (Segal 9) by testing his resolve and ensuring his moral growth. The hero must endure multiple cycles of initiatory death and rebirth in all their quasiritual forms.[18] These are foreshadowed for the napping Peter, whose sleep is conventionally the brother to death, in his dream as the solitary traveler, guarded by the nurse. Emerging from a Dantean dark wood, he passes through amniotic waters to the figure of a mother, thus experiencing a symbolic death and rebirth (85-88). Although "falling asleep is a tragically heroic necessity" in the *Odyssey* (Friederich 21), his return to consciousness is a rebirth. Similarly, Septimus Smith as a foil for Peter illustrates Lucretius's drowned sailor, the infant who gives birth (as a rebirth) to himself: "He strained; he pushed" (104, 140; Lucretius *De Rerum Natura* 5.222-27). Even as the newborn infant is a shipwrecked sailor on the beach, so also the shipwrecked sailor is an infant, newly born or reborn. Whether or not Peter's adventure fits this pattern remains to be revealed.

The novel's surface simplicity, like that of the *Odyssey*, "disguises the depth of its thoughts" (Segal 12). Yet, in view of Peter's apparently insignificant existence in a seemingly meaningless text, his search for the truth is as meaningless as his perception of his future rolling down to him like the stone that Sisyphus has just rolled up (75). This is one of the solar myths with which Homer's epic is involved. The disparity between Peter's reality and his imaginary life, involving the marriage theme and the nautical motif that are relevant to the elegiac *Odyssey*, derives from imposing "form on an essentially formless reality" (Iser, *Implied Reader* 193). Peter, like Odysseus, tells the stories of his past by flashback during and as a part of the story of his "odyssean" present, erotic stories that begin with Clarissa whose paradisiac childhood home is a *locus amoenus* like Calypso's: "It was a nice place, a very nice place" (83).[19] Calypso's flourishing grove and shining fountains are secondary to the immortality she would confer on her lover. But reprimanded by Hermes, who says she must allow the hero to depart, she is conscious of the double standard that demands chastity of women (even goddesses) and allows the gods their promiscuity, and so she must release Odysseus—just as Clarissa expostulates, "the gods, who never lost a chance of hurting, thwarting and spoiling human lives were seriously put out if, all the same, you behaved like a lady" and let him go (*Odyssey* 5.118-32; *MD* 117). The garden world of Bourton ends when Clarissa refuses Peter, though they remain friends. Eventually, Clarissa sees Peter off to India with "her little attentions—cigars, notes, a rug for the voyage" (120). This is a bon voyage, a *propemptikon* or send-off convention that is reminiscent of Calypso, who actually helps Odysseus build the ship besides stocking it with provisions (*Odyssey* 5.234-68).

India eventually provides a "Penelope" for Peter—Daisy, a married woman who is being courted by two suitors in his absence, Major Orde and Major Simmons. In her letter Daisy gives an account of their meetings and, like the elegiac Penelope of Ovid's *Heroides* I, line 91, "said it to make him jealous" (121). Like Penelope, Daisy is as crafty as Odysseus: "She flattered him; she fooled him" (*Odyssey* 2.88; *MD* 68). Peter, preeminently enamored of married women, is apparently expecting to settle with Daisy in London. His age suggests that she, an elegiac *puella* stereotype, would be a "widow with a past one of these days, draggling about in the suburbs" (239), suggesting the Roman *subura*, the red-light district, which reflects upon Peter as a strumpet's fool—"look at the women he loved" (192). Having returned to London, however, he visits Clarissa and tells her of Daisy and, as though he is begging leave of Calypso to return to his wife, he bursts into tears, following the elegiac imperative and the weeping Odysseus. Peter's visit with Clarissa also parodies another Homeric allusion, however.

It begins in Clarissa's drawing room, simulating Odysseus's visit in Helen's chamber when he reveals the Greek strategy, presumably the Trojan Horse (*Odyssey* 4.251-56). As Odysseus creeps into the city in disguise, recognized only by Helen, not the defenders, before the conclusion of the Trojan War, Peter suggests: "Nobody yet knew he was in London" (77). Peter makes a clean breast of it, not of the wooden horse but of Daisy, and marks the cryptic Homeric source by saying he "told her everything as usual" before the battle (64-73). Clarissa's persona as Helen has been planted in Peter's mind by none other than Sally Seton, who "implored him, half laughing of course, to carry off Clarissa, to save her from the . . . 'perfect gentlemen' who would 'stifle her soul'" (114), reminiscent of the abduction of Helen (25). This is the same Helen whose powers of imitation and deception are still remarkable 20 years later (*Odyssey* 4.277-89). Clarissa introduces yet another *propempticon*. "As if he were starting directly upon some great voyage," she responds with her conventional propemptic plea: "Take me with you" (70).

Clarissa's ad hoc personae encompass another formidable Mediterranean divinity suggested when Peter thinks, "Clarissa had sapped something in him permanently" (241). The comparison implies that Peter will not be able to string Odysseus's bow (Adams 21). Although Odysseus fears that Circe would unman him, not make him a pig as she did his crew (*Odyssey* 10.301, 341), Peter is victim to the fate the hero escaped; the boating on the lake is encoded intercourse, giving an incongruous impression of Peter's imitation of antiquity's favorite superstud: "Richard rowed them back" (94-95).[20] This reminiscence concludes with an echo of the quarrel over a girl between Agamemnon and Achilles in the *Iliad*: "He deserved to have her" (74-75) (the word *have* bears the same sexual connotations in antiquity as it does today). As in Homer's Circean episode, transformations of men to swine represent an initiation that restores youthfulness: "he had not felt so young for years" (78). "To have been a sacred animal . . . is to have been given a second chance of sorts" (Skulsky 19, 23, 227n20); it appears that Peter's second chance will be justified, if not his youthfulness. Oddly, Peter's view of Clarissa, whether as Helen, Calypso, or Circe, makes her an elegiac mistress "with the tears running down her cheeks" when it is he who sheds elegiac tears (69, 236).

Whereas a Calypso would elevate Odysseus to the level of divinity and a Circe would degrade him to bestiality, other beings in the *Odyssey* merely think of him as dinner. The girl shedding veil after veil, reminiscent of Leukotheia's lifejacket (*Odyssey* 5.346), suggests a Salome whom Peter follows from Trafalgar square, completing her seductive dance abruptly in his hotel where the next visitor, like St. John the Baptist (a solar figure whose beheading is to be commemorated on June 24), might appear as "a joint of meat to be served on a perfectly clean platter" (*MD* 78-79, 235; Harrison, "The Head of John the Baptist" 218). For Peter, life is clearly not "plain sailing" (for "plain sailing," see *MD* 184, 238); for the Homeric hero sailing a Euclidean "plane" world, matters are difficult enough. Peter, a buccaneer among marching soldiers, acutely aware of the "troubles of the flesh" (77), is "sailing" a non-Euclidean spherical text as he retraces the hero's elegiac, not heroic, path.

The Homeric journey typically includes "the crossing of water, the change of clothes, the sharing of food" (Segal 66). Peter Walsh, like Odysseus (Block), acquires new clothing from time to time, his outward appearance suggesting that each ordeal has wrought some internal change. In Clarissa's drawing room he wears "the same check suit" (60). On the street he sees himself as "a man in a tail-coat with a carnation in his button-hole" (72). In Regents Park somewhat later, Septimus and Rezia see him as a man in a gray suit (105). Septimus believes that this is Evans, his deceased war companion, "But no mud was on him; no wounds; he was not changed." Septimus's perception quotes and reverses the dream of Aeneas in which Hector is

> black with bloodied dust; his swollen feet were pierced by thongs. Oh this was Hector, and how different he was from Hector back from battle. . . . His beard unkempt, his hair was thick with blood, he bore the many wounds he had received around his homeland's walls. (*Aeneid* 2.376-84; trans. Mandelbaum)

Furthermore it establishes the Hector persona as Septimus's as well; he (a self-taught poet like Phemius in *Odyssey* 22:346-47) who left Stroud because of his mother, and coming down to tea "with his hands unwashed" (*MD* 127), simulates Hector who tells his mother he cannot pour a libation to Zeus "with hands unwashed," all spattered with blood and muck (*Iliad* 6.264-68; trans. Lattimore). Septimus, a patriotic volunteer soldier, is pointedly different from the draft dodgers Ulysses and Achilles (Frazer, "Epitome" 3.6-7, 177).

Here it seems that Peter is in a kind of Underworld where as Odysseus he sees Septimus Smith who is reminiscent of Elpenor ("not sound in his wits"—*Odyssey* 10.553; Segal 41), first having been made a swine and now a shade who died falling from Circe's roof, a free-fall ending in Hades. This Underworld is both an analeptic allusion to Peter's self-reference "He was in Hell" and anticipates Septimus's "falling down, down into the flames" (*Odyssey* 10.559-60; *MD* 93, 213). Those who have gone down to the Underworld and return are twice dead and twice born, as Circe observes (*Odyssey* 12.21-23), and participate in the cyclic pattern of loss and renewal in Homer's poem and in *Mrs. Dalloway*.

Oddly, the Warren-Smiths are the only Londoners who seem to notice Peter, as if he were invisible (like Odysseus) most of the day. His invisibility may be a function of his hat, a cap of invisibility, which he holds in his hand and puts on as he leaves Regents Park. At this point he hears the Siren singing, but wisely does not pause to listen. This Siren, an ornithomorphic creature such as Homer's Sirens, sings with her birdlike twitter not of the Trojan War but, in proper elegiac terms, of love in a Homeric flowery meadow (Regents Park), yet in very watery, Pindaric circumstances:[21] "The old bubbling, burbling ['swee to'] song" ("Love's Old Sweet Song") with "the earthly vacuity of what is long dead" (Segal 101) "streamed away in rivulets over the pavement" (*MD* 122-24).

The Siren, a midday demon (Harrison, *Prolegomena* 202-03), interrupts Peter's thoughts of Daisy and of seeing lawyers about his divorce from the woman he married on his passage to India (10, 285). The wedding theme in *Mrs. Dalloway* is universally applied even in the negative—Peter's divorce. When he arrives in Bloomsbury, he has seen the divorce lawyers and presumably left things in their hands. Yet his brief thought about "dead bodies" (229) reveals that he is still preoccupied with divorce. Oddly, the matter of dead bodies skillfully links the wedding theme with the nautical motif in the unlikely hands of Aristotle and Milton. Aristotle's *Protreptikos*, illustrating the predicament of the prisoners in Plato's Cave, mentions "the vivid simile of the torture inflicted by the Etruscan pirates who bound their victims face to face with corpses" (Aristotle fragment 60, Rose). The simile enters Peter's consciousness through Milton, who used it "when in the Divorce Tracts he spoke of an unhappy marriage as being 'as if a living soul were bound to a dead body'" (Guthrie 157).[22] At this point Peter is also impressed with the triumph of civilization.

Peter's awareness of civilization becomes significant because for him this next episode as for Odysseus represents a transition between the dangers of life on the street, such as being killed by a falling tree (improperly loaded onto its truck—Juvenal, *Third Satire*, c. line 257) or even being struck down by diseases or knocked over at a crossing, and his return from fantasy to "reality." Packing up his knife, his watch, seals, and note case, Peter effects the "arming of the hero" (241). His discourse at dinner with the Morrises—whose name suggests William Morris's remarkable translation of the *Odyssey* and his utopian scenarios (49) in *News from Nowhere* and *The Earthly Paradise*—recalls Homer's "civilized" Phaiakians of Scheria inhabiting an earthly paradise where fruit trees, especially pear trees, bear their fruit year round. Like the Phaiakians, the Morrises derive from a thalassocratic culture (at Liverpool). Relations between the Morrises are perfect; that is, they simulate the harmonic likemindedness, the *homophrosune*, of the ataraxic royal couple Alcinous and Arete, which is nonexistent between Sally's parents (48, 243). This *homophrosune* is also shared by Clarissa when she contemplates the suicide, Septimus Smith, a tempting "suitor": "She felt somehow very like him." For her, "Nothing could be slow enough; nothing last too long" (282, 283), as when Athena lengthens the night of Odysseus's passionate reunion with Penelope (*Odyssey* 23.241-348).

Homer's Odysseus in Scheria is treated hospitably, although, like Peter, he dines apart from the Court. The Homeric hero begs leave to eat before responding to the conventions of Greek hospitality by telling his story. Odysseus is here especially ruled by his belly (*Odyssey* 7.215-21). Peter, however, prefers to give the appearance of "addressing himself seriously, not gluttonously, to dinner" (242), for which the Morrises respect him: "They liked him, he felt." Moreover, "they felt he counted on their support . . .; was champion of a cause which immediately became their own" (243). Thus, simulating the ultracivilized Phaiakians who aid Odysseus on the last leg of his "adventurous, long, long voyage," the Morrises are "glad to do any little service such as lend a time-table [a "Bradshaw"] or impart useful information" (247, 242). Like the lord of Ithaca, Peter has ways "that won him respect"; the Phaiakians almost immediately ponder the suitability of Odysseus as husband for young Nausicaa, who discovers Odysseus at the water's edge while doing the laundry, perhaps simulated by Elaine Morris who is "training for the family business" (243).

Morris, however, "mends the boots on Sunday" (244), not unlike Eumaeus the pig farmer (also possibly "the family business" [243] unless the Morrises run a laundry) whose "hut is a kind of rustic Phaiakia" (Segal 164) and whose roots are also utopian (*Odyssey* 14.23, 403-11; 15.407). When Peter and the Morrises separate, the narrative indicates they will meet again, as though he will come back and meet them later. The Phaiakian reunion will instead take a different form. Admittedly it's all made up "as one makes up the better part of life" (81) that Peter has previously considered an "exquisite amusement."

Of the alternative plans he makes for the evening ("he might go to Clarissa's party, or he might go to one of the Halls, or he might settle in and read an absorbing book" [239, 244]), he suddenly decides, without motivation, to attend Clarissa's party, to which he has been explicitly denied an invitation—Clarissa's letter contains no hint of an invitation: "How heavenly it was to see him. She must tell him that! That was all"

(234; for the "uninvited," see Proust, 1: 927; 2: 771, 1091; 3: 217 ff.).[23] This curious situation hinges on Clarissa, who has told about burning her candle ad infinitum. This bit of Circean sorcery simulates the homeopathic procedures of Simaitha, who burns wax and asks the moon to beckon Delphis: "'Simaitha wants you to come' and bring him here" (Theocritus *Idyll* 2; trans. Barriss Mills). A similar spell is also successfully cast in Virgil's *Eclogue*, line 8.[24] In Clarissa's case, with the candle half burnt, "she could just hear the click of the handle released as gently as possible by Richard, who slipped upstairs in his socks and then as often as not, dropped his hot-water bottle and swore! How she laughed!" (47). It seems that in Peter's case Clarissa's been burning candles again.

When Peter thinks "one might weep if no one saw," now his eye is "a cup that overflowed" (230, 250). His elegiac cup runneth over. As a part of "the whole of London in little boats moored to the bank, tossing on the waters as if the whole place were floating off in carnival" and in cabs "rushing round the corner, like water round the piers of a bridge" (249-50), Peter sails back, not to Ithaca but to Clarissa's house. He arrives with his pocketknife (his "far-shadowing spear"—*Odyssey* 22.95, 97; 24.519, 522); the party seems to be falling flat, when Clarissa like a good hostess merely wants everyone to be themselves and have a good time. The party is rescued by an explosion (255) reminiscent of the thundering sneeze from Telemachus that makes Penelope laugh, analogous to Clarissa's laughter in the presence of the malodorous Miss Kilman, hated and loved (for "laughter," see *MD* 190, 194, 195, 266; *Odyssey* 17.541-42). Here the noise is a gust of "wind" so great that it blows out the curtains—twice.[25] In an Aristophanic context, such omens suggest crepitation, an occasion of harmless amusement and laughter making it possible "to say things you couldn't say anyhow else" (*MD* 259; Henderson 195n15, par. 422, 423). It blows in the utopian birds of paradise as well (*MD* 256-58; Proust 2: 40 ff.), suggesting several Homeric oracular birds (*Odyssey* 2.146-54; 15.160, 525; 20.242). As a bird omen, a portent often encountered in comic Aristophanic utopias, it augurs well for the success of Clarissa's party—"So it wasn't a failure after all" (Harrison, *Themis* 98-99; Aristophanes *Birds*, line 717—"if it's an omen you call it a bird"). This paradise is familiar territory for Peter. Rather than quickening his apparently lost innocence (unlike Dickens he has no "very great expectations" [247]), it seems to offer little hope that any paradise (Miltonic or otherwise) can be regained, that the party will be any more rewarding than the series of imaginary constructs from which he has just emerged.

He encounters a Circean Aunt Helena, famous for pulling up testicular orchids by the roots,[26] Lady Bruton who threatens him with lunch, and Clarissa's impersonation of a sea nymph in her "silver mermaid's dress. . . . Lolloping on the waves and braiding her tresses" (264). Typically she gives Calypso's send-off ("and good luck to him"—*merde* [*MD* 265]) to the prime minister, Stanley Baldwin. Peter and Sally together recreate the Teichoscopia from *Iliad* 3.166 ff.[27] Peter identifies various guests for Sally's benefit, as Helen does for Priam: "Tell me do. Who is this?" (It was Mrs. Hilbery.) "Who was that?" (Ellie Henderson.) And Richard, "Who was he talking to?" (Sir William.) The catechesis begun at Bourton, "Who is *that*?" (Sappho LP 31), now extends to Richard Dalloway: "Who is that lovely girl?" (48, 295, 296). Finally Peter briefly reports the erotic news from India as he did for Clarissa—Daisy, that is, who brackets his section of the novel (290-93, 295).

Sally's passing quotations—"did absence matter?" (Propertius 2.33, 43), that is, *semper in absentis felicior aestus* (absence makes the heart grow fonder); Tennyson's "it is better to have loved [and lost]"; and Matthew Arnold's poem "Growing Old"; such that Elizabeth "feels not half what we feel"—illustrate her elegiac preoccupations with eroticism and the abbreviation typical of elegy, not going into everything (for these allusions see *MD* 10, 287, 292, 295). Furthermore it is, perhaps, astonishing for Peter to find that Sally now lives in an earthly paradise with "plants, hydrangeas, syringas, very, very rare hibiscus lilies that never grow north of the Suez Canal" (290) that afford her the Epicurean ataraxia, the peace "which men and women never gave her" (Hawley 74; Propertius 3.21, 25-26; *MD* 293-94). Having five sons identifies her as an allomorph of the Phaiakian queen, Arete of Scheria, and Nausicaa as well. Sally may be 55 in body as she claims, "but her heart was like a girl's of twenty" (294); that is, she is both the older and younger form of the same persona (Harrison, *Prolegomena* 274). Peter and the Phaiakians have met again. Sally's tempting invitation to the wandering hero, "no home, nowhere to go to" (289), may suggest something more than a casual visit to this predatory woman, who after a barbed attack on Clarissa—she was a snob, she lacked something, was hard on people—twists her elegiac weapon in the wound: "What does the brain matter . . . compared with the heart" (296).

For Peter, this elite culture simulates Scherian culture and recapitulates the end of his day in London. His peregrinations that led him away from Helen of Troy to various outposts in the Mediterranean, ending with the Phaiakians at Scheria, now only lead him to the walls of Troy and the comforts of Scheria once more, a story that like the *Odyssey* moves in a textual circle (Thalmann 67), a comprehension that begins only at the end of the reading. The fairyland he had fantasized is again materialized, surrounded, as Mrs. Hilbery reports, by Clarissa's "enchanted garden. . . . But she was a magician!" (291), and Peter is as much a captive as ever insofar as discourse confirms its own truth.

The surroundings, including the party, simulate the scene of what has been called a "courtship dance" in the *Odyssey* that restores the antebellum friendship between the hero and his wife; "they reverse roles, take risks, dominate and outwit each other, until finally they reunite" (Felson-Rubin 22-25; *Odyssey* 18-23). Penelope intermittently withdraws to her room, eventually allowing Odysseus his epic battle with the suitors. While Clarissa has withdrawn to her little room, there is in place of a battle Sally's attack on Clarissa and her temptation of Peter until, with a Propertian twist, Clarissa returns, having found her lost youth (282). There she was, at last, saying she would buy the flowers herself, asserting her victory over Sally's floral seductiveness. Effectively, she joins the end to the beginning, and restores the status quo with flowers of her own.

Interpreting *Mrs. Dalloway* is facilitated by recontextualizing several elusively shifting elements, among them the irreverently transmigrated Homeric facet of otherwise uninterpreted events, the frame that a fragmentary expression of the mediating vision has dislocated, and from within which a meaningful reading must be made. It is perforce a requirement that readers should recollect the parts and recognize this intertextual relation. The author is aware that comprehension depends on recognizing Odysseus even if Clarissa's guests do not (86, 288). Readers must be capable of grasping such subtleties and willing to laugh. It is "revealing to those who know the original, but hermetic to the uninitiated," and it "can only hope to appeal to a highly educated and critically perceptive minority" (Riewald 131).

Although *Mrs. Dalloway* is a fiction critical of Joyce's *Ulysses*, like *Ulysses* it is constructed from and mirrors classical literature. The necessary absurdities that are manifest in this parody reflect the fact that Virginia Woolf's reading of *Ulysses* was not a sympathetic one. The Homeric device not only mocks Joyce as part of its own comedy, and cleverly evades the obscenity charges to which he was subject, but also serves to satirize its modern dramatis personae. Furthermore, it shows that a brief but coherent narrative can parody just as much as a long one and can be equally as obscure without being totally unintelligible.

As misleadingly simple as the *Odyssey, Mrs. Dalloway*'s other creative ruses are many. Its staples are indirection, preterition, disguise, subterfuge, and guile; it is demanding yet enriching while giving the reader "an ever-increasing responsibility to share the work of creation" (Worcester 166). It is as cannibalistic a creature as the *gaster*, the belly that drives Odysseus (Segal 17)—a Homeric monster that feasts on "recondite knowledge and recherché wit" (Zanker 16), first devouring the components, then regurgitating the tale. Most of all, however, it is clear from the elegiac imperative that *Mrs. Dalloway* is of the erotic party of Sappho (LP 16), whose conception of beauty is not a cavalry or marching soldiers, as some say, but is instead clearly a matter of what you love.

From *Twentieth Century Literature* 45.2 (Summer 1999): 186-209. Copyright © 1999 by *Twentieth Century Literature*. Reprinted with permission of *Twentieth Century Literature*.

Notes

1. Very much in the mold of Wyndham Lewis is William Jenkins, who concludes that Woolf was "influenced by that which she ostensibly rejected" (519). William York Tindall, less acerbic than Lewis but equally incorrect, says that *Mrs. Dalloway* "is indebted primarily to Joyce" (Heilbrun 72). Kelly Anspaugh says Lewis "is defending *Joyce*" and exposing "plagiarism by Woolf" (371). DiBattista and Pearce seem stranded on a dichotomy; it must be either Joyce or Woolf. Hugh Kenner, like Lewis, stoops to insult for lack of insight: Virginia Woolf "is an English novelist of manners writing village gossip from a village called Bloomsbury" (37). Carolyn Heilbrun wisely says, "No critical display is more offensive than that which praises one author only by damning another, as though critical judgement were a seesaw on which one reputation cannot rise unless another is lowered" (67). Virginia Woolf's version of the *Odyssey*, however, is one of those circular phenomena described from within a discourse which determines what counts as phenomena in the first place.

References to *Mrs. Dalloway* will be indicated by *MD*, references to *The Common Reader* by *CR*.

2. Jenkins gleefully mentions the incriminating water closet as an item Woolf cribbed from Joyce's *Ulysses* without noticing that it is also a prominent fixture in Proust (1: 530, 715). He takes no notice of "Waterloo" as a part of the subtle garderobe humor; it had been a perfectly acceptable word for some time. In *Mrs. Dalloway* there are several direct quotes "cribbed" from the "Nausicaa" chapter of *Ulysses*, suggesting that Lewis et al. are rather like Peter's nurse, waving at the wrong window (78). There are also 25 references to other authors.

3. The chiasmus, or hysteron proteron:

A dog that p's, a man that forths = Joyce
An airplane that forths, a man that p's = Woolf

4. Bruns writes: "The true writer is he who conceals his plagiary by artful and unprecedented imitation" (97). Conte (23-24) cites thereby "the simultaneous presence of two different realities." Clarke mentions "a metamorphic recycling of prior texts into newly imagined combinations" (32). Bing includes "the necromantic urge, that desire to reanimate the past" (83). Booker includes parody and plagiary in the reper-

toire of carnival and transgression. Hebel says of quotation, it is "a device for activation of two texts" (6).

5. Eliot says: "Immature poets imitate; mature poets steal. . . . The good poet welds his theft into a whole of feeling which is unique, utterly different from that from which it was torn" (*Sacred Wood* 125). He also says, somewhat overstating it,

> Mr. Joyce is pursuing a method which others must pursue after him. They will not be imitators, any more than the scientist who uses the discoveries of an Einstein in pursuing his own independent, further investigations. (*Selected Prose* 177)

6. Douglas Frame includes under the heading of solar symbolism the return from death as a return from darkness, blinding as a solar motif, the stages of the Ciconian battle that follows the course of the sun, and "kindle" (*MD* 3) as a return to light/life. Max Müller's solar mythology includes India and the Vedic god of fire ("rubbing stick to stick" [*MD* 282]). The mythology of Palmer analyzes the solar character of Sampson (*MD* 274), in Dorson 28 and 55n22. Apparently the circular life of salmon marks them as solar fish.

7. The number refers to a line. References to volume, chapter, and line in classical literature are given, for example, as Propertius 2.1.50.

8. Latin elegy, in general, is love poetry written in couplets, one line in hexameter, one in pentameter. The implied unevenness of metrical feet has suggested that elegy "limps" like Gerty MacDowell in *Ulysses*. See also the limping Sara in *The Years* (see Cramer). It has no relation with pastoral elegy (see Veyne). Benediktson (*Propertius: Modernist Poet* 135) indicates that Joyce employed (plagiarized?) Propertius 4.7. Callimachus

> founded an aesthetics based upon a semiotic fact: the independence of the literal meaning; an exercise in equilibrium and therefore in gracefulness, a text that, far from being a mirror to reality, is equivocal to the point of dizziness; a form of writing that is sufficient unto itself because it does not explain anything. (Veyne 19)

See also Cameron 52, 471-83. Callimachus, a librarian who did not care for big books, *mega biblion/mega kakon*, preferred Homer to the Hellenistic imitations of Homer in his own time.

9. Propertius typically mentions Homer by way of elegiac convention, praising Ulysses's sexual partner who waited for him, and his happy return in spite of difficulties (2.6.23, 2.9.3-7, 2.14.3, 2.26.37, 3.7.41), and his weeping at the death of his crew. Propertius 3.12.23-36 follows some unknown tradition, as Benediktson notes. Propertius mentions Helen in relation to elegiac conventions instead of the epic Trojan War (2.1.50, 2.15.18, 2.31.32, 2.34.5). Once he summarizes the features of the Trojan War by way of a parasiopesis, the parts he will pass over. In the poems of Propertius, the speaker, hence the distancing "*persona loquens*," is not always to be construed as the poet. These are not confessional poems.

10. Miss Kilman, whose smell is noticeable, like the wound of the tormented Greek hero Philoctetes, like him learns through suffering the Greek commonplace *pathein/ mathein* (Sophocles, *Philoctetes* lines 537-38): "No one knew the agony" (*MD* 196, 199).

11. According to Austin (106-07), the Homeric *thumos* is variously located in the chest or lungs. When the person is in doubt, it can split in two. It functions as a receptacle of intellectual activity and as a source of emotion—joy, anger, desire, and grief. It can be "diminished or wasted by grief, filled or satiated with food, grief, or weeping, can be storm-tossed, stirred up, melted, bewitched by eros." It also "orders, urges, hopes, restrains, flutters with anxiety, rejoices, exalts, forbids, has volition and daring, can be arrogant and intransigent, credulous or incredulous." See also Padel 21-29.

12. There had been several novels, including D. H. Lawrence's 1920 novel *Women in Love*, in which portraits of Ottoline Morrell were offensive. In 1917, Woolf told Ottoline that "when she wrote her great Garsington novel there would be a streak of white lightning—and that would be Ottoline" (Darroch 212). Kilman's "éclair," in French, is "lightning," a better reference to Ottoline than Sally Seton's "in a flash of lightning" but very carefully camouflaged indeed (*MD* 53, 199).

13. It is doubtless troubling to Septimus Smith that the Cyclops's preferred diet is milk.

14. For boiling back to life, see Detienne 243-45 and Frazer, "Appendix" 1.359 ff.

15. For such conventions, see Cairns. These conventions are extremely mannered, however natural they may seem to the uninitiated, and they draw attention to the form more than to the matter.

16. Ellman cites the book by Maurice Clare (May Byron) as an allusion mentioned in Joyce's *Ulysses*. Clarissa's morning walk also suggests this little work. It is also a June morning for "Shakespeare," whose lavish freehandedness is in opposition to Clarissa's frugality. He visits the booksellers at St. Paul's Churchyard, comparable to Clarissa's Hatchard's. He is anachronistically concerned with the ongoing performance of *Hamlet*, which is of thematic interest in *Ulysses*, whereas Clarissa becomes preoccupied with *Cymbeline*. While walking, he broods over his marriage and his affair with the Dark Lady as Clarissa broods over Richard and Peter. He enjoys writing about flowers—daffodils, violets, lilies, roses, daisies, carnations—and he eventually arrives at the herbalist's, Gerard's (Clarissa's Mulberry's), where he inhales "the warm June scents" and has lunch as all the clocks strike 12. He meets his brother Edmond as Clarissa meets Hugh (Clare 1-26). Even Shakespeare had been accused of plagiarism, styled an upstart crow beautified with borrowed feathers that had been "crudely treated by his predecessors" (Clare 7).

17. A distinction is also made between monologues—always spoken aloud in Homer, used "when a character is alone, cannot be heard by others, and hence can utter what he thinks"—and embedded focalization—"used when other characters are present" and "not meant to overhear his thoughts" and "only the reader is informed of these perceptions and feelings, and not the characters in the story" (de Jong 30, 43). Hence, when Peter says, "Nobody yet knew he was in London" (77), his monologue is spoken aloud. Miss Kilman ("Fool! Simpleton!" etc.—*MD* 189) exemplifies embedded focalization. Some extracts from *Mrs. Dalloway* are given by de Jong in addition to the

relevant Homeric quotations. Compare Peter's Homeric "turn for mechanics" (73) with "Odysseus of the many devices" (*polymechanos*) (*Odyssey* 14.486).

18. Cramer, who has said that the Homeric tales and most Greek drama "sought to inspire masculine aggression in the service of the state" (206), reveals thereby a perspective that apparently conforms to her preconceived ideological preoccupations. She has further difficulty in interpreting the work of Jane Ellen Harrison regarding ritual and Greek literature.

19. The Phaiakian utopian world features fertility, including fruit trees and a vineyard that are never exhausted. Calypso's flourishing grove of trees with birds, viniculture, and kitchen garden is comparable. Many of the Homeric islands feature endless fertility and growth without cultivation (making the plow superfluous). These all conform to the conventional *locus amoenus*. In London, as well, the garden world is typical: St. James's Park, Green Park, Hyde Park, Kensington Gardens, Regents Park. Italy also features the Milan gardens (*MD* 34).

20. West notes that "whenever a ship metaphor is applied to a woman the tone is scurrilous" (69).

21. Svenbro says: "Ever since Homer and Hesiod, a voice was envisioned as something that 'flowed,'" and for Pindar, "speech is frequently liquid." See Svenbro (88 and n35) for his examples.

22. Being bound face to face also suggests the Wars of Venus and hand-to-hand combat.

23. Lady Bruton is similarly of two minds. "She might come; or she might not come" (see Penelope in Homer's *Odyssey* 19.524; Sappho LP 51 [LP is a current designation for fragments of the poetry of Sappho and Alcaeus. It functions as a title.]). A similar scenario appears in Terence's *Eunuchus:* "She takes the trouble to ask me over, do I go? . . . Locks me out . . . summons me back? She can go down on her knees; I'm not coming back." Eventually it is insinuated that the woman in question might rub her eyes and "squeeze out a dribble of moisture" (Terence, *Eunuchus* 1-69; trans. Douglass Parker). Horace's parody of this episode has the scorned lover "wondering if he should or shouldn't go. . . . But now, now that she's asked me, should I go? . . . She rejects me, recalls me. Go back? No, not if she begs" (Horace, *Satires* 2.3, lines 260-64; trans. Jacob Fuchs).

24. The Homeric odyssey of Virgil's hero Aeneas is said to be imitated in the first six books of the *Aeneid*. The odyssey of Apuleius's hero (*The Golden Ass*) is performed after he has been transformed into an ass by a witch. Peter Walsh, like Hugh Whitbread, is reduced to a "whimpering, snivelling old ass" (for "asses" see *MD* 121, 173, 179). In the *Satyricon*, Petronius characterizes "Encolpius as a comic version of Odysseus persecuted over land and sea by the wrath of Priapus (rather than Poseidon) and obsessed with his beautiful but fickle girlfriend Kirke" (Brilliant 167). Homer's *Odyssey* is a popular comic vehicle.

25. The wind pertains to Ralph Lyon ("lyin'"), as in Henry James's "The Liar," suggesting the "false word" (a fart), and the eponymous character is true to his name. This draws attention to the stories of the *Odyssey*, the heroic master of lies and disguises, his epic, and this novel, all of which are "a paradoxical mixture of truth and false appearances" (Segal 183). Woolf comments on

a passage in the *Odyssey* where laughter begins to steal upon us. . . . To laugh instantly it is almost necessary (although Aristophanes may supply us with an exception) to laugh in English. Humour, after all, is closely bound up with a sense of the body. (*CR* 36)

In Greek, *bronte* (like "Emily Brontë"—*MD* 285) is *vox propria* for crepitation (Henderson 195n14).
26. See Hansen on orchids. My thanks to Professor David Payne for this reference and other helpful suggestions. For orchids in Proust, see 1: 253, 2: 565, 650, 654. In Proust, "Burma" appears as "Berma" the actress.
27. The well-known Homeric View from the Walls is parodied in Shakespeare's *Romeo and Juliet* 1.5.128-30, in Surtees's *Mr. Sponge's Sporting Tour* at the racetrack (ch. 68), and in Flaubert's *Sentimental Education* (2.1) at a society party in which the wind blows open the curtains and birds from an adjacent aviary invade the room. At the end of the party, things are scattered on the floor.

Works Cited

Adams, J. N. *The Latin Sexual Vocabulary*. London: Duckworth, 1982.

Anspaugh, Kelly. "Blasting the Bombardier: Another Look at Lewis, Joyce, and Woolf." *Twentieth Century Literature* 40 (1994): 365-78.

Austin, Norman. *Archery at the Dark of the Moon: Poetic Problems in Homer's Odyssey*. Berkeley: U of California P, 1975.

Bassett, Samuel Eliot. *The Poetry of Homer*. Berkeley: U of California P, 1938.

Benediktson, D. Thomas. "Propertius' 'Elegiacization' of Homer." *Maia* 37-38 (1985-86): 17-26.

_____. *Propertius: Modernist Poet of Antiquity*. Carbondale: Southern Illinois UP, 1989.

Bergren, Ann L. T. "Odyssean Temporality: Many (Re)Turns." *Approaches to Homer*. Ed. Carl A. Rubino and Cynthia W. Shelmerdine. Austin: U of Texas P, 1983: 38-73.

Bing, Peter. *The Well-Read Muse: Present and Past in Callimachus and the Hellenistic Poets*. Göttingen: Vandenboeck and Ruprecht, 1988.

Block, Elizabeth. "Clothing Makes the Man: A Pattern in the *Odyssey*." *Transactions of the American Philological Association* 115 (1985): 1-11.

Booker, M. Keith. *Techniques of Subversion in Modern Literature: Transgression, Abjection and the Carnivalesque*. U of Florida P, 1991.

Brilliant, Richard. "Kirke's Men: Swine and Sweethearts." *The Distaff Side: Representing the Female in Homer's Odyssey*. Ed. Beth Cohen. New York: Oxford UP, 1995. 165-74.

Bruns, Gerald L. "A Short Defense of Plagiary." *The Review of Contemporary Fiction* 1 (1981): 96-103.

Cairns, Francis. *Generic Composition in Greek and Roman Poetry*. Edinburgh: Edinburgh UP, 1972.

Cameron, Alan. *Callimachus and His Critics*. Princeton: Princeton UP, 1995.

Clare, Maurice [May Byron]. *A Day With William Shakespeare*. Np: Hodder and Stoughton, 1913.

Clarke, Bruce. *Allegories of Writing: The Subject of Metamorphosis*. Albany: SUNY P, 1995.

Conte, Gian Biagio. *The Rhetoric of Imitation: Genre and Poetic Memory in Virgil and Other Latin Poets*. Ed. Charles Segal. Ithaca: Cornell UP, 1986.

Cramer, Patricia. "Loving in the War Years: The War of Images in *The Years*." *Virginia Woolf and War: Fiction, Reality, and Myth*. Ed. Mark Hussey. Syracuse: Syracuse UP, 1991. 203-24.

Culler, Jonathan. *Structuralist Poetics: Structuralism, Linguistics, and the Study of Literature*. Ithaca: Cornell UP, 1975.

Darroch, Sandra Jobson. *Ottoline: The Life of Lady Ottoline Morrell*. London: Cassell, 1976.

de Jong, Irene J. F. "Between Word and Deed: Hidden Thoughts in the *Odyssey*." *Modern Critical Theory and Classical Literature*. Ed. Irene J. F. de Jong and J. P. Sullivan. New York: Brill, 1994. 27-50.

Detienne, Marcel, and Jean-Pierre Vernant. *The Cuisine of Sacrifice Among the Greeks*. Trans. Paula Wissing. Chicago: U Chicago P, 1989.

DiBattista, Maria. "Joyce, Woolf, and the Modern Mind." *Virginia Woolf: New Critical Essays*. Ed. Patricia Clements and Isobel Grundy. Totowa: Barnes and Nobel, 1983. 96-114.

Dorson, Richard. "The Eclipse of Solar Mythology." *Myth: A Symposium*. Ed. Thomas A. Sebeok. Bloomington: Indiana UP, 1958. 25-63.

Eliot, T. S. *The Sacred Wood: Essays on Poetry and Criticism*. London: Methuen, 1920.

_____. *Selected Prose of T. S. Eliot*. Ed. Frank Kermode. New York: Harcourt, 1975.

Ellman, Richard. *The Consciousness of Joyce*. New York: Oxford UP, 1977.

Felson-Rubin, Nancy [N. F. Rubin]. *Regarding Penelope: From Character to Poetics*. Princeton: Princeton UP, 1994.

Frame, Douglas. *The Myth of Return in Early Greek Epic*. New Haven: Yale UP, 1978.

Frazer, J. E., ed. and trans. "Epitome." *Apollodorus*. 2 vols. The Loeb Classical Library. London: Heinemann, 1931.

Friederich, Reinhard H. "Fortuna's Journeymen in the Abyss of Sleep." *Kenyon Review* 5.3 (Summer 1983): 8-22.

Guthrie, W. K. C. *Orpheus and Greek Religion: A Study of the Orphic Movement*. New York: Norton, 1966.

Hansen, Eric. "The Flower of Frozen Desserts." *Natural History* (Apr. 1997): 76-79.

Harrison, Jane Ellen. *Epilegomena to the Study of Greek Religion and Themis*. New Hyde Park: University Books, 1962.

_____. "The Head of John the Baptist." *Classical Review* 30-31 (1916-17): 216-19.

_____. *Prolegomena to the Study of Greek Religion.* 3rd ed. New York: Meridian, 1955.

Hawley, Richard. "The Problem of Women Philosophers in Ancient Greece." *Women in Ancient Societies: An Illusion of the Night.* Ed. Leonie Arden, Susan Fischler, and Maria Wyke. New York: Routledge, 1994. 70-87.

Hebel, Udo. *Intertextuality, Allusion, and Quotation: An International Bibliography of Critical Studies.* New York: Greenwood, 1989.

Heilbrun, Carolyn. *Hamlet's Mother and Other Women.* New York: Ballantine, 1990.

Henderson, Jeffrey. *The Maculate Muse.* New Haven: Yale UP, 1975.

Hoff, Molly. "Woolf's *Mrs. Dalloway.*" *Explicator* 50.3 (Spring 1992): 161-63.

Iser, Wolfgang. *The Act of Reading: Theory of Aesthetic Response.* Baltimore: Johns Hopkins UP, 1978.

_____. *The Implied Reader: Patterns of Communication in Prose Fiction from Bunyan to Beckett.* Baltimore: Johns Hopkins UP, 1974.

Jenkins, William D. "Virginia Woolf and the Belittling of *Ulysses.*" *James Joyce Quarterly* 25.4 (1988): 513-19.

Kenner, Hugh. "The Making of the Modernist Canon." *Mazes: Essays by Hugh Kenner.* San Francisco: North Point, 1989. 28-42.

Lewis, Wyndham. "Virginia Woolf." *Men Without Art.* Ed. Seamus Cooney. Santa Rosa: Black Sparrow, 1987. 131-40.

Newton, Rick M. "The Rebirth of Odysseus." *Greek, Roman, and Byzantine Literature* 25 (1984): 5-25.

Oettli, Simone. "The Maze Maker." *Kenyon Review* 5.1 (Winter 1983): 67-84.

Padel, Ruth. *In and Out of the Mind: Greek Images of the Tragic Self.* Princeton: Princeton UP, 1992.

Pearce, Richard. "Who Comes First, Joyce or Woolf." *Virginia Woolf: Themes and Variations.* Ed. Vara Neverow-Turk and Mark Hussey. New York: Pace, 1993. 57-67.

Proust, Marcel. *Remembrance of Things Past.* Trans. C. K. Scott Moncrief and Terence Kilmartin. 3 vols. New York: Random, 1981.

Redfield, James. "The Economic Man." *Approaches to Homer.* Ed. Carl A. Rubino and Cynthia W. Shelmerdine. Austin: U of Texas P, 1983: 218-47.

Richter, Harvena. "The *Ulysses* Connection: Clarissa Dalloway's Bloomsday." *Studies in the Novel* 21.3 (Fall 1989): 305-19.

Riewald, J. G. "Parody as Criticism." *Neophilologus* 50 (1966): 125-48.

Rose, Margaret A. *Parody/Metafiction: An Analysis of Parody as a Critical Mirror to the Writing and Reception of Fiction.* London: Croom Helm, 1979.

Segal, Charles. *Singers, Heroes, and Gods in the Odyssey.* Ithaca: Cornell UP, 1994.

Skulsky, Harold. *Metamorphosis: The Mind in Exile.* Cambridge: Harvard UP, 1981.

Svenbro, Jesper. *Phrasikleia: An Anthropology of Reading in Ancient Greece.* Trans. Janet Lloyd. Ithaca: Cornell UP, 1988.

Thalmann, William G. *The Odyssey: An Epic of Return.* New York: Twayne, 1992.

Veyne, Paul. *Roman Erotic Elegy: Love, Poetry, and the West*. Trans. David Pellauer. Chicago: U of Chicago P, 1988.

West, David. *Horace, Odes I, Carpe Diem*. Oxford: Clarendon, 1995.

Woolf, Virginia. *The Common Reader*. Ed. Andrew McNeillie. London: Hogarth, 1984.

_____. *The Diary of Virginia Woolf*. Ed. Anne Olivier Bell and Andrew McNeillie. 5 vols. Vol. 2. New York: Harcourt, 1984.

_____. *The Essays of Virginia Woolf*. 3 vols. Vol. 2. Ed. Andrew McNeillie. New York: Harcourt, 1987.

_____. *The Letters of Virginia Woolf*. 6 vols. Ed. Nigel Nicholson and Joanne Trautmann. New York: Harcourt, 1980.

_____. *Mrs. Dalloway*. New York: Harcourt, 1925.

Worcester, David. *The Art of Satire*. New York: Harvard UP, 1940.

Zanker, Graham. *Realism in Alexandrian Poetry: A Literature and Its Audience*. London: Croom Helm, 1987.

"A Direction of One's Own":
Alienation in *Mrs. Dalloway* and *Sula*_____

Lorie Watkins Fulton

Before Toni Morrison became *the* goddess of contemporary literature, she was Chloe Ardellia Wofford, a graduate student at Cornell
who, in 1955, completed a master's thesis exploring manifestations of
alienation in the works of William Faulkner and Virginia Woolf.
Therein, Morrison defines alienation, with its attendant isolation, as
the defining literary theme of the twentieth century, and explores the
two authors' differing treatments of it in Woolf's *Mrs. Dalloway* and
two of Faulkner's novels ("Treatment" 1). She begins by theorizing
that Woolf's characters only become self-aware when isolated, and
that Faulkner's characters can never attain self-knowledge in isolation
(2-3). Ultimately, she determines that while Faulkner and Woolf seek
the same ends, the "answer to the questions of death, life, time and morality," they disagree on "what pattern of existence is most conducive
to honesty and self-knowledge" (39).

Morrison privileges Faulkner's emphasis on communal connection
by reading his position as the "antithesis" to Woolf's (4), and, after all,
her later writings clearly reveal the value she places on community.
Alienation, writes Morrison, "is not Faulkner's answer" to the problems
of modern life (3), and it hardly seems to be hers either.[1] Although Morrison has doubtlessly revised many of the opinions she expressed in her
thesis, she continues to tout the dangers of isolation.[2] This apparent rejection of Woolf's preferred strategy for attaining self-knowledge does
not, however, mean that Woolf exerts less influence on Morrison's
work than does Faulkner, although the lack of critical commentary to
that effect might suggest as much.[3]

Although fewer scholars have addressed the topic, Morrison's fiction similarly explores some of Woolf's key themes in ways that allow
her characters successfully to navigate the problems of modernity that
her thesis identifies. In fact, biographical and theoretical connections

suggest that Morrison's work might even have stronger ties to Woolf than to Faulkner.[4] At any rate, such a relationship seems most textually evident between Woolf's *Mrs. Dalloway* and Morrison's *Sula*. Though the two novels differ in many respects, at base, they share strikingly similar plots. *Mrs. Dalloway*'s main action reveals much through its depiction of Clarissa Dalloway's interaction with friends and family throughout a day filled primarily with preparations for the party she gives at the novel's conclusion. In the background, one subplot details the last day in the life of Septimus Warren Smith, a World War I veteran suffering from the symptoms of post-traumatic stress that ultimately lead to his suicide, and another deals with Clarissa's girlhood romance with Peter Walsh and friendship with Sally Seton. At the party, Clarissa learns of Septimus's suicide from his doctor, Bradshaw, and feels an uncanny connection to him and his tragic end. In *Sula*, Morrison utilizes time differently; rather than relying, as Woolf does, on memory to keep the narrative action in the present, Morrison follows her title character for several years. She tells the story of Sula's life, though, in Woolf fashion, by outlining Sula's relationships with her one great love and only true friend, and, much like Clarissa's connection to Septimus, Sula shares a deep revelatory bond with Shadrack, a veteran of the first world war who exists in a state of altered reality quite similar to the one that traps Septimus.

By noting such likenesses, I do not mean to suggest that Morrison simply retells Woolf's narrative in an African American context; in fact, she does precisely the opposite. Henry Louis Gates, Jr., speaks to such revisions in *The Signifying Monkey* when he suggests that African American writers often rewrite western texts with "a compelling sense of difference" (xxii). In his study of *Mrs. Dalloway* and alienation, Jeremy Hawthorn determines that while the novel "can present the unsatisfactoriness" of alienation, it "includes no real solution to it" (94).[5] In *Sula*, however, Morrison gets around such limitations via the revolutionary sense of revision that Gates references: she resolves in her fiction the same problems inherent in alienation for Woolf's char-

acters that her graduate thesis addresses. An examination of the reso-
nant connections between the two novels and the specific ways that
Morrison reworks the theme of alienation in a similar narrative setting
leads to a greater understanding of both texts; Morrison perhaps en-
courages such connections, despite her protestations about the anxiety
of influence (McKay 151-52).

Morrison begins her thesis chapter on Woolf by quoting a diary entry that Woolf dated October 25, 1920: "Why is life so tragic; so like a
little strip of pavement over an abyss . . . its unhappiness is everywhere
("Treatment" 5). Early in *Sula* Morrison pointedly utilizes a similar cement walkway as a metaphor when the military hospital releases
Shadrack because there "was clearly a demand for space":

> When he stepped out of the hospital door the grounds overwhelmed him:
> the cropped shrubbery, the edged lawns, the undeviating walks. Shadrack
> looked at the cement stretches: each one leading clearheadedly to some
> presumably desirable destination. There were no fences, no warnings, no
> obstacles at all between concrete and green grass, so one could easily ig-
> nore the tidy sweep of stone and cut out in another direction—a direction
> of one's own. (10)

Shadrack declines to take the path defined by the sidewalk. Instead, he
takes off in what Morrison describes as "a direction of one's own," a deliberately placed phrase that necessarily calls to mind Woolf's *A Room
of One's Own*. In much the same fashion, Morrison's novel disregards
the limitations of alienation that characterize *Mrs. Dalloway*; Morrison
defies the inherent tragedy of life as Woolf represents it, builds a sidewalk of her own over that rhetorical abyss by posing alternatives to
such alienation. And though Woolf surely never anticipated becoming
a foremother to an African American novelist, she alludes to such a
possibility in *A Room of One's Own* when she writes, "For books continue each other, in spite of our habit of judging them separately. And I
must also consider her—this unknown woman—as the descendant of

all those other women whose circumstances I have been glancing at and see what she inherits of their characteristics and restrictions" (80). Although Woolf actually speaks of Mary Carmichael, she could just as easily have referred to Morrison, her own literary descendent.[6]

* * *

Morrison challenges the inevitability of alienation in several ways, but she defies it most dramatically through her revision of the figure of the veteran suffering from post-traumatic stress in order to, as Eileen Barrett puts it, make "literal the mindlessness of war" (27).[7] In reference to another alienated figure, Sula, Patricia McKee argues that the people of Medallion do not ostracize her because of her difference, but rather integrate her as a necessary communal figure, one that "occupies the place of absences people cannot afford to miss" (40). Sula, McKee contends, "is not placed outside the group" because the members come "to depend on her for their own sense of place" (55). Shadrack seems to occupy a similar position. Unlike Septimus, who has so fully withdrawn from the world that he communicates only with the dead and thinks of his wife as "the unseen" until the brief moment of lucidity just before his death (*Dalloway* 25), Shadrack has a definite communal connection. He has a home to return to after the war (*Sula* 14), unlike Septimus who fought valiantly for "an England which consisted almost entirely of Shakespeare's plays and Miss Isabel Pole in a green dress walking in a square" (*Dalloway* 86).

Morrison similarly reworks the connection between her veteran and his psychic double. In *Mrs. Dalloway*, this connection remains completely one-sided as Clarissa imagines Septimus's suicide and subsequently experiences the epiphany that allows her to surmount her fear of death by somehow placing it into a larger context. Septimus's suicide causes her to "feel the beauty" and "feel the fun" of life by juxtaposing it with death (186), and makes her realize that, by taking his own life, Septimus "preserved" the meaningful core of his existence:

A thing there was that mattered; a thing, wreathed about with chatter, de-faced, obscured in her own life, let drop every day in corruption, lies, chatter. This he had preserved. Death was defiance. Death was an attempt to communicate; people feeling the impossibility of reaching the centre which, mystically, evaded them; closeness drew apart; rapture faded, one was alone. There was an embrace in death. (184)

However, Clarissa alone reaps the benefits of this revelation; Woolf never allows Septimus to meet her, much less derive similar benefit from their connection.

Conversely, Morrison constructs a mutually advantageous bond by allowing Shadrack and Sula to share a similar moment. After the small boy named Chicken Little drowns while playing with Sula and Nel on a riverbank, Sula is spurred by a child's terror of being caught in an act of wrongdoing and runs to Shadrack's house to see if he witnessed the event. When Sula enters the house, its order and "restfulness" amaze her. While taking in this initial lesson about the inaccuracy of precon-ceptions, she speculates, "Perhaps this was not the house of the Shad. The terrible Shad who walked about with his penis out, who peed in front of ladies and girl-children, the only black who could curse white people and get away with it" (61-62). Shadrack then returns to find Sula in his home and, rather than scolding her, he "nodded his head as though answering a question, and said, in a pleasant conversational tone, a tone of cooled butter, 'Always'" (62).

While telling Nel about the exchange, Sula thinks that Shadrack "had answered a question she had not asked, and its promise licked at her feet" (63); thus, Morrison initially leads readers to believe that Shadrack's "always" means that he will always keep Sula's secret. Later, however, it becomes clear that his remark means something quite different to both him and Sula. Near the novel's end, we learn that Shadrack treasures the purple and white belt that Sula lost as she ran from his cabin as "the one piece of evidence that he once had a visitor in his house" (156), apparently for him a symbol of her effort to reach out to him. Shadrack knows that Sula "had wanted something—from him. Not fish not work, but something only he could give" (156), and he decides that she wants him to reassure her of the existence of an afterlife. Consequently, he says "always" so that "she would not have to be afraid of the change—the falling away of skin, the drip and slide of blood, and the exposure of bone underneath. He had said 'always' to convince her, assure her, of permanency" (157). Shadrack, then, effectively answers a question that Sula did not even think to ask, one concerning Chicken Little's fate, and his answer somehow helps her and Nel to live with the consequences of their actions. At Chicken's funeral, "They held hands and knew that only the coffin would lie in the earth; the bubbly laughter and the press of fingers in the palm would stay aboveground forever" (66). Shadrack thus assures Sula of the inability of death to conquer all in much the same way that Septimus provides Clarissa a similar security; however, Morrison's relationship seems far more reciprocal, and Shadrack, in turn, does not exist in the same state of alienation that so fully traps Septimus.

The methods by which each man seeks to impose order upon chaos also reflect Shadrack's more connected existence. In his isolated state, Septimus becomes enthralled by the "message hidden in the beauty of words" (*Dalloway* 88), and he accordingly tries to harness that power to write his own "revelations on the backs of envelopes" (24). Only Rezia, his wife, ever sees his messages, though, and while she does not understand them in the way that Septimus wants her to, she does, at least, think some of them "very beautiful" (148). Shadrack, however, spreads his message throughout Medallion by instituting National Suicide Day, a holiday that Katy Ryan describes as "a 'sane' institution to counter the insanity of war" (402). The holiday grows out of Shadrack's struggle to "order and focus experience"; he realizes (as, of course, does Clarissa in *Mrs. Dalloway*) that it "was not death or dying that frightened him, but the unexpectedness of both." Subsequently, he decides, "if one day a year were devoted to it, everybody could get it out of the way and the rest of the year would be safe and free." National

Suicide Day operates, at first, as a rite, a representational exercise that Shadrack enacts on the third day of January each year by walking "through the Bottom down Carpenter's Road with a cowbell and a hangman's rope calling the people together. Telling them that this was their only chance to kill themselves or each other" (*Sula* 14). Gradually, Shadrack achieves his purpose and makes a formal acknowledgement of death a part of life as the people of Medallion absorb his message "into their thoughts, into their language, into their lives" (15). Morrison writes, "Easily, quietly, Suicide Day became a part of the fabric of life up in the Bottom of Medallion, Ohio" (16).

For years, Shadrack continues to perform this ritual alone until a few other outcasts gradually join him (*Sula* 41). By novel's end, though, Morrison takes the holiday beyond the symbolic. After Sula dies, Shadrack, as if mourning his one human connection, begins "to miss the presence of other people" (155). Though disheartened, he manages to take up his bell and rope and begin his pilgrimage yet again (158). Some combination of a winter thaw and a desire to look "at death in the sunshine" while "being unafraid" draws a record crowd to the parade, and by "the time Shadrack reached the first house, he was facing a line of delighted faces" (159). Their eager display, which frightens him from the beginning, culminates in tragedy as the group faces "the tunnel they were forbidden to build" (161), a project the community once thought would bring new life to the Bottom but instead soured into a "leaf-dead promise" when the contractor would hire African American workers only for the most menial jobs (162). The participants, in their desire to "kill" the tunnel, "kill it all," go down into it and, instead, lose their own lives (161-62). Lisa Williams interprets this final parade as "a protest against the violence of social hierarchy that refuses these black men work" (121), but Ryan takes the idea of protest a step further to suggest that the deaths fulfill the requirements for a "revolutionary suicide": the individual deaths become subsumed into "a political protest in which identity is collective" (401). By provoking such response, Shadrack spreads his message far more successfully than does Septimus, for while Septimus touches only one woman, Shadrack changes the consciousness of an entire community.

* * *

Most obviously, though, Morrison challenges the concept of alienation by appraising the value of female friendship. She spoke of its potential in her interview with Claudia Tate:

> Friendship between women is special, different, and has never been depicted as the major focus of a novel before *Sula*. Nobody ever talked about friendship between women unless it was homosexual, and there is no homosexuality in *Sula*. Relationships between women were always written about as though they were subordinate to some other roles they're playing. This is not true of men. (157)

Morrison did not set out to explore the possibilities of women's friendships and even told Tate, "I was half-way through the book before I realized that friendship in literary terms is a rather contemporary idea" (157).[8] Nevertheless, the force of her revisioning lies in the relationship that she establishes between best friends Sula and Nel. In many ways, it resembles the childhood relationship between Clarissa and Sally when the two share a similarly non-sexual closeness while they sit, "hour after hour, talking in her [Clarissa's] bedroom at the top of the house, talking about life, how they were to reform the world" (*Dalloway* 33).

Clarissa admires Sally for her daring, what she terms, "a sort of abandonment, as if she [Sally] could say anything, do anything; a quality much commoner in foreigners than in Englishwomen" (*Dalloway* 33). Clarissa values Sally not only for the daring that inspires her to run naked through the hall after forgetting her bath sponge, but also for her smaller violations. In one instance, Clarissa admires Sally's willingness to experiment with flowers, to "cut their heads off" and make "them swim on the top of water in bowls" in a fashion that horrifies stodgy old Aunt Helena (34). The differences that Woolf establishes between the two girls must seem obvious to all onlookers in the novel because Peter Walsh, who notices practically nothing, thinks of Sally as "Clarissa's greatest friend, always about the place, totally unlike her" (59).

Following—or rather surpassing—Woolf, Morrison also portrays her characters as different from one another. From girlhood, Sula exhibits a nature far more daring than Sally's; for example, she persuades Nel to join her in confronting the bullies who loiter on Carpenter's Road and prevent the girls from taking the shortest route home. When the boys block the gate to the path one day, Sula pulls Eva's paring knife from her pocket and "pressed her left forefinger down hard on its edge." Morrison writes, "Her aim was determined but inaccurate. She slashed off only the tip of her finger" (54). Though Sula seems to have planned to cut off even more of her finger, the boys stare "open-mouthed at the wound." Sula asks them, "If I can do that to myself, what you suppose I'll do to you?" (54-55). Morrison similarly casts Nel as a sort of Clarissa figure in that her repressed mother has driven "her daughter's imagination underground" (*Sula* 18), so that Nel, like Clarissa, has become an "unimaginative" and "prudish" victim of what Peter calls "The death of the soul" (*Dalloway* 59). Largely because of Sula's friendship, Nel finally finds the courage to dissociate from her mother, and Morrison writes that the two girls somehow complete each other. Their bond creates a "safe harbor of each other's company" where they can "afford to abandon the ways of other people and concentrate on their own perceptions of things" (*Sula* 55).

The intense friendships in both Woolf's and Morrison's novels contain at least the potential for romantic love. In *Mrs. Dalloway*, a crucial moment occurs as the two girls walk along the terrace at Bourton:

She and Sally fell a little behind. Then came the most exquisite moment of her whole life passing a stone urn with flowers in it. Sally stopped; picked a flower; kissed her on the lips. The whole world might have turned upside down! The others disappeared; there she was alone with Sally. And she felt that she had been given a present, wrapped up, and told just to keep it, not to look at it—a diamond, something infinitely precious, wrapped up, which, as they walked (up and down, up and down), she uncovered, or the radiance burnt through, the revelation, the religious feeling!—when old Joseph and Peter faced them. (35-36)

Williams speculates that such memories of her relationship with Sally allow Clarissa finally to "admit to herself that her feelings for Sally constitute the deepest, most exquisite passion of her life, and her mind's avid descent into the past represents Clarissa's wish to revisit that lost feeling" (86). While that seems true enough, within the confines of the novel, Clarissa looks back upon her relationship with Sally, much as she does her failed affair with Peter, as a temporary bond made possible only by the impetuousness of youth: "it had a quality which could only exist between women, between women just grown up. It was protective, on her side; sprang from a sense of being in league together, a presentiment of something that was bound to part them" (*Dalloway* 34). Just as old Joseph and Peter interrupt the moment that the girls share on the terrace, life and marriage do indeed part them, and Clarissa laments the loss of friendship more than anything else. She thinks, "The strange thing, on looking back, was the purity, the integrity, of her feeling for Sally" (34). While Clarissa remembers their kiss as "the most exquisite moment of her whole life," it could also qualify as the most tragic, because it marks the point at which her only true friendship dies and Sally becomes just another potential lover that Clarissa must reject to preserve her solitude.

Although Morrison insisted during the Tate interview that there "is no homosexuality in *Sula*" (157), she nevertheless depicts a similarly climactic, if only symbolic, scene between Nel and Sula when the girls join together in what they call "grass play":

In concert, without ever meeting each other's eyes, they stroked the blades up and down, up and down. Nel found a thick twig and, with her thumbnail, pulled away its bark until it was stripped to a smooth, creamy innocence. Sula looked about and found one too. When both twigs were undressed Nel moved easily to the next stage and began tearing up rooted grass to make a bare spot of earth. When a generous clearing was made, Sula traced intricate patterns in it with her twig. At first Nel was content to do the same. But soon she grew impatient and poked her twig rhythmically and in tensely into the earth, making a small neat hole that grew deeper and wider with the least manipulation of her twig. Sula copied her, and soon each had a hole the size of a cup. Nel began a more strenuous digging and, rising to her knee, was careful to scoop out the dirt as she made her hole deeper. Together they worked until the two holes were one and the same. (58)

Rather than allowing this erotic "grass play" to move from the representational to the actual as Woolf does, Morrison metaphorically buries the potential for a sexual relationship between her two characters. When Nel's twig breaks she throws the pieces into the depression with "a gesture of disgust" (58). Sula throws hers in as well and, together, the two girls "replaced the soil and covered the entire grave with uprooted grass. Neither one had spoken a word" (59). Shortly thereafter, the girls witness a literal death, Chicken Little's drowning, the event that marks their entrance to adulthood and foreshadows their later destructive romantic relationships with men.

Clarissa's relationships with men hardly seem more productive. Woolf makes it clear that Clarissa chooses to marry Richard because he presents a safe alternative to Peter, who thinks, "everything had to be shared; everything gone into" (*Dalloway* 8). With Richard, Clarissa can easily maintain what Peter terms her "impenetrability" (60), a quality that she thinks of as "a dignity in people; a solitude" that prevents a completely open connection to another person (120). In her marriage to Richard, she maintains the "little independence" that she thinks must exist "between people living together day in day out in the same house; which Richard gave her, and she him" (7-8). Clarissa's choice leads scholars such as Hawthorn to speculate that Woolf disapproves of consuming passion "because it consumes" (51). In any case, Clarissa cuts herself off from the very possibility of a fulfilling (much less consuming) connection, and Woolf hints that Clarissa chooses such remoteness in her marriage not from some theoretical commitment to independence, but because of a perceived lack within herself: "She could see what she lacked. It was not beauty; it was not mind. It was something central which permeated; something warm which broke up surfaces and rippled the cold contact of man and woman, or of women together." Because of this lack, Clarissa thinks that she has "failed" Richard (*Dalloway* 31), but, more importantly, that she has failed herself.

In her master's thesis, Morrison speculates that the death of Clarissa's sister, Sylvia, spurs her emotional withdrawal and that the effects of her detachment first appear in her relationships with Sally and Peter (9). Whatever the reason, Clarissa clearly cuts herself off from the possibility of any sort of deep, meaningful relationship, inside or outside of marriage. She goes from believing, as a girl, that "one must seek out the people who completed them; even the places" (*Dalloway* 153), to taking her husband quite for granted in the novel's present action, and thinking, when she unexpectedly meets Sally at the party after a separation of several years, only of how the "lustre had gone out of her" (171). Clarissa's self-imposed isolation is particularly poignant given that, in her own estimation, her "only gift was knowing people almost by instinct. . . . If you put her in a room with some one, up went her back like a cat's; or she purred" (9). Thus Woolf creates in Clarissa an impossible conflict between her impulse toward people and her need to preserve the "solitude" that, for her, makes "self-respect" possible (120); this tension transforms Clarissa's "gift" into something more akin to a burden marking the totality of her isolation.

While Morrison has no more hope than Woolf does for the success of a marriage built on consuming passion, her female characters do not experience the personal lack that Clarissa faces because they maintain an abiding, though troubled, friendship.[9] Like Clarissa and Sally, Nel and Sula separate as mature adults, but Morrison tellingly displaces the blame for the suspension of their friendship when she notes that "Nel's *response*" to her future husband, Jude, "selected her away from Sula" (emphasis mine, *Sula* 84).[10] As a consequence to Nel's withdrawal, Sula disappears from Medallion after the wedding and does not return for 10 years. Though Morrison leaves vague the specifics of Sula's absence, we do know that she attended college during that period of time (99). Morrison makes Sula's purpose during those absent years, however, eminently clear. She spent the time trying to replicate in a heterosexual romantic relationship the closeness that she had felt with Nel: "She had been looking all along for a friend, and it took her a while to discover that a lover was not a comrade and could never be—for a woman" (121). With this discovery, Morrison saves Sula from a fate similar to the one that awaits Sally Seton when she marries a Manchester man who owns cotton mills, becomes Lady Sally Rosseter, and delights most in her "five enormous boys" (*Dalloway* 171).

After learning the lesson of women's primary intimacy with one another, Sula returns to Medallion and Nel's friendship. The two fall back into their easy relationship and former closeness; as Nel puts it, "Talking to Sula had always been a conversation with herself" (*Sula* 95). Morrison, though, subjects their friendship to a test far more difficult than the simple endurance of time and distance when Nel happens upon her husband and Sula "down on all fours naked, not touching except their lips right down there on the floor" (105). Morrison said in her "Conversation" with Gloria Naylor that she wanted to establish that strong friendship and then "have one [of the women] do the unforgivable thing to see what that friendship was really made out of" (200). At first, it seems that the friendship is not made of very strong stuff at all, and Nel feels doubly deprived at the loss of both her husband and best friend: "Here she was in the midst of it, hating it, scared of it, and again she thought of Sula as though they were still friends and talked things over. That was too much. To lose Jude and not have Sula to talk to about it because it was Sula that he had left her for" (*Sula* 110).

Throughout the rest of the novel, Morrison deconstructs the affair in light of Sula and Nel's friendship. Ultimately, in the person of Sula, Morrison creates a character that ascribes to an alternative morality not all that different from the Bloomsbury sexual ethos that informed the behavior of Woolf's most intimate circle of friends.[11] Morrison writes that Sula leads "an experimental life" (118), and has "no affection for money, property or things, no greed, no desire to command attention or compliments—no ego" (119). Morrison displays this Bloomsbury influence most prominently in Sula's reasoning about the affair:

> She had clung to Nel as the closest thing to both an other and a self, only to discover that she and Nel were not one and the same thing. She had no thought at all of causing Nel pain when she bedded down with Jude. They had always shared the affection of other people: compared how a boy kissed, what line he used with one and then the other. Marriage, apparently, had changed all that, but having had no intimate knowledge of marriage, having lived in a house with women who thought all men available, and selected from among them with a care only for their tastes, she was ill prepared for the possessiveness of the one person she felt close to. (119)

Three years later, after learning that Sula has become gravely ill, Nel finally confronts her, "What about me? Why didn't you think about me? Didn't I count?" When Nel points out that Sula "didn't love me enough to leave him alone. To let him love me. You had to take him away," Sula offers a shocking reply: "What you mean take him away? I didn't kill him, I just fucked him. If we were such good friends, how come you couldn't get over it?" (144, 145).

* * *

By posing the radical possibility that women friends could and should share male lovers, even in the context of wedlock, Morrison intentionally creates and endorses an alternative to heteronormative romantic love based in jealous possession. As she told Naylor:

> You see, if all women behaved like those two, or if the Sula point of view operated and women really didn't care about sharing these things, everything would just crumble—hard. If it's not about fidelity and possession and my pain versus yours, then how can you manipulate, how can you threaten, how can you assert power? I went someplace once to talk about *Sula* and there were some genuinely terrified men in the audience, and they walked out and told me why. They said, "Friendship between women?" Aghast. Really terrified. (200)

Like Morrison, Sula realizes that the world—or more singularly, Nel—cannot yet accept such a philosophy. On her deathbed, she tells Nel that after something, some violent event, turns the world upside down, "then there'll be a little love left over for me. And I know just what it will feel like" (146). After that, she fades into drugged, hazy memories of her own and Nel's shared childhood, remembering "the days when we were two throats and one eye and we had no price" (147). Sula then dies and realizes "that there was not going to be any pain" and that she "was not breathing because she didn't have to. Her body did not need oxygen. She was dead." The depth of her bond with Nel becomes apparent when, significantly, Sula thinks of Nel as she passes from this life and enters the next: "Well, I'll be damned . . . it didn't even hurt. Wait'll I tell Nel" (149).

Nel comes to appreciate Sula's perspective, but only after Sula dies. As she returns from the funeral, Nel senses the presence of Sula's spirit and finally realizes that while "all that time, I thought I was missing Jude," she actually longed for Sula, her best friend, the other half of her soul. The acknowledgement of her loss causes her to cry out, "O Lord, Sula . . . girl, girl, girlgirlgirl" (174), and the two again merge, visually and textually, into the oneness of friendship as the sound of Nel's lamentation fades away. Morrison describes Nel's wail as "a fine cry—loud and long," and notes that "it had no bottom and it had no top, just circles and circles of sorrow" (174). Morrison, in her thesis, tellingly mentions an associated metaphor of Woolf's and determines that "Big Ben, chopping the day into sections, is not time as change, but time as destroyer" (22). Although Morrison does not comment on it, Woolf represents Big Ben's echoes as "leaden circles dissolved in the air" (*Dalloway* 4), an image that Morrison probably noticed. In *Sula*, Morrison takes those defunct circles and uses them to find a way to outwit time, not through suicide, as *Mrs. Dalloway* proposes, but through a friendship that survives death. The circles of Nel and Sula's friendship do not spiral outward, to eventually dissolve like the sounds of Big Ben, but instead repeat upward and outward, endlessly throughout time like William Butler Yeats's gyres. Through her friendship with Nel, Sula finally achieves the sort of immortality that the young Clarissa Dalloway believed possible before she detached from the world. Peter says of Clarissa's abandoned belief:

It ended in a transcendental theory which, with her horror of death, allowed her to believe, or say that she believed (for all her scepticism), that since our apparitions, the part of us which appears, are so momentary compared with the other, the unseen part of us, which spreads wide, the unseen might survive, be recovered somehow attached to this person or that, or even haunting certain places after death . . . perhaps—perhaps. (153)

Morrison makes such an extension possible for Sula as Nel detects the presence of her spirit in the novel's final pages, and a similar type of continuation perhaps exists for Clarissa even in her isolation, though by novel's end she clearly has given up any hope or conscious desire for extraordinary intimacy. Peter says that Clarissa "had influenced him more than any person he had ever known" (*Dalloway* 153), and Sally similarly puts their friendship first when she "counted up her blessings" because she "had owed Clarissa an enormous amount. They had been friends, not acquaintances, friends" (191, 188). Perhaps, in this way, Clarissa can similarly outwit time by continuing to inspire the same admiration in others that Peter and Sally feel ultimately feel for her. Indeed, she continues to exist and to touch readers, for Morrison taps into her power and transforms it in *Sula*, an exploration of intimacy that proves Woolf's theory: one book can clearly continue another.

Notes

1. Williams mentions that Morrison's thesis deals with "*Mrs. Dalloway* and the theme of alienation," and adds, "It is, however, important to point out that as a mature novelist herself, Morrison went on to rewrite and re-envision Woolf's idea of isolation" (2). Morrison's descriptions of other alienated literary characters also indicate where her sympathies lie: "The characters created by Thomas Wolfe, T. S. Eliot, Aldous Huxley, James Joyce and Ernest Hemingway, to mention a few, evoke images of solitary, alienated people who, together, form a community of the isolated" ("Treatment" 1). She tellingly suggests that even isolated characters form some sort of community with each other.

2. Morrison told Elizabeth Farnsworth in a 1998 *Online NewsHour* interview concerning *Paradise* that isolation "carries the seeds of its own destruction." Moreover, Richard Misner even says in that novel, "Isolation kills generations. It has no future" (*Paradise* 210).

3. In comparison to the veritable wealth of criticism about the Faulkner/Morrison connection, only Williams has attempted a book-length examination of Woolf and Morrison. Indeed, much of my own thinking about this essay grew out of connections I first made between Morrison's reading of Quentin Compson in her thesis and her own *Song of Solomon*. Her sensitivity to such comparisons also warrants notice. For example, in a 1983 interview with Nellie McKay, she emphatically remarked, "I am not *like* James Joyce; I am not *like* Thomas Hardy; I am not *like* Faulkner. I am not *like* in that sense" (152).

4. Christian suggests that Morrison wrote her thesis on Faulkner because there "was no such thing as African American literature—studying Faulkner was what they call in the music business, a cover" (486), and goes on to outline intersections between Morrison's and Woolf's lives and fictions. Most notably, she observes that their fic-

tions resist stereotypes such as the "angel in the house" versus "the mammy in the Big House" (487), create novels "bracketed by war" (489), explore new forms for the novel (491), illustrate the disconnect between the inner lives and outer worlds of characters (492), connect their characters' belief systems to nature (496), and, most importantly, always keep "pushing against" what they had already learned (497).

5. Hawthorn does not actually use the term "alienation" in his discussion of dissatisfaction, but the term's meaning clearly informs his argument. Rather, he makes reference to Georg Lukács's criticism of Modernist writing "because in it the interaction of social forces remains unseen and characters 'act past one another'" (93). This acting "past one another," as Hawthorn relates it to *Mrs. Dalloway*, functions as the end result of self-interest and alienation.

6. For my thinking about such continuation, I am indebted to Barrett.

7. Barrett points to the similarities between Shadrack and Septimus. I shift her focus slightly to examine how Morrison revises the figure to emphasize his communal connection. As Williams notes, "Morrison creates characters, who, while alienated, can also find acceptance and solace within the surrounding African-American community. Woolf's characters, on the other hand, are usually completely alone, without any type of community or often even friends" (2).

8. Morrison works with a similar theme in her later novel, *Love*. Although *Love* explores another friendship between two women, Christine and Heed Cosey, Morrison, at least theoretically, extends her belief in the power of friendship to include men as well, as long as the bond forms early enough. Morrison's ghostly narrator, the "L" or "Love" of the title says about early friendships, *"If such children find each other before they know their own sex, or which one of them is starving, which well fed; before they know color from no color, kin from stranger, then they have found a mix of surrender and mutiny they can never live without. Heed and Christine found such a one"* (199).

9. In *Love*, Christine Cosey says that her marriage built on a desire "so instant it felt like fate" made for a terrible marriage: "As couplehood goes, it had its moments. As marriage goes, it was ridiculous" (93). Williams points out that Morrison deliberately inverts the notion of friends leaning on each other when she writes that Nel and Sula use "each other to grow on" (Williams 109; *Sula* 52). According to Williams, this quality makes the friendship, "in itself, subversive" because the girls use it to replace "an unsatisfactory mother/daughter bond as well as future heterosexual relations" (109).

10. In *Love*, Morrison's female characters are aware of their own roles in sacrificing their friendship for love. As Christine tells Heed, "it's like we started out being sold, got free of it, then sold ourselves to the highest bidder" (185).

11. In "Clive Bell and Duncan Grant," Garnett alludes to the policy of "deferment," a term that Bell adopted and popularized for the group's policy of refusing to acknowledge the tension generated when sexual relationships between individual members posed a conflict. Garnett says of the triangular relationship between Clive and Vanessa Bell and Duncan Grant: "Between Clive and Duncan there was not the faintest show of jealousy—indeed it seems absurd to mention such a thing" (221). In his essay titled "Bloomsbury," Bell describes the basis of this policy as a shared "taste for discussion in pursuit of truth and a contempt for conventional ways of thinking and feeling—con-

tempt for conventional morals if you will" (119-20). Morrison further underlines this Bloomsbury connection by writing that Sula, "like any artist with no art form . . . became dangerous" (121).

Works Cited

Barrett, Eileen. "Septimus and Shadrack: Woolf and Morrison Envision the Madness of War." *Virginia Woolf: Emerging Perspectives*. Eds. Mark Hussey and Vara Neverow. New York: Pace UP, 1994. 26-32.

Bell, Clive. "Bloomsbury." Rosenbaum 114-23.

Christian, Barbara T. "Layered Rhythms: Virginia Woolf and Toni Morrison." *Modern Fiction Studies* 39.3-4 (1993): 483-500.

Farnsworth, Elizabeth. "Conversation: Toni Morrison." *Online NewsHour*. 9 Mar. 1998. PBS. 30 June 2002. <http://www.pbs.org/newshour/bb/entertainment/jan-june98/morrison_3-9.html>

Garnett, Angelica. "Clive Bell and Duncan Grant." Rosenbaum 215-22.

Gates, Henry Louis, Jr. *The Signifying Monkey: A Theory of Afro-American Literary Criticism*. New York: Oxford UP, 1988.

Hawthorn, Jeremy. *Virginia Woolf's* Mrs Dalloway: *A Study in Alienation*. London: Chatto and Windus, 1975.

McKay, Nellie. "An Interview with Toni Morrison." Taylor-Guthrie 138-55.

McKee, Patricia. "Spacing and Placing Experience in Toni Morrison's *Sula*." *Toni Morrison: Critical and Theoretical Approaches*. Ed. Nancy J. Peterson. Baltimore: Johns Hopkins UP, 1997. 37-62.

Morrison, Toni. *Love*. New York: Knopf, 2003.

_____. *Paradise*. 1997. New York: Plume, 1999.

_____. *Sula*. 1973. New York: Plume, 1982.

_____. [Chloe Ardellia Wofford]. "Virginia Woolf's and William Faulkner's Treatment of the Alienated." Master's thesis. Cornell University, 1955.

Naylor, Gloria. "A Conversation: Gloria Naylor and Toni Morrison." Taylor-Guthrie 188-217.

Rosenbaum, S. P., ed. *The Bloomsbury Group: A Collection of Memoirs and Commentary*. Toronto: U of Toronto P, 1995.

Ryan, Katy. "Revolutionary Suicide in Toni Morrison's Fiction." *African American Review* 34 (2000): 389-412.

Tate, Claudia. "Toni Morrison." Taylor-Guthrie 156-70.

Taylor-Guthrie, Danille, ed. *Conversations with Toni Morrison*. Jackson: UP of Mississippi, 1994.

Williams, Lisa. *The Artist as Outsider in the Novels of Toni Morrison and Virginia Woolf*. Westport, CT: Greenwood, 2000.

Woolf, Virginia. *Mrs. Dalloway*. 1925. San Diego: Harcourt, 1990.

_____. *A Room of One's Own*. 1929. First Harvest ed. San Diego: Harcourt, 1989.

Reinventing Grief Work:
Virginia Woolf's Feminist Representations of Mourning in *Mrs. Dalloway* and *To the Lighthouse*_____

Susan Bennett Smith

Freud, in his studies of hysterics, and the contemporary nerve specialists George Savage and Silas Weir Mitchell, in case studies, treat bereaved women as mentally unbalanced. They assume a causal link between grief and madness without any analysis or explicit justification. Because women had traditionally been the primary mourners, they became the primary patients of rest cures and talking cures. As one of Savage's patients and as the subject of much biographical writing, Virginia Woolf embodies the effects of this easy correlation between madness and grief. In Woolf's case, the issue becomes crystallized in a specific moment: why was the family physician called in to treat the thirteen-year-old Virginia Stephen after her mother died? That moment marks a break with Victorian mourning ritual, and makes vivid the transition from social grief practices to medical and psychological therapies. Her own writings, both autobiographical and fictional, offer a critique of this transition and describe a post-Freudian form of grief work. In *Mrs. Dalloway* Woolf tells a cautionary tale of the fatal results of the feminization and medicalization of grief, but offers no viable alternative. In *To the Lighthouse* she removes mourning from the realms of femininity and medicine, and provides a positive model for grief work.

As is well documented, her mother's death triggered Virginia's first breakdown; her father's death when she was twenty-two precipitated a severe breakdown and a suicide attempt. Recent theorists consider eating and sleep disorders, hallucinations, anger, and depression to be non-pathological manifestations of grief.[1] Bereavement which prompts a suicide attempt is pathological, but short of that, what constitutes disordered grief? This question becomes particularly difficult to answer when we compare the reactions of Virginia and Leslie Stephen to Julia's death. According to Quentin Bell, both experienced their bereavement as a kind of imitation death, but while Leslie's was comprehensible in terms of Victorian mourning ritual, his daughter's was not. "For a long time he abandoned himself to grief; his life, like his writing paper, was confined within a deep black border" (1:40). Virginia's "breakdown" was "a great interval of nothingness, a kind of positive death which cannot be described and of which Virginia herself probably knew little" (1:44). In Bell's words, Leslie "broke down utterly" after Julia's death, but he did not suffer a "breakdown." There is a fine but definite line between "broke down" and "breakdown," between what can be described in terms of social conventions and what cannot.

In "Reminiscences" Woolf compares her father's grief unfavorably to her own and that of her sisters and brothers. In her analysis it is Leslie's grief that is transgressive. She felt that the "Oriental gloom" which her Victorian father imposed on the household was excessive: his "groans [and] passionate lamentations . . . passed the normal limits of sorrow" (*Moments of Being* 40). She characterizes his expression of grief as both foreign and feminine, as inappropriate; he is like "a Hebrew prophet" (40) and "the Queen in Shakespeare" (94) in his self-dramatization. But Woolf's notion of "the normal limits of sorrow" is very different from her father's Victorian idea. Leslie Stephen was a distraught widower, living in a conventionally darkened house, visited by female relatives and friends who offered sympathy and comfort. The trappings of "Oriental gloom" were the trappings of Victorian mourning ritual. Woolf's insistence on the strangeness of her father's behavior manifests her complete rejection of nineteenth-century modes of grief as emotionally oppressive, excessive, and perhaps even pathological.

The profound difference between Leslie's and Virginia's bereavements was both gendered and generational. Woolf's rejection of her father's Victorian bereavement is characteristic of her generation's wholesale rejection of things Victorian, but to her family and to many of her critics Virginia's grief was a disease; Leslie's was normal.[2] No one suggests that Adrian or Thoby were traumatized by the deaths in the family, but Stella, Vanessa, and Virginia were, some argue, tragically affected. Louise DeSalvo claims that Vanessa, like Virginia and in "the pattern of perpetual mourning and profound depression of her mother," suffered from an inability to complete her mourning for her parents: "Vanessa lived out her whole life in a state akin to mourning" (75, 77). Critics' failure to examine the boys' reactions to the deaths reflects the bias that women are more likely to suffer from pathological grief than are men.

The family doctor was called in to treat Virginia's nervousness, excitability, and depression after her mother's death. "Dr. Seton . . . put a stop to all lessons, ordered a simple life and prescribed outdoor exercise" (Bell 1:45). Considerations of medicine, not mourning, decree that Virginia is to rest her mind and exercise her body. Presumably, "a simple life" does not include existential angst, depression, or feelings of despair. When worried about his daughter, the agnostic Leslie Stephen called the doctor; ministers had no role in the Stephen household. Physicians believed that by tending to the body they were tending to the mind.[3]

Dr. Savage ordered rest in the country for Virginia after Leslie's death. In a letter to Violet Dickinson written seven months after his death, she reflects on her bereavement "Sorrow, such as I feel now for Father, is soothing and natural, and makes life more worth having, if sadder" (*Letters* 1: 143). She gives the rest cure credit for helping her.[4]

> You will be glad to hear that your Sparroy feels herself a recovered bird. I think the blood has really been getting into my brain at last. It is the oddest feeling, as though a dead part of me were coming to life. I can't tell you how delightful it is—and I don't mind how much I eat to keep it going. All the voices I used to hear telling me to do all kinds of wild things have gone—and Nessa says they were always only my imagination. (1:142)

Virginia Stephen here attests to the success of her rest cure in the doctors' terms of fat and blood, in the triumph of the disciplined body over the unruly mind.[5] The voice of the doctor has prevailed over the wild voices, and she is thankful.

If Virginia's disorder was grief, why might the rest cure have been therapeutic?[6] Virginia, accompanied by a hired nurse, stayed with Violet Dickinson, then with her aunt, Emelia Stephen. The seclusion of their homes, the company of sympathetic women, and the cessation of public activities combine to approximate a medical version of traditional mourning ritual. Both the rest cure and mourning ritual require a reduced existence for a fixed period of time.

The symbolic resonance of the imitation deaths imposed on women by both the rest cure and Victorian mourning ritual held true not only for Virginia Stephen, but for many other patients as well. Feminist critics have found the rest cure to be a form of Victorian moral medicine which enforced the doctor's domination over rebellious women.[7] That its patients were primarily women has been established; that its patients were very often bereaved has not been explored. In his popular textbook *Insanity and Allied Neuroses* (1907) George Savage lists grief as one of the "psychical exciting causes" of insanity (46). Savage's case histories of grief-induced neurosis are almost all women, a pattern which could be found in other well-known texts of its day. But grief is no more than an "exciting cause"; it is endowed with no further explanatory power. Neither Savage nor other physicians acknowledged bereavement as a period of mental and physical disruption. Their focus was on disease and on the importance of the doctor/patient relationship, a relationship which must be free of interference from family and friends. The physician quietly took over the former roles of minister and family as social grief practices waned and medical discourse became increasingly powerful.

In *Mrs. Dalloway* Woolf explores the debilitating effects of feminizing and medicalizing grief that leave Septimus without any legitimate means to express his sorrow. She reveals in her Introduction to a

Modern Library edition of the novel that Septimus "is intended to be [Clarissa's] double" (36). One of the ways to interpret the Doppelgänger theme is to see Septimus and Clarissa as mourners and potential patients for the rest cure.[8] From this perspective Clarissa represents sane bereavement, whereas Septimus's mourning is pathological. In Freud's terms, he is suffering from melancholia. Because Septimus has internalized an excess of stoicism in the Great War, he reacts by expressing his grief in self-abnegation. Men, especially soldiers, don't cry. The authoritarian rest cure will not help him; Septimus's own way out is suicide.

Septimus suffers hallucinations; he mistakes the grey-suited Peter Walsh for his dead comrade Evans in a ghostly vision of revelation:

> A man in grey was actually walking towards them. It was Evans! But no mud was on him; no wounds; he was not changed. I must tell the whole world, Septimus cried, raising his hand (as the dead man in the grey suit came nearer), raising his hand like some colossal figure who has lamented the fate of man for ages in the desert alone . . . and with legions of men prostrate behind him he, the giant mourner, receives for one moment on his face the whole— (105-06)

But the revelation breaks off at the crucial moment. Septimus is imaged as an Ozymandias, not full of pride but of despair. The oddity of this somewhat martial figure conveys Septimus's mental imbalance, but it also suggests the absence of models for male mourning in Western culture. The image evokes the colossal problem of mourning the dead of the War. How can Septimus (or anyone) mourn the "legions of men prostrate behind him"? The magnitude of that sorrow is too great to bear.

Unmanned by his grief, Septimus is feminized by his tears and excluded from being an acknowledged mourner by his gender.[9] Lady Bexborough, whom Clarissa admires for carrying on with a charity bazaar after receiving word that her son had been killed, is an example of restraint, which, were Septimus able to follow it, would only reinforce his emotional numbness.[10] The War made traditionally feminine mourning unpatriotic and promoted the more manly virtues of fortitude and devotion to duty—Lady Bexborough's qualities. The Victorian Leslie Stephen's demonstrative grief would no longer be acceptable in this context. Septimus's outbursts meet with disapproval, not with sympathy. The only aid offered him is a rest cure in a private institution where he would be separated from his wife and subject to the doctor's disciplinary gaze (a much less congenial prospect than the rest Virginia Stephen had with friends). "Anxieties about masculinity" and a general "feminine aspect" were commonly diagnosed features of shell-shock victims (Showalter 172). Any sign of emotion such as tears would be interpreted as pathological: how then was a soldier to grieve? Rezia feels she must conceal Septimus's threats of suicide: "'Septimus has been working too hard'—that was all she could say to her own mother" (33). Overwork was the typical diagnosis of male patients who underwent the rest cure, but it clearly does not apply to Septimus. For men, carrying on with one's work, rather than staying home with the women, was standard grief practice.

Having established the cause of Septimus's trauma, Woolf satirizes the obtuseness of the medical profession in the figures of Dr. Holmes, a general practitioner; and Sir William Bradshaw, the Harley Street nerve specialist. They fail to find the cause of his misery; in fact, they discourage him from thinking about himself at all (137-39, 149). Woolf makes it clear that the rest cure relies upon the principle of control and that the physician functions as a moral agent. She also portrays the rest cure as an instrument of repression that can only harm Septimus; Woolf puts the blame, at least in part, on Holmes and Bradshaw for Septimus's suicide.[11] In the novel Woolf does not explore the potential benefits of the rest cure as a substitution for mourning ritual—even Holmes's home would provide a retreat from the ongoing life of the city. One would never guess from reading *Mrs. Dalloway* that she had ever found a version of the rest cure helpful.

By the 1920s, medicine had implicitly replaced mourning ritual, and grief had become virtually unmentionable. Then, as now, physicians considered it their duty to aid the grief-stricken, but without acknowledging the source of the pain. That Holmes treats Rezia as his patient after Septimus's leap is indicative of this encroachment on mourning ritual. He gives her a sleeping draft, a chemical version of the rest cure, for her grief (227).

Clarissa's uncanny empathy with Septimus is based, at least in part, on her familiarity with prescription rest. She understands the threat which Sir William Bradshaw's moral medicine poses to his patients' integrity. Rest is recommended to Clarissa for physiological reasons, but both her illness and the cure have emotional resonances as well. Her heart is affected. Peter thinks that "Clarissa was as cold as an icicle" (121-22); she is "unmaternal," "a snob" (290). Clarissa is aware of this deficiency in herself: "She could see what she lacked. It was not beauty; it was not mind. It was something central which permeated; something warm which broke up surfaces and rippled the cold contact of man and woman, or of women together" (46). Clarissa's heart, her emotional well-being, was irritated by the influenza: "for at any moment the brute would be stirring, this hatred [for Miss Kilman], which, especially since her illness, had power to make her feel scraped" (17). The narrator connects Clarissa's need for rest and seclusion not with a cure but with death. "There was an emptiness about the heart of life; an attic room. . . . Narrower and narrower would her bed be. . . . For the House sat so long that Richard insisted, after her illness, that she must sleep undisturbed" (45-46). Her attic bedroom is as isolated as possible from the rest of the house. Rest is imagined as preparation for death, the bed becoming the grave. Clarissa's mild experiences with the rest cure make clear the emotional affinities to the imitation death expressed by the conventions of Victorian grief practices: seclusion and the wearing of black.

Such a mild form of the rest cure is not available to Septimus, whose lower-class status dictates rougher treatment. Moreover, his condition is much worse than Clarissa's: he suffers from a classic case of melancholia, as Freud describes it. The fall in self-esteem that distinguishes the melancholic from the mourner is strongly marked in Septimus; he denounces himself as a criminal (137, 145, 148). Septimus's symptoms correspond to Dr. Savage's observation that the pathologically bereaved "conjure up all sort of imaginary crimes that they have committed" (47). His suicidal impulses are the extreme form of the melancholic's loss of self-esteem (Freud *Collected* 4:155-56). Shell-shocked soldiers in Britain did benefit from the talking cure. Septimus, inspired by a vision of Evans, mutters, "Communication is health," which would be a good slogan for psychoanalysis (141). The talking cure might have helped someone like Septimus, although Freud felt that melancholia, as one of the narcissistic disorders, was unamenable to transference, and hence unamenable to treatment (5:124).

Septimus is unable to overcome his hallucinations of Evans or to accept the reality that Evans is dead. His marriage to Rezia right after Evans's death offers him a substitute, but he fails to respond to her. In Freud's terms, he cannot free his libido from Evans (4:154). But according to Woolf's early notes for the novel, this model for the relinquishment of grief is not entirely desirable. "He must somehow see through human nature—see its hypocrisy, & insincerity, its power to recover from every wound, incapable of taking any final impression. His sense that this is not worth having" (Notebook 12; qtd in Zwerdling 131). Clarissa serves as an example of nonpathological mourning that does not depend upon Freud's formula of the ultimate freedom of the ego from the lost love object.[12] In Freud's sense, her mourning remains uncompleted. She does not sever her ties with what is lost upon testing reality; instead, she makes an effort to maintain those connections.

Clarissa's "odd affinities" with strangers and ongoing connections with her distant friends structure the novel (231). Peter and Sally, who had been lost to her for many years, return as if they were ghosts. Even before they surprise Clarissa by their actual appearances, Clarissa has been thinking of them (4, 48). "The unseen part" is not to be relinquished. "With the two of them (more even than with Richard) she shared her past; the garden; the trees. . . . A part of this Sally must always be; Peter must be" (277). Time does temper her memories somewhat, but it does not lessen them: "some days, some sights bringing him [Peter] back to her calmly, without the old bitterness; which perhaps was the reward of having cared for people; they came back in the middle of St. James's Park on a fine morning—indeed they did" (9). Clarissa thus doubles Septimus: she has her own sane version of his hallucinatory visions of Evans in the park. She maintains the connections, even the visions; her present is composed of her past.

But the return of Peter and Sally into Clarissa's life is not entirely analogous to Septimus's vision of Evans; they travel from India and Manchester, not from the afterlife. The "raising of the dead" which J. Hillis Miller describes in *Mrs. Dalloway* is not to be taken literally in Clarissa's case (176-202). The childhood death of Clarissa's sister Sylvia marks her as a mourner who will not cease to feel grief, but Sylvia gets only a brief mention and does not reappear in the novel (117). Clarissa's transcendental theory does not bring back the dead; *Mrs. Dalloway* is no ghost story. Even Evans's appearance in the park is a case of mistaken identity: Peter Walsh is the man in the grey suit (105-06). The conflation of Peter and Evans makes Peter more of a ghost and Evans less of one; they are easily explained away. The appearances of her old friends validate Clarissa's sense of connectedness with the past, but no such validation is possible for Septimus. Thus, Clarissa is an inadequate model of sane bereavement to counter Septimus's insane grief.[13] Death puts too great a burden on her web of connections, although she does achieve a feeling of connectedness with the dead Septimus.

The nature of Septimus's relationship with Evans complicates his bereavement. He fits Freud's definition of melancholia in the additional respect of having ambivalent feelings for his friend (*Collected* 4:167). Septimus's unacknowledged homoerotic feelings for Evans make it difficult for him to come to terms with his death:[14] "He drew the attention, indeed the affection of his officer, Evans by name. It was a case of two dogs playing on a hearth-rug. . . . They had to be together, share with each other, fight with each other, quarrel with each other" (130). Dr. Holmes's exclamation, "The coward!" upon Septimus's suicide (226) supports this interpretation: "When military doctors and psychiatrists dismissed shell-shock patients as cowards, they were often hinting at effeminacy or homosexuality" (Showalter 171). The sexual component of Septimus's war neurosis seems to confirm Freud's suggestion that war neuroses, like all other neuroses, have a sexual etiology (5:83-87). I would argue, however, that sexuality is secondary to bereavement in Septimus's case as well as in Freud's case studies of hysterics.

Psychoanalytic studies of hysterics often include bereavement as a contributing factor, but, like the nerve specialists, Freud considers it of minor importance. Both Anna O. and Dora suffered from recent bereavements, a fact which Freud considered a noteworthy causative factor, but not relevant to the treatment. Unlike the nerve specialists, Freud does address the question of the distinction between normal and pathological mourning. For him it is not a matter of the severity of the symptoms, but rather a matter of their composition or longevity. While Freud considers mourning a normal process, he argues for early therapeutic intervention in the case of Anna O. to prevent a long-term pathological fixation (*Five* 17). The psychoanalyst is to replace the ministrations of family, friends, clergy, and nerve specialists. Like the rest cure, the talking cure adopts elements of traditional mourning ritual. Freud defines the proper length of a "normal period of mourning" as "from one to two years," a definition which corresponds to the Victorian period of bereavement for a close relative. The innovation of the talking cure—the talk itself—can be seen as a legacy of the expressive nature of Victorian mourning ritual. The elaborate symbolism of the mourning clothes as well as the custom of expressing sympathy in visits and in letters allowed grief and sympathy voice. Psychoanalysis treated the same population of upper-middle-class women as the rest cure. The emphasis on expression in psychoanalysis contrasts strongly with the repressive rest cure, but the psychoanalytic couch is a lasting symbol of Freud's early debt to the techniques of the rest cure.

Virginia Woolf was never psychoanalyzed, but she did claim to have undergone a successful talking cure. By writing *To the Lighthouse*, "I suppose I did for myself what psycho-analysts do for their patients. I expressed some very long felt and deeply felt emotion. And in expressing it I explained it and then laid it to rest." What she laid to rest was her mother's ghost: "When it was written, I ceased to be obsessed by my mother. I no longer hear her voice; I do not see her" (*Moments* 81). Woolf viewed the writing of *To the Lighthouse* as grief work which freed her from obsession. Her assessment corresponds to Freud's idea of grief work as freeing the libido from the lost love object.[15] The novel itself, however, describes varieties of grief work which establish some distance between the dead and the living without completely severing the connections.

Woolf, like the nerve specialists and psychoanalysts, borrows from traditional mourning ritual for her model of grief practices. The setting of the vacation house offers a retreat from public life and a venue for the visits of family and friends. The community offers each other sympathy and support, though the expression is often tacit due to Woolf's rejection of the conventions of Victorian mourning ritual. She also deviates from tradition by not designating women chief mourners and by not feminizing male mourners. Mr. Ramsay tries to impose the traditional burden of comforter on Lily Briscoe, but she refuses it. Nor is grief pathological in the novel. Cam and James object to their father's selfish grief, but it is clear that this is a generational difference rather than one of mental health. No doctors or therapists need be called in.

Woolf makes the work of mourning literal in *To the Lighthouse*. "The Window" establishes the gendered opposition between work and sympathy, which will later be resolved in a new idea of grief work. Despite the setting at a summer house, Mr. Ramsay, Charles Tansley, and

William Bankes have all brought their work with them. Lily, too, has brought her work, although given the social devaluation of the work women do, it comes as a revelation to her "that she had her work" (128). When, in the last section, Mr. Ramsay is threatening to interrupt her in order to extract womanly sympathy, Lily is reduced to "playing at painting, playing at the one thing one did not play at, and it was all Mrs. Ramsay's fault. She was dead" (224). It is her fault because she did not respect Lily's work ("One could not take her painting very seriously" [29]), and because she catered to her husband, who expects sympathy from all women.

In "The Window" work and sympathy belong to separate gendered spheres represented by Mr. and Mrs. Ramsay.[16] Mr. Ramsay, Charles Tansley, and William Bankes all crave attention from the beautiful Mrs. Ramsay; their work is not enough. Nor is sympathy, the art of human relations, enough for Mrs. Ramsay; she is somewhat envious of her husband's greater hopefulness because "he had always his work to fall back on" (91). The word "work" is not used to describe Mrs. Ramsay's activities of mothering eight children and a husband, running a large household, looking after the comfort of her guests, matchmaking, and visiting the sick and the poor. She feels "passionately" about "hospitals and drains and the dairy. . . . A model dairy and a hospital up here—those two things she would have liked to do, herself. But how? With all these children?" (89). Her interest in social issues is not taken any more seriously than she takes Lily's painting. During dinner she begins to speak about "the iniquity of the English dairy system, and in what state milk was delivered at the door, and was about to prove her charges, for she had gone into the matter, when all round the table . . . her children laughed; her husband laughed; she was laughed at" (155-56).

Mrs. McNab, a member of the working class, makes it clear that the apparent gender division between beautiful sympathy and work represented by the Ramsays is class-specific.[17] The unlovely Mrs. McNab must work, even as an old woman. Her work opposes the forces of "loveliness and stillness" that have descended on the unoccupied house (195). But her work is not without a spiritual dimension: she does the work of mourning. In her efforts to put the deserted house to rights she envisions the ghostly presence of Mrs. Ramsay: "She could see her now, stooping over her flowers; and faint and flickering, like a yellow beam or the circle at the end of a telescope, a lady in a grey cloak, stooping over her flowers, went wandering over the bedroom wall, up the dressing-table, across the wash-stand, as Mrs. McNab hobbled and ambled, dusting, straightening" (205). While Mrs. McNab's vision of Mrs. Ramsay is not an artist's epiphany, hers is a kind of grief work which evokes the dead as a welcome presence by means of tasks related to them.[18] She is "something not highly conscious . . . something not inspired to go about its work with dignified ritual or solemn chanting" (209). Her work is unadulterated by conventions or ritual; like Lily's painting, it is the thing itself. In the figure of Mrs. McNab, Woolf represents an unmediated and unconscious ideal of grief work which salvages the past in the interests of the present. The slow and painful work of Mrs. McNab and Mrs. Bast allows the others to do theirs.

Lily takes over the work of mourning from Mrs. McNab; unlike the weary, witless "care-taking woman" (196), she is "Awake" (214). But Lily does not at first know what to do with her morning; she is in a quandary, "wondering whether, since she had been left alone, it behooved her to go to the kitchen to fetch another cup of coffee or wait here. . . . For really, what did she feel, come back after all these years and Mrs. Ramsay dead? Nothing, nothing—nothing that she could express at all" (217). Sitting at the table reminds Lily of the "moment of revelation" she had had ten years previously about her painting: "she would paint that picture now" (220). A desire to escape Mr. Ramsay's emotional demands triggers her memory: "She must escape somewhere, be alone somewhere. Suddenly she remembered" (220). She thinks of her work as a haven from sympathy, but it becomes clear that the two are necessary to each other.

Even with her easel set up and brush in hand, Lily is still vulnerable to the nakedness of Mr. Ramsay's needs (223): "An enormous need urged him, without being conscious what it was, to approach any woman, to force them, he did not care how, his need was so great, to give him what he wanted: sympathy" (225). Woolf's terms here suggest rape, a suggestion which condemns the traditional sexism that makes women answerable for men's emotions: "A man, any man, would staunch this effusion, would stop these lamentations. A woman, she had provoked this horror; a woman, she should have known how to deal with it. It was immensely to her discredit, sexually, to stand there dumb" (228). Woolf critiques the tradition of placing the burden of mourning on women: "She could not sustain this enormous weight of sorrow, support these heavy draperies of grief (he had assumed a pose of extreme decrepitude; he even tottered a little as he stood there) a moment longer" (227). Mr. Ramsay, of course, bears a strong likeness to Leslie Stephen, and his demands correspond to those Leslie made of his daughter Stella (*Moments* 94). Mr. Ramsay's behavior strikes Lily as insincere: "(He was acting, she felt, this great man was dramatising himself)" (227). His bereavement is very much a Victorian one; Lily's reactions belong to Woolf's generation.

The somewhat comic solution to this gendered and generational impasse is to discuss a work of beauty:

> "What beautiful boots!" she exclaimed. She was ashamed of herself. To praise his boots when he asked her to solace his soul . . . deserved, she knew, and she looked up expecting to get it, in one of his sudden roars of ill-temper, complete annihilation.
>
> Instead, Mr. Ramsay smiled. His pall, his draperies, his infirmities fell from him. Ah, yes, he said, holding his foot up for her to look at, they were first-rate boots. (229)

The boots are associated with Mr. Ramsay's own egotism rather than with Mrs. Ramsay; they offer a diversion.[19] That Lily and Mr. Ramsay

---

land on "the blessed island of good boots," becomes less trivial, less puzzling, and less ironic when seen in light of workmanship, beauty, and the sympathy that binds the two together.[20] Mr. Ramsay has invested his own work in these beautiful boots: first in finding the only man capable of making them, and second in devising an original and superior method for tying the laces. Mr. Ramsay expands to his professional self as teacher to instruct Lily how to tie a knot. In the contemplation of his boots, Mr. Ramsay forgets the excesses of his grief; his ability to attend to the material reality of the boots indicates that his grief has eased a bit. Woolf uses boots as a symbol of death at the end of *Jacob's Room*. Here, because the owner of the boots still lives, they maintain their usefulness; they are a part of life.

Lily, having ministered to Mr. Ramsay, is free to paint. Her unconscious takes over, just as it did for Woolf in the quick, bubbling composition of the novel itself (*Moments* 81): "As she lost consciousness of outer things . . . her mind kept throwing up from its depths, scenes, and names, and sayings, and memories and ideas, like a fountain spurting over that glaring, hideously difficult white space, while she modeled it with greens and blues" (*Lighthouse* 238). The work of memory is inseparable from her art: "And as she dipped into the blue paint, she dipped too into the past there. Now Mrs. Ramsay got up, she remembered" (256). Lily's memory finally summons Mrs. Ramsay's ghost as manifested by "an odd-shaped triangular shadow over the step" where she had been sitting years before for Lily to paint her (299). Lily envisions Mrs. Ramsay knitting in her chair, at work on charity socks. The woman artist invokes not her beauty but her work. Lily's vision is simultaneously the extremity of her grief and its abatement. The fact of Mrs. Ramsay's death is now "part of ordinary experience"; the work of mourning is done (300). All that is left is to put the final stroke on the painting in concert with the arrival of the Ramsays at the lighthouse. Of course Lily's painting is not a conventional portrait "of" Mrs. Ramsay. Instead she produces a respectful depiction of Mrs. Ramsay as an abstract shape which expresses her grief without clothing it in the hated Victorian conventions. Lily is a modernist in both art and mourning; she wants to express "the thing itself before it has been made anything" (287).

The Ramsays are also engaged in a work of mourning. The trip to the lighthouse fulfills the aborted journey discussed in "The Window," and in doing so honors both Mrs. Ramsay's beauty and her social work. James has the work of steering the boat and remembering his mother, in the same scene that Lily remembers, but the focus for James is on his father's interruption of his shared moment with his mother (252). James's resentment of his father is overcome when Mr. Ramsay praises his skillful handling of the boat. As the leader of the expedition, Mr. Ramsay recapitulates the work of his earlier philosophical journey: his attempted intellectual journey from "Q" to "R" is "a desolate expedition across the icy solitudes of the Polar region," and Mr. Ramsay himself is "the leader, the guide, the counselor" on whose bravery and strength it all depends (54). His mourning abates when he recognizes the deaths of sailors as an ordinary, workaday event: "Naturally men are drowned in a storm, but it is a perfectly straightforward affair, and the depths of the sea (he sprinkled the crumbs from his sandwich paper over them) are only water after all" (306). As with Lily's painting, work enables the acceptance of death for both James and Mr. Ramsay.

The action in *To the Lighthouse* takes place in a single symbolic day: it begins in the afternoon and ends at noon after a long, dark night that spans ten years and many deaths. The work of mourning takes place, appropriately, in the morning. That the novel ends in the full light of day enhances the optimistic consummations of Lily's and Mr. Ramsay's projects. Woolf aimed at the effect of simultaneity, which suggests that their projects are fundamentally the same (*Diary* 3:106). The works of mourning are complete.

My reading of the novel as a symbolic day suggests that it is ahistorical, that the night might be arbitrarily long, that the mourning will dispel the darkness into noon. There is a sense in which this is the case: the community of the vacation house, composed of friends, relations, and servants, enacts what Philippe Aries terms the "pre-Romantic" mourning of the whole community for its dead: "It is this model that might, because of its extreme age and stability, be compared to a state of nature" rather than the model of Victorian mourning ritual (581-82). The roles of Lily Briscoe and Mrs. McNab as mourners follow this much older tradition; the Victorian conventions did not recognize the deaths of any but relatives. In *To the Lighthouse* Woolf employs this quality of pre-Romantic mourning in defining a new mode of mourning. She rejects the gendered role-playing of conventional sympathy, as well as the psychoanalytic concept of grief work which demands complete detachment from the dead. Instead she advocates meaningful work, as appropriate to both the bereaved and the dead. Women are no longer to be merely the objects of art, or the servants of men; Woolf's feminist consciousness shapes her conception of the work of mourning. Lily Briscoe and Mr. Ramsay take separate journeys, not because of gender difference, but because of their differing talents and interests. Both a work of art and artful work allow grief to be expressed and worked through.

To the Lighthouse offers a defeminized and demedicalized model for grief practices. From this point of view, it presents a more developed thinking with regard to grief than is expressed in *Mrs. Dalloway*. In the earlier novel Woolf thoroughly critiques the medical establishment as oppressive and insensitive, but she accepts its diagnosis of grief as a disease. Septimus is mad, and his madness derives from his inability to feel anything for Evans's death. Furthermore, she accepts the traditional model of grief as feminine: Septimus is feminized as a measure of his mental disorder. In *To the Lighthouse* Woolf expresses grief without conventions, without doctors and without therapists. She expresses grief in work.

From *Twentieth Century Literature* 41.4 (Winter 1995): 310-327. Copyright © 1995 by *Twentieth Century Literature*. Reprinted with permission of *Twentieth Century Literature*.

Notes

1. See John Bowlby (98), George L. Engel (18), and Geoffrey Gorer (49) for discussions of the range of nonpathological reactions to grief.

2. It has been suggested that Woolf inherited her mental instability from Leslie, but he is not typically labeled "mad." In his biography of Stephen, Noel Annan makes clear the distinction between Virginia Woolf and Leslie Stephen: "Virginia went mad. Her father did not" (136). But he does relate that Stephen suffered a "breakdown" in 1888 from overwork which was "serious" (112). Grief did not cause his breakdown. Katherine C. Hill shares Annan's position and suggests that the sources of Leslie and Virginia's mental instability are obsessions with work and with grief (33, 36). Louise DeSalvo considers Leslie to have been "seriously suicidal" and recounts the history of mental illness in the Stephen family, with special mention of Leslie's nephew, J. K. Stephen, who committed suicide by starvation in an asylum (114, 136). Roger Moss posits an Oedipal relationship between father and daughter which includes an inheritance of mental instability (53). Thomas C. Caramango draws a mood-disorder family tree for the Stephens, and argues that Woolf inherited her manic-depressive disorder primarily from her father, but that her mother, as a depressive, contributed as well (98-112). Roger Poole (22) and Stephen Trombley (8-9, 83), among others, claiming that her bereavements were not abnormal, argue that Woolf was not mentally ill.

3. As the inventor of the rest cure, Silas Weir Mitchell, put it, "You cure the body and somehow find that the mind also is cured" ("Treatment" 2037).

4. Woolf's resistance to the rest cure is well known, but she also felt at times that she needed it. See *Letters* 1:434 and 2:592 for other references to the rest cure's having been efficacious.

5. Mitchell outlines the rest cure in *Fat and Blood*.

6. Without reference to grief, Caramango argues that the rest cure was beneficial for Woolf because manic depressives respond favorably to sleep therapy: "Recent studies at the National Institute of Mental Health showed that restructuring a manic-depressive's sleep cycle can effect at least a temporary remission of symptoms" (19).

7. There are several excellent feminist critiques of the rest cure which analyze its political and psychosexual implications for women. Gail Parker points out that the emphasis on milk drinking in the rest cure infantilizes patients, making them dependent on their doctors (49). Ann Douglas Wood considers the rest cure, with its symbolic replication of the conditions of pregnancy, to have been a kind of punishment for women who failed in their womanly duties (9-10). Elaine Showalter also detects a sexual dynamic, "a kind of eroticism in the rest cure," which for Woolf, as for Charlotte Perkins Gilman, involved "romantic implications of [a] quasi-courtship" between doctor and patient (144).

8. In his analysis of Woolf's alleged "lifelong inability to grieve" (which results in a "lifelong inability to love"), Mark Spilka considers grief to be the important link between Septimus and Clarissa, but in his view Septimus's abundance of grief makes up for Clarissa's lack (9). Spilka's reading of Woolf's novels as a mirror of her psychic life is necessarily speculative and does not address the question of normative standards of grief.

9. See Susan Squier for a discussion of how Septimus fatally "confounds customary gender roles, social positions, and psychological states" (110-15). Elaine Showalter also discusses the inappropriateness of Septimus's "feminine" feelings of grief for Evans (193).

10. Alex Zwerdling finds that Lady Bexborough's stoicism and Septimus's mad outbursts are both "failures to maintain a natural flow of response commensurate with the occasion" (136). Although Zwerdling recognizes the social regulation of emotion, he maintains the notion of a "natural" expression which is problematical in light of the novel's focus on the social determinants and consequences of emotion.

11. Showalter interprets Septimus's suicide as a response to his doctors: "Cornered by the implacable team of Holmes and Bradshaw, Septimus leaps from a window to escape them. Such cases were not uncommon among returning soldiers" (193).

12. John Bowlby explicitly disagrees with Freud on this point: "Findings in regard both to the prevalence of a continuing sense of the presence of the dead person and to its compatibility with a favourable outcome give no support to Freud's well-known and already quoted passage: 'Mourning has a quite precise psychical task to perform: its function is to detach the survivor's memories and hopes from the dead' (*SE* 13: 65)" (100).

13. On Freud's model of mourning, Clarissa's affinity for ghosts is an indication of failure. But her "transcendental theory" corresponds quite strikingly with another theory Freud was also working on in the late teens: transference. Freud used the word "*revenants*" to describe the ghostly repetition of a past relationship in a present one. See Reinhard and Lupton for a discussion of the centrality of mourning to the development of Freud's theories. They note the important role of ghosts in the concept of "*revenants*" (53, 60).

14. Several critics have discussed Septimus's possibly erotic love for Evans. See Nancy Topping Bazin for a Freudian interpretation of Septimus's feelings (110). Emily Jensen analyzes the homoerotic aspects of the novel; she argues that Clarissa shares Septimus's repressed homosexuality (162).

15. In later private correspondence, ten years after his daughter's death, Freud no longer feels that complete detachment from the dead is necessary or even desirable: "Although we know that after such a loss the acute state of mourning will subside, we also know we shall remain inconsolable and will never find a substitute. No matter what may fill the gap, even if it be filled completely, it nevertheless remains something else. And actually this is how it should be. It is the only way of perpetuating that love which we do not want to relinquish" (qtd. in Freeman and Strean 72).

16. See Zwerdling for a discussion of the division between work and family life in the novel (180-209). He compares Mr. and Mrs. Ramsay to Leslie and Julia Stephen in order to show how the fictional couple is a simplified version of Woolf's parents. However, I think that Zwerdling oversimplifies Mrs. Ramsay by characterizing her as completely disassociated (and self-dissociated) from the male arena of work (188).

17. In Woolf's recurrent figure of the charwoman, Jane Marcus identifies the "origins of art in women's work" and associations with "death and resurrection" (11). "In 'Time Passes,' then, Virginia Woolf has written a socialist feminist dialectic on life and death, a world view that includes the mystical and the material, an aesthetic that relates

the poet's 'single voice piping clear and sweet' to the moan of a charwoman's music-hall song" (14).

18. The spirituality of Woolf's charwomen is available only to observers; epiphanies are not ascribed to them. In Woolf, privileged moments are for the privileged classes. The modernist celebration of primitivism, as represented by Mrs. McNab, depends upon the reader's faculty for appreciation.

19. In Lucio Ruotolo's analysis the boots offer a means for "mutual self-forgetfulness" which allows a moment of connection between Lily and Mr. Ramsay (138).

20. A similar combination of qualities appears early in the novel. William Bankes had admired Lily's shoes: "Her shoes were excellent, he observed. They allowed the toes their natural expansion" (31). This observation contributes to his respect for Lily; it helps establish sympathy between them and allows Lily to feel comfortable sharing her work with him.

Works Cited

Annan, Noel. *Leslie Stephen*. London: Weidenfeld, 1984.

Aries, Philippe. *The Hour of Our Death*. Trans. Helen Weaver. New York: Knopf, 1981.

Bazin, Nancy Topping. *Virginia Woolf and the Androgynous Vision*. New Brunswick: Rutgers UP, 1973.

Bell, Quentin. *Virginia Woolf*. 2 vols. New York: Harcourt, 1974.

Bowlby, John. *Loss, Sadness and Depression*. New York: Basic, 1980. Vol. 3 of *Attachment and Loss*. 3 vols. 1980.

Caramango, Thomas C. *The Flight of the Mind*. Berkeley: U of California P, 1992.

DeSalvo, Louise. *Virginia Woolf: The Impact of Childhood Sexual Abuse on Her Life and Work*. Boston: Beacon, 1989.

Engel, George L. "Is Grief a Disease?: A Challenge for Medical Research." *Psychosomatic Medicine* 23 (1961): 18-22.

Freeman, Lucy, and Herbert S. Strean. *Freud and Women*. New York: Continuum, 1987.

Freud, Sigmund. *Collected Papers*. 5 vols. Ed. James Strachey. London: Hogarth, 1950.

_____. *Five Lectures on Psycho-Analysis*. Trans. James Strachey. New York: Norton, 1977.

_____. *The Standard Edition of the Complete Psychological Works of Sigmund Freud*. 24 vols. London: Hogarth, 1953-1974.

Gorer, Geoffrey. *Death, Grief, and Mourning*. New York: Arno, 1977.

Hill, Katherine C. *Virginia Woolf and Leslie Stephen: A Study in Mentoring and Literary Criticism*. Diss. Columbia U, 1979. Ann Arbor: UMI, 1979. DDJ7916419.

Jensen, Emily. "Clarissa Dalloway's Respectable Suicide." *Virginia Woolf: A Feminist Slant*. Ed. Jane Marcus. Lincoln: U of Nebraska P, 1983. 162-79.

Marcus, Jane. *Virginia Woolf and the Languages of Patriarchy*. Bloomington: Indiana UP, 1987.

Miller, J. Hillis. *Fiction and Repetition*. Cambridge: Harvard UP, 1982.

Mitchell, Silas Weir. *Fat and Blood: An Essay on the Treatment of Certain Forms of Neurasthenia and Hysteria*. 7th edition. Philadelphia: Lippincott, 1898.

_____. "The Treatment by Rest, Seclusion, etc., in Relation to Psychotherapy." *The Journal of the American Medical Association* L(25) 20 June 1908: 2033-37.

Moss, Roger. "*Jacob's Room* and the Eighteenth Century: From Elegy to Essay." *Critical Quarterly* 23 (1981): 39-54.

Parker, Gail. *The Oven Birds: American Women on Womanhood 1820-1920*. Garden City, NJ: Anchor, 1972.

Poole, Roger. *The Unknown Virginia Woolf*. 3rd ed. Cambridge: Cambridge UP, 1990.

Reinhard, Kenneth, and Julia Lupton. "Shapes of Grief: Freud, *Hamlet*, and Mourning." *Genders* 4 (1989): 40-67.

Rutolo, Lucio P. *Interrupted Moment*. Stanford: Stanford UP, 1986.

Savage, George H. *Insanity and Allied Neuroses*. Chicago: W. T. Keener, 1907.

Showalter, Elaine. *The Female Malady: Women, Madness and English Culture 1830-1980*. New York: Penguin, 1985.

Spilka, Mark. *Virginia Woolf's Quarrel with Grieving*. Lincoln: U of Nebraska P, 1980.

Squier, Susan. *Virginia Woolf and London: The Sexual Politics of the City*. Chapel Hill: U of North Carolina P, 1985.

Trombley, Stephen. *All That Summer She Was Mad*. New York: Continuum, 1982.

Wood, Ann Douglas. "'The Fashionable Diseases': Women's Complaints and Their Treatment in Nineteenth Century America." In *Clio's Consciousness Raised*. Eds. Mary S. Hartman and Lois Banner. New York: Harper, 1974. 1-22.

Woolf, Virginia. *The Diary of Virginia Woolf*. 5 vols. London: Hogarth, 1977-1984.

_____. Introduction. *Mrs. Dalloway*. New York: Modern Library, 1928. Rpt. in *Virginia Woolf: A Collection of Criticism*. Ed. Thomas S. W. Lewis. New York: McGraw-Hill, 1975. 35-37.

_____. *The Letters of Virginia Woolf*. 6 vols. New York: Harcourt, 1975-1980.

_____. *Moments of Being*. New York: Harcourt, 1976.

_____. *Mrs. Dalloway*. New York: Harcourt, 1925.

_____. Notebook, Nov. 9, 1922-Aug. 2, 1923. Berg Collection, New York Public Library.

_____. *To the Lighthouse*. New York: Harcourt, 1927.

Zwerdling, Alex. *Virginia Woolf and the Real World*. Berkeley: U of California P, 1986.

From Text to Tableau:
Ekphrastic Enchantment in *Mrs. Dalloway* and *To the Lighthouse*

Kathryn Stelmach Artuso

> Words move, music moves
> Only in time; but that which is only living
> Can only die. Words, after speech, reach
> Into the silence. Only by the form, the pattern,
> Can words or music reach
> The stillness, as a Chinese jar still
> Moves perpetually in its stillness.
> —T. S. Eliot, "Burnt Norton" (V)

> For most of us there is only the unattended
> Moment, the moment in and out of time,
> The distraction fit, lost in a shaft of sunlight,
> The wild thyme unseen, or the winter lightning
> Or the waterfall, or music heard so deeply
> That it is not heard at all, but you are the music
> While the music lasts. . . .
> The hint half guessed, the gift half understood, is
>   Incarnation.
> Here the impossible union.
> —T. S. Eliot, "The Dry Salvages" (V)

Near the end of her life, Virginia Woolf intensified her search for a newly patterned literary language capable of synaesthetically blurring sensory boundaries and merging the fleeting temporality of music and poetry with the spatial substance of painting and sculpture. In her final novel, *Between the Acts* (1941), Woolf vividly inscribes the central artistic paradoxes that invigorated and exasperated her career, paradoxes she explores in *Mrs. Dalloway* (1925) and *To the Lighthouse* (1927) but comes close to reconciling in the fragmented dramatic representation that "break[s] the rhythm and forget[s] the rhyme" at the close of *Between the Acts* (187). Early in the novel, Woolf outlines her attempt to create a spatio-temporal continuum through her description of a vase and the dining-room painting of a mythical Diana figure, a scene which recalls the still-life imagery in the "Time Passes" section of *To the Lighthouse*:

> In her yellow robe, leaning, with a pillar to support her, a silver arrow in her hand, and a feather in her hair, she led the eye up, down, from the curve to the straight, through glades of greenery and shades of silver, dun and rose into silence. The room was empty.
>
> Empty, empty, empty; silent, silent, silent. The room was a shell, singing of what was before time was; a vase stood in the heart of the house, alabaster, smooth, cold, holding the still, distilled essence of emptiness, silence. (36-37)

Momentarily suspended beyond the succession of historical human activity, the dually valenced "shell" of a room parallels the empty alabaster vase, which sits at the "heart of the house" and prevails over the scene similar to the manner in which Wallace Stevens's jar takes "dominion" over the surrounding landscape. The room paradoxically sings in its stillness, revealing the essential, living presence behind works of art that appear frozen beyond sequential movement. While the painting of the mythical woman with her silver emblem of chastity invites the viewer to step through the frame into a natural world leading into the heart of silence, the alabaster vase spatially surrounds a "distilled" silence, suggesting a living fluidity rather than a frozen density. Merging painting, sculpture, and song in an effort to transcend the confines of space and the slipperiness of time, Woolf reveals that the essence of silence and of artistic representation is not death but a "still movement" of life. Through her potentially paronomastic use of the word "still," Woolf evokes both Keats's Grecian urn, the "still unravish'd bride of quietness," and Eliot's "Chinese jar" that "still moves perpetually in its stillness." She creates a moment of complex ekphrastic suspension that seeks to translate the visual representations of plastic art into a verbal representation. She also attempts to transcend the distinctions between temporal fluidity and spatial substance by blurring and ultimately reversing the visual-to-verbal pattern of earlier literary forms of ekphrasis.

From the musical "composition" of *The Voyage Out* (1915) to the metadramatic representation of *Between the Acts*, Woolf sought to mingle various art forms by blurring boundaries and employing a defamiliarizing framing technique, which coalesces into the visionary mediation of thresholds to suspend liminal moments of epiphanic and ekphrastic revelation. Woolf foregrounds the transition between forms of art as well as the restorative transformations in the minds of her characters. Wary of complete static suspension, Woolf instead sought a new art form that would reverse the ekphrastic moment and move beyond the confines of space and time into the paradoxical *tableau vivant*, often re-composed by the imaginative motion of memory. Woolf's epiphanic "moments of being"—the enchanted tableaux of reverse ekphrasis—arise in the midst of sacrificial displays of generosity, fusing motion with stasis and freezing the frame at the height of energetic expenditure. The extravagant generosity of female characters such as Mrs. Dalloway and Mrs. Ramsay provides a parallel with Woolf's own linguistic extravagance, which enacts the same process of redemptive defamiliarization. As she pursues linguistic re-enchantment and communal solidarity in an effort to restore and to unite aesthetic contemplation, Woolf draws upon the literal and symbolic sense of liminality to convey the state of ecstatic self-sacrifice, which often remains resistant to verbal representation. The paradox of "reverse ekphrasis" reinscribes itself within the storehouse of memory, which functions as another site of perpetual motion and stasis. Characters later revivify scenes suspended in the mind's eye, often envisioning the scenes as paintings and reading them as texts. In the face of impending failure, since she must still render a visual picture within the verbal flow and since language can never attain corporeal presence, Woolf ultimately underscores the endlessly cyclical nature of ekphrasis: tableaux and texts become virtually indistinguishable as they oscillate between the realms of spatial imagination and sequential narration.

Drawing upon both James Heffernan's concise definition of ekphrasis and Murray Krieger's awareness of the transubstantiating power of art, I would maintain that Woolf's "reverse ekphrases"—as foregrounded in her framed tableaux—arise from female generosity and lead to communal and linguistic re-enchantment through the joint act of aesthetic contemplation. The verbal representation of a visual representation ultimately turns back upon itself to transmute the fleeting power of language into the paradox of the still living *tableau vivant* that is suspended beyond the confines of space and time and often—but not always—brought to life through the imaginative motion of memory. Unlike Keats's "Ode on a Grecian Urn" or Yeats's "Lapis Lazuli," which seek to envoice an art object or bring it to life, Woolf's intensely lyrical prose renders ekphrases that arise from the transformative estrangement of excessive expenditure, arresting the linear passage of time in a framed epiphanic moment and then enacting an immediate return to time. Such "moments of being" reveal the evanescent wonder inherent in seeing life as a cyclical "*pattern* of timeless moments"—to borrow Eliot's phrase (144)—rather than as a sequence or "*series* of gig-lamps symmetrically arranged" (Woolf, "Modern Fiction" 1924, my emphases). In a letter to Duncan Grant in 1938, Woolf underscored her preference for language that aspires to spatial form: "Like all painters, your sense of words is plastic, not linear, and I am on the side of the plastic myself" (qtd. in Torgovnick 67).[1]

Woolf's novels thus offer an innovative angle on the vexed notion of ekphrasis, a term given currency in the mid-twentieth century by a handful of New Critics and formalists who used it to refer to poetry that seeks to envoice an art object.[2] In the early Hellenistic denotation, however, "ekphrazein" referred to a rhetorical strategy of elaboration or "reporting in detail," and today it remains defined in the discipline of rhetoric as a "self-contained description, often on a commonplace subject, which could be inserted at a fitting place in a discourse" (qtd. in Golahny 12, Heffernan 191).[3] Such definitions nonetheless rely upon the power of words to convey an image, a notion first articulated by Plutarch, who cites Simonides as drawing the analogy between picture and word, claiming that painting is mute poetry, and poetry is a speaking picture (Hollander 6, Golahny 11-12). Horace's enigmatic phrase "ut pictura poesis" ("as in painting, so in poetry") proved far more influential throughout the centuries for critics comparing verbal and visual representations, even though ekphrasis by the third century C.E. had come to designate descriptions of visual art, such as Homer's famous excursus on the shield of Achilles (Golahny 11-12, Heffernan 191). Not until Murray Krieger's influential 1967 essay, which challenged Gotthold Lessing's indivisible barrier between temporal and spatial art, did ekphrasis enter critical vocabulary as the oxymoronic "still movement" of visual and artistic experience (266, Golahny 12). Krieger envisioned ekphrasis as a moment in which language seeks to appropriate sculpture's plasticity through the use of formal patterns that create a "circular repetitiveness within the discretely linear" (265).

Dissatisfied with Krieger's theory, which he thought would "seal literature within the well-wrought urn of pure, self-enclosed spatiality, where the ashes of New Criticism . . . now repose," James Heffernan in 1991 instead defined ekphrasis as the "verbal representation of visual representation" (2-3) and drew upon W. J. T. Mitchell's theories, deliberately emphasizing the difference between the image and the word in a paragonal contest and in an intensely gendered fashion that not only interrupts but also challenges the narrative (1, 191; see Mitchell's *Iconology* and "Spatial Form"). Mitchell sought to stage ekphrasis as a competition between the feminine image and the masculine word, a conflict he witnessed most clearly in Keats's ode, where the male poet forces the "still unravish'd bride" to speak (*Picture* 170-71). Despite

Heffernan's critique, Krieger's structuralist analysis resists the very closure of which Heffernan accuses it by underscoring the illusionary nature of the nostalgic quest for a "natural sign" of corporeal presence, remaining aware of the mirage of seeking to "represent the unrepresentable," and acknowledging that the ekphrastic poet tries and fails to work the "magical transformation" (Krieger 2, 10).

Both upholding and undermining Mitchell's ekphrastic theory, which posits a struggle for dominance between the feminine image and the masculine word, Woolf underscores gender rivalries even as she envisions a friendlier relationship and yearns for a synaesthetic and androgynous blurring of boundaries between the visual and the verbal arts, an aspiration heralded in "A Sketch of the Past":

> If I were a painter I should paint these first impressions in pale yellow, silver, and green. There was the pale yellow blind; the green sea; and the silver of the passion flowers. I should make a picture that was globular; semitransparent. I should make a picture of curved petals: of shells; of things that were semitransparent; I should make curved shapes, showing the light through, but not giving a clear outline. Everything would be large and dim; and what was seen would at the same time be heard; sounds would come through this petal or leaf—sounds indistinguishable from sights. (1991)

Numerous critics have cited this passage to link Woolf's work to aesthetic theories of Impressionism and Post-Impressionism, to the influence of formalist art critics such as Roger Fry and Clive Bell, and to the influence of her sister, the painter Vanessa Bell.[4] They have noted how Woolf referred to several of her works as "canvases"; they have pointed to the architectural and sculptural metaphors that underlie most of her novels; and they have frequently analyzed Woolf's Impressionistic and Post-Impressionistic use of color and imagery as it relates to Clive Bell's theory of "significant form." Yet these critics have neglected the subtle connection Woolf draws between ekphrasis and memory, which she reveals in a sculptural metaphor that she used to illustrate her earliest recorded sensation of hearing the ocean as she fell asleep at St. Ives: "If life has a base that it stands upon, if it is a bowl that one fills and fills and fills—then my bowl without a doubt stands upon this memory" (1990). Resembling more a holy grail than a Grecian urn, this sculptural image indicates the sense of plasticity, endurance, and aesthetic wholeness that Woolf accords her memories, which "can still be more real than the present moment" (1992). Woolf grants this figurative sculptural form both stability and movement, as it remains grounded in a past memory and simultaneously overflowing with continual action, a thematic duality that lends structural unity to *Mrs. Dalloway* and *To the Lighthouse*.

"For there she was": Freezing the Frame on Clarissa

Seeking to transcend individual isolation, the incommunicability of experience through speech, and the fragmented nature of language within sequential time, Woolf in *The Voyage Out* (1920) highlights language as a frame that can surround an idea or reality but never approach its true substance: "So beautiful was the sound of their voices that by degrees they scarcely listened to the words they framed"; "not only did the silence weigh upon them, but they were both unable to frame any thoughts" (283, 270). In contrast to the unsubstantial imprecision of language and speech, Woolf elevates both the temporal and spatial substance of music, which "goes straight for things" by saying "all there is to say at once" (212). In her attempt to blur the distinctions between various forms of art and to make writing approach the integrated wholeness of music, Woolf establishes in this novel the framing technique that recurs throughout all her works and that simultaneously underscores and transcends individual isolation. When Helen and Rachel surreptitiously gaze through the windows of the hotel, they frame distinct *tableaux vivants* within their visions and enact a process of estrangement that parallels the defamiliarizing power of art; indeed,

Rachel later realizes that "the most familiar view seen framed through glass has a certain unfamiliar distinction" (233).

In *Mrs. Dalloway* (1925), Woolf continues this framing technique, opening the novel by dissolving all barriers between the interior and the exterior as Clarissa plans to have the doors removed from their hinges to allow freedom of movement at her party. Just as Clarissa strives to create a space for unimpeded communal fellowship, so Woolf attempts to remove the barriers between individual minds. She smoothly weaves in and out of the consciousnesses of all her characters, erasing the distinction between speech and thought through her use of free indirect discourse, blurring the boundaries between the individual and the community, and dissolving the doors but retaining the framed threshold as a site of liminal revelation.[5] Creating a frame within a frame at the beginning of her journey, Clarissa throws open a window upon the past and upon a new day: "What a lark! What a plunge! For so it had always seemed to her when . . . she had burst open the French windows and plunged at Bourton into the open air" (1).[6] At the florist's shop, Woolf sets up another frame within a frame as Clarissa and the florist look out the window at the window of the car that perhaps contains the Queen, the "enduring symbol of the state" (16). Yet this moment of ritual, communal solidarity, in which the group should focus upon its totemic representative, is ultimately upstaged as the group's attention is magnetized by an advertisement in the sky. In the face of this fetishized commodity, this new totem of the "awe-stricken" masses below, Woolf embarks on an effort to re-enchant language and establish genuine communal solidarity in a world desacralized by the anomie of modernity, the mechanized slaughter and shell-shock of modern warfare, and the acquisitive mentality of the capitalist marketplace, which has made a Toffee advertisement the modern sacred.

Such a reading supports the contentions of Vincent Pecora, who draws upon Emile Durkheim, Georges Bataille, and the anthropological underbelly of modernity to argue that literary modernism's "extravagant displays of the artistic word" parallel the nostalgia for a pre-capitalistic enchanted economy in which excessive, sacrificial expenditure—a symbolic exchange without production—represented a noble gesture that modernism adopted to oppose to the narrow utilitarianism of a Calvinist marketplace (xi). The sense of aesthetic wholeness pursued by Woolf appears to oppose Bataille's theories of expenditure, where he elevates the redemptive power behind the non-productive use of luxury and art and envisions the "drive within language toward rational closure" as a "barrier to sovereignty" (qtd. in Pecora 250-51). Yet the concepts of excess and integration are not incompatible since Woolf upholds the paradox of the suspended moment in the midst of superfluous generosity, which fuses effervescence with endurance, and she resists rational closure through her endlessly circling aesthetic that continually oscillates between text and tableau.[7]

Woolf's project of collective and aesthetic re-enchantment certainly does not belong in the hands of a Miss Kilman, who embodies the pinched life of sterile asceticism and whose inward absorption and rejection of mystery makes her an unfit candidate for restoring communal fellowship and a revivified sense of the sacred. Trapped in the world of commodities and envy that she ceaselessly strives to transcend, Miss Kilman lacks the generosity, child-like wonder, and concrete substantiality of Clarissa; indeed, others in the church see Miss Kilman only as a "soul cut out of immaterial substance," who agonizes on the "threshold" of the religious "underworld," unable to blur the rigid boundaries she has established for herself or "aspire above the vanities, the desires, the commodities" of this world (149-150). Because Miss Kilman cannot engage in a superfluous expenditure of imaginative exuberance, the tautly wound simplicity of her consciousness leaves no ground for metaphor and is reflected in the terse, simpler sentences Woolf uses to describe her mental processes: "She despised Mrs. Dalloway from the bottom of her heart. She was not serious. She was not good" (144).

Nor can the process of re-enchantment be ascribed to a character like Septimus Warren Smith, whose dehumanization during the War and subsequent inability to feel isolates him completely. Woolf's recurring trope of windows figures this separation, but without the potential for the dissolution of barriers or the estranging power of art: "(b)eauty was behind a pane of glass" for Septimus, and he entertains the possibility, "looking at England from the train window," "that the world itself is without meaning" (97, 98). No longer able to engage in aesthetic play or freely squander his emotions and imagination, Septimus reveals his detachment from language through his disenchantment with Shakespeare: "the intoxication of language . . . had shriveled utterly. How Shakespeare loathed humanity" (98). Despite this detachment, Septimus still maintains a visionary capacity in which he occasionally experiences raw synaesthesia. In the moment of his death, Septimus symbolically breaks through the frame and pane, stepping over the threshold that has separated him from the world by throwing himself through the window, an act that simultaneously affirms and abolishes human relatedness and communication. Musing on the implications of his suicide, Clarissa thinks that "death was defiance. Death was an attempt to communicate, people feeling the impossibility of reaching the center which, mystically, evaded them: closeness drew apart; rapture faded; one was alone" (208). In the very act of disrupting human privacy and solitary vision, Septimus destroys any capacity for reintegration within the community by enacting a self-sacrifice that maintains individual isolation.[8] Before he commits suicide, he notices that "coming down the staircase opposite an old man stopped and stared at him," but this framed moment of spontaneous contact with a watching stranger fails to save him, as it will later save Clarissa, from the debilitating fear of coerced conformity and proportion that Dr. Bradshaw and Dr. Holmes epitomize (168). Woolf intimates that the accidental social encounters of strangers who retain their independent integrity and communicate wordlessly may provide a hedge against the alienation of the urban landscape that has created such a suffocating sense of mass conformity and individual isolation.

In contrast to the tense asceticism of Miss Kilman and the be-numbed attitude of Septimus, Clarissa breaks thresholds and crosses flames in a manner that reinforces communal solidarity as she sacrifi-cially offers herself to the crowded party, giving herself away freely and unreservedly in an outward-looking fashion. She had that "ex-traordinary *gift*," thinks Peter Walsh, "that woman's *gift*, of making a world of her own wherever she happened to be. She came into a room; she stood, as he had often seen her, in a doorway with lots of people round her. But it was Clarissa one remembered . . . she never said any-thing specially clever; there she was, however; there she was" (84, my emphases). Framed in the doorway, Clarissa suspends time and mem-ory in this liminal, ekphrastic moment, hesitating on the threshold in a manner that creates a sense of communal solidarity for all who have seen and can remember her. Unlike Isabel Archer, whom Henry James continually depicts standing in doorways and hesitating on the thresh-old of her life to symbolize her rite of passage, Clarissa instead frames the moment and her life to enable communal fellowship and a collective consciousness to arise from her extravagant expenditure—a Durkheimian effervescence—and from the joint act of aesthetic ap-preciation. This motif will later recur in Mrs. Ramsay's dinner party scene as the group gazes at the cornucopia centerpiece on the table. In-deed, Clarissa's ability to create a frozen moment later brought to life through the imaginative motion of memory also parallels Mrs. Ramsay's ability to "mak[e] of the moment something permanent" (*Lighthouse* 161).

As the totemic representative of the group, Clarissa gives her parties as sacrificial offerings, as a noble gesture of superfluous expenditure since "she felt quite continuously a sense" of the fragmented existence of isolated lives: "she felt what a waste: and she felt what a pity; and she felt if only they could be brought together; so she did it. And it was an offering; to combine, to create; but to whom? An offering for the sake of offering, perhaps. Anyhow, it was her gift" (136-137). Clarissa thus becomes the sovereign individual, in Georges Bataille's terms, who embodies "life beyond utility" (*Accursed* 198), blurring boundaries and creating room for aesthetic play and imaginative exuberance in an anomic world significantly bereft of such capacities. By the end of the novel, Mrs. Hilbery describes Clarissa as an enchantress who has transformed the mundane into the magical: "Did they know, she asked, that they were surrounded by an enchanted garden? Light and trees and wonderful gleaming lakes and the sky. Just a few fairy lamps, Clarissa Dalloway had said, in the back garden! But she was a magician! It was a park" (215). Reflecting on Clarissa's magical ability to conjure moments from the past, Peter had earlier thought how "it was awfully strange" that "she still had the power, as she came tinkling, rustling, still had the power as she came across the room, to make the moon, which he detested, rise at Bourton on the terrace in the summer sky" (51).[9]

Clarissa's imaginative ability to squander sacrificially without a thought for reciprocation derives from a moment early in the novel when Sally Seton had kissed her on the terrace at Bourton:

> Then came the most exquisite moment of her whole life passing a stone urn with flowers in it. Sally stopped: picked a flower; kissed her on the lips. The whole world might have turned upside down! The others disappeared; there she was alone with Sally. And she felt that she had been given a present, wrapped up, and told just to keep it, not to look at it—a diamond, something infinitely precious, wrapped up, which as they walked (up and down, up and down), she uncovered, or the radiance burnt through, the revelation, the religious feeling!—when old Joseph and Peter faced them:
> "Star-gazing?" said Peter.
> It was like running one's face against a granite wall in the darkness! It was shocking: it was horrible! (38)

In passing the "Grecian urn," the two women enter an atemporal moment of sculptural ekphrasis that unites them in sororal solidarity. Although critics have often read this as a Sapphic moment—perhaps indexed by the Grecian urn itself—a closer look reveals that this fleeting instant embodies a moment of ekphrastic suspension that upholds the potential for speechless communication. Clarissa is not so much irritated by the entrance of Peter as male, as by the fact that he replaces this maternally creative moment within time and places it prematurely before the public gaze, disrupting and ironizing her private epiphany. When—and only when—Clarissa is ready to do so, she takes the private gift of the suspended moment and transubstantiates it into the public sphere as she throws her parties and stands at the top of the stairs, becoming the diamond gift herself, offered freely to others, transmuting the private into the public in the same way that modernist authors offer their private epiphanies to the public sphere.[10]

In perhaps the most regenerative vision of ekphrastic enchantment in the novel, Clarissa looks out the window at the sky after hearing of the death of Septimus, encountering the estrangement of the unexpected since the "solemn sky" she thinks she will find is not there; instead, "it was new to her" (209-10). By breaking out of the frame that separates him from the outer world, Septimus provokes the process of defamiliarization in Clarissa's mind as she cleanses the Blakean "doors of perception" and removes the frames separating herself from the private mystery of the soul embodied in the old woman next door: "in the room opposite, the old lady stared straight at her. . . . Could she see her? It was fascinating, with people still laughing and shouting in the drawing-room, to watch that old woman, quite quietly, going to bed alone" (209-10). Earlier in the novel, Clarissa had identified the old woman as an emblem of the "miracle" and "mystery" of life, of the "privacy of the soul" that defies neatly packaged religious explanations: "Why creeds and prayers and mackintoshes? [W]hen, thought Clarissa, that's the miracle, that's the mystery. . . . here was one room; there another. Did religion solve that, or love?" (143). In the face of the isolating distances between the paired window frames and the separate minds, Clarissa watches the old woman watch her as the reader watches them both. Creating an endless mediation of framing devices that paradoxically upholds the potential for human communication in the face of the private mystery of the soul, Woolf reveals the redemptive power of aesthetic vision to unite the disparate fragments of individual lives into an integrated wholeness.

In a complex ekphrastic moment that suspends both spatial and temporal elements, Woolf takes the *tableau vivant* of the woman next door, lifts it out of time, and then immediately replaces it within time: "The clock was striking. The leaden circles dissolved in the air" (210). Describing the clock's loud sound as creating "leaden circles" implies a cyclical spatiality that situates this ekphrasis within a moment that Mircea Eliade would term "sacred time" (68) or Walter Benjamin would term "liturgical" or "calendrical time" (261). The recurrence of redemptive moments, set apart in a ritualized fashion, is underscored by Woolf's cyclical repetition of the same sentence ("the leaden circles dissolved in the air" [2, 105, 210]) throughout the course of the novel. The spatial image of expanding concentric circles recalls the plunging metaphor at the opening of the novel and emblematizes the subtle connections beneath the surface of society, connections Clarissa associates with her mystical, "transcendental theory" of the afterlife, in which the "unseen part of us, which spreads wide, the unseen might survive" (172). Clarissa had earlier thought that the "gigantic" force of time mysteriously remained connected to the old woman next door; indeed, as soon as Clarissa's consciousness momentarily freezes the frame on the woman, "down, down, into the midst of ordinary things the finger [of time] fell making the moment solemn" (142-143). Even as Clarissa attempts to remove the tableau from the sequential movement of time, the sudden entrance of the clock's sound allows her to appreciate the transient nature of life, a life strangely re-enchanted by the free will displayed in Septimus's death and by the mysterious wonder and grace embodied in the older, mirror image of herself next door.[11]

Watching the woman next door, Clarissa experiences a visionary "moment of being," one of the "little daily miracles, illuminations, matches struck unexpectedly in the dark" that parallels the Joycean epiphany (*Lighthouse* 161). Like Joyce's "bird-girl" epiphany in *A Portrait of the Artist as a Young Man* that merges the sensual and the spiritual into an aesthetic vision of frozen ekphrastic proportions, like Faulkner's suspension of the death of the bear in *Go Down Moses*, and like Lily Briscoe's juxtaposition of the butterfly wing upon the cathedral arch, Woolf briefly arrests the wonder of the timeless moment in the midst of mortality. The novel closes in another tableau frozen upon the figure of Clarissa who has again paused on the threshold of the room, merging both time and space, offering herself unreservedly to her friends, and invoking all the terror, ecstasy, and excitement of a mystical state of enchantment. "For there she was," the novel concludes, deliberately repeating the phrase that earlier ran through Peter's mind when he imagined Clarissa standing in the doorway, "making a world of her own" by her mere presence (84, 219). Woolf's use of free indirect discourse in this final line now suggests a wholly unified collective consciousness as Peter and the others jointly gaze upon Clarissa, who stands on the threshold of the room. Like Clarissa, Woolf becomes the magician with the ability to re-enchant a desacralized world, an artist with a new extravagance of the literary word, stepping across isolating thresholds, freely expending her imagination in the realm of aesthetic play, and creating a revivified sense of wholeness in a fragmented world.

Butterfly Wing and Cathedral Arch

As she carries these motifs into her composition of *To the Lighthouse* (1927), Woolf relocates Clarissa's sacrificial expenditure of energy and "unnecessary expense of emotion" within the character of Mrs. Ramsay, whose sympathetic nature and outward-looking absorption provides sustenance for her family and friends and for the budding artist, Lily Briscoe, who is drawn "like a bee, drawn by some sweetness or sharpness in the air" to the "dome-shaped hive" of Mrs. Ramsay (16,

51). Lily desires a mystical unity with Mrs. Ramsay that she knows she will never achieve even as she attempts to paint the triangular, dome-shaped essence of Mrs. Ramsay into her non-representational art, an art that opposes the pastel Impressionism of Mr. Paunceforte:

> . . . she imagined how in the chambers of the mind and heart of the woman who was, physically, touching her, were stood, like the treasures in the tombs of kings, tablets bearing sacred inscriptions, which if one could spell them out, would teach one everything, but they would never be offered openly, never made public. What art was there, known to love or cunning, by which one pressed through into those secret chambers? What device for becoming, like waters poured into one jar, inextricably the same, one with the object one adored? (51)

According to Jesper Svenbro, the first examples of Greek alphabetic documents appeared on tablets, tombstones, or statues inscribed with epigrams that envoice the object they adorn (3, 9). Indeed, the very heart of Mrs. Ramsay holds ekphrastic epigrams, tablets inscribed with the words that could reveal her primal, essential nature if anyone could see and interpret the signs. Yet these private signs will always remain a mystery to the outside world and to Lily, who perpetually hums about the intricately chambered hive of Mrs. Ramsay and who desires the thousand eyes of Argus to view Mrs. Ramsay from every conceivable angle. Lily also desires a unity of consciousness that parallels Woolf's own desire to fuse the spatiality of sculpture (jar) with the temporality of language (water) as she endeavors to enter the intricate chambers of the hearts of all her characters.

In contrast to the excessive expenditure of Mrs. Ramsay's imagination, Mr. Ramsay's monumental intellect demands ceaseless reinforcement and continual soothing from his wife. As he debates his status within the archives of philosophical greatness and agonizes over the next step in the metaphysical progression along the alphabet of logic, Mr. Ramsay stands near a stone urn and enters a sculpturally ekphrastic moment that arrests his thought processes in a paralytic fashion. Knowing that he will never reach the end of the philosophical quest and that he will never be the genius of the age, Mr. Ramsay still refuses to "die lying down; he would find some crag of rock, and there, his eyes fixed on the storm, trying to the end to pierce the darkness, he would die standing" (35). Like a courageous leader of a doomed expedition or a heroic king of an ancient epic, Mr. Ramsay "squared his shoulders and stood very upright by the urn" (36), entering the stony state of suspension symbolized by an urn that—in this negative context—connotes ashes and death rather than artistic wholeness. While Clarissa and Sally enter the "still movement" of ekphrastic suspension that embodies the aesthetic transcendence of a circling Keatsian urn, Mr. Ramsay instead enters a frozen moment of immobility. Yet Mr. Ramsay knows that this response to art, sensation, and intellect can never prove fruitful, and he immediately re-enters the movement of living temporality by turning to view his wife and son who are framed in the window of the house like a *tableau vivant*. The very structure of the paragraph replicates this framing process as it opens and closes with the same phrase:

> *Who shall blame him*, if, so standing for a moment, he dwells upon fame. . . . Who will not secretly rejoice when the hero puts his armor off, and halts by the window and gazes at his wife and son, who, very distant at first, gradually come closer and closer, till lips and book and head are clearly before him, though still lovely and unfamiliar from the intensity of his isolation and the waste of ages and the perishing of the stars, and finally putting his pipe in his pocket and bending his magnificent head before her—*who will blame him* if he does homage to the beauty of the world? (36, my emphases)

Opting not for individual isolation or granite immobility but rather for the framed *tableau vivant* of wife and child, Mr. Ramsay finds rejuvenation in the aesthetic appreciation of breathing beauty, as he refuses the negating arrest of death and philosophical permanence and instead exalts the living, vibrant picture that "still" moves within its frame and within its spatio-temporal continuum.[12] As he approaches his wife, Mr. Ramsay pleads for an outpouring of sympathy, and Mrs. Ramsay expends herself without reservation, bringing him within the tableau and surrounding him with the frame of her creative love:

> So boasting of her capacity to surround and protect, there was scarcely a shell of herself left for her to know herself by; all was so lavished and spent; and James, as he stood stiff between her knees, felt her rise in a rosy-flowered fruit tree laid with leaves and dancing boughs into which the beak of brass, the arid scimitar of his father, the egotistical man, plunged and smote, demanding sympathy. . . .
>
> Immediately, Mrs. Ramsay seemed to fold herself together, one petal closed in another, and the whole fabric fell in exhaustion upon itself . . . while there throbbed through her, like the pulse in a spring which has expanded to its full width and now gently ceases to beat, the rapture of successful creation. (38)

Employing lavish, sensual metaphors, Woolf underscores the interpenetration of artistic and maternal creation and of the ecstatic rapture of self-sacrificially offering one's energy and imagination. She reveals that the finest creators and authors ultimately become both the giver and the given, the creator and the crucified, both the priest who transubstantiates the word into flesh and the expended sacrifice itself. While this scene appears to uphold theories of the struggle for dominance between the feminine image and the masculine word, Mr. and Mrs. Ramsay's interactions here and throughout the novel instead reveal a reciprocity in which neither character completely subsumes the individual integrity of the other, but rather creates a space in which speechless communication occurs: "She had not said it [that she loved him]: yet he knew" (124). Perhaps this view overly romanticizes a relationship about which the text often remains ambiguous and circumspect, but it nevertheless offers a corrective to a critical tradition that has tended to overly ironize the Ramsays' bourgeois domesticity.

When Mrs. Ramsay's sacrificial ecstasy—the "rapture of creation"— and the outward absorption fade away, so too does the excess of language, which grows terse, taut, and denotative when Mrs. Ramsay's focus turns inward: "She had been admired. She had been loved. She had entered rooms where mourners sat. Tears had flown in her presence. . . . It injured her that [Carmichael] should shrink. It hurt her" (41). Such occasions of inner absorption prove rare for Mrs. Ramsay, however, and Lily describes Mrs. Ramsay's creative and sacrificial gift of love as something that "never attempted to clutch its object; but, like the love that mathematicians bear their symbols, or poets their phrases, was meant to be spread over the world and become part of the human gain" (47).

Mrs. Ramsay's imaginative ability to frame moments of aesthetic appreciation that become a treasured part of the onlooker's memory appears early in the novel during her trip to town with Charles Tansley, perhaps the most self-absorbed character in the text. As they make their journey, Mrs. Ramsay frames the moment by pointing out the painters to her companion, by erupting in "childlike exultation" over the arrival of a circus, and by creating a haven of respite for Charles from his normally bruised ego (11). Suddenly filled with an unprecedented and "extraordinary emotion," Charles waits for Mrs. Ramsay during her visit to an invalid and then sees her stand "quite motionless for a moment against a picture of Queen Victoria" (13-14).[13] During this ekphrastic moment of framed suspension, Charles realizes that Mrs. Ramsay is the "most beautiful person he had ever seen." His consciousness waxes rhapsodic, though a bit clichéd, as her exquisite beauty gives him a new ground for metaphor, thereby transforming his normally terse and academic language into a poetic discourse. He thinks of something other than himself for the first time in the text: "Stepping through fields of flowers and taking to her breast buds that had broken and lambs that had fallen; with the stars in her eyes and the wind in her hair—He took her bag" (14). Just as Mrs. Ramsay soothes the flaring temperaments of Charles and her husband, so she ameliorates the disappointment of her son James by helping him find pictures to cut out while simultaneously becoming a portrait that will long remain in his memory. With her knitting in hand and her head "outlined absurdly by the gilt frame," Mrs. Ramsay embodies a poetic picture of a mythical weaver, framed for a liminal moment to create a sense of aesthetic wholeness and permanence woven in the midst of the fragmented and the fleeting (30).

Nowhere is Mrs. Ramsay's power of aesthetic enchantment more prevalent than in the dinner party scene, where the verbal representation of a dinner party and of individual thoughts slowly transforms into a visual representation and into a collective consciousness. The scene emulates a painting framed through the window, illumined by the flickering, chiaroscuric play of light and dark, and centered upon the "still"-life cornucopia in the middle of the table.[14] Like Clarissa Dalloway, Mrs. Ramsay fears that her party has failed before it has even begun, and the prose again grows taut: "Nothing seemed to have merged. They all sat separate. And the whole effort of merging and flowing and creating rested on her" (83). Through the imaginative motion of memory that Mr. Bankes's discussion of a mutual friend elicits, Mrs. Ramsay replays from the past a day permanently suspended in her mind's eye: "it fascinated her, as if, while she had changed, that particular day, now become very still and beautiful, had remained there, all these years. . . . It was like reading a good book again, for she knew the end of that story" (87, 93). The treasured day exists as both a stilled tableau and as a text made narratable by the action of memory, reinforcing the ultimate interdependence of the verbal and the visual in Woolf's endlessly circling aesthetic. The tableau, suspended in time and brought to life through her memory's motion, provides Mrs. Ramsay with the hope that her own dinner party will also become wound round in the participants' hearts, "however long they lived" (113).

Before the group unites in communal fellowship, the "monumental and contemplative" (96) Augustus Carmichael, the symbolic house-hold god often associated with Neptune, asks for another bowl of soup as he revels in the available abundance set before him. And then the lighting of the candles focuses the group's collective attention in a moment of aesthetic contemplation by suddenly revealing a magical cornucopia as the centerpiece of the table:

> What had she done with it, Mrs. Ramsay wondered, for Rose's arrangement of the grapes and pears, of the horny pink-lined shell, of the bananas, made her think of a trophy fetched from the bottom of the sea, of Neptune's banquet, of the bunch that hangs with vine leaves over the shoulder of Bacchus (in some picture), among the leopard skins and the torches lolloping red and gold. . . . Thus brought up suddenly into the light it seemed possessed of great size and depth, was like a world in which one could take one's staff and climb hills, she thought, and go down into valleys, and to her pleasure (for it brought them into sympathy momentarily) she saw that Augustus too feasted his eyes on the same plate of fruit, plunged in, broke off a bloom there, a tassel here, and returned, after feasting, to his hive. That was his way of looking, different from hers. But looking together united them. (97)

As an emblem of Dionysian ecstasy and of a ritualized harvest ceremony, the cornucopia unites the group in a communal fellowship of joint aesthetic appreciation and evokes images not only of Caravaggio's painting of Bacchus with its chiaroscuric interplay of light and dark, but also of Cézanne's still-life paintings that Woolf admired. Although each observer has a different "way of looking," their common focus on a central totemic object unites them against the outer fluidity of time and change symbolized by the dark night "now shut off by panes of glass, which, far from giving any accurate view of the outside world, rippled it so strangely that here, inside the room, seemed to be order and dry land; there, outside, a reflection in which things wavered and vanished, waterily" (97). Suddenly spared the ravages of time and transience, the dinner party scene transforms into an enchanted tableau that is framed against the window and defamiliarized by the estranging power of glass and light, a moment that arises from the lighting of the candles and the collective fusion of aesthetic contemplation. This timeless moment revolutionizes earlier literary forms of ekphrasis because it no longer seeks to envoice an art object through the spoken word, but rather relinquishes all speech in favor of silent aesthetic contemplation, where visual imagery predominates so strongly that the scene could easily be reproduced as a painting. Yet the visual ultimately remains rendered in the verbal since Woolf equates reading a book with contemplating a painting, an equation that sustains the inevitable inseparability of the two modes and the final failure of creating a transubstantive language of corporeal and synaesthetic presence. In contrast to the presumed struggle between the feminine image and the masculine word, Woolf instead merges masculine and feminine aesthetic vision on a central totemic object, creating collective solidarity coupled with the uniqueness of individual vision rather than a gendered semiomachia.

Just when Mrs. Ramsay thinks that Minta and Paul should arrive, they appear as if by magical wish fulfillment, a motif derived from Shakespeare's late romances and one that paints Mrs. Ramsay as a Prospero-like enchantress. In her role as a priestess, Mrs. Ramsay feels rising within her a "curious sense" of

> celebrating a festival, as if two emotions were called up in her, one profound—for what could be more serious than the love of man for woman, what more commanding, more impressive, bearing in its bosom the seeds of death; at the same time these lovers, these people entering into illusion glittering eyed, must be danced round with mockery, decorated with garlands. (100)

Seeking to celebrate the profound wonder and absurdity of human love, ultimately as illusionary as a work of art, Mrs. Ramsay turns the dinner into a ceremonial ritual of Dionysian ecstasy, venerating the cornucopic abundance of life and casting a spell of enchantment upon them all. "There was something frightening about her," Lily thinks, because in her role as enchantress, Mrs. Ramsay "was irresistible. . . . She put a spell on them all, by wishing, so simply, so directly, and Lily contrasted that abundance with her own poverty of spirit" (101). As she carries on a conversation about something as mundane as vegetables, Mrs. Ramsay looks like a priestess leading her victims to the altar; indeed, in the face of such a beautiful, charismatic leader, all of her followers symbolically become insensible to everyday troubles and to the pain of sacrifice. By invoking the image of a priest leading others to a sacrifice, by describing lovers in the throes of unconsummated desire, and by summoning images of ecstatic rituals of Dionysian frenzy, Woolf not only suspends the dinner party in a *tableau vivant* but also creates a moment of reverse sculptural ekphrasis through her vivid echoes of Keats's "Ode on a Grecian Urn." With its "wild ecstasy," its lovers "forever panting and forever young," and its picture of a sacred procession following a priest leading the "heifer lowing at the skies" with "all her silken flanks with garlands drest," Keats's urn becomes the perfect emblem for the still movement of liturgical, circular repetition that is embodied in the "eternal now" of the dinner party scene, which even has its own sacrificial heifer—the intricately garlanded Boeuf en Daube. Even Lily feels the scorching heat of "human passion" that leaves her "heart high-sorrowful and cloy'd" and gives her "a burning forehead and a parching tongue" (Keats, ll. 29-31) when Paul "turn[s] on her cheek the heat of love, its horror, its cruelty, its unscrupulosity," which burns her with its power (*Lighthouse* 102). Like Keats's urn that merges Apollonian form with Dionysian content, Mrs. Ramsay's dinner party fuses the living sacrificial ceremony with the spatial plasticity of painting and sculpture.

Having created a secular communion, Mrs. Ramsay sits back to enjoy the rising fragrance of successful sacrifice and exalt in the permanence that has arisen spontaneously in the midst of transience. She elevates the "still space that lies about the heart of things," the moment "immune from change" that shines out "in the face of the flowing, the fleeting, the spectral, like a ruby" (105). Yet she knows that this patterned timeless moment will soon be replaced within the flux of sequential time. As Augustus Carmichael and her husband begin chanting "Luriana Lurlilee," they enact a liturgical benediction to close the ritual. Carried outside of herself through the incantatory sweep of the benediction, Mrs. Ramsay can no longer identify the speaker or the meaning of the words as she watches Augustus Carmichael, looking like a chanting priest in a "long white robe," pay her homage and open the door for her. Hesitating on the threshold in a liminal moment between the two worlds of past and future, between timelessness and temporality, Mrs. Ramsay becomes a Janus figure, watching a "scene which was vanishing even as she looked"; "it had become, she knew, giving one last look at it over her shoulder, already the past" (111).[15] The sudden entrance of an image of death, the "horrid skull" hanging in the children's bedroom, immediately counterbalances the serene beauty of the dinner party scene, even as it creates a new tableau of Arcadian proportions that evokes Poussin's and Guercino's pastoral paintings, in which shepherds discover a skull or tomb in the midst of a paradisal landscape, near which is carved the words, "Et in Arcadia ego." Though she attempts to cloak its presence, the pig's skull acts as a *memento mori* that undermines Mrs. Ramsay's desires to transcend transience, and it foreshadows the shocking events of "Time Passes," which create nostalgia for a lost idyllic existence. While the novel makes every effort to prove the contrary, the skull suggests that the only "moment immune from change" may in fact be death.

Woolf's motif of the liminal moment of framed suspension recurs in the formal composition of Lily's painting, which seeks to figuratively fuse the evanescence of a butterfly's wing upon the strength of a cathedral arch. The arching compositional structure parallels the design of Woolf's text, which is grounded in the two framing side sections of "The Window" and "The Lighthouse" and held together by the rounded middle section of "Time Passes."[16] By creating an entrance or archway through which the reader must pass, Woolf embeds the concept of liminal space in the formal structure of the text, a threshold and archway ultimately translated ekphrastically into Lily's own painting, which visually represents Woolf's verbal representation. In "Time Passes," Woolf's intensely lyrical prose renders still-life imagery that counterpoises decay with beauty: "Now, day after day, light turned, like a flower reflected in water, its sharp image on the wall opposite" (129). Woolf also broadens the scope of her ekphrastic endeavor to include architecture, depicting the house as a giant sculpture hovering on the threshold of disintegration, whose decline and resurrection parallels the near destruction and subsequent restoration of post-war Europe. Having shattered the Enlightenment ideals of the inherent goodness of humanity, the rightness of reason, and the inevitability of progress, the Great War also breaks the mirror between humanity and nature, fracturing all notions of artistic mimesis. As the anonymous mystic paces the beach searching for answers, he spots the "silent apparition of an ashen-colored ship" followed by a sunken submarine's "purplish stain upon the bland surface of the sea" (133-134). Such intrusions into a "scene calculated to stir the most sublime reflections" made it difficult to "marvel how beauty outside mirrored beauty within. . . . to pace the beach was impossible; contemplation was unendurable; the mirror was broken" (134).

In the face of this fragmentation and nihilism, Lily nonetheless returns to the house and returns to her painting, striving to comprehend what remains changeless in the midst of mutability. Seeking to juxtapose beauty of form with strength of content in her desire to conflate the motion of a butterfly's wing with the spatial solidity of an arch, Lily also endeavors to fuse the pattern with the sequence, the permanent with the fleeting, the Dionysian with the Apollonian, and the imaginative play of Mrs. Ramsay with the unflinching realism of Mr. Ramsay.[17] Grappling with the "problem of space" just as Mrs. Ramsay had wrestled with the fluidity of time, Lily fashions a moment of ecstatic creation that recalls Mrs. Ramsay's maternally sympathetic effervescence in the first section of the novel. Unable to give Mr. Ramsay the all-encompassing comfort he demands in person, Lily later enacts an aesthetic expenditure that frames the moment around Mr. Ramsay's journey. Her realization at the end, that "whatever she had wanted to give him, when he left her that morning, she had given him at last" (208), forms a distinct parallel with Mrs. Ramsay's own ability to surround her husband with the flame of her love and draw him into a living tableau. As Lily enters the Dionysian "exciting ecstasy" and "dancing rhythmical movement" of artistic creation, exposing her "unborn soul" to "all the blasts of doubt," Woolf not only transmutes Mrs. Ramsay's struggle to achieve permanence in the midst of instability, but also attempts a reverse ekphrasis as she translates her own struggle to cover the blank page into Lily's struggle to fill the blank canvas (157-158).

As she loses her sense of self and "loses consciousness of outer things" during her act of creation, Lily's mind casts up "from its depths" a frozen tableau brought to life by the motion of her memory, a tableau of a visit to the beach with Mrs. Ramsay and Charles Tansley, where Mrs. Ramsay again functions as the totemic representative around which the group coalesces, as the one who creates a sense of communal fellowship and unity in the face of pettiness and isolation (159). Lily revives this moment of spontaneous joy frozen in the depths of time, discovering that the same unnecessary and unifying generosity created by Mrs. Ramsay also accompanies the creation and aesthetic contemplation of works of art:

. . . what a power was in the human soul! she thought. That woman sitting there writing under the rock resolved everything into simplicity; made these angers, irritations fall off like old rags; she brought together this and that and then this, and so made out of that miserable silliness and spite . . . something—this scene on the beach for example, this moment of friendship and liking—which survived, after all these years complete, so that she dipped into it to re-fashion her memory of him, and there it stayed in the mind *affecting one almost like a work of art*. (160, my emphasis)

While Mrs. Ramsay replays the past as a narratable text, Lily instead contemplates the *tableau vivant* as a template into which she can figuratively dip her brush to restore and "re-fashion" her fading memory of Charles. In the face of an anomic world fragmented by grief and war, in which the mirror between humanity and nature has shattered, Lily celebrates a superfluous moment of human fellowship eternally framed beyond the confines of space and time and brought to life through the imaginative motion of memory. Although Mrs. Ramsay assumes that her dinner party will be woven into the participants' hearts, Lily instead recalls another tableau, an act that both confirms and ironizes Mrs. Ramsay's belief in eternal return. While Mrs. Ramsay's gift of the dinner party acquires overtones of a Dionysian sacrificial ceremony that must die in time to be returned as memory, Lily instead revives the Dionysian ritual in another form of aesthetic creation and through another memory. Ironically, only the housekeeper Mrs. McNab recalls the dinner party scene, remembering that "she had seen them once through the dining-room door all sitting at dinner" (140), framing yet another memory as an artistic tableau.

Accepting that the "great revelation" of the meaning of life will perhaps never come, Lily instead exalts the sudden revelatory moments of being, the

little daily miracles, illuminations, matches struck unexpectedly in the dark; here was one. . . . Mrs. Ramsay bringing them together; Mrs. Ramsay saying "Life stand still here"; Mrs. Ramsay making of the moment something permanent (as in another sphere Lily herself tried to make of the moment something permanent)—this was of the nature of a revelation. In the midst of chaos there was shape; this eternal passing and flowing . . . was struck into stability. (161)

In the face of fragmentation and cacophony, Mrs. Ramsay's ceaseless capacity to give to others freezes the frame in a manner that parallels Lily's own artistic creation, her own superfluous gift. The incantatory sweep of the preceding passage, Lily's liturgical repetition of Mrs. Ramsay's name, and her ecstatic overflow of artistic expenditure again create an enchanted tableau that magically transubstantiates the word into flesh as Lily brings Mrs. Ramsay to life and envisions her seated within the frame of the window. As Lily attains a sudden visionary epiphany, James simultaneously approaches the lighthouse and sees its present-day black-and-white reality coupled with the lighthouse of his youth's imagination. In this double vision he unites the unflinching realism of his father with the exuberance of his mother, realizing that "nothing was simply one thing" (186). Acknowledging that life can only be a "miracle" and an "ecstasy," Lily merges the mundane and the miraculous, transfiguring even the most commonplace events into revelatory moments of enchantment, accepting and continuing the legacy left behind by Mrs. Ramsay. As all promises finally reach fulfillment, Lily stands near Augustus Carmichael, who again represents a classical sea god and who crowns the occasion and closes the moment with a silent benediction, thus translating the journey and the novel into a unified liturgical ceremony. Exalting the visual over the verbal, both characters relinquish speech in the face of a sacred vision that merges classical imagery with biblical allusion and places them outside of linear time into a patterned, mythical moment of enchantment:

> "He has landed," she said aloud. "It is finished." Then, surging up, puffing slightly, old Mr. Carmichael stood beside her, looking like an old pagan god, shaggy, with weeds in his hair and the trident (it was only a French novel) in his hand. . . . Now he has crowned the occasion, she thought, when his hand slowly fell, as if she had seen him let fall from his great height a wreath of violets and asphodels which, fluttering slowly, lay at length upon the earth. (208)

Transcending all gendered divisions between the image and the word, Woolf androgynously merges masculine and feminine perception, enabling Lily and Mr. Carmichael to communicate wordlessly without subsuming the individual integrity of each other: "They had not needed to speak. They had been thinking the same things and he had answered her without her asking him anything" (208). Through the ambiguous nature of Lily's final vertical line, Woolf underscores both the potential and the failure of the ekphrastic attempt to transmute language into synaesthetic and corporeal presence, at once revealing the redemptive power of mutual aesthetic vision and the inherent multiplicity of interpretation that will follow.[18] As she makes the final vertical mark on her canvas, Lily not only closes the framing arch of her painting and the arc of the novel but also draws a connecting line between the sea and sky, between the secular and the sacred, coming as close as possible to completing the reverse ekphrastic transubstantiation of the verbal into the visual, as the book and painting together approach the "impossible union" of incarnation, as the completed tableau enters the memory and imagination of the reader.

Notes

1. Torgovnick notes that Woolf developed a theory of perception and memory as rooted in visual images, and she identifies the "pictorial" impulse in Woolf's writing but fails to link it to ekphrasis or to Woolf's attempt to create "spatial form."

2. See Hagstrum (18n, 49-50), who offers one of the narrowest definitions of ekphrasis, using it to refer only to those poems that seek to envoice an art object and speak to the reader. He reserves the label "iconic" for poems that merely describe an art object and do not give it a voice. See Hollander for a discussion of the distinctions between actual and "notional" ekphrasis, the latter referring to art that exists only in the poet's imagination (4).

3. Golahny's introduction provides the most helpful overview of the muddled history and critical theory surrounding ekphrasis.

4. See especially Gillespie, Goldman, Goring, McLaurin, Quick, Stewart, and Torgovnick.

5. My discussion of Woolf's use of the literal and symbolic sense of liminality supports Smith who draws upon Kristevan theory to foreground abjection and androgyny in the works of Woolf and Katherine Mansfield. While Smith generates a feminist reading of the two authors' "refusal of masculine hieratic value" (26), I instead maintain that Woolf transcends these standard gender dichotomies in her attempt to create communal aesthetic contemplation and to merge various art forms. My reading seeks to rectify the imbalance currently prevalent in Woolf criticism, where the pervasive desire to read Woolf only through the lens of gender has marginalized other theoretical angles on her work. Joyce and Faulkner, Woolf's stream-of-consciousness counterparts have not been locked into such theoretical straitjackets.

6. This text is based on the original British (Hogarth) edition rather than the American (Harcourt) edition. The British edition proves more accurate, for reasons explained below in n. 11.

7. Bataille envisioned poetry as synonymous with sacrificial expenditure and loss ("Notion" 120). Underscoring the connection between religious and artistic sacrifice, Bataille claimed that

> literature is in fact religion's heir. A sacrifice is a novel, a story, illustrated in bloody fashion. Or rather a rudimentary form of stage drama reduced to the final episode where the human or animal victim acts it out alone until his death. Ritual ceremonies are certainly dramatic versions repeated on a certain date, of a myth, of the death of a god. There is nothing here that should surprise us. In a symbolic form this happens every day at the sacrifice of the mass. (*Death* 87)

8. Woolf's earlier draft of the suicide scene reveals an overt parallel to the scene near the end of the novel, where Clarissa stands at her window staring at the old woman next door, but in the proofsheets sent to Harcourt and to her friend Jacques Raverat in February 1925, Woolf re-wrote the suicide scene in a slightly subtler fashion, changing the sentence, "But look at the old man in the house opposite, staring at him!" to "Coming down the staircase opposite an old man stopped and stared at him" (225). The earlier version suggests that Septimus saw the old man framed in the window across the way, just as Clarissa will later see an old woman framed in the window of the house next door.

9. Like Clarissa and Mrs. Ramsay, Miss La Trobe in *Between the Acts* appears as a shamanic, gift-giving artist, as one who "seethes wandering bodies and floating voices in a cauldron, and makes rise up from its amorphous mass a re-created world" (153).

10. I am seeking to offer a corrective to the critical traditions that have dismissed or demythologized the bourgeois domesticity of Mrs. Dalloway and Mrs. Ramsay, traditions that have neglected to see any redemptive or aesthetic enchantment in the lives of the two generous women.

11. Following "The leaden circles dissolved in the air," the oddly shallow line, "He made her feel the beauty; made her feel the fun" appears in all the American editions published by Harcourt, but it did not appear in the first British edition published by Hogarth Press (Wright 213). Woolf continued to make corrections on the proofs for the Hogarth edition *after* she had mailed another set of proofs to Harcourt in late February

or early March 1925, and thus the first British edition represents a more reliable source than the American edition, even though the British and American editions were both published on the same day: May 14, 1925 (Wright 176). The deletion of "He made her feel the beauty; made her feel the fun" appears to have been made by Woolf after February 1925, and such a deletion preserves the consistency in tone since it proves "gratuitous to have her think that Septimus' suicide 'made her feel the fun,'" given the serious import of Clarissa's meditations at this point (Wright 213). In the proofs she sent to her friend Jacques Raverat. currently housed in the Special Collections of the University Research Library at UCLA, the line is not deleted, but instead reads "He made her feel the beauty; the fun" (281). See also *Mrs. Dalloway: The Definitive Collected Edition*, Wright, ed.

12. Woolf's stylistic framing devices extend even to punctuation and to chapter breaks, as evidenced by the excursus of chapter 24's beach expedition, which is entirely enclosed in parentheses and framed by Mrs. Ramsay's question at the end of chapter 23 and Prue's response at the beginning of chapter 25. Like Mr. Ramsay turning away from the granite immobility of the urn of death, so Miss La Trobe at the end of *Between the Acts* watches a woman approaching a burial urn, considers whether the sacrificial expenditure of art truly proves redemptive, and then sees the tree of birds explode into a celebration of rhapsodically wasteful "life without measure," embodying a useless and fragmented song of delight (209).

13. Winston offers an ekphrastic reading of Empire in *To the Lighthouse*, using this quotation as the primary support for her argument that Mrs. Ramsay is an allegorical representation of Queen Victoria.

14. Although Goldman argues that Woolf sought to overturn the traditionally masculine imagery of chiaroscuro through her feminized Post-Impressionist use of color, this scene clearly demonstrates the use of chiaroscuro for a dramatic effect that poses the warmth and light of the interior against the exterior darkness. Goldman does not address this scene in her book.

15. In *The Hours*, Michael Cunningham recreates this scene in a reflexive fashion by depicting a birthday party thrown by an unhappy wife in late 1940s Los Angeles, merging both the temporal and the spatial as he too conflates the text with the tableau by portraying a fleeting, if more ironic, moment "immune from change":

> it seems she has succeeded suddenly, at the last minute, the way a painter might brush a final line of color onto a painting and save it from incoherence: the way a writer might set down the line that brings to light the submerged patterns and symmetry in the drama. . . . The room seems almost impossibly full: full of the lives of her husband and son; full of the future. It matters: it shines. Much of the world, whole countries, have been decimated, but a force that feel unambiguously like goodness has prevailed. . . . Laura reads the moment as it passes. Here it is, she thinks; there it goes. The page is about to turn. (207-08)

In addition to creating a postmodern retelling of *Mrs. Dalloway*, Cunningham merges a plot line about Mrs. Brown that echoes elements from *To the Lighthouse*.

16. Woolf indicated in her preliminary notes for the novel that she envisioned the

design of her novel as an **"H"** shape, as "two blocks joined by a corridor" (qtd. in Goring 223).

17. While Lily's agonizing and ecstatic struggle to fill the blank canvas parallels Woolf's own struggle to cover the blank page, it proves too simple to claim, as many critics have done, that Lily stands as Woolf's primary spokesperson in the text. Mrs. Ramsay's struggle to achieve permanence in the midst of instability also enacts an aesthetic, ekphrastic expenditure, and Mr. Ramsay's heroic, tragic quest for philosophical greatness parallels Woolf's own fear of failing or being forgotten.

18. I am following Goring's claim for the indeterminacy of Lily's final mark, rather than McLaurin's claim that she paints a tree or Harrington's claim that she draws the lighthouse.

Works Cited

Bataille, Georges. *The Accursed Share*. Trans. Robert Hurley. New York: Urzone, 1989.

_____. *Death and Sensuality: A Study of Eroticism and the Taboo*. New York: Walker, 1962.

_____. "The Notion of Expenditure." *Visions of Excess: Selected Writings 1927-1939*. Trans. Allan Stoekl. Minneapolis: U of Minnesota P, 1985. 120.

Benjamin, Walter. *Illuminations*. Trans. Harry Zohn. New York: Schocken, 1969.

Cunningham, Michael. *The Hours*. New York: Picador, 1998.

Eliade, Mircea. *The Sacred and the Profane: The Nature of Religion*. Trans. Willard R. Trask. New York: Harcourt Brace, 1959.

Eliot, T. S. *The Complete Poems and Plays, 1909-1950*. New York: Harcourt Brace, 1980.

Gillespie, Diane. *The Sisters' Arts: The Writing and Painting of Virginia Woolf and Vanessa Bell*. Syracuse: Syracuse UP, 1988.

Golahny, Amy, ed. *The Eye of the Poet: Studies in the Reciprocity of the Visual and the Literary Arts from the Renaissance to the Present*. Lewisburg: Bucknell UP, 1996.

Goldman, Jane. *The Feminist Aesthetics of Virginia Woolf: Modernism, Post-Impressionism, and the Politics of the Visual*. Cambridge: Cambridge UP, 1998.

Goring, Paul. "The Shape of *To the Lighthouse*: Lily Briscoe's Painting and the Reader's Vision." *Word and Image* 10.3 (1994): 222-29.

Hagstrum, Jean. *The Sister Arts: The Tradition of Literary Pictorialism and English Poetry from Dryden to Gray*. Chicago: U of Chicago P, 1958.

Harrington, Henry R. "The central line down the middle of *To the Lighthouse*." *Contemporary Literature* 21.3 (1980): 363-82.

Heffernan, James. *Museum of Words: The Poetics of Ekphrasis from Homer to Ashbery*. Chicago: U of Chicago P, 1993.

Hollander, John. *The Gazer's Spirit: Poems Speaking to Silent Works of Art*. Chicago: U of Chicago P, 1995.

Keats, John. "Ode on a Grecian Urn." 1820. *Norton Anthology of English Literature*. Ed. M. H. Abrams, et al. 6th ed. Vol. 2. New York: Norton, 1993.

Krieger, Murray. *Ekphrasis: The Illusion of the Natural Sign*. Baltimore: Johns Hopkins UP, 1992.

McLaurin, Allen. *Virginia Woolf: The Echoes Enslaved*. Cambridge: Cambridge UP, 1973.

Mitchell, W. J. T. *Iconology: Image, Text, Ideology*. Chicago: U of Chicago P, 1986.

_____. *Picture Theory: Essays on Verbal and Visual Representation*. Chicago: U of Chicago P, 1994.

_____. "Spatial Form in Literature: Toward a General Theory." *The Language of Images*. Ed. W. J. T. Mitchell. Chicago: U of Chicago P, 1980.

Pecora, Vincent. *Households of the Soul*. Baltimore: Johns Hopkins UP, 1997.

Quick, Jonathan. "Virginia Woolf, Roger Fry and Post-Impressionism." *MA Review* 26.4 (1985): 547-70.

Smith, Angela. *Katherine Mansfield and Virginia Woolf*. Oxford: Clarendon, 1999.

Stewart, Jack. "Color in *To the Lighthouse*." *Twentieth-Century Literature* 31.4 (1985): 438-58.

_____. "Impressionism in the Early Novels of Virginia Woolf." *Journal of Modern Literature* 9.2 (1982): 237-66.

_____. "A 'Need of Distance and Blue': Space, Color, and Creativity in *To the Lighthouse*." *Twentieth-Century Literature* 46.1 (2000): 78-99.

_____. "Spatial Form and Color in The Waves." *Twentieth-Century Literature* 28.1 (1982): 86-107.

Svenbro, Jesper. *Phrasikleia: An Anthropology of Reading in Ancient Greece*. Ithaca, NY: Cornell UP, 1993.

Torgovnick, Marianna. *The Visual Arts, Pictorialism, and the Novel: James, Lawrence, and Woolf*. Princeton: Princeton UP, 1985.

Winston, Janet. "'Something Out of Harmony': *To the Lighthouse* and the Subject(s) of Empire." *Woolf Studies Annual* 2 (1996): 39-70.

Woolf, Virginia. *Between the Acts*. 1941. New York: Harcourt Brace, 1970.

_____. "Modern Fiction." 1919. *Norton Anthology of English Literature*. Ed. M. H. Abrams, et al. 6th ed. Vol. 2. New York: Norton, 1993. 1921-1926.

_____. *Mrs. Dalloway*. 1925. New York: Alfred A. Knopf, 1993.

_____. *Mrs. Dalloway*. 1925. Set of proofs sent to Jacques Raverat. Special Collections of University Research Library, University of California, Los Angeles. Special collections #170.

_____. "A Sketch of the Past." 1939. *Norton Anthology of English Literature*. Ed. M. H. Abrams, et al. Vol. 2. 6th ed. New York: Norton, 1993.

_____. *To the Lighthouse*. 1927. New York: Harcourt Brace, 1989.

_____. *The Voyage Out*. 1915. London: Harcourt Brace, 1948.

Wright, G. Patton, ed. *Mrs. Dalloway: The Definitive Collected Edition*. London: Hogarth, 1990.

Mrs. Dalloway, the Dictator, and the Relativity Paradox _____

Christopher Herbert

Walter Pater, a keen observer of contemporary trends and a writer for whom Virginia Woolf had close affinities,[1] declared in 1865 that the defining feature of modern thought was "its cultivation of the 'relative' spirit in place of the 'absolute'" (*Appreciations* 66). This statement is bound to seem enigmatic, since the great philosophical, scientific, and polemical movement that took place in the second half of the nineteenth century under the banner of the relativity principle—the principle that nothing exists but relations—has yet to be redeemed from the oblivion into which, for various ideologically inflected reasons, it fell after the turn of the century. Yet relativity, along with evolution, to which it was so closely tied as often to be nearly synonymous with it, was well recognized at the time as the distinctive theme of much of the Victorian avant garde. It was proclaimed as such by Herbert Spencer, the most eminent early spokesman of relativity, in his once-famous manifesto *First Principles* (1862) and by a constellation of other distinguished Victorian radicals and freethinkers including, to name only a few, the psychologist Alexander Bain, the mathematician W. K. Clifford, the statistician Karl Pearson, the economist W. S. Jevons, and the theorist of physics J. B. Stallo. These writers set forth the doctrine of what Bain called as early as 1855 "the law of RELATIVITY" (*Senses* 8) and, later, the "principle of Universal Relativity" (*Logic* 1: 255) as the foundation of a newly rigorous scientific rationality, one emancipated from the reign of "metaphysical" absolutes unable to give logically coherent accounts of themselves. Restoring this movement to view is indispensable to a fully articulated understanding of modernist, and thus post-modernist, intellectual culture; and restoring Virginia Woolf's great novel *Mrs. Dalloway* (1925) to its connection with the philosophical tradition of relativity is necessary—so I argue in this essay—to understanding it in its full historical matrix.

There may be little need at this late date to challenge once again, as many Woolf scholars now have, Lukács's implausible idea of her as a writer of hermetically self-enclosed "subjective experience" and as an instance of the modernist "negation of history" (51, 21); but her important link to the nineteenth-century relativity movement and, in particular, its bearing upon her literary experimentalism, have yet to be brought to light.[2]

From the start, this movement of radical intellectual reconstruction was a moral and political movement as well. In attributing the rise of relativity thinking to "the influence of the sciences of observation," Pater makes the point clearly, rebutting in advance the thesis, widely asserted subsequently, that scientific relativity and "moral relativism" were separate and independent things.[3] As a function of the development of the antiabsolutistic premise, he says, contemporary thinkers have begun "a new analysis of the relations of . . . good and evil," and "[h]ard and abstract moralities are yielding to a more exact estimate of the subtlety and complexity of our life" (*Appreciations* 66, 67). When Edward Westermarck in *The Origin and Development of the Moral Ideas* (1906-08) and in *Ethical Relativity* (1932) dismantles systematically "[t]he supposed objectivity of moral judgments" in order to vindicate a sweeping theory of "ethical subjectivism and relativity" (*Ethical* 3, xviii), he builds in fact on a long-established if always volatile and perplexed tradition of the radical Victorian intelligentsia. "There is no absolute code of morality, no absolute philosophy nor absolute religion," declares Karl Pearson in 1887, for example (428). Westermarck gives this tradition his own sharp polemical twist by maintaining that moral systems even at advanced levels of civilization are rooted in a primitive basis of resentment, retribution, and "the instinctive desire to inflict counter-pain . . . that gives to moral indignation its most important characteristic," and by protesting against the persecution in Christian society of such harmless taboo behaviors as homosexuality (*Ethical* 85).[4] So, too, when Woolf herself, in a 1932 essay, identifies Laurence Sterne's innovations in relativistic fictional technique with the principle that "there is . . . no universal scale of values" (*Collected* 1: 97), she is highlighting not only the radical character of her own novelistic enterprise—her idea of fiction as an instrument for revising the fundamental moral behavior of her society (including the anathematizing of homosexuality)—but also the derivation of her radical outlook from that of the Victorian age that so often, in the defining polemical gesture of modernism, she disavows.[5]

The critique of "hard and abstract moralities" takes its political form in Victorian relativity discourse as a credo of resistance to what these writers regarded as the acute contemporary menace of authoritarianism and dogmatic absolutism. This theme is prominent, for example, in the work of George Grote, radical Benthamite politician, eminent historian of Greece, and militant spokesman for the relativity movement. Grote never tires of exhorting his readers to beware the moment when "the dogmatist enacts his canon of belief as imperative, peremptory, binding upon all" (*Plato* 3: 153), for this, he says, is the fatal moment when persuasion and rationality are abolished and "you leave open no other ascendancy over men's minds, except the crushing engine of extraneous coercion with assumed infallibility" (*History* 7: 41-42n). Rejecting the almost universal vilification of Protagoras the Sophist, the original formulator of relativity, by nineteenth-century philosophical commentators, Grote exalts him for proclaiming what he declares to be the one genuine creed of human liberty: "the negation of the absolute, and the affirmation of universal relativity in all conceptions, judgments, and predications" (*Plato* 3: 127). By way of contrast, Grote stresses the image of Plato as he appears in his late treatise the *Laws*, a promoter of a totalitarian dictatorship devoted to the brutal repression of all deviations from official thinking (*Plato* 3: 148). According to Grote, some such political system is implied necessarily by any invocation of that purely ideological and anti-scientific category, to the demolition of which Protagoras devoted his intellectual life, "Truth Absolute" (*Plato* 3:138).

As for Pater, he raises the prospect of dictatorship and coercion only in a far less polemical—though ultimately equally provocative and scandalous—form. "Beauty, like all other qualities presented to human experience, is relative," he says in the opening paragraph of the preface to *The Renaissance* (1873), defining the principle from which his aesthetic theory flows. He concludes that all attempts "to find some universal formula" for defining beauty are futile—that the question of "what beauty is in itself, or . . . its exact relation to truth" is a "metaphysical" one and thus "as unprofitable as metaphysical questions elsewhere" (xix, xx). In the Paterian aesthetic field, therefore, there are no privileged reference frames and no principles of dogmatism or sectarian exclusion: to one who has embraced the new way of thinking, "all periods, types, schools of taste, are in themselves equal" (xxi).[6] The vocation of the critic whose basic postulate is that "beauty . . . is relative" is thus not to strive to determine the inherent or absolute properties of art objects, for no such properties exist, but to cultivate as keen, as generous, and as impartial a sensitivity as possible to all manifestations of that thing indefinable "in itself," beauty. No attitude is more alien to this one than the idea of criticism as an agency for the purification of taste or for the enforcing of fixed codes of values. Predictably, the Paterian doctrine of impartiality and cultivated pleasure seemed to guardians of orthodoxy to be a form of immoralism and an incitement to perversion (specifically pederasty) and provoked the same calls for the violent repression of deviancy in the name of social hygiene that relativity never has failed to provoke since the exiling of Protagoras and the burning of his works, including his famous lost treatise *On Truth*, by the Athenian police. Hence the criticism deployed, for example, by Leslie Stephen, Woolf's father, in an essay condemning the relativistic aestheticism of Pater himself (though without mentioning him by name). When an author proposes "sentiments which imply moral disease," says Stephen, then "the critic should step in and administer the lash with the full strength of his arm. The harder he hits and the deeper he cuts the better for the world" (94, 92).

In marked contrast to this imagery of the sadistic official violence that always is implicit, according to partisans of relativity, in absolutist theories, being in fact the result that the theories exist to produce, Pater promotes an idea of criticism as a mode of analysis in which "the instinctive desire to inflict counter-pain . . . that gives to moral indignation its most important characteristic" is entirely in abeyance. This is no incidental aspect of his thinking, which appears on the Victorian cultural scene specifically as a challenge to the ascendancy of a puritanical mentality in which moral indignation and the love of inflicting pain ("the justice that desires to hurt culprits as much as they deserve to be hurt," as George Eliot puts it in *The Mill on the Floss* [48]) were widely diagnosed as paramount. For a critic under Pater's dispensation, "the negation of the absolute" implies the ideal of riskily experimental, nondogmatic, ever-mobile freethought articulated by the line of culturally dissident writers that runs from J. S. Mill and Clifford to their latter-day disciple, the late Paul Feyerabend. "What we have to do," says Pater, "is to be for ever curiously testing new opinions and courting new impressions, never acquiescing in a facile orthodoxy" (*Renaissance* 189).[7] Such, in part, is the moral theory, pledged to the potentially severe perturbation of the status quo and keyed to a mission of resistance to the ideology of purificatory violence, that is given extended fictional form in *Mrs. Dalloway*. To trace the logic of its exposition in Woolf's text is to discover there a line of concerted philosophical intention that most commentary on the novel heretofore—Lukács's first and foremost—would not prepare us to find.

* * *

Not to seek to reduce this richly multifarious book to a diagram, but merely to make its affiliation with Victorian relativity literature stand out as clearly as possible, we may imagine it as envisioning two opposed zones of experience: on the one hand, that of coercion and violence; on the other, that of relativity.

It would be hard to name many novels—Bram Stoker's *Dracula* (1897) might be one—in which imagery of physical violence is more startling, more expressive of the appalling, intolerable character of violence, than in *Mrs. Dalloway*. That this is so is testimony not so much to the absolute content of violence in this work as to the principle that fictional effects are as subject to Bain's "law of RELATIVITY" as are "all other qualities presented to human experience." The violence in Woolf's novel takes on its peculiar intensity of effect, that is, by appearing as the antithesis and the nullification of a fictional scene defined by a radically different system of imagery—imagery, for example, of partygiving (of exquisite domestic refinements, of floral displays and polished silver, of ceremonious social intimacy) and of the delightfully animated London scene out of doors. Both of these settings radiate in *Mrs. Dalloway* an atmospherics of paradisal beauty and happiness probably without an equivalent in any other serious novel except for the first half of *Du côté de chez Swann*. "Never had he seen London look so enchanting," thinks Peter Walsh, sounding the distinctive note of feeling in this novel: "—the softness of the distances; the richness; the greenness; the civilisation" (*Dalloway* 107). The juxtaposition of this system of effects and its opposite, the ugly horror of violence, forms in effect the central trope of the novel. Clarissa Dalloway herself feels it keenly at the moment when the news of Septimus Smith's death, with all its imagery of a shattered, "horribly mangled" (227) human body, erupts with obscene effect in the midst of the rarefied setting of her party (279-80).

Smith's suicide by impaling himself on the spikes of Mrs. Filmer's area railings (226) forms the most graphic epiphany of violence in the novel, but it signifies from a wider perspective just one minor aftershock of the vast system of organized violence represented by the Great War of 1914-18. Though the shooting stopped five years previously, war still overshadows the scene.

For it was the middle of June. The War was over, except for some one like Mrs. Foxcroft at the Embassy last night eating her heart out because that nice boy was killed and now the old Manor House must go to a cousin; or Lady Bexborough who opened a bazaar, they said, with the telegram in her hand, John, her favourite, killed; but it was over; thank Heaven— over. (5)

In other words, the carnage of the world war is not over at all, but renews itself daily, all these years later, in the private lives of innumerable survivors. Septimus Smith's anguished hallucinations of his dead army comrade Evans express this theme in its most drastic form and illustrate the prevalence throughout the novel of an unstable psychic state marked by uncontrollable mood swings between euphoria and sudden piercing sensations of grief, dread, and desolation. This is the symptomology, we come to realize, of a sort of all-pervading and seemingly indelible shell shock that affects everyone in deeply traumatized postwar society, ex-combatants and civilians alike. In its searching diagnosis of this syndrome, *Mrs. Dalloway* rehearses a fantasy of impending European cataclysm, of what Spencer called prophetically "a return to barbaric principles of government" (*Study* 244), that haunts the literature of the Victorian relativity tradition and forms, in fact, one of its most insistent motifs. W. K. Clifford, for example, warns repeatedly of a revival of religious powers claiming "to declare with infallible authority what is right and what is wrong," a development that would raise the prospect of a "civilisation perverted to the service of evil"; in such a case, he declares, "the wreck of civilised Europe would be darker than the darkest of past ages" (2: 224, 234, 256). This motif appears in *Mrs. Dalloway* not in the form of a dire premonition but in that of a compulsive, lacerating memory. The two versions, the prophetic and the recollective, are essentially equivalent, not only imagistically but because the traumatic memory that haunts the minds of Woolf's characters does constitute a kind of prophecy after all; or rather, it carries a dreadful awareness that the prophecy has perhaps not ceased to be operative just because it has already come true. It conveys a warning too appalling to be stated outright, and all too prescient, that the demon of military violence may not have been exorcised for good, as everyone longs to believe, but may only be awaiting the chance to break out from a temporary phase of latency into terrible action once again.[8]

Never are we far in *Mrs. Dalloway* from shocking eruptions of imagery of violence that make the novel's celebration of delightfully festive social intercourse seem fragile and precarious, if not delusional. Clarissa thus reflects briefly amid her party preparations on the genocidal violence inflicted on the Albanians—or was it the Armenians?—"[h]unted out of existence, maimed, frozen, the victims of cruelty and injustice" (182); Peter Walsh thinks in the same way of "the rascals who get hanged for battering the brains of a girl out in a train" (263). Vindictive savagery like this may seem altogether alien to the genteel social environment in which the novel is mainly set, but it is not. Clarissa herself suffers from her own rasping hatred of Miss Kilman, which seems to her like a "brutal monster" in her own heart (17); and Miss Kilman, seething with resentment and religious righteousness, reciprocates, savoring the imaginary pleasure of scourging Clarissa in much the same sadistic terms in which Leslie Stephen imagined inflicting punishment on Walter Pater: "there rose in her an overmastering desire to overcome her; to unmask her. . . . If only she could make her weep; could ruin her; humiliate her; bring her to her knees crying, You are right!" (189). This is "the instinctive desire to inflict counter-pain" in shocking, undiluted form.

The syncretic structure of Woolf's novel intimates as one of its most pressing suggestions that violence in its many forms, from the geopolitical to the private and the intimately personal, is always the same thing, always springs from the same fundamental psychosocial structure. This submerged train of thought in *Mrs. Dalloway* is later theorized at length in *Three Guineas* (1938), in which Woolf meditates particularly on the link between military violence and the violence pervasively inflicted, as she claims, upon the female sex in English society. Both are defined by her as expressions of a primitive "desire to impose authority" (*Three* 155n) that allegedly is fundamental to male psychology in Western society. This propensity is incarnated for Woolf in the archetypal figure of the Dictator, whose fictionalized and real avatars as cited by her include Sophocles's Creon, Hitler, and Mussolini, but who is no less distinctly embodied, she says, in a host of subsidiary tyrants like the Rev. Patrick Brontë or Mr. Barrett, the "monster of Wimpole Street" (*Three* 132). This menacing figure "is called in German and Italian Führer or Duce; in our own language Tyrant or Dictator" (142); he personifies in his various guises the total concentration of human energy upon "the repulsive task of coercion and dominion" (185n) and upon replacing all possibilities of variety, multiplicity, and creative improvisation in human life with rigid uniformity. In all this exposition, Woolf again makes one think of Bram Stoker's fable of the clandestine invasion of England by a monstrous tyrant who boasts of his ancestral descent from the dictator Attila, who is venerated as "dear Master" by his followers, and who seemingly is driven by no other motives than a pure mania to subjugate others, and women particularly, to his all-powerful will (60, 137). But the clearest foreshadowings of Woolf's polemics against dictatorship are found, as we have seen, in nineteenth-century relativity literature, with its insistent warnings about the coming to power of "the dogmatist [who] enacts his canon of belief as imperative, peremptory, binding upon all" (Grote, *Plato* 3:153).

It may or may not be reckoned a shortcoming of Woolf's account of this type in *Three Guineas* that it is, like Stoker's and Grote's, relentlessly simplistic, positing as it does a monolithic will to domination, or that it contradicts the Foucauldian model according to which the ancien regime of brutally vindictive state power exercised directly on human bodies has been eclipsed by a postcarceral regime of more sophisticated, more pervading and diffusive institutions of supervision and control (institutions that Woolf by no means discounts and, in fact, investigates intensively). This model is to some extent danger-ously naive, she would presumably insist. What it leaves out, treats as obsolete, is precisely the pathological dynamic of *violence*. The insti-tution that in fact overshadows modern society in the aftermath of the collapse of the divine right of autocracy is that of the megalomaniacal Plato-like dictator, she argues, and dictators by their nature are insatia-bly prone to violence. To some degree (so her work, like Hannah Arendt's, lets us speculate), the prospect of a totally docile, indoctri-nated, disciplined populace actually runs counter to the craving of dictatorship to inflict murderous reprisals on real or make-believe enemies.[9]

Mrs. Dalloway's unforgettable incarnation of the Dictator is the Harley Street psychiatrist Sir William Bradshaw, "a great doctor yet to [Clarissa] obscurely evil, without sex or lust, extremely polite to women, but capable of some indescribable outrage—forcing your soul, that was it" (*Dalloway* 281). Sir William figures in literary his-tory as one of the last and scariest exemplars of the lineage of vampire-like soul-destroyers, "those spectres who stand astride us and suck up half our life-blood, dominators and tyrants" (*Dalloway* 16-17), who emerge from Victorian fiction in a host of sinister forms—Mr. Murdstone, St. John Rivers, Mr. Casaubon, Angel Clare, Dracula—as something like the archetypal modern personality. (Of course, this per-sonality is intimately interlocked at every turn with its necessary com-plement, that of the victim, such as Lady Bradshaw, who willingly ac-quiesces in the structure of domination, finding in it a perverse kind of self-aggrandizement.) Sir William worships two great deities: Propor-tion (the principle of normalcy and of the strict repression of emotion and imagination) and, especially, Conversion (the principle of evan-gelical religiosity). His religion professes altruistic ideals but is, in fact, like that of his immediate literary ancestor, Count Dracula, a cult of sheer domination. "Conversion," which "feasts on the wills of the weakly," says Woolf's narrator, "offers help, but desires power." She is active in building churches and hospitals, "[b]ut conversion, fastidious

Goddess, loves blood better than brick, and feasts most subtly on the human will" (*Dalloway* 151-52).

With this concentrated imagery of epicurean cannibalistic or vampiric perversion, Woolf seems to allude back beyond Bram Stoker to the work that figures (as I do not have space here to demonstrate) as something like the ur-text of Victorian relativity thinking, Feuerbach's *Essence of Christianity* (1841). "There lurks in the background of [Christian] love," Feuerbach said, "an unloving monster, a diabolical being, whose personality, separable and actually separated from love, delights in the blood of heretics and unbelievers,—the phantom of religious fanaticism" (52-53). Woolf also seems to evoke another nineteenth-century Feuerbachian refraction, Nietzsche's morbidly diseased ascetic priest, whose "awful historic mission" it is to exercise "*lordship over sufferers*" and who must be "impregnable . . . in his will for power, so as to acquire the trust and the awe of the weak so that he can be their hold, bulwark, prop, compulsion, overseer, tyrant, god." He comes in this role, says Nietzsche, "to represent practically a new type of the beast of prey," one who is "venerable, wise, cold, full of treacherous superiority" (162-63). Stoker's, Feuerbach's, and Nietzsche's tyrannical monster, the incubus of nineteenth-century nightmares, takes on a recognizable contemporary image in the form of the great medical researcher Doctor Benjulia in Wilkie Collins's 1882 novel *Heart and Science*. Benjulia is a specialist, like Sir William Bradshaw, in "brain disease"; his "hideous secret" is that he runs a vivisection laboratory and confesses in an unguarded moment that his greatest longing is to put not just animals but living human beings on his "torture table" for experimental purposes. "A scrupulously polite man," says Collins's narrator, in language that Woolf echoes closely, "he was always cold in his politeness" (Collins 183, 247, 190, 99). Undoubtedly Woolf's portrait of Sir William, the quintessential Dictator, derives in some degree from her own unhappy experiences with psychiatrists, as commentators have said;[10] first and foremost, however, he is a deeply characteristic emanation of the nineteenth-century fictional and philosophical imagination. In a 1910 preface, James Frazer comments implicitly on this native mythographic tradition in declaring, in a definitive formula, that his central subject in *The Golden Bough* is "men who have masqueraded as gods" (*Magic* 1: ix). Such men are driven to excesses of sadism, we may intuit, by the maddening awareness that their claim to divinity is only a masquerade after all. They inflict torture on the helpless to keep at bay the knowledge of their own common humanity: such is the insight that this complex of uncannily prophetic fictional imagery gives us into multiplying twentieth-century incarnations of the "diabolical being," from Adolf Hitler and the ultimate avatar of the medical monsters of literature, Josef Mengele, to Jim Jones, the genocidal psychiatrist Radovan Karadzic, and others of their type.

In her fixation on the terrifying dangers of tyranny and coercion, Woolf distinctly aligns herself, in any case, with the Victorian avant-garde tradition of Feuerbach, Spencer, Clifford, Grote, Pater, and others: modernistic and experimental as her fiction may be from a technical point of view, in this thematic respect it is old-fashioned. Like the writers of the nineteenth-century tradition, too, she explicitly identifies the prospect of a restoration of human freedom and of humane social life with the radical transformative power of the principle of relativity—the principle, in the Protagorean phrase, that "nothing is one thing just by itself" (Plato 17), that "Truth Absolute" is a chimera, and that all frames of reference are equally valid.

At least part of this philosophical argument is spelled out, again, in the indispensable companion text for *Mrs. Dalloway, Three Guineas*. Woolf's guiding axiom, as she here states repeatedly (*Three* 5, 18, 23), is the one that is enunciated by Feuerbach (4-5) and then by one writer after another in Victorian relativity literature: the axiom that differently positioned observers will perceive and understand the world differently. If only her contemporaries could be led to grasp fully this one supreme principle, Woolf's insistent stress on it implies, a revolutionary change would follow.

It seems plain that we think differently according as we are born differently; there is a Grenfell point of view; a Knebworth point of view; a Wilfred Owen point of view; a Lord Chief Justice's point of view and the point of view of an educated man's daughter. All differ. But is there no absolute point of view? Can we not find somewhere written up in letters of fire or gold "This is right. This wrong"?[11]—a moral judgment which we must all, whatever our differences, accept? (9-10)

But the quest for the "absolute point of view" is futile and misguided, she concludes. She illustrates the point by noting that contemporary Anglican bishops, the official moral custodians of English society, are "at loggerheads" among themselves about so pressing and definite an issue in 1938 as that of the acceptability of pacifism. "It is distressing, baffling, confusing, but the fact must be faced," she concludes, in terms that again echo the long rhetorical tradition of Victorian freethought; "there is no certainty in heaven above or on earth below" (*Three* 10).

The doctrine of the inescapability of differing points of view and thus of the decisive abandonment of the ideal of "certainty"—that is, of discovering true interpretations of things to which everyone must subscribe—in all matters of serious concern is not a formula of pessimism or passivity for Virginia Woolf; it does not mean, as it is often misread to mean, that one is helpless to understand the world or to find meaningful grounds for moral agency. On the contrary, it is the formula of emancipation from the ideology that sustains dominators like Sir William Bradshaw. It is the same militant formula that underlies, for example, the pragmatist philosopher and arch-relativist F. C. S. Schiller's extended 1912 critique of syllogistic logic as "a machine for yielding categorical certainty." Schiller declares that any rigorously relativistic science will treat its analytical operations "with the utmost freedom, and will recognize no finality about them," for wherever antirelativistic finality and certainty prevail, he says, repression by the constituted authorities is sure to follow (224, 55). A closely similar argument pervades *Three Guineas*, where Woolf declares that embracing a relativistic moral theory—one void of privileged reference frames and therefore of certainty and finality—offers the best possible warrant "to experiment freely in altering current values" (117). Specifically, such a theory forms the very precondition of an activist program that one fulfills, as she says, not shying away from the statement of what may almost seem a naive or sentimental political creed, "by protecting the rights of the individual; by opposing dictatorship; by ensuring the democratic ideals of equal opportunity for all" (*Three* 100).

Such is the line of argument that is played out very fully in *Mrs. Dalloway*, where it is expressed, however, not for the most part in the form of philosophical dicta and logical demonstrations but figuratively, in a constellation of metaphor and allegory. Logical arguments may in fact be of limited efficacy in arousing resistance to the idolatry of certainty and of its accompanying apparatuses of coercive violence, the novel suggests, though it does so without reference to Schiller's claim that logic by its very nature is inscribed with the ethic of dictatorship. Everyone who comes near him may find Sir William Bradshaw repellent and threatening, but the cult of dogmatic science and dogmatic moral authority that he embodies is so revered that even Clarissa, who instinctively loathes him, has no choice but to receive him as an honored guest at her party—an anomaly expressing in vivid form the irresistible and irrational character of ideological compulsion. No theoretical critique will overthrow this system; what is needed is a more fundamental reeducation of cultural imagination and the moral sensibilities. Such is the premise on which Woolf seems to base the freely experimental method of this great novel, which dismantles much of the structure of traditional prose fiction as part of a radical strategy for "altering current values" and forming a new contemporary mentality, one wholly alien, above all, to the mentality of dictatorship.

Hence Woolf's disestablishment, in the name of a symbolic imagery of "utmost freedom," of the chief institution of narrative in the tradition of realistic fiction to which *Mrs. Dalloway* (which has distinct thematic similarities to *Middlemarch*, say) belongs: the institution of the single controlling point of view. Rather than vesting the storytelling function in one central consciousness, she distributes it among a fluid consortium of eighteen or so major and minor characters who take turns reciting the tale—except that it is barely a tale (consisting as it mainly does of events that would seem unworthy of narration by the standards of conventional fiction) and that it never occurs to these narrators to assert the formal prerogatives and the declarative voice of a storyteller; they merely meditate inwardly on their experiences and immediate surroundings in a way that we are somehow, inexplicably, enabled to overhear. The most striking stylistic effect of the novel by far is thus the constant fluctuation of its point of view. The central story line of the opening episode is that of Clarissa's outing on foot to buy flowers for her party, for example, but this line is punctuated by a series of narratorial shifts. For one thing, it diverges persistently into Clarissa's freely meandering stream of consciousness, a medley of spontaneous memories and reflections triggered by sometimes labyrinthine associations with stimuli such as the squeak of a door hinge (*Dalloway* 3). Further, Clarissa's point of view alternates contrapuntally with those of a random-seeming series of onlookers and passersby: people outside the shop gazing at a mysterious motor-car idling portentously in Bond Street (19); Septimus Smith and his wife Lucrezia (20-21); spectators in the bow-windowed precincts of Brooks's overlooking the street (26); Moll Pratt, a sidewalk flower-vendor (27)—and so on.[12]

Woolf constructs this fluid fictional universe in order to investigate (among other things) the ideological structures implicit in conventional novelistic form and particularly in that unchallengeable source of knowledge known as the omniscient narrator or the "implied author." This numinous figure presides over a conventional novel as its supreme agency, possessing sole authority to dictate the interpretation of the events in question and, in Clifford's phrase, "to declare with infallible authority what is right and what is wrong." Just as Paul de Man says, giving the point his own polemical import, "the fallacy of a finite and single interpretation derives . . . from the postulate of a privileged observer" (11). Given the constitutional primacy of the privileged observer (that metaphysical wraith who in the field of physics is abruptly dissolved in 1905 in the founding act of Einsteinian special relativity) in orthodox fictional narrative and in the criticism it fosters, one might hazard a definition of this mode of fiction as precisely *that form of narrative that is based in principle on the subjection of the reader to the sovereign authority of the narrator. Mrs. Dalloway* makes this definition suddenly legible by seeming to constitute a revisionary response to it.

In the voluminous critical literature devoted to this novel, one or two scholars have called attention to the effect just mentioned, though without developing the point very fully. "In *Mrs. Dalloway*," as Patricia Matson thus says, "no one point of view dominates"; Woolf in this way "mocks the conventional authority of the omniscient narrator" (171, 173).[13] In echoing and amplifying this observation, I seek to make a number of interconnected points, each arising from the close historical nexus that I have sought to draw between the novel and the Victorian relativity tradition that it strives to incorporate.

The first emphasizes the drastic character of Woolf's experimentation and the resistance that any interpretation of the novel—this one or any other—fully consonant with relativity theory is bound to encounter. Such resistance is implicit, for instance, in a work itself deeply shaped by the relativity tradition, M. M. Bakhtin's *The Dialogic Imagination*. "The prerequisite for authentic novelistic prose," he claims (264), almost as though he had *Mrs. Dalloway* in mind, is that centrifugal, multiply stratified condition of language called "heteroglossia." The primordial function and the genius of the novel as a genre is to give a full registration of a symphonically rich multiplicity of competing voices or points of view, of "heteroglot, multi-voiced, multi-styled and often multi-languaged elements" (265). Bakhtin accordingly proposes a definition of the genre that seems contradictory to the authority-centered one I have ventured above but is so only in appearance. "The novel can be defined as a diversity of social speech types (sometimes even diversity of languages) and a diversity of individual voices," he states, but then adds the crucial qualifier, "artistically organized" (262). This function of artistic organization poses a theoretical difficulty, for it signifies in fact nothing other than *a subduing and disciplining* of heteroglossic impulses. The multiple and dissident voices that Bakhtin means to affirm are finally compressed in this model within a single linguistic structure. Novelistic heteroglossia is in the last analysis inevitably subject, Bakhtin says, to "the style of the whole" and inevitably "participates in the process whereby the unified meaning of the whole is structured and revealed." This "combining of languages and styles into a higher unity" is precisely what novelistic form is designed to do (262, 263). No provision is finally made in Bakhtin's theory for refractory, dissident, unmanageable elements that might strive to resist being subsumed into the "unified meaning of the whole," as Septimus Smith, for instance, strives desperately to resist being subsumed into the interpretive patterns dictated by Sir William Bradshaw.

The ideological secret of all fiction set under the sign of "higher unity," so *Mrs. Dalloway* seems designed to intimate, is that it gives idealized symbolic form to the great principle that Herbert Spencer, one of the first analysts and decriers of its dominant role in modern society, called "centralized administration and . . . compulsory regulation" (*Principles of Sociology* 1: 570). Imaginative literature produced under this regime trains the reader at least subliminally in unquestioning subservience to the voice of authority, through which some definite body of meaning makes itself known. The training process is vested much more distinctly, obviously enough, in the institution of literary criticism, based as it is on that "desire to account for the totality of a given work" by constructing "a total reading" of it that J. Hillis Miller, for example, holds up in his discussion of *Mrs. Dalloway* as the critical ideal (17, 18). It is just this pedagogical apparatus and all its sustaining rhetoric of higher unities and total readings that Woolf attempts to overthrow in *Mrs. Dalloway*. This she does, as the present essay argues, in obedience to her insight that every assertion of an "absolute point of view" has its affiliation with the great network of violence. The chief textual sign of the overthrow is precisely the relativity effect: a multiplication of independent points of view and a reestablishment of something like heteroglossia. Similarly, the effect of rational coherence or "artistic unity" that in conventional narrative is synonymous with the narrator's steady intentionality is disrupted in this book by an outbreak of haphazard, prankish, irrational-seeming fictive phenomena—Moll Pratt's sudden appearance in the role of privileged observer, for example—that no narrator conscious of his important administrative and regulatory functions would ever tolerate and that finally has a deeply troubling effect on the resemblance of this novel to a canonical precursor text such as *Middlemarch*.[14]

In arguing for an uncompromisingly relativistic reading of *Mrs. Dalloway*, one needs again to distinguish such a reading from any species of philosophical pessimism and thus from the provocative accounts of the book given by Patricia Matson and Pamela Caughie. In seeking to depict a "subversive" (Matson 163) antiauthoritarian Woolf, these scholars have tended to identify her proleptically with a certain strain of nihilistic postmodernism. In *Mrs. Dalloway*, says Matson, "meaning cannot be pinpointed with any certainty"; Woolf disavows "consistency" and "clarity," fills her tale with "incoherencies" and by such means "inserts a degree of confusion (of nonsense) into the text" (170, 171). "The text continually proposes that nothing can be pinpointed with any certainty" (Matson 165). "Equivocation . . . is for Woolf a stance against . . . certainty, a guard against the desire to prevail" (Caughie 8). These comments raise a tricky set of issues for relativity theorists in general and for Woolf in particular. There is no doubt of the essential role played by nihilistic language in the relativity movement surveyed in the first part of this essay. We have seen that Karl Pearson, for instance, takes relativity to be equivalent to the doctrine that "there is no absolute code of morality, no absolute philosophy nor absolute religion," and that Woolf laments in *Three Guineas* the "distressing, baffling, confusing" fact that "there is no certainty."

As one of its cardinal artistic effects, therefore, her novel does indeed baffle all attempts to derive "certain"—in the prejudicial sense of "imperative, peremptory, binding upon all"—interpretations from it. For instance, the reader has no way of knowing in an "absolute" sense whether Clarissa's party is as a matter of fact as wonderfully successful as she thinks. Evidently she is the only observer to perceive its epiphanic beauty, as Septimus Smith is the only one, as far as we know, to hear the sparrows in Regent's Park rapturously singing "there is no death" in Greek (36). Is Clarissa's perception of the splendor of her party anything more than a kind of hallucination of her own, a sign of the "intoxication of the moment" (265)? The truth is that there is no such thing as absolute reality in the radically relativistic world of this novel, where "no absolute point of view" can possibly be set up to measure and evaluate the shifting pattern of observers' differing perceptions. It would be alien to Woolf's conception for a reader to ask whether the party "really" possesses the magical beauty that it (momentarily) seems to possess from its hostess's point of view. Pater's dictum is precisely germane to the stern epistemological discipline enforced throughout *Mrs. Dalloway*: "what beauty is in itself, or . . . its exact relation to truth" is a "metaphysical" question that is "as unprofitable as metaphysical questions elsewhere." Similar caveats apply to all—or nearly all—the broader interpretive issues raised in this novel. Is Clarissa a figure of redemptive spirituality and the moral touchstone of the novel that bears her name or, as various observers in the novel assert, "'spoilt'" and "worldly," "simply a snob" (182, 115, 183)? Does she stand for the affirmation of "life," as Avrom Fleishman and other scholarly interpreters categorically assert, or for the affirmation of death, as J. Hillis Miller asserts no less categorically?[15] Is Peter Walsh a second-rater and a "warped personality" (Fleishman 77) or, as he seems to his fellow hotel guests who overhear the magnificent manner with which he orders his Bartlett pears (*Dalloway* 242-43), a noble "champion," a model of manliness and integrity? The opening tableaux in *Mrs. Dalloway* of Londoners puzzling over the decipherment of the skywriter's ambiguous message and over the identity of the great personage of uncertain sex glimpsed (perhaps) in the motorcar in Bond Street (19-32) clearly are to be taken as, among other things, cautionary parables of the interpretive reading of *Mrs. Dalloway* itself, with its relativistic collage of discrepant points of view that seem designed with such a palpable intent to frustrate the interpretive will to power.[16]

Nothing was more vital to relativity theorists of the nineteenth century, however, than the need to deny that the rejection of categorical or "absolute" knowledge implied a disavowal of knowledge itself. They made precisely the opposite claim, that it was the mirage of non-relativistic knowledge that plunged mental life inevitably into mystification and muddle, at the same time as it lent itself to a syndrome of moral and political perversions. They took as their creed (and Woolf inscribed in her novel) not a nihilistic praise of ambiguity and "equivocation," but what could be called Poincaré's Principle, though the great scientist Henri Poincaré, the co-discoverer of special relativity, was not the first to state it: the principle that there is not a single true explanatory theory of any given set of facts, but that innumerable theories will always prove to correspond to it (Poincaré 168, 222). It is not that things cannot be known, not that we are helpless observers of the indeterminacy of meaning and hostage to "confusion" and the want of "clarity," but, rather, that things may always be known in various competing ways among which it will not ultimately be possible to decide on empirical grounds. This postulate of the irreducibility of different perspectives and the equal legitimacy of different reference frames will seem like "equivocation" or "uncertainty" only to one who begins with the assumption that there must exist a single true interpretation of things, if only we could discover it. Relativity literature insists on abandoning this assumption as the prerequisite of any sound and unmystified analytical method.

The argument underpinning Woolf's novel, then, is that it is possible to inhabit a thoroughly relativized world without giving up the ideal of genuine knowledge—or rather, that to move into such a world constitutes in fact a tremendous *expansion* of the possibility of knowledge, and that not to do so is to remain in a state of permanently impaired understanding. Definitive value judgments of characters and their actions may scarcely be attainable in *Mrs. Dalloway*, but nothing could be clearer than that this impossibility does not entail any paralysis of moral insight. Moral problems such as the question of Clarissa's alleged superficiality are not rendered futile or meaningless by the relativistic form of Woolf's novel; on the contrary, they are at the foreground at every moment and are investigated with the greatest possible acuity—all under the aegis of the principle that in the absence of an ultimate and privileged authority, no final, categorical answers to them can possibly be forthcoming. Different observers will inescapably come to differing conclusions; there is no such thing as "a moral judgment which we must all, whatever our differences, accept" (*Three* 10). This is not confusion but rigorous clarity, precisely the mode of rationality according to which "hard and abstract moralities" may be made to yield, as Pater said, "to a more exact estimate of the subtlety and complexity of our life." To defend the mode based on the ideology of total readings, on the other hand, is to render thought hostage to "the repulsive task of coercion and dominion" and finally, Woolf suggests, to participate however unwittingly in the maintenance of "the whole iniquity of dictatorship" (*Three* 103) in human society. It is to reinforce the authority of the "judges," who, as Septimus Smith phrases it, "saw nothing clear, yet ruled, yet inflicted" (*Dalloway* 225). This is Woolf's insistent and of course almost unacceptably tendentious intimation to the critical reader of *Mrs. Dalloway*.

In constructing her novel according to "the negation of the absolute," Woolf does of course proclaim one absolute: the rejection of absolutism itself. In a world where all nonrelativistic truth has been abolished, the relativity principle itself is proclaimed as a universal verity. This is one version of the paradox that inhabits every species of relativity and that antirelativists from Plato onward have declared to constitute a fatal logical self-refutation. (If all propositions are relative, how can one frame such a proposition to begin with?) Woolf, unwilling to finesse any problem, seems to go out of her way to acknowledge this one by causing the abolished omniscient narrator suddenly to reappear in her text for the specific purpose of analyzing and denouncing Sir William's perverted cult of Proportion and Conversion, according to which no relativistic indeterminacy is allowed (*Dalloway* 149-54). The jarring effect produced in the novel at this moment is Woolf's signal of the logical difficulty implicit in any program of rigorously relativistic thinking (and implicit, for example, in the present essay, which invokes the emancipatory motive of relativity while insisting on one privileged reading of a novel that is open, as Poincaré's Principle decrees, to any number of other legitimate readings). Those in sympathy with Woolf's mode of thinking will conclude with her that it is precisely the overshadowing problem of violence in human life that requires us to free ourselves from making a supreme idol of logical coherence. *Mrs. Dalloway* implies that a certain quotient of incoherence is simply the toll to be paid for deliverance from "the repulsive task of coercion and dominion" and that the dream of a philosophical outlook cleansed of paradox is finally a sinister one fundamentally incompatible with the creation of a humane social world.

It may never be possible to expunge dictatorship altogether from any social construction (such as a literary text). If only because *Mrs. Dalloway* is intensively concerned with the theme of abusive intrusions on personal privacy, or because the Victorian relativity literature to which Woolf's imagination is so deeply attuned is itself preoccupied with the theme of "invasions of State power" (Spencer, *First* 6), a reader is compelled to wonder, for example, about the harmlessness of the invasive imaginary apparatus by which the secret thoughts of so many characters are discovered and laid open to public view and to wonder whether the system of organization figuratively represented by this model of narration may not be preyed upon after all by an indelible internal contradiction. Yct the overthrow of constituted narrative authority that is carried out in *Mrs. Dalloway* is not fatally compromised by such anxieties. Chiefly it yields a radical enfranchisement of individual characters to express their views of the world free of censorship or coercive "unification." Even characters widely deemed by their acquaintances to be mediocrities, like Clarissa Dalloway and Peter Walsh, even so unsympathetic a figure as Miss Kilman, even insignificant bystanders like Scrope Purvis, Moll Pratt, Maisie Johnson, Mrs. Dempster, and Ellie Henderson (*Dalloway* 4, 27, 37-41, 256-57)—all are allowed to manifest themselves and to participate freely in narrating a novel that seems designed as the symbolic equivalent of a tolerant, egalitarian community, one dedicated to "protecting the rights of the individual," "opposing dictatorship," and vindicating in the most straightforward terms possible—by letting everyone share in the telling—"the democratic ideals of equal opportunity for all." The ideal collectivity that Clarissa strives to create in her party is in this sense realized at least partially in the novel itself and is identical with its commitment to the principle of relativity.

What follows from the enactment of this policy of novelistic emancipation is an outpouring of "irrepressible, exquisite delight" (*Dalloway* 78). Living in a fictional world where the dictatorial narrator has been stripped of his powers and where freedom prevails seems to the characters themselves like a glorious, unprecedented adventure. "What a lark! What a plunge!" thinks Clarissa on the first page, as she sets forth on her errands. Moll Pratt has a delirious impulse to fling one of her precious bunches of roses into the street "out of sheer lightheartedness and contempt of poverty" (27), ostensibly to honor the Prince of Wales but in effect to express her glee at finding herself in a novel able to allow even the likes of her a moment of narratorial glory. The mood of exhilarated freedom is picked up vividly in the episodes of delightfully impulsive forays through London undertaken in turn by Clarissa, Peter, and Clarissa's daughter Elizabeth (3-42, 78-81, 205-11): *free movement* represents a primary symbolic motif of the novel, that is, as it does also in Woolf's handling of stream of consciousness and of narrative point of view. The euphoric mood that goes along with this sense of freedom is experienced repeatedly in the novel as a mystical revelation of "divine vitality" (9) and of joy and beauty in almost ineffably vivid forms. The urban scene as represented in traditional British fiction is transformed as a result. Compare, for example, Dickens's vision of "the roaring streets" of a prisonlike Victorian London, where "the noisy and the eager, and the arrogant and the forward and the vain, fretted, and chafed, and made their usual uproar," in the final sentence of *Little Dorrit* (1855-57), with Clarissa Dalloway's delighted sense of "the bellow and the uproar" that she adores in the same streets (5) or with her daughter Elizabeth's rapture at finding herself amid the hubbub of Fleet Street, which signifies to her, precisely, the presence of a utopian democratic community. "She liked the geniality, sisterhood, motherhood, brotherhood of this uproar. It seemed to her good. The noise was tremendous" (209). One thinks of newsreels of crowds of Berliners dancing in the streets to celebrate the collapse of the Wall in 1989. These rapturous revelations are always fragile and unstable in *Mrs. Dalloway*, but they are central to the strains of feeling that surge into the world of this novel in the wake of the liberation of fictional narrative from the model of despotic authorial control.

The antiauthoritarian principle that thus seems implicit in the whole form of the work is articulated cogently—though with an anguished sense of precariousness—by Clarissa. She inscribes at the top of her tablet of moral commandments the necessity of preserving inviolate "the rights of the individual," and her most profound and permanent moral intuition is that these rights can only be preserved by an uncompromising defense of personal autonomy against all invasions, even well-meaning ones. "[T]here is a dignity in people; a solitude; even between husband and wife a gulf; and that one must respect, thought

Clarissa . . . for one would not part with it oneself, or take it, against his will, from one's husband, without losing one's independence, one's self-respect—something, after all, priceless" (181). In a wonderful essay that seems almost like a commentary on *Mrs. Dalloway*, Hannah Arendt glorifies her hero Lessing as a champion of liberty who "not only wanted no one to coerce him, but . . . also wanted to coerce no one, either by force or by proofs" and whose only goal was to provoke people "'to think for themselves'" and to preserve at all costs their "freedom of movement" (*On Humanity* 9). Lessing regarded the use of logical arguments to compel anyone's assent to anything, she says, as an especially pernicious form of "the repulsive task of coercion and dominion." In obedience to this same radical moral imperative, Clarissa in her passionate love of independence and her hatred of every form of dictatorship instinctively recoils from all attempts to change others' minds. "Had she ever tried to convert any one herself? Did she not wish everybody merely to be themselves?" (191). For her, in opposition to the malign cultural principle incarnated in such figures as Doctor Benjulia, Count Dracula, and Sir William Bradshaw, what she calls "the privacy of the soul" is sacrosanct (192).

Yet she also dreads solitude and (in another manifestation of the foundational paradox of relativity thinking) venerates communication and combination—specifically, in her case, the activity of bringing separate individuals, by the exercise of an irresistible influence that she possesses, into unified collectivities, even if only for the duration of an evening's party. "It was an offering; to combine, to create," she thinks to herself, echoing Septimus Smith's intuition that "[c]ommunication is health; communication is happiness" (185, 141). This theory translates into an expressly moral proposition the general axiom of relativity: that *nothing is one thing just by itself* and that a thing cut off from communication with other things, as the early relativity theorist J. B. Stallo declared in 1881, refuting a famous thought experiment of C. G. Neumann's, would simply cease to exist (Stallo 212-15). Clarissa defies the threat of solitude and annihilation by giving her party, where she is overjoyed to hear again, as Elizabeth does in Fleet Street, the roaring sound of unstinting human interrelation: "Clarissa turned, with Sally's hand in hers, and saw her rooms full, heard the roar of voices, saw the candlesticks, the blowing curtains, and the roses which Richard had given her" (261). In her combinatory genius, she seems to demonstrate, as her creator puts it in *Three Guineas*, "the capacity of the human spirit to overflow boundaries and make unity out of multiplicity" (143).

In the final extension of its guiding line of thought, *Mrs. Dalloway* thus plays audaciously on the relativistic conundrum that individual points of view, the preservation of which in their unimpaired state is the most important thing of all, can only achieve their full value, can only in fact exist, by being brought into reciprocity and democratic communion with others. Inviolable solitude and unimpeded, unprejudiced communication need each other: somehow the state of wonderfully free movement that this novel opposes to the state of dictatorship and violence consists in the paradoxical coexistence of the two opposite terms. To grant preference to one or the other would be, the novel suggests, to create one of those "hard and abstract moralities" that, according to Pater, were yielding in modern times to the influence of "the 'relative' spirit"; it would in fact be symptomatic of that "desire to dominate" that blights, Woolf says, every dimension of modern existence (*Three* 181n). This is the desire that is both intensively portrayed and, for a brief imaginary moment corresponding to a radical experiment with the ideology of narrative form, suspended in *Mrs. Dalloway*.

Notes

1. For an extended study of the relation between Woolf and Pater, though one that does not consider the themes highlighted here, see Meisel.

2. In the opening paragraphs of this essay and to a lesser extent later on, I draw on materials more fully developed in *Victorian Relativity*.

3. For one example of this cardinal doctrine of twentieth-century intellectual history, see Toulmin 1: 89.

4. See also *Ethical* 258 and *Origin* 2: 456-89.

5. See, for example, Woolf's evocation of the nineteenth century as an age of rampant dampness, rot, and suffocation in chapter 5 of *Orlando*. For an illuminating study of Woolf's indebtedness to Victorian writing, see Beers "The Victorians in Virginia Woolf: 1832-1941" in *Arguing with the Past*. "The Victorians are not simply represented . . . in her novels," says Beer; "the Victorians are also *in* Virginia Woolf. They are internalized, inseparable, as well as held at arm's length" (139).

6. Need one comment that when Einstein subsequently proposes as the basis of a new physics the principle of "the equal legitimacy of all inertial systems" (*World* 69), he transposes the Paterian theme—no doubt mediated for him by a host of intervening cultural agencies—fairly directly from an extrascientific context into a scientific one? Gross's and Levitt's claim that it is "wildly implausible" that relativity theory in physics was affected by "something in the ambient culture" (*Higher Superstition* 103) is itself rendered implausible by such evidence as this.

7. For a disapproving latter-day account of Pater's relativity, see Small 91-111.

8. While Woolf was composing her novel, Adolf Hitler was composing his own meditation on the unhealed wounds of the world war, *Mein Kampf*, in the fortress prison at Landsberg. The two books, each in its own idiom conjuring the specter of a new age of military violence, were published in the same year of 1925.

9. Once Hitler ran out of Jews and Slavs to massacre, says Arendt, he would inevitably have begun slaughtering ordinary Germans, because "terror . . . is the very essence" of the totalitarian form of government (*Origins* 344; see also 391, 411, 416n, 424).

10. See Gordon 64, Trombley 95-106, and Showalter 277-78.

11. "Faith discriminates thus: This is true, that is false. And it claims truth to itself alone" (Feuerbach 248).

12. In inventing this multiperspectival method for *Mrs. Dalloway*, Woolf no doubt shows indebtedness to Joyce's *Ulysses*, first published three years before, in 1922. For a stimulating account of her ambivalence toward Joycean novelistic experimentation, see DiBattista.

13. The same point is made by Mepham 140.

14. A kind of vestigial omniscient narrator does persist throughout *Mrs. Dalloway*, and J. Hillis Miller has focused a striking essay upon this figure and its supposed functions. In what seems to me to be a vain attempt to reduce Woolf's tale to the workings of a mechanistically explicable model, Miller very emphatically inscribes it within a set of assumptions about the necessarily authoritarian and panoptical character of fictional narration. See Miller 178-81. His account of Woolf's novel and mine begin with similar preoccupations and come to sharply divergent conclusions.

15. "It is at the end of this prolonged transaction with death that Clarissa chooses life" (Fleishman 87). On the contrary, claims Miller, "[t]he climax of *Mrs. Dalloway* is not Clarissa's party but the moment when, having heard of the suicide of Septimus,

Clarissa . . . [recognizes that] [d]eath is the place of true communion." This is "the moment of her greatest insight" (196-97). As John Henry Newman explained in *Grammar of Assent* (1870), in any matter of interpretation—that is, in any scientific inquiry in a world where relativity prevails—experts are bound to disagree (287-89).

16. Fleishman nullifies Woolf's carefully calculated effect of indeterminacy by struggling to show that the occupant of the mysterious car is in fact the Prime Minister (75n).

Works Cited

Arendt, Hannah. "On Humanity in Dark Times: Thoughts about Lessing." *Men in Dark Times*. Trans. Clara and Richard Winston. New York: Harcourt, n.d. 3-31.

_____. *The Origins of Totalitarianism*. New York: Harcourt, 1966.

Bain, Alexander. *Logic*. 1870. 2nd ed. 2 vols. London: Longmans, 1873.

_____. *The Senses and the Intellect*. 1855. 3rd ed. New York: Appleton, 1874.

Bakhtin, M. M. *The Dialogic Imagination*. Ed. Michael Holquist. Trans. Caryl Emerson and Michael Holquist. Austin: U of Texas P, 1981.

Beer, Gillian. *Arguing with the Past: Essays in Narrative from Woolf to Sidney*. London: Routledge, 1989.

Caughie, Pamela L. *Virginia Woolf & Postmodernism: Literature in Quest & Question of Itself*. Urbana: U of Illinois P, 1991.

Clements, Patricia, and Isobel Grundy, eds. *Virginia Woolf: New Critical Essays*. London and Totowa, NJ: Vision and Barnes & Noble, 1983.

Clifford, William Kingdon. *Lectures and Essays*. 1879. Ed. Leslie Stephen and Sir Frederick Pollock. 2 vols. New York: Macmillan, 1901.

Collins, Wilkie. *Heart and Science: A Story of the Present Time*. 1882-83. Ed. Steve Farmer. Peterborough: Broadview, 1996.

de Man, Paul. *Romanticism and Contemporary Criticism: The Gauss Seminar and Other Papers*. Ed. E.S. Burt, Kevin Newmark, Andrzej Warminski. Baltimore: Johns Hopkins UP, 1993.

DiBattista, Maria. "Joyce, Woolf and the Modern Mind." *Virginia Woolf: New Critical Essays*. Ed. Clements and Grundy. 96-114.

Dickens, Charles. *Little Dorrit*. 1855-57. Ed. Harvey Peter Sucksmith. Oxford: Oxford UP, 1982.

Einstein, Albert. *The World as I See It*. New York: Covici Friede, 1934.

Einstein, Albert, and Leopold Infeld. *The Evolution of Physics: The Growth of Ideas from Early Concepts to Relativity and Quanta*. New York: Simon and Schuster, 1942.

Eliot, George. *The Mill on the Floss*. 1860. Ed. Gordon S. Haight. Boston: Houghton Mifflin, 1961.

Feuerbach, Ludwig. *The Essence of Christianity*. 1841. Trans. George Eliot. New York: Harper, 1957.

Fleishman, Avrom. *Virginia Woolf: A Critical Reading*. Baltimore: Johns Hopkins UP, 1975.

Frazer, James George. *The Magic Art and the Evolution of Kings*. 1911. 2 vols. London: Macmillan, 1917.

_____. *Taboo and the Perils of the Soul*. 1911. London: Macmillan, 1919.

Gordon, Lyndall. *Virginia Woolf: A Writer's Life*. New York: Norton, 1984.

Gross, Paul R., and Norman Levitt. *Higher Superstition: The Academic Left and Its Quarrels with Science*. Baltimore: Johns Hopkins UP, 1994.

Grote, George. *A History of Greece; From the Earliest Period to the Close of the Generation Contemporary with Alexander the Great*. 1846-56. 4th ed. 10 vols. London: Murray, 1872.

_____. *Plato, and the Other Companions of Sokrates*. 1865. 2nd ed. 4 vols. London: Murray, 1888.

Herbert, Christopher. *Victorian Relativity: Radical Thought and Scientific Discovery*. Chicago: U of Chicago P, 2001.

Kern, Stephen. *The Culture of Time and Space, 1880-1918*. Cambridge: Harvard UP, 1983.

Lukács, Georg. *Realism in our Time: Literature and the Class Struggle*. Trans. John and Necke Mander. New York: Harper, 1971.

Matson, Patricia. "The Terror and the Ecstasy: The Textual Politics of Virginia Woolf's *Mrs. Dalloway*." *Ambiguous Discourse: Feminist Narratology & British Women Writers*. Ed. Kathy Mezei. Chapel Hill: U of North Carolina P, 1996. 162-86.

Meisel, Perry. *The Absent Father: Virginia Woolf and Walter Pater*. New Haven: Yale UP, 1980.

Mepham, John. "Mourning and Modernism." *Virginia Woolf: New Critical Essays*. Ed. Clements and Grundy. 137-56.

Miller, J. Hillis. *Fiction and Repetition: Seven English Novels*. Cambridge: Harvard UP, 1982.

Newman, John Henry. *An Essay in Aid of a Grammar of Assent*. 1870. Garden City: Doubleday, 1955.

Nietzsche, Friedrich. *The Genealogy of Morals: A Polemic*. Trans. Horace B. Samuel. New York: Russell and Russell, 1964.

Pater, Walter. *Appreciations with An Essay on Style*. 1865. Evanston: Northwestern UP, 1987.

_____. *The Renaissance: Studies in Art and Poetry*. 1893. Ed. Donald L. Hill. Berkeley: U of California P, 1980.

Pearson, Karl. *The Ethic of Freethought: A Selection of Essays and Lectures*. London: Unwin, 1888.

Plato. *Theaetetus*. Trans. John McDowell. Oxford: Clarendon, 1973.

Poincaré, Henri. *Science and Hypothesis*. 1902. Trans. W.J.G. London: Scott, 1905.

Schiller, F. C. S. *Formal Logic: A Scientific and Social Problem*. London: Macmillan, 1912.

Showalter, Elaine. *A Literature of Their Own: British Women Novelists from Brontë to Lessing*. Princeton: Princeton UP, 1977.

Small, Ian. *Conditions for Criticism: Authority, Knowledge, and Literature in the Late Nineteenth Century*. Oxford: Clarendon, 1991.

Spencer, Herbert. *First Principles*. 1862. 6th ed. London: Williams and Norgate, 1908.

_____. *The Principles of Sociology*. 1876-96. 3rd ed. 3 vols. London: Williams and Norgate, 1897-1906.

_____. *The Study of Sociology*. 1872-73. 22nd ed. London: Kegan Paul, n.d.

Stallo, J. B. *The Concepts and Theories of Modern Physics*. 1881. Ed. Percy W. Bridgman. Cambridge: Harvard UP, 1960.

Stephen, Leslie. "Art and Morality." *Cornhill* 32 (1875): 91-101.

Stoker, Bram. *Dracula*. 1897. Ed. Glennis Byron. Peterborough: Broadview, 1998.

Toulmin, Stephen. *Human Understanding*. Vol. 1. Princeton: Princeton UP, 1972.

Trombley, Stephen. *"All that Summer She was Mad": Virginia Woolf and Her Doctors*. London: Junction, 1981.

Westermarck, Edward. *Ethical Relativity*. New York: Harcourt, Brace, 1932.

_____. *The Origin and Development of the Moral Ideas*. 1906-08. 2nd ed. 2 vols. London: Macmillan, 1926.

Woolf, Virginia. *Collected Essays*. 4 vols. London: Hogarth, 1966.

_____. *Mrs. Dalloway*. New York: Harcourt, 1925.

_____. *Three Guineas*. 1938. New York: Harcourt, 1963.

Virginia Woolf's *Mrs. Dalloway*: "A Well of Tears"

George A. Panichas

I

The Great War of 1914-1918 is also on occasion referred to as "The Great War for Civilization." It was a commonly held belief that this was a war to save civilization from destruction and, in effect, to preserve and to strengthen the foundations of Europe's legacy to the world. By the end of the war and stretching well into the 1930s, the noble word civilization was increasingly replaced by another word, a word signifying bleakness and heartbreak: "Disenchantment," which was often used to describe the social, physical, and moral horrors that came to pass once the conflict came to its ignominious end on November 11, 1918.

The British writer C. E. Montague (1867-1929) poignantly describes this debasing process in an acclaimed book that appeared in 1922, *Disenchantment*. To read Montague's text regarding his own personal experiences in the war and how "handsome and boundless illusions" transformed into cynicism, dejection, disappointment returns us to Ezra Pound's earlier famous words in his poem, *Hugh Selwyn Mauberley* (1920), describing how "The Men of 1914" had "walked eye-deep in hell/ believing in old men's lies, then unbelieving/ came home, home to old lies, and new infamy." Montague astonishingly replicates Pound's feelings about the magnitude of losses and the spirit of lostness, and underlines an equivalent tone of dismay and despair in these words: "The lost years, the broken youth, the dead friends, the women's overshadowed lives at home, the agony and bloody sweat— all had gone to darken the stains which most of us had thought to scour out of the world that our children would live in."[1]

Montague's words help to gauge the temper of the modern world as it would be rendered in remarkable poems and fiction written in the English language during the early decades of the twentieth century. A novel that communicates this temper in general and the feelings of disenchantment in particular, in personal and sociological and one could even say epochal contexts, is Virginia Woolf's *Mrs. Dalloway* (1925). This novel also tells us much about the war and the postwar years, about human feelings and relationships, and about the malaise that would afflict individual and collective life in the era between the two world wars.[2] In this novel the reader is able to gauge the mood of the times, in terms of both the human personality and the historical situation, as these were inevitably intertwined. What we recognize above all is a broken world and broken sensibilities impelled by the annihilative effects of war on both the human consciousness and the human soul. And, too, we witness the human condition in crisis in an epochal context of debasement and deterioration.

How inner human emotions, and particularly how love and death evince the consequentiality of a murder-war, is clearly a heart-word in the literature of disenchantment that Woolf registers in her novel, in which feelings of forlornness, desperation, deprivation are prevalent, and in which, to employ a Dickens phrase, we see how "a crestfallen, disenchanted man" emerges to characterize the modern age in transition. Romanticism itself, it can be said, comes of age in a world now abruptly shorn of illusions, dreams, promises of greatness. Human destiny, it seems, is arrested as men and women now confront their own souls—and their innermost *angst*.

History in life and life in history are irreducible phenomena in these years of crisis. The English novelist focused on in this essay ultimately provides a tragic vision of a society and culture not only under violent physical attack but also in moral disarray and dissolution. The men and women we meet in *Mrs. Dalloway* are casualties of their time, physically and emotionally wounded, and badly paralyzed by the power of might that is beyond comprehension. Disillusionment is akin to a sentence of death that has no surcease and that pervades their thoughts and actions, from "sickness unto death." Their demons of fate roam in the dissimulative shape of those invidious forms of disenchantment that

T. S. Eliot, in 1914, had prophesied in his poem on J. Alfred Prufrock, who is constitutionally incapable of overcoming hopelessness and lovelessness, and whose internal monologue embodies what Russell Kirk speaks of as "the intellectual and moral struggles of our time." This is the Prufrock ("pinned and wriggling on the wall") who lies transfixed in a modern hell, who knows the full pain of "voices dying with a dying fall," and who lacks "the strength to force the moment to its crisis."

Prufrock's agonizing dilemma helps objectify the experience of the hollow men and women in the early decades of the twentieth century destined to suffer the madness of the Great War, and also to enact the feelings of laceration and derangement in post-war society. The raging battles of the war were to extend far beyond trench warfare and to become a battleground for the minds and souls of those who were to find themselves trapped in a situation over which they lacked the capacity to exert control. The tendency to play down the larger spiritual dimension of the human spectacle and instead to choose to concentrate on human patterns of behavior, sometimes to an extreme clinical degree, is bound to be one-dimensional. Eros, for example, is counted as an exclusive expression of *physis* in critical assessments, for instance, of Ernest Hemingway's "inward terrain" and "the violence of our own inner nature."[3]

Secular tendencies and habits that ignore the spiritual nature of ourselves, even when the spiritual substance is itself indiscernible or indefinable, fail to gauge the full force and effects of interior, invisible warfare as these encompass the human psyche and condition. As a result the total picture of the human drama that evolved during and after the Great War is never fully comprehended when spiritual essences, both seen and unseen, are barely invoked or examined. Critical imbalance tends, as a result, to characterize literary discourse as a whole because of hostility to spiritual truths within a secular milieu. Indeed, the secular and secularizing view that pervades the intellectual realm in our time—and it is a view that promotes itself zealously—is ultimately advanced by zealous ideologues who rule over the cultural scene at large. This selfsame view, widely held and imperiously espoused, simply refuses to consider the origins and spread of the pervasive disenchantment in those early decades of the twentieth century.

To correct this critical imbalance is a central task here if the disenchantment that seemed to spread like a cancer in modern society after the war is to be perceived in its full power and complexity. "Enemies of the permanent things" should not be allowed to have the last word in twentieth-century life, literature, and thought, and in effect to denude the life of the soul in direct relation to the depth and magnitude of disenchantment as a symptom and portent of the spiritual malaise that deepened and accelerated after 1914-1918. The disenchantment that novelists like a Virginia Woolf, an Ernest Hemingway, and an F. Scott Fitzgerald elicit in their fiction has an immediacy that, in the course of time, underscores the prophetic element and ramifications.

The modern age, it can even be said, begins on a note of disenchantment that great imaginative novelists and poets portray in its specificities—a process that history amply confirms in the continuity of false beliefs. In a sense, it can be said, disenchantment emblematizes the deaths of belief that now define postmodern attitudes and habits, in those advanced forms of nihilism and anarchy that bring the Enlightenment to its final dismal hours of agony. Today great humanistic artists (and critics) are thus being steadily replaced by "talents and technicians" who infect the literary scene with their dissonant sensibility. "We have suffered a paralysis or eclipse of imagination before the nightmare of history in this age," the American critic John W. Aldridge notes in words that have a sad and harsh relevance.[4]

Virginia Woolf reminds us dramatically how great imaginative fiction unites social history and the truths of reality in memorable, enduring ways, conjoining moral intensity and civilized sensibility. To read the text of *Mrs. Dalloway* is to reexperience the full violence of war inflicted on body and soul and mind; to comprehend the ravages of cruel history; and, above all, to rediscover how disenchantment swept over the human personality and the state of humanity in a time of un-alleviating tragedy. That we are, it appears, at the beginning of a new age, a new social order, underlies the prophetic truths that great imaginative literature reveals to us in pensive words and voices that do not necessarily seek to define the phenomenon of disenchantment, but instead to render the experience in prose and in poetry, and in effect to reflect, in the more subtle tones of a growing awareness, the jarring rhythm of disintegration in modern existence.

A humane literary genius is actively at work in a novelist like Woolf as a moral realist who communicates her version of "the fate of man in the modern world," unto "the end of our time," what the Russian philosopher Nicolas Berdyaev in the thirties spoke of as "the internal apocalypse of history." Contemporary critics, furiously "at war with the word," generally choose to play down or to reject outrightly intricate connections and interconnections that render issues and concerns that are the stuff of the imagination and of that shaping spirit of modern fiction, in form, in composition, in values, identified and interpreted in this essay.[5] Readers are today prone to assuming and accepting the death of great literature as it has been dictated by postmodern literary theorists and deconstructors. The theme of disenchantment, the text chosen to illustrate it, and the moral interpretation of both theme and text in the ensuing discussion, revolve around what one young critic, Mark C. Henrie, writes in an admirable essay entitled "The Refreshment of the Humanities": "The best defense of the humanities is the activity itself. . . . The way for humanists to recover their cultural authority [and patrimony] is by doing what they do best: reading and explaining and criticizing the old books."[6]

II

Virginia Woolf's *Mrs. Dalloway* portrays the acute physical and psychic effects, and the sundry ramifications of disenchantment in the post-1918 years. It shows in the most vivid and heartbreaking of ways how the experience and suffering of the battlefields of the European War wreaked havoc; how the combatants who survived the holocaust then struggled wearily to understand their civilian surroundings; how, in short, they "coped," or failed to cope, with the realities and the demands of civic society. Even if the late War and the Armistice were now simply a memory, painful memories of the war resonated among those survivors seeking to go about the business of human existence in peacetime.

Woolf's novel has as one of its primary reference points the life and fate of a psychologically maimed soldier who has returned from the Western Front. Years after the cessation of the war, he is seen struggling frantically to come to terms with and then to overcome his experience of war and death, and then of disenchantment and madness. His name is Septimus Warren Smith, whom we see in the final day of his life on a Wednesday in June 1923; he is drawn in direct and tangential relation to the other central and secondary figures in the novel, as well as to the chain of events transpiring on a "hot June day, with the bees going round and about and the yellow butterflies." Indeed, his character is dominant both in the overall consciousness of the novel's fictive world and in the personal histories of the figures who appear in the events of the novel, as these are enacted in the city of London, in the district of Westminster, in which Big Ben (and Saint Margaret's) tolls with precision and regularity: "There! Out it booms. First a warning, musical; then the hour, irrevocable."[7]

Time passes, it seems, unmitigably as the human spectacle and human fate inevitably interact in the framework of routine conditions and circumstances of present history, which is, nonetheless, indelibly still launched by the memory of the Great War: "This late age of the world's experience had bred in them all, all men and women, a well of tears." Clearly, whatever peacetime happenings and ambitions and hopes constitute the novel's soul, as it were, the resonances of war cannot be entirely erased, or forgotten even years later, for somehow the war revisits human consciousness and relationships in the visible forms of remembrance of things past. To be sure, five years have passed by since military operations ended, but for "the men of 1914" the Great War was, in the words of a French combatant, Henri Massis, "the home of our youth" and "would never cease to mark our work and our days."[8]

The truth of Massis's statement permeates the whole of *Mrs. Dalloway* and is personified, continuously and pitilessly, from the beginning to the end of the novel, by Septimus Warren Smith—"aged about thirty, pale-faced, beak-nosed, wearing brown shoes and a shabby overcoat, with hazel eyes which had that look of apprehension in them which makes strangers apprehensive, too." It is precisely the overarching note of apprehensiveness that captures and conveys the basic temper of *Mrs. Dalloway*, and that, in the end, testifies to the disenchantment that post-war literature (and society) was to highlight, with the inextinguishable power and acuity that were to earmark the modern age in its origins and developments since 1918.

It could even be said that Septimus is a representative figure in the pantheon of those early "moderns" who survived but who also lost their souls on the fighting fronts of the Great War, and who lacked, or perhaps rejected, the fundamental capacity and self-assurance, the faith, to refurbish and regain their equilibrium in an age that announced its unique ascendancy in the post-war years. Not only is Septimus a prescient historical figure and force, but also, in *Mrs. Dalloway*, a powerful presence that refuses to disappear, either in suicide or in death. To be sure, Clarissa Dalloway is the substantive character and center of Woolf's novel, but Septimus Warren Smith is its fictive coadjutor (or "double") without whom neither the role of Clarissa nor the full significance of the novel can be completely grasped. Indeed, as one critic observes, Septimus "is more closely identified with Woolf herself than is Clarissa."[9] In fact, Septimus unifies the novel in its parts and whole; consummates the burden of its vision; extends and rarefies its rendition; and, in sum, attenuates a "gradual drawing of everything to one centre."

Septimus was one of the first to volunteer after the outbreak of war on August 4, 1914. "He went to France to save an England which consisted almost entirely of Shakespeare's plays and Miss Isabel Pole who, before the war, had deeply impressed a shy, stammering, "half-educated, self-educated" Septimus, newly arrived in London from Stroud. She "lit in him such a fire as burns only once in a lifetime," exciting deep feelings, love, and idealism, and an aspiration to make something of himself, even to be someday an important literary figure. This early phase of his life was filled with poetry and enthusiasm, and was a portent of Septimus's future as his London employer, Mr. Brewer, believed. "Something is up" in Septimus, an enthusiastic Mr. Brewer said, as he gauged his young employee's character and prospects. Indeed, those brilliant portents, no less than his pre-war world, would soon turn into ashes, as that "monstrous" August of 1914 seemed to announce an eventual crumbling of modern civilization.

What D. H. Lawrence has likened to a "disintegrating autumnal process"[10] now began to take hold as the "prying and insidious . . . fingers of the European War . . . smashed a plaster cast of Ceres, ploughed a hole in the geranium beds, and utterly ruined the cook's nerves at Mr. Brewer's establishment at Muswell Hill," to recall here Woolf's words in *Mrs. Dalloway.* Septimus Warren Smith was to epitomize a way of life that would undergo cataclysmic changes and that would never return when the maroons boomed on November 11, 1918.

To be sure, Septimus, once he returned to England, and resumed his position under Mr. Brewer, was "advanced to a post of considerable responsibility. They were proud of him; he had won crosses." Septimus and Rezia, who trims ladies' hats for an occupation, now rent from a kindly Mrs. Filmer, "admirable lodgings off the Tottenham Court Road." But it was by now too late, too late for Septimus, for whom Shakespeare and "the intoxication of language . . . had shrivelled utterly"—and "the world itself is without meaning." An "appalling fear" had taken possession of him, at once choking and reducing him to bitterness and denial: "The secret signal which one generation passes, under disguise, to the next is loathing, hatred, despair." For Septimus the drama of the horrors of 1914-1918 was to be not simply a "Great Interruption," as Henry James called it, but the unbearable experience of a "murder war"—an eternity of darkness, emptiness, desolation.[11]

In Septimus Warren Smith we view conterminously a frozen heart and a stricken soul. Since his return from the war—now married for five years to twenty-four year old Rezia, from Milan—his life has been increasingly drab and unfulfilling, struggling as always to make sense of things, but without real success, except for some sporadic moments of clarity and self-understanding. "For he was gone, she thought—gone, as he threatened, to kill himself—to throw himself under a cart." His mind and heart remain captives of his war sufferings, which he never transcends, such are their conscious and unconscious ache and pain. His affliction is unassuaging no matter where he happens to be, or what he happens to be doing, even as his relation to others (and to his wife) is null and non-existent—content as he is, it appears, "to talk to himself, to talk to a dead man [Evans], in the seat over there."

Rezia's own fate, "rocked by this malignant torturer," is heightened progressively by her husband's undulant pattern of mental behavior. His few moments of clarity, as, for example, when he feels that "Beauty was everywhere," are invariably followed by discordant thoughts and gestures: "He had grown stranger and stranger." For Rezia, and for Septimus, there is no possibility of full solace, coherence, salvation. Even in the midst of a luminous moment of quietude and reasonableness, he steadily descends "into the flames"; sees "faces laughing at him, calling him horrible disgusting names," and a Skye terrier turning into a man; hears sparrows in Regents Park in the Broad Walk singing "in voices prolonged and piercing in Greek words."

Woolf's description of Septimus's condition is astonishing in its dispassionate power of insight and also of sympathy as she depicts him before and after the war, when he is sinking inexorably into an abyss of nothingness and desolateness. The fact is that Septimus never escapes from no-man's-land, that his only future is the death that, as the soldier-poet Sir Herbert Read has observed, he even now shares intimately with all those before him who had fought and died in the trenches.[12] Septimus, to be sure, was a brave warrior, but he had expended all his bravery in the war, as well as his love for his fellows. There was nothing left for him now: all his human concerns and literary ambitions were to count for him nothing in postwar English society, and he could not connect with other human beings or with the postwar world: "His body was macerated until only the nerve fibres were left. It was spread like a veil upon a rock." The spectre of his commanding officer, Evans ("a quiet . . . red-haired man"), killed at the front just before the Armistice, stubbornly and mysteriously clung to Septimus and haunted his thoughts: "A man in grey was actually walking towards them. It was Evans! But no mud was on him; no wounds; he was not changed."

In the war Septimus "developed manliness; he was promoted; he drew the attention, indeed the affection of his officer, Evans by name." Clearly Septimus's friendship with Evans is a "sacramental" one, of the ethereal kind that developed among the combatants, now necessarily free of class distinctions, confronting a common enemy and a common danger, with a common loyalty and solidarity. But the shock of warfare and its grim consequences in the end robbed Septimus of his human feelings: "For now that it was all over, truce signed, and the dead buried, he had . . . these sudden thunder-claps of fear. He could not feel." His view of the world of men and women, then, is a disordered one, indelibly warped by a war that was to ordain disillusionment and cynicism that will not go away: "For the truth is . . . that human beings have neither kindness nor faith, nor charity. . . . They hunt in packs. Their packs scour the desert and vanish screaming into the wilderness."

Septimus's shell-shocked consciousness deteriorates in his postwar setting, as "he descended another step into the pit. . . . he dropped his head on his hands. Now he had surrendered; now other people must help him." Dr. Holmes, a kindly, amiable, but hopelessly imperceptive and inept general practitioner, who also happens to be Mrs. Filmer's physician, is now called on to examine Septimus: "There was nothing whatever the matter, said Dr. Holmes," who is totally oblivious of the young man's "degradation." Perfunctorily, he brushes aside the "headaches, sleeplessness, fears, dreams—nerve symptoms and nothing more, he said." Septimus's internal condition gets worse, in the meantime, notwithstanding Holmes's forty years' medical experience: " . . . Holmes himself could not touch this last relic straying on the edge of the world, this outcast. . . ."

And once again we hear the voice from behind the screen: "Evans was speaking. The dead were with him." Having no real confidence in Dr. Holmes, who has been treating him for six weeks, and with Septimus's condition steadily reaching a breaking point, the "Warren Smiths walked down Harley Street," this time to consult with an eminent specialist, Sir William Bradshaw, who has attained "the reputation (of the utmost importance in dealing with nerve cases) not merely of lightning skill, and almost infallible accuracy in diagnosis but of sympathy; tact; understanding of the human soul."

Sir William "was certain directly he saw the man; it was a case of extreme gravity. . . . [a] complete physical and nervous breakdown, with every symptom in an advanced stage." For Septimus, as indeed for a neurasthenic like Virginia Woolf herself, Sir William's is the voice of *thanatos*, the voice of the world, unrelenting in its authority, cold and matter-of-fact, dogmatic in conviction, the last word in disenchantment. "Shortly and kindly Sir William explained to her [Rezia] the state of the case": Septimus had threatened to kill himself. "There was no alternative. It was a question of law."

In short, Septimus Warren Smith, "the drowned sailor; the poet of the immortal ode; the Lord who had gone from life to death," was condemned by Sir William to "go into a home" in the country, where he would learn to rest. "Really he was not fit to be about." ("The fellow made a distasteful impression" on the famous specialist, in whom there was "a grudge, deeply buried, against cultivated people who came into

his room and intimated that doctors . . . are not educated men.")
Septimus's own instinctive perception of what Sir William represents
is sharply expressed in his interior thoughts on the hard-nosed "ar-
rangements" for his rehabilitation (for the sake of "divine proportion"): "Once you fall, Septimus repeated to himself, human nature is
on you. Holmes and Bradshaw are on you. They scour the desert. They
fly screaming into the desert. The rack and the thumbscrew are applied. Human nature is remorseless."

Sir William's meeting with Septimus and Rezia, which comes at the
novel's mid-point, contains Woolf's conception of alienation in its
modern constituents, as these are transcribed in an urban metropolis
that, from the standpoint of human warmth and compassion, is cold
and unfeeling, even indifferent to the possibility of suicide and death.
If anything, the city of London in *Mrs. Dalloway* has the underlying
look and feel of a necropolis and magnifies the sense of alienation that
oppresses men and women who live in its houses, walk on its streets,
meet and interact with others, hear sounds and words, and see things
that are transient in context and meaning. The Smiths/Bradshaw meeting manifests the mood and temper of alienated men and women—
skeptical, estranged, or withdrawn, or withered in feeling or affection.
This dramatic meeting, which has incalculable effects, as evidenced in
its immediate scenes and dialogue, leads Rezia to conveying her most
frightening inner feelings of disenchantment and, ultimately, of disconnection: "Sir William was not a nice man." "He had failed them!"
"They had been deserted."

III

In the presence of Sir William Bradshaw one finds one's self in an
intimidating and menacing milieu; he is the epitome of a world in
which Septimus can find no meaning and in which he becomes its
helpless victim. Bradshaw, "this man being the ghostly helper, the
priest of science," is the inescapable nullity and way to death. His very

presence is fraught with all the trappings of negation. On the surface his diagnosis of things is adroit; it is the product both of his power to judge absolutely and to decide human fate, and of his self-certainty in categorizing the state of Septimus's "case." Even in his own state of confusion, Septimus intuits the negatives that are ultimately at the core of Bradshaw's diagnostic power. Indeed, even Sir William's medical notes, written in pencil on pink cards, are confirmations of his remorseless "verdicts." "'Try to think as little about yourself as possible,'" he advises the young man—but, *"Really, he was not fit to be about."* Bradshaw has full trust in his findings: "'Trust everything to me,'" he says, knowing as he does that his authority is unchallengeable and that no dissension can be booked, such is his absolute confidence in treating a patient's illness: "order rest in bed; rest in solitude; silence and rest; rest without friends, without books, without messages. . . ."

His professional success, which he has gained by "sheer ability" has grown by leaps and bounds, and he is honored by those who admire his reputation, and who can also afford his "very large fee." In the meanwhile, when Sir William's own wife waits for him to conclude one of his distant visits to the rich and affluent, she thinks of "the wall of gold, mounting minute by minute," which her husband is steadily building "in dealing with nerve cases," as he ministers to his patients far and wide. And he savors his power over life, makes his unilateral judgments and decisions, as he carefully doles out his time ("[t]o his patients he gave three-quarters of an hour"). His general attitude is gallant, condescending, and always self-satisfying in knowing the worth of his medical judgments and decisions in the eyes of his peers.

As Sir William prospered, he knew, too, that he "made England prosper, secluded her lunatics, forbade childbirth, penalized despair, made it impossible for the unfit to propagate their views." He knew only too well that his paramount function was to protect the citizenry from those who would enfeeble a civic society's resolve to press on with its material fortunes and identity; that he would be thanked and rewarded "for insisting that these prophetic Christs and Christesses [such as Septimus Warren Smith], who prophesied the end of the world, or the advent of God, should drink milk in bed, as Sir William ordered."

Sir William does not personify a metaphysics of evil that one encounters, say, in some of Fyodor Dostoevsky's and Joseph Conrad's villains, who essentialize abstract and extraworldly essences of a demonism that places them somewhere between heaven and hell.[13] His Goddess was one of "proportion, divine proportion," whom he evokes again and again; this is the Goddess who conveys Sir William's public persona and mythifies his accomplishments. It is, so to speak, his calling card as a physician who has profound insight and helps to undo the blunders of general practitioners like Dr. Holmes.

But as Woolf's narrative makes unmistakably clear, there is another Goddess, "Conversion is her name," whom he worships. "Less smiling, more formidable," this sister Goddess, like the prince of this world, is found everywhere, and is "even now engaged in dashing down shrines, smashing idols, and setting up in their place her own stern countenance." It is this Goddess of Conversion, as Rezia "divines," who not only dwells in Sir William's heart "under some plausible disguise; some venerable name; love, duty, self sacrifice," but also who best defines and dominates his innermost motives: to vanquish human wills and to nourish his imperial self. The "great," self-serving doctor, in fact, though he outwardly professes belief in the classical virtue of measure, places his full and final faith in a totalitarian temper, in that other "Goddess" whose "lust is to override opposition, to stamp indelibly in the sanctuaries of others the image of herself."

His goal is to embrace and to advance unilaterally the diverse agencies of power so as to make his patients (and his own wife) capitulate to the sovereignty of his will. He is, as his very gestures and declarations demonstrate, the "master of his own actions," as he "swooped; he devoured. He shut people up." The power to control others' fate, to make his word absolute, to silence all opposition, to dominate human life: that was his constant goal. The pursuit of power best describes his creed of faith and his *raison d'être*. Both Rezia and Septimus, whatever their anguish and the degree of their *ressentiment*, recognize Sir William's power to judge and to prevail.

It is precisely his insatiable appetite for the acquisition of power and dominion that furnishes Sir William with the trappings of wealth, fame, esteem, influence, dominion. It is not so much, then, that he is a representative of evil ends as that he is also the incarnation of raw power to manipulate lives and shape destiny, and as such to judge and to overrule others and to apportion punishment to the weak, the infirm, the debile, even as he simultaneously championed proportion as a way of life. Insidiously, meretriciously, he maneuvers to attain his vision of power within his own profession as a special healer of the bodies and the minds of combatants who have somehow survived military carnages only to be continuously haunted by "the images of war."

In word and attitude, Sir William is the archetype of a scientific elite as distinguished from other intellectual and social groupings; in this he manifests a modern state of mind empowered by its specialized view of the modern conditions and realities of material existence. His diagnosis of and his prescription for Septimus's rehabilitation are in the end barren of understanding the depth of the disease of disenchantment that the soldier-poet Wilfred Owen designated as the "undone years" and "the hopelessness" that the combatants experienced.

Woolf employs a very fitting concrete symbol of Sir William's success and affluence, his grey motor car parked in front of his house on Harley Street: "low, powerful, grey with plain initials interlocked on the panel." He often uses this motor car to travel sixty miles or more into the country to visit wealthy patients as his "work grew and grew." To match its "sober suavity," "grey furs, silver grey rugs were heaped in it, to keep Lady Bradshaw warm while she waited" for her husband to parcel out his "infallible" medical advice. Seated within the motor car, "she felt wedged on a calm ocean, where only spice winds blow," thinking at this point of the narrative of their marriage, with her only child, "a boy doing well at Eton," and how "respected, admired, envied" she was, "with scarcely anything left to wish for, though she regretted her stoutness."

Sir William has provided his family with material satisfaction; "no longer young," "with his grey hair," he had been knighted and has acquired a look of distinction, "a heavy look, a weary look," "the responsibilities and privileges of his profession [being] so onerous." Almost predictably, following consultation with Sir William, who informs Mrs. Warren Smith that her husband must go into one "of *my* homes," where he will be taught to rest, Septimus's condition is precarious. We see him next, having returned to his lodgings, "lying on the sofa of the sitting-room," as he has become suddenly more "excited." "That man, his friend who was killed, Evans, had come, he said. He was singing behind the screen." With tears now running down his cheeks, Septimus is radically incoherent: "he would cry that he was falling down, down into the flames."

At this pivotal juncture, Dr. Holmes again appears on the scene; he is, for Septimus, "the brute with the blood-red nostrils," as on an earlier occasion Septimus pictured him in his mind: "Once you stumble, Septimus wrote on the back of a card, human nature is on you." Indeed, Septimus never gets over the morbid feeling that both Holmes and Bradshaw are pursuing him as agents of "human cruelty." They were his judges who "saw nothing clear, yet ruled, yet inflicted." The scene here has an electrical intensity, and marks the moment when Rezia and Septimus are to be separated. As she prepares to pack Septimus's things to take with him to one of Bradshaw's "homes," she hears voices from below and then goes downstairs, thinking perhaps that it was Dr. Holmes who had come. "Septimus could hear her talking to Holmes on the staircase. 'My dear lady, I have come as a friend,' Holmes was saying." Rezia, who intuits danger to her husband in the bedroom, tries to bar his way, but "a powerfully built" Holmes puts her aside.

Septimus is in a state of frenzy, fearing as he does that Holmes is about to burst open the door and to deliver a fearsome "verdict."

Thoughts of how to bring an end to his life surge up in him:—with Mrs. Filmer's "nice clean bread knife"? or by gas fire? or with a razor? "But it was too late now. Holmes was coming." For Septimus there "remained only the window, the large Bloomsbury-lodging house window. . . . Holmes was at the door. 'I'll give it to you!' he cried, and flung himself vigorously, violently down on to Mrs. Filmer's area railings." Agitation, shock, "thumping and whispering," "running up and down stairs" fill this grim scene, concluding with Dr. Holmes sedating Rezia so that she will not have to see her husband's "horribly mangled body." The "sweet" potion lulls Rezia into a strange, uneasy slumber, as she finally beholds the shadow of Holmes's "body standing dark against the window. So that was Dr. Holmes."

At Clarissa Dalloway's party that same evening, Sir William and Lady Bradshaw, who are among the invited guests, pass along, rather perfunctorily, to Clarissa the news of Septimus's suicide, which she now envisions in harrowing detail: "He had thrown himself from a window. Up had flashed the ground; through him, blundering, bruising, went the rusty spikes. There he lay with a thud, thud, thud in his brain, and then a suffocation of blackness. So she saw it." For Clarissa "her party," for which she has been meticulously preparing, is of major personal importance, to be attended by great personages, "old friends," dignitaries, Ladies and Gentlemen, and, yes, the Prime Minister himself,—"this majesty passing; this symbol of what they all stood for, English society." His presence, obviously, incarnates not only the success of the party, but of Clarissa as the paragon hostess.

Sir William's presence, in sharp contrast,—"There were the Bradshaws, whom she disliked."—brings in a note of terror. Although Clarissa recognizes his fame, "[a] man absolutely at the head of his profession, very powerful, rather worn," she nonetheless would not want to fall into his clutches: "No; not that man." At one time, in fact, she had gone to him for a consultation. "But heavens—what a relief to get out to the street again!" Her own earlier experience with Sir William now connects her to Septimus, and also confirms those same fears that the Smiths were to express in their dealings with Sir William. Clarissa cannot put her finger on what exactly she disliked in him; her husband, Richard, also shares this dislike of Bradshaw, for he himself "'didn't like his taste, didn't like his smell.'"

In any event, the Bradshaws are, for Clarissa, nocturnal conduits of terrible news. "Oh! Thought Clarissa, in the middle of my party, here's death, she thought." Sir William is for her, then, a dark and threatening force, and the sight of him "curl[s] her up." Yes, she thinks, he is an "extraordinarily able" doctor, but "yet to her obscurely evil, without sex or lust, extremely polite to women, but capable of some indescribable outrage—forcing your soul, that was it. . . ." Sir William's news of Septimus killing himself strikes fear in her—"her dress flamed, her body burnt." And as she dwells on the details of Septimus's suicide, the news of which darkens and tarnishes for her the "success" of her party and interjects the grim scene of death: "It was her punishment to see sink and disappear here a man, there a woman, in this profound darkness. . . ."

In Septimus, Clarissa not only sees her own mortality but also feels the fleetingness and fragility of human existence: "Death was defiance. Death was an attempt to communicate; people feeling the impossibility of reaching the centre which, mystically, evaded them." Indeed, though death signified for her that "one was alone," it also signified that there "was an embrace in death." The mood of *Mrs. Dalloway* is pensive and even elegiac in reflection, invariably touching on the everlasting questions—sin, guilt, evil, death, redemption.

Virginia Woolf's concentration on evil in this novel is especially intensive as she demonstrates in her graphic portrayal of Sir William Bradshaw. Even in the last three pages of the novel it is Bradshaw who is startlingly *there*; it is as if Mrs. Woolf cannot ignore, or dismiss, or forget, or escape him, such is the elemental power of his presence as an "enemy": "this distinguished-looking man and his rather common-looking wife . . . what could one know about people like that?" For Richard Dalloway, who is casually observing the Bradshaws, "they're damnable humbugs." For Virginia Woolf, however, William Bradshaw is far more than simply a humbug, a deceiver, a fraud, or a sham. He *is*, as E. M. Forster emphatically remarks in *Abinger Harvest* (1936), "uninterruptedly and embracingly evil."[14] Clearly, Sir William Bradshaw is Woolf's quintessential metaphor for evil.

To be sure, *Mrs. Dalloway* is a novel about what Virginia Woolf has termed in one of her celebrated essays, "Mr. Bennett and Mrs. Brown" (1924), "the spirit we live by, life itself."[15] In the more immediate context of the novel's story line, it is about "this hot June day," "this moment in June," with its "myriad impressions." In a deeply metaphysical sense, however, it is a novel that transports us into the kingdom of enmity and that, simultaneously, contemplates the horror of evil: its sensations, motions, forms, enticements, consequences; its dynamic of oppressive brutality and violence and death. Its contemplation of evil makes *Mrs. Dalloway* a modern classic that speaks in a universal language and has universal meaning, known to and felt by humankind in all countries and climes.

Notes

1. New York, 230.
2. For a thorough examination of the conflict's impact on Woolf's war consciousness, see Karen Levenback, *Virginia Woolf and the Great War*, 1st ed. (Syracuse, N.Y., 1999).
3. See Richard B. Hovey, *Hemingway: The Inward Terrain* (Seattle and London, 1968).
4. See his *Talents and Technicians: Literary Chic and the Assembly-Line Fiction* (New York, 1992); and also his *The American Novel and the Way We Live Now* (New York and Oxford, 1983).
5. See R. V. Young, *At War with the Word: Literary Theory and the Liberal Imagination* (Wilmington, Del., 1999).
6. *Modern Age: A Quarterly Review* (Spring 2003), 178.
7. All quotations from *Mrs. Dalloway* (1925) found in the text of this essay are

from the Harvest Book edition of the novel published by Harcourt, Brace & World, Inc. (New York, 1953).

8. "The War We Fought," *Promise of Greatness: The War of 1914-1918*, edited by George A. Panichas, with a foreword by Sir Herbert Read (New York and London, 1968), 284.

9. Peter Filkins, "Virginia Woolf's *Mrs. Dalloway*," *British Writers Classics*, Vol. II (New York, 2004), 198.

10. Quoted in George A. Panichas, "D. H. Lawrence's War Letters," *The Courage of Judgment: Essays in Criticism, Culture, and Society*, with a foreword by Austin Warren, 1st ed. (Knoxville, Tenn., 1982), 220-231. The essay that immediately follows, "In Retreat," 232-237, should also be of interest.

11. For Henry James's reactions to World War I, see George A. Panichas, "Henry James and Paradigms of Character," *The Critic as Conservator: Essays in Literature, Society, and Culture* (Washington, D.C., 1992), 57-76.

12. Sir Herbert Read, Foreword, *Promise of Greatness*, v-vii.

13. See George A. Panichas, "Chapter Three: Satanism," *The Burden of Vision: Dostoevsky's Spiritual Art* (Grand Rapids, Mich., 1977), 89-112; and also his "Moral Warfare in Joseph Conrad's *Victory*," *Modern Age: A Quarterly Review* (Summer 1999), 240-251.

14. "The Early Novels of Virginia Woolf" (New York, 1955), 108.

15. *Collected Essays*, Vol. 1 (New York, 1967), 319-337.

Mrs. Dalloway:
A Study in Composition _____

Nathalia Wright

An examination of Virginia Woolf's technique in the construction of *Mrs. Dalloway* reveals a novel which is primarily neither a narrative nor a character sketch. It is a thematic study, juxtaposing certain patterns for purely aesthetic ends. These patterns are not themes in the traditional sense; that is, none constitutes a text, upon which a story, like *Vanity Fair* or *The Scarlet Letter*, may be told. They are, more properly, elements of composition, bearing a structural relationship to one another and involving no plot at all.

These elements—of characters, psychological states, sounds, and colors—are not unique in Mrs. Woolf. The presence of each may be pointed to in all her novels and, indeed, in many other novels of the present century. However, in *Mrs. Dalloway* their recurrence as themes is most deliberate and their ultimate synthesis one of her most brilliant achievements.

I

Four character groups are distinguishable in *Mrs. Dalloway:* the group of Clarissa, Richard, and Elizabeth Dalloway, Hugh and Evelyn Whitbread, Sally Seton, Lady Bruton, and Doris Kilman; the group of Peter Walsh and Daisy Simmons; the group of Septimus and Lucrezia Warren Smith, Dr. Holmes, Sir William and Lady Bradshaw, and Evans; and the group of 116 minor characters.

The primary position of the Clarissa theme is obvious: it occurs in the title, at the beginning and end of the book, and on more than half the pages. By manipulation it also appears for a moment in a third place of prominence in the novel—the exact middle, at a prominent hour, high noon—thus dividing in half the book and the day.

The secondary nature of the Peter Walsh theme is evident in the relationship that exists between him and Clarissa. In the early days of their acquaintance "they went in and out of each other's minds without any effort." And, though "they might be parted for hundreds of years," Clarissa would suddenly wonder what Peter would say of this or that, and Peter would have an abrupt vision of their last meeting:

> . . . . In absence, in the most unlikely places, it would flower out, open, shed its scent, let you touch, taste, look about you, get the whole feel of it and understanding, after years of lying lost.

The third theme is the complement of the first. That Septimus and Mrs. Dalloway are doubles and that in the first version, in which Septimus did not exist, Mrs. Dalloway was to kill herself, has been acknowledged by Mrs. Woolf.[1] The most overwhelming internal evidence of this relationship occurs when Clarissa, postulating three reasons for ending her own life, hits in the middle upon the very one which had driven Septimus to fling himself down upon the railings: the intolerable pressure exerted upon the soul by passionless men. Her other reasons—fear and the impossibility of communication—were also problems of Septimus', who feared the world's coming to an end before his eyes and whose poems and drawings failed so desperately to pluck the truth from the universe. Thus brooding, Mrs. Dalloway felt "somehow it was her disaster—her disgrace"; and again "she felt somehow very like him—the young man who had killed himself."[2]

The summarizing fourth theme—the theme of the English national character—is represented by the entire group of minor characters. Throughout the novel Mrs. Woolf exhibits a Shakespearean penchant for individualizing unimportant people. Of the crowds that throng the pages of *Mrs. Dalloway*, 116 are named and in varying detail epitomized.

Thus, to enumerate a few, Mrs. Filmer's serving girl is Agnes, the housemaid at Bourton who saw Sally Seton run naked down the hall was Ellen Atkins, and in his dream Peter calls for Mrs. Turner to clear the things away. Lady Bruton's secretary is Milly Brush, whose brother is doing poorly in Portsmouth. Mrs. Carrie Dempster—watching the airplane—has bad feet, and her nephew is a missionary. The child with her nurse in Regent's Park is Elise Mitchell, Daisy's husband is Major Simmons, and her friend in Peter's absence is Major Orde. Even Elizabeth's dog Grizzle and Lady Bruton's pony Patty are named.

The peculiarity of this fourth theme lies in its relationship to the other three. Characteristically, it does not run parallel but cuts across them at right angles, that is, individual minor characters are constantly crossing the paths of Clarissa or Peter or Septimus, but, without altering their courses, they immediately pass from sight.[3] More than a hundred such encounters may be noted. In this fashion, although never continuing long at a time, the fourth theme appears a far greater number of times than any other. Its parallel treatment, on the other hand, occupies only about one-fifth of the book. On two occasions major and minor characters are gathered into one group—at the strategic positions of the opening and closing of the book.

From the beginning to the end of the novel, thirteen major shifts of character theme may be noted, exclusive of the incidental appearances of minor characters.[4] They occur in this order: Clarissa, English national character, Septimus, Clarissa, Peter, Septimus, Peter, Septimus, Clarissa, Septimus, Peter, Clarissa, English national character; which, when broken down, appears as a distinct scheme:

a b   c a   d c   d c   a c   d   a b.

For the most part, only one theme occurs at a time. However, on occasion two and three appear simultaneously and at the end all four in a grand finale.[5]

II

Likewise, four psychological themes may be noted in the novel, corresponding, in general, with the characters Clarissa, Peter, Septimus, and the English national character.

The consciousness of the self—the problem preoccupying not only Mrs. Woolf but most important novelists since Proust—receives in the character of Clarissa full embodiment.[6] Her transcendental theory of personality, shared with Peter, grows out of her own heightened sensibility. It is described while she is looking in the mirror:

> . . . . Clarissa . . . . plunged into the very heart of the moment, transfixed it, there—the moment of this June morning on which was the pressure of all the other mornings, seeing the glass, the dressing-table, and all the bottles afresh, collecting the whole of her at one point (as she looked into the glass), seeing the delicate pink face of the woman who was that very night to give a party; of Clarissa Dalloway; of herself.
>
> How many million times she had seen her face, and always with the same imperceptible contraction! She pursed her lips when she looked in the glass. It was to give her face point. That was her self—pointed; dartlike; definite. That was her self when some effort, some call on her to be her self, drew the parts together, she alone knew how different, how incompatible and composed so for the world only into one centre, one diamond, one woman who sat in her drawing-room and made a meeting-point . . . . for the lonely to come to. . . . .

The secondary theme of memory, essentially part of the whole problem of consciousness, is recognized in more than one relationship of Peter Walsh. In the Bourton retrospect, which forms so large a part of the novel, Peter is the central character. He and Clarissa think of each other only in terms of the past. Peter is also, in the role of a Britisher returned home after some years, constantly comparing the times:

Those five years—1918 to 1923—had been, he suspected, somehow very important. People looked different. Newspapers seemed different. Now for instance there was a man writing quite openly in one of the respectable weeklies about water-closets. That you couldn't have done ten years ago—written quite openly about water-closets in a respectable weekly. And then this taking out a stick of rouge, or a powder-puff and making up in public. On board ship coming home there were lots of young men and girls—Betty and Bertie he remembered in particular—carrying on quite openly; the old mother sitting and watching them with her knitting, cool as a cucumber. The girl would stand still and powder her nose in front of every one. And they weren't engaged; just having a good time; no feelings hurt on either side.[7]

The theme of self-annihilation, personified in Septimus,[8] is the complement of the theme of consciousness. Their relationship is symbolized in the psychological, though never physical, contact of Clarissa and Septimus. Part of Clarissa's self-consciousness is the anticipation of its dissolution. Two quotations recur in her mind, much as the deceased Evans recurs to Septimus: "Fear no more the heat o' the sun" and "If it were now to die, 'twere now to be most happy." The former is once transferred without motivation to Septimus' consciousness,[9] and his motives for suicide are transferred to her.

In the minds of both Septimus and Clarissa there are two aspects of annihilation, one more terrifying than the other: the death of the body and the death of the soul. It is to save his soul, which is menaced by Holmes and Bradshaw with their "must," "must," that Septimus destroys his body. To Septimus' disordered brain these two appear as brutes preying upon him—an image essentially shared by Clarissa, Rezia, and Bradshaw's other patients. In the picture of the sister-goddesses, Proportion and Conversion, the whole hideous process of overpowering the human will is laid bare, and in Lady Bradshaw the results so greatly feared by Septimus are exhibited.

In Clarissa's circle it is Miss Kilman who threatens the soul:

Love and religion! thought Clarissa, going back into the drawing-room, tingling all over. How detestable, how detestable they are! For now that the body of Miss Kilman was not before her, it overwhelmed her—the idea. The cruelest things in the world, she thought, seeing them clumsy, hot, domineering, hypocritical, eavesdropping, jealous, infinitely cruel and unscrupulous, dressed in a mackintosh coat, on the landing; love and religion. Had she ever tried to convert any one herself? Did she not wish everybody merely to be themselves? And she watched out of the window the old lady opposite climbing upstairs. Let her climb upstairs if she wanted to; let her stop; then let her, as Clarissa had often seen her, gain her bedroom, part her curtains, and disappear again into the background. Somehow one respected that—that old woman looking out of the window, quite unconscious that she was being watched. There was something solemn in it—but love and religion would destroy that, whatever it was, the privacy of the soul. The odious Kilman would destroy it.

In Peter Walsh's mind, by a curious return of the circle, it is Clarissa herself who is identified with spiritual death. Awakening from his dream in the park, he finds himself repeating the words, "the death of the soul," and associating them with an occurrence at Bourton: Clarissa's discovery that an acquaintance of hers had given birth to a child out of wedlock:

He hadn't blamed her for minding the fact, since in those days a girl brought up as she was, knew nothing, but it was her manner that annoyed him; timid; hard; something arrogant; unimaginative; prudish. "The death of the soul." He had said that instinctively, ticketing the moment as he used to do—the death of her soul.

Finally, there is the theme of nationalism, introduced by the minor characters. Taken as a group they represent the complete structure of English society—lords, ladies, a prime minister, colonels, majors, shopkeepers, artists, a professor, doctors, ministers, lawyers, politicians, housemaids, butlers. Of the 116, 12 are from the serving class, 36 from the bourgeois, and 68 from the aristocracy.

In this populous world of English society, the relatively few major characters of *Mrs. Dalloway*—there are at most 16—come and go. They are never far out of it, and at times they lose themselves in it to become temporarily mere British subjects.[10]

III

Whereas the themes of character and psychological states are matters of content, the theme of sound, or time, is formal. Though highly emotional in substance, in form Mrs. Woolf is a classicist, imposing upon her characters' streams of consciousness a strict limitation.

The form in *Mrs. Dalloway*, undivided as the novel is by chapters, consists of certain periods of time, intellectually conceived and repeatedly defined. Following the compressed tradition of *Ulysses*, the novel opens with Big Ben sounding 10:00 A.M. and closes on the stroke of three the following morning. Fifteen times the sound of clocks striking reverberates through the book, noting, in all, ten different hours and accompanied by two repeated images: "The leaden circles dissolved in the air" and "the sound fading up there among the gulls." These nine divisions of time are: 10:00-11:00, 11:00-11:30, 11:30-11:45, 11:45-12:00, 12:00-1:30, 1:30-3:00, 3:00-3:30, 3:30-6:00, 6:00-3:00. Reduced to minutes the pattern is

60   30   15   15   90   90   30   150   540.

A progression is immediately apparent: the time being reduced by half in the first three divisions, then repeated, then stepped up to equal the first two, then repeated. The nine-hour division at the end is virtually the total of the preceding eight divisions.

Between these divisions of time and the alternating appearances of the characters there is a general correspondence. Whereas at each sound of the clock there is a shift from one character to another, there are seven shifts unaccompanied by clocks. In any case the functional relationship between the two remains the same: the consciousness of the characters is not allowed to wander on freely in time and space but is recalled periodically by the confinement of a particular moment.

Further examination of the relationship between the characters and these periods of time into which the novel is divided demonstrates Mrs. Woolf's theory, expounded in *Orlando*, of the "discrepancy between time on the clock and time in the mind." Although the external action of the book occupies only seventeen hours—about eleven devoted to Clarissa, ten to Peter, six to the English national character, and three to Septimus—the time covered simultaneously within the minds of the characters is about sixty years, or from Lady Bruton's Devonshire childhood.

Recollections of this past are diffused through the novel from two points, the summer of 1889 at Bourton and the war years of 1914-18; and, though it is impossible to isolate all these memories, the occurrence of protracted retrospects may be noted. They have a rhythmical pattern of their own, their extent varying inversely with the time divisions simultaneously noted by the clocks:

minutes . . .	60	30	15	15	90	90	30	150	540
pages	2	9	10	19	1	2	2	4	7

As the present becomes shorter, the past becomes longer. Whereas the account of Lady Bruton's luncheon, for example, occurring between the hours of 1:30 and 3:00, is related at the rate of twenty-four pages to ninety minutes, the Smiths' fifteen-minute walk from Regent's Park to Harley Street takes up the same amount of space. The difference is to be accounted for by the fact that more than half the pages are devoted to a résumé of Septimus' life and cover a period of over ten years.[11]

IV

The thematic use of color in *Mrs. Dalloway* is another matter of form. Opening with the riot of hues in Mulberry's flower shop, the book closes in the midst of the bright costumes of Clarissa's guests. Between the two, an extrication of certain colors and an association of them with certain characters or character groups take place.

The color for Clarissa is green. Seven times the color of her green evening dress, upon which she sews in the morning and which she wears at night, is remarked; in it she is described as a mermaid. Earlier she is compared to a "blue-green" jay. The Dalloway house has green lights and green linoleum on the bathroom floor. Peter remembers "the vivid green moss" near the fountain, where she refused to marry him. Miss Kilman, a member of the Clarissa group, wears a green mackintosh, and Elizabeth Dalloway is compared to a hyacinth, "sheathed in glossy green."

For Peter the color is blue—the color lying next in the spectrum. In Sally Seton's mind he is associated with the image of blue hydrangeas. He blows rings of blue smoke from his cigar in the park. He receives a letter from Clarissa written on blue stationery; they sit on a blue sofa together; and the evening through which he walks to her party is compared to a woman in blue and pearls.

Red is the color associated with Septimus. He has a persistent image of the world bursting into flames before his gaze and another of being pursued by a beast with "blood-red nostrils." His bedroom is papered with red roses, and he once imagines red flowers are growing up through him. His friend Evans, part of the Septimus group, was red-headed. In his end the color of blood is implied. In connection with the relatively small amount of space and time occupied in the book by Septimus, an admittedly vital character, this choice seems significant. For red has the strongest wave length in the spectrum, ranging from 0.723 to 0.647 mm. as compared with 0.575-0.492 for green and 0.492-0.455 for blue.

These three colors are complementary. In order to complete the symbolism, therefore, white should be associated with the English national character. Although this image is not so dominant as the other three, it does appear. The airplane, upon which the attention of all London is fixed, flies into and out of white clouds, writing in white smoke; when Elizabeth mingled with the crowds in the Strand "the clouds were of mountainous white"; Peter sits next to a "grey nurse" in the park; the upholstery of the royal motor car is grey; from it "the pale light of the immortal presence fell upon them"; and Clarissa thought she knew who was inside, for

> she had seen something white, circular, in the footman's hand, a disc inscribed with a name,—the Queen's, the Prince of Wales, the Prime Minister's?—which, by force of its own lustre burnt its way through (Clarissa saw the car diminishing, disappearing), to blaze among candelabras, glittering stars, breasts stiff with oak leaves, Hugh Whitbread and all his colleagues, the gentlemen of England, that night in Buckingham Palace.

In addition to these simple parallels between colors and characters, there appears to be an attempt to connect Mrs. Dalloway and Septimus Smith by means of an intermediate color. Whereas the use of green, blue, and red is largely confined to the three major characters, yellow, lying between red and green in the spectrum, is applied equally to Clarissa and Septimus. She wears a yellow hat, her living room has yellow curtains, her husband, who is fair-haired, has yellow gloves, her daughter rides a yellow bus. Septimus, on the other hand, notices yellow flowers from the top of a bus, repeatedly looks at the yellow bananas on the sideboard, watches the sunlight making a gold spot on the wall.[12]

V

The coherence of *Mrs. Dalloway* is the more remarkable for the kaleidoscopic nature of its parts. Characters, psychological states, sounds, and colors are taken up in no logical sequence. They are introduced irregularly, abruptly dropped, and intertwined with a good deal of complexity. To relate these fragments Mrs. Woolf has been assiduous in employing unifying devices. First among these is the theme of nationalism, its function inherent in its very nature. A second is the theme of time, which, also reiterated, brings certain characters together by appointment, accounts for the transition made from one psychological theme to another, and is on the mind of every major character.

There is, finally, the use of mechanical links, without which no shift is made from one character to another: the simple meeting of two persons,[13] the joining of two people by a third,[14] and, most contrived of all, the use of inanimate objects to connect people. Of the latter Mrs. Woolf employs a notable variety: the motorcar, the airplane, the clocks of Harley and Oxford Streets, the clouds in the sky over the Strand, and the ambulance. None of these objects, unless it is the ambulance, bears any internal relation to the characters or possesses inherent value as a conjunction. The selection is entirely arbitrary; but, once made, each is converted by purely intellectual processes into a pertinent symbol.

Far above these joints of the novel, however, a greater unity is achieved by the author's method of dealing with her elements of composition. Mrs. Woolf's style is not fluid; one character does not merge into another, or one theme or one moment into another. Her novel is distinctly put together of parts, but recurring and interrelated parts. Her style is contrapuntal, and the unity of the novel is not one of flow but of rhythm.

The counterpoint of *Mrs. Dalloway* is most distinct between the character appearances and the time divisions, a relationship which may be pictured by setting down the two patterns:[15]

60 minutes. . . .30	15 15 90 90 30 150 540
2 pages. 9	10 19 1 2 2 4 7
\			/
abc	a, d c d, c a c dab

While time and personality are the main rhythms in *Mrs. Dalloway*, they are not the only ones. There are the additional rhythms of recurring psychological themes and color themes. These four alternate simultaneously with one another, within themselves, and within their subdivisions. In the rhythms which are thus created, correspondence and antithesis are as great factors as repetition: the correspondence between certain characters, certain psychological states, and certain colors; the antithesis of Clarissa and Septimus, of the themes of consciousness and dissolution, of the past and present in inverse ratio, of the complementary colors red and blue-green, of emotional substance and intellectual form.

Mrs. Dalloway, indeed, is an easier novel to diagram than to summarize. If it does have a text it must be something like this: Every British subject has two possessions which are in a curious way one—consciousness and memory—both of which he will one day be deprived of by the death of the body.

A book which has this for a story, in which characters are ultimately reduced to shades of the spectrum and time to the striking of clocks, it is impertinent to abstract. Only the recurring themes of personality, of mental states, of colors and sounds may be charted. The composition is the thing.

From *College English* 5.7 (April 1944): 351-358. Copyright © 1944 by the National Council of Teachers of English. Reprinted with permission of the National Council of Teachers of English.

Notes

1. *Mrs. Dalloway* ("Modern Library" ed.), p. vi.
2. See also pp. 142, 279-82; their attentions are united by the motorcar and the airplane; Peter Walsh and Sir William Bradshaw go back and forth between them.
3. Pp. 42, 59, 97, 203, 242-44.
4. Whereas, of a total of 293 pages, Clarissa occupies 153, Peter 123, the English national character 69, and Septimus 64, the actual number of appearances of Clarissa is 4, of Septimus 4, of Peter 3, and of the English national character 2.
5. Pp. 19-42, 59-72, 250-96.

6. The contrast may be noted throughout the book of normal consciousness, from the dullest to the most sharpened, with Septimus' abnormal consciousness, Peter's dream consciousness, and consciousness of the past.

7. The interplay of past and present is constant throughout the book: in the reminiscences of Clarissa walking up Bond Street, the character of Sally Seton-Lady Rosseter, Lady Bruton's memories of her childhood, the hallucinations of Septimus Smith, the conversion of Miss Kilman, and the general disillusion of the war still shadowing English life.

8. It is nonetheless present at each of the thirteen major shifts of character (see pp. 13, 23, 33, 46, 88, 100, 117, 118, 139, 192, 226, 231, 271, 275, 280-82).

9. P. 211.

10. See pp. 5, 19-42, 209, 210, 275. Other manifestations of this theme, like the other three diffused through the novel, are the symbolic motorcar, the projects of Lady Bruton, the background presence of British India, Richard Dalloway's love of monarchy, Clarissa's love of London, Peter Walsh's love of British civilization, and the presence of Minister Baldwin at Clarissa's party—the "symbol of what they all stood for, English society."

11. The theme of time is also notable in the date (Wednesday, mid-June, 1923), in the three appointments around which the action eddies (12:00, 1:30, and [9:00], if the last hour may be assigned to Clarissa's party), and in the sense of time on the minds of all the major characters (see pp. 44, 74, 75, 83, 170, 192, 193, 208, 210).

12. Unlike the color symbolism in *To the Lighthouse*, these colors do not possess independent meaning; that is, green does not symbolize consciousness, or blue memory, or red death; they match the character themes rather than the psychological themes of the book.

13. Pp. 59, 106, 250 ff.

14. Pp. 98, 122-24.

15. This relationship has been analyzed by Mr. Daiches in a diagram illustrating the regular alternation of the categories of time and space, or personality (*The Novel and the Modern World* [Chicago: University of Chicago Press, 1939], pp. 174-76). Actually, his is more of a formula than a chart, emphasizing the alternation of two themes rather than the simultaneous movement of several.

A-linear Time and Stream of Consciousness _____
Teresa Prudente

I have so far attempted to define the experience of an exit from the linearity of time as represented in Virginia Woolf's work. This has involved the consideration of the relation connecting the changes in perception experienced by the subject in *moments of being* and the possibility of re-creating them in writing. The ineffability inherent in the experience of ecstasy has led me to analyze the way in which in *To the Lighthouse* Woolf challenges the limits of language in order to achieve a re-presenting of *moments of being* through art. The third part of my analysis will continue focusing on Woolf's narrative choices, now shifting from examination of the writer's stylistic features (the structuring of sentences and the polysemy of vocabulary) to the wider consideration of Woolf's narrative structures.

This final part of my analysis will then involve a theoretical level of reflection which, in comparing Virginia Woolf's and André Gide's narrative choices, will suggest the various and different modalities in which the novel can convey the experience of a-linearity of time. This chapter will therefore take into consideration Woolf's employment of the *stream of consciousness*[1] techniques, which appear fundamental in transposing my analysis of the literary re-creation of *moments of being* to the level of an inquiry into the expressive potentialities of the novel.

Nevertheless, *Mrs Dalloway*, the novel on which I will focus in this chapter, requires that I briefly return to a thematic examination before extending the analysis to the level of structural reflection. The 1925 novel offers several elements which suggest and invite re-discussion of the concept of a-linearity and its implications. In *Mrs Dalloway*, the mirror imaging of the two characters of Clarissa Dalloway and Septimus Smith stimulates not so much a re-definition, but rather a further process in the breaking up of the concept of a-linearity as I have so far defined it. The analysis of *Orlando* and *To the Lighthouse* has in fact established a relation between a-linearity and the experience of ecstasy, in underlining how the subject experiences in *moments of being* a perceptual expansion and a temporal transformation which make him perceive a sense of *eternity*. *Mrs Dalloway*[2] seems instead to portray the experience of a-linearity of time as broken up in different and opposing modalities, which open the concept to further complex implications. As I will show, this does not imply a definition of a-linearity in terms which are opposed to the ones that I have so far proposed. This refinement seems instead to complete Woolf's portrayal of a-linearity, in presenting it as composed by contradictory and yet complementary elements.

The two characters Mrs. Dalloway and Septimus Smith, who never meet throughout the narrative and are nevertheless connected by a system of relations and coincidences[3], thus function as essential elements for breaking up the experience of a-linearity in its complex and apparently contradictory components. As is well-known, Woolf herself declared that the character of Septimus was conceived by her as the double of Clarissa Dalloway, with the intention of changing the tragic destiny that she had initially reserved for this second character: "in the first version Septimus, who later is intended to be her double, had no existence; and Mrs. Dalloway was originally intended to kill herself, or perhaps merely to die at the end of the party."[4] The acceptability of this version provided by Woolf on the conception of *Mrs Dalloway* is questioned by some critics, who refer to "Mrs Dalloway in Bond Street," the 1923 short-story from which the novel originated.[5] Nevertheless, the careful and profound alignment of the two characters is certain, and it is the interdependent relation between the two which allows Woolf to show in this novel the unfolding of two simultaneous and opposite points of view on reality. Woolf's intention while conceiving *Mrs Dalloway* in fact was to achieve a breaking up of the narrative point of view; as I will show, this appears to convey not so much two contradictory perceptions of time, but rather two aspects of the same experience of a-linearity: "I adumbrate here a study of insanity and suicide; the world seen by the sane and the insane side by side."[6]

Since the very beginning of the novel the character of Mrs. Dalloway presents features which are similar to those that Woolf will later attribute to Mrs. Ramsay in *To the Lighthouse*. This is particularly true with regards to the two characters' ability to balance the interaction between on the one hand the perception of external reality and self-exploration on the other. While wandering in the streets of London and absorbing the stimuli offered by the city, Mrs. Dalloway experiences a sense of solemnity and peace. This temporal suspension is cyclically spaced out by the intermittent beating of Big Ben, which brings the character back to the linear flowing of time. The marking of time does not, however, prevent Mrs. Dalloway from feeling an organic sense composing the dynamic and contradictory elements of her perception into a coherent design. In this sense, Clarissa embodies the positive and stimulating aspects of life in the city which Woolf had underlined in the essay "The Narrow Bridge of Art"[7], while Septimus, as we will see, represents the opposite, the inability to overcome the impact of modernity on the perceptual faculties of the sensitive subject:

> an indescribable pause; a suspense (but that might be her heart, affected, they said, by influenza) before Big Ben strikes. There! Out it boomed. First a warning, musical; then the hour, irrevocable. The leaden circles dissolved in the air. In people's eyes, in the swing, tramp, and trudge . . . was what she loved, life; London; this moment of June.[8]

Instead of suggesting the inescapable passing of time, the striking of the hours produces in Mrs Dalloway a suspension[9] and the sense of a pause in the rhythm of the city which transform the linear beating of time into the perception of a cyclic temporality. This circularity is dissolved by the irrevocable sound of the bells, conveyed by Woolf with the recurrent image of a vibration which combines the immateriality of the sound (the "circles" of vibration which allude to cyclic time) with the materiality of its origin ("leaden"). The sound of the bells thus appears not only to anchor the character absolutely in the present time ("this moment of June"), but also to be endowed with two different and contradictory implications, which allude equally to a-temporal suspension and to linear progression in time. This is paralleled in *To the Lighthouse* in the scene which depicts Mrs. Ramsay experiencing the sense of a double and contradictory significance in listening to the sound of the waves.[10] Similar to the passage quoted from *Mrs Dalloway* in which two opposite feelings are perceived by the subject as closely related to each other ("First a warning, musical; then the hour, irrevocable"), in *To the Lighthouse* cyclic temporality and irrevocable beating of time are portrayed as interacting. The co-existence of the two perceptions of time thus leads Mrs. Dalloway, like Mrs. Ramsay in *To the Lighthouse*, to achieve an exhilarating balance between the stimuli offered by external reality and her consciousness. The chaotic accumulation of heterogeneous elements which characterize the city produces in the character the sense of a coinciding and osmosis between external and interior perception. Mrs. Dalloway appears to plunge spontaneously into the life of the city to the point of feeling her personality dissolving into the magma of external reality:

> She would not say of any one in the world now that they were this or were that. She felt very young; at the same time unspeakably aged. She sliced like a knife through everything; at the same time she was outside looking on. She had a perpetual sense, as she watched the taxicabs, of being out, out, far out to sea and alone . . . she would not say of Peter, she would not say of herself; I am this, I am that.[11]

The essence of Mrs. Dalloway's balanced relation with the external world seems to reside in the character's ability to plunge into experience and to absorb the stimuli while also maintaining that distance which allows the subject to hold a proportioned point of view. Similar to Lily's stepping back from her canvas in *To the Lighthouse*, this act of distancing helps the subject to place experience in perspective and gain rational control on the chaos of perception. The co-existence of *immer-*

sion into and *distancing* from immediate perception stimulates in Mrs. Dalloway the sense of a blurring of the boundaries of her personality, a process which, as I have stated in the previous chapters, acts as fundamental also in *To the Lighthouse*. The impossibility of achieving a stable self-definition works in both novels as a determining element, which exposes the subject to the awareness of the complexity and inexplicability inherent in the processes of consciousness. Like the two female characters in *To the Lighthouse*, Mrs. Dalloway does not appear engaged in the quest for a general and all-encompassing answer able to provide a theorized explanation of her perception, but rather focuses on the "little daily miracles"[12] which over time compose a fragmented whole of significance:

> It was not beauty; it was not mind. It was something central which permeated; something warm which broke up surfaces and rippled the cold contact of man and woman, or of women together . . . It was a sudden revelation . . . Then, for that moment, she had seen an illumination; a match burning in a crocus; an inner meaning almost expressed. But the close withdrew; the hard softened. It was over—the moment.[13]

The moment of illumination manifests itself in the form of a brief parabola which presents features of unpredictability and instantaneity. Revelation emerges without apparent reason and gives origin to the movements of progressive intensification and expansion of perception which culminate in the metaphorical breaking of the surface of experience. The moment is dominated by a sense of evanescence which immediately raises for the subject the question of how to crystallize such flowing and illuminating instants ("an inner meaning, almost expressed"). The image of "a match burning in a crocus" anticipates the metaphor in *To the Lighthouse* of "matches unexpectedly struck in the dark"[14]; even if here the process of burning seems to suggest a temporal prolonging of the moment of revelation compared to the instantaneous quality of the image in *To the Lighthouse*, the evanescent nature of these moments is indeed emphasized by the mention of the "crocus."[15] The appearance of significance behind reality does not lead to the subject's appropriation of a definitive and stable explanation, but rather acquires the form of a fleeting fragment of revelation. In this sense, the *moment of being* maintains an unfathomable quality, and this makes the subject perceive how these instants hold a mysterious nucleus ("something central, something warm") which can only be conveyed by lytosis through *negation* ("it was not beauty, it was not mind") and sensorially grasped through *impressions* ("some astonishing meaning").

The character of Septimus appears different from Mrs. Dalloway (and from the later characters of Mrs. Ramsay and Lily Briscoe) in virtue of his particular reactions to these perceptual transformations, which in him structure a radically opposite experience of a-linearity. While the female characters mentioned prove to find in the exit from habitual lines of perception the chance to experience an extra-temporal dimension which also leads them to the revelation of the complexity and multiple significances in reality, this same alteration of reality instead acts in Septimus as a disorientating and dramatic experience. The sense of loss of control on reality is not transformed by the subject into the fertile redefinition of his relation with the external world, but seems instead to ignite a tragic tension between consciousness and reality. Since his first appearance in the novel, Septimus is characterized by a hyper-sensitivity which does not lead him to the intensification and expansion of the *moment of being*, but which makes him feel his perpetual sensitiveness as unbearable:

Septimus Warren Smith, aged about thirty, pale-faced, beak-nosed, wearing brown shoes and a shabby overcoat, with hazel eyes which had the look of apprehension in them which makes complete strangers apprehensive too. The world has raised its whip; where it will descend? Everything had come to a standstill. The throb of the motor engines sounded like a pulse irregularly drumming through an entire body . . . and this gradual drawing together of everything to one centre before his eyes, as if some horror had come almost to the surface and was about to burst into flames, terrified him. The world wavered and quivered and threatened to burst into flames. It is I who am blocking the way, he thought. Was he not being looked at and pointed at; was he not weighted there, rooted to the pavement, for a purpose? But for what purpose?[16]

Woolf operates here a rapid shift from the external description of the character to the insight into his consciousness and both points of view seem to underline Septimus's peculiarities in perception. The temporal suspension produced by the event in the scene ("everything had come to a standstill"), the reverberation of the sound and the crowding of people originate in Septimus a terror which takes the form of an uncontrolled and deformed acceleration of time.[17] The chaotic experience of the city which stimulates Mrs. Dalloway to perceive the multitude of stimuli and the fertile combination of her thoughts thus seems to act differently in Septimus originating the sense of an excess in perception which leads to paralysis. Similarly, the sense of fluctuation of reality is not transformed into the revelation of new significances as in Mrs. Dalloway, but rather originates in Septimus only negative sensations which make him experience his body to be overwhelmed and immobilized by fear. The emergence on the surface of a hidden reality thus coincides in this character not with Mrs. Dalloway's insight of "something central" and essential, but with its opposite: the appearance of a terrifying truth. The images which convey Septimus's transformations in perception do not refer to a sense of expansion, as they do for the character of Mrs. Dalloway, but instead allude to dramatic scenes of annihilation. Furthermore, the temporary loss of meaning which represents for Lily Briscoe the first step toward the revelation of a *different* order, originates in Septimus ("for a purpose? But for what purpose?") a dramatic confrontation between the self and the perceived world. The momentary breaking up in perception and appearance of new significances do not thus culminate for Septimus in the temporary re-composition of reality, which seems instead to remain insanely de-structured and fragmented.

In the second event which catalyzes the attention of the crowd, the passage of an airplane which traces words in the sky[18], Septimus's process of deconstruction in perception takes the form of a feeling of coincidence with external reality. This does not however stimulate in the character the rise of a range of new significances, but rather implements Septimus's difficulty in dealing with his raw and over-sensitized perception:

> "K . . . R . . . " said the nursemaid. And Septimus heard her say "Kay Arr" close to his ear, deeply, softly, like a mellow organ, but with a roughness in her voice like a grasshopper's, which rasped his spine deliciously and sent running up into his brain waves of sound which, concussing, broke.[19]

Language itself is here disarticulated into its single phonic components and this shows how Septimus proves to be sensitive to the hidden supra-semantic potentialities of words. This attitude is not transmuted in Septimus, as happens in other Woolfian characters, into the possibility of entering a different and more significant communicative system, but rather marks the subject's increasing separation from reality. The sounds of the letters, and especially the "R" which produces a physical reaction in the character, provoke a crowd of sensations which unveil Septimus's amplified and distorted perception, conveyed in the text by Woolf's recurrent image of waves breaking in the mind.[20] Though similar to the ones undergone by Woolf's other characters experiencing *moments of being*[21], these transformations in perception do not coincide in Septimus with a process of transfiguration of reality ending with the subject's return to ordinary perception. On the contrary, Septimus's experience of moments of hyper-significance seems to lead the character to a more and more progressive and definitive abandonment of reality and alteration in perception. When, in fact, Rezia, Septimus's wife, puts her hand on her husband's knee, this small gesture acts as the only element able to anchor the subject to the solidity of reality; in this sense the verb "to transfix," often employed by Woolf in conveying *moments of being*, unveils its double significance here, showing how the crystallization of time holds the potential to lead not only to the feeling of ecstatic revelation but also to a dramatic sense of petrification. The subject is clearly represented here as experiencing a progressive effacement of the real world, which is obscured by a more and more consistent vision, reproduced in the text by the rapid succession of coordinates sentences conveying the suspense and the violent caesura of the final statement "would have sent him mad."[22]

Septimus's excessively consistent vision does not take the form, as in Clarissa and in *To the Lighthouse*, of a temporary instant of revelation, but rather imposes itself as an incumbent deformation which marks the subject's increasing separation from reality.[23] In this sense, Septimus's exit from linear perception does not lead the subject to the redefinition of his relation with reality, but rather implements the definitive separation between his subjective perception and an objective act of apprehension:

> The sparrows fluttering, rising, and falling in jagged fountains were part of the pattern; the white and the blues, barred with black branches. Sounds made harmonies with premeditation; the spaces between them were as significant as the sounds. A child cried. Rightly away a horn sounded. All taken together meant the birth of a new religion.[24]

Septimus's plunge into his vision thus acquires the character of a radical alienation which does not lead the subject to a more intense perception of reality, but instead stimulate the growth of a *different* reality. This visionary process sees an opposition between the subject's mental reality and objective perception and in this sense the real world is felt as violently breaking into and interrupting[25] the subject's vision, which has become for him the only and most consistent reality. Septimus perceives the revelation of a hidden pattern behind reality and this, as I have underlined in analyzing *To the Lighthouse*, represents the subject's potential to establish new and significant connections linking the elements of perception, and build a new and temporary system of interpretation. As in several of Woolf's characters, in Septimus we see the unfolding of a process of osmosis which leads the character to perceive a reverberation of meaning also in the small and inanimate details of perception. The trees, the leaves, the branches and the sparrows, with their movements and their spatial dispositions, become parts of the secret design revealed to the subject. In Woolf's description these single elements notably shift from juxtaposition to a simultaneous convergence which results in their meeting within the metaphorical space of the subject's body, and this shows how the elements are transformed from random and disconnected stimuli to essential and organic parts of a hidden pattern. The subject thus functions as the meeting-place of the "dissemblables"[26] in reality and acts as the re-elaborating centre where different and fragmented elements are collected and reordered into a design which is meaningful to him. As recurrent in Woolf's atomist view, the individual stimuli are depicted as interacting and, as I have shown in *To the Lighthouse*, emptiness and fullness work as closely interconnected ("the spaces between them were as significant as the sounds"). In this sense, the experience of the character of Septimus does not differ from Woolf's other portrayals of instants of revelation and is here again represented as a temporary converging of the elements in a significant re-composition. On the contrary, the transformations undergone by Septimus in his perception of time acquire very specific features, which stimulate further re-discussion of the notion of a-linearity.

In the previous chapters we have seen how *moments of being* bring about a sense of *eternity* which is felt by the subject not in terms of extension of time, but rather as a feeling of expansion of these instants in a continuous present. This amplification of time does not appear to take place in Septimus, who in the significant moments proves to enter a timeless dimension which coincides for him with an *eternal suffer-*

ing. In the scene mentioned above, Rezia's voice is perceived by Septimus as transfigured[27] and this is underlined by Woolf's shift from direct to indirect speech, a narrative passage which marks the character's inability to allow external stimuli to enter his consciousness without translating them into the *different* voice in his mind. Reality appears to be pressing on the character and calling on his reluctant attention, while Septimus shows himself to be far from proportion in his perception and to oscillate between a sense of omnipotence and the opposite feeling of passivity and impotence. Septimus's exit from linear perception of time[28] thus coincides with a revelation which does not take the form, as in Clarissa, of a co-existence of and circular passage from internal to external time, but is rather transformed into a dramatic tension between the sense of eternity and the marking of chronological time. As Paul Ricoeur states, the confrontation between these two manifestations of time, which he defines as *mortal* and *monumental*, does not take the form in this novel of a simple opposition, but rather re-creates the two extremities within which a wide range of different temporalities unfolds.[29] As shown in the previous chapters, it is the presence of death which operates a temporary conjunction between mortal and eternal temporalities, by unveiling the relation of interdependence which connects *the end of time* with *endless time*. In *Mrs Dalloway*, death is present in the form of Septimus's hallucinations about his deceased friend Evans and, later in the novel, in the character's suicide. Both manifestations contribute to the spreading for the character of a disorientating loss of significance, which, as happens in *To the Lighthouse*, acts as the origin not only of a painful awareness, but also of a process of re-definition of the experience of time. In this sense, death is shown by Woolf as imminent in life and as holding the potentialities of a double-sided significance. Nevertheless, in *Mrs Dalloway* the releasing of new significance originating from the subject's relation with death, conceived as the *other* than time, deploys its potentialities only for the character of Clarissa. The echo of Septimus's suicide opens in Clarissa Dalloway the way to a re-definition of the concept of death which leads her to perceive how the end of life holds the potential to function in consciousness not as negation of time, but rather as a more intense perception of the instant in the present: "Death was defiance. Death was an attempt to communicate, people feeling the impossibility of reaching the centre which, mystically, evaded them; closeness drew apart; rapture faded; one was alone. There was an embrace in death."[30]

Though being the origin of this revelation, Septimus appears unable to reconcile both the discrepancy between his mental vision and reality, and the gulf separating his internal a-temporal dimension and chronological time:

> "It is time," said Rezia.
>
> The word "time" split his husk; poured its riches over him; and from his lips fell like shells, like shavings from a plane, without his making them, hard, white, imperishable, words, and flew to attach themselves to their places in an ode to Time; an immortal ode to Time.[31]

The return to reality and to the perception of linear time proves to be impossible for the character of Septimus and this defines his dramatic internal split. In entering Septimus's perception, the word "time" produces an image similar to that arisen from the previous explosion of an engine; the subject perceives the sense of the breaking of a surface ("splits its husk"[32]) and a new process of internal fragmentation of language ("like shells, like shavings from a plane . . . words"). Words acquire an existence which proves to be autonomous and independent of the subject ("without his making them") and spontaneously start moving and combining. Finally, in Septimus's perception words compose an Ode to Time which, by evoking the presence of Evans, again links death to immortality ("hard, white, imperishable") and the end of time to endless time. As Paul Ricoeur comments, the character of Septimus exemplifies a revelation which sees death connected to eternal time and *monumental time* as contrasting the subject's access to the a-temporal dimension.[33] In this sense, Septimus differs from Woolf's other characters who in *moments of being* experience a temporary significant recomposition in perception which makes them perceive how the contradictory elements in reality can be re-composed into a constellation of meanings. In Septimus the exit from linear perception does not originate a temporary suspension and expansion of time which ends in a redefinition of ordinary perception, but instead marks a more radical and definitive alienation from reality. Septimus's process of breaking up in perception does not culminate in a more significant re-interpretation of reality, but rather takes the form of the dramatic revelation of a total *absence of meanings*:

> He could reason; he could read Dante for example, quite easily ("Septimus, do put down your book," said Rezia, gently shutting the *Inferno*), he could add up his bill; his brain was perfect; it might be the fault of the world then—that he could not feel . . . It might be possible, Septimus thought . . . it might be possible that the world itself is without meaning.[34]

The existential opposite to the character of Clarissa Dalloway, and to Mrs. Ramsay and Lily Briscoe in *To the Lighthouse*, Septimus proves to experience a drastic dissociation between his sensorial perception and the re-elaboration operated by his mind. While in the three other characters mentioned moments of ecstasy are structured on a close interdependence between the act of sensorial apprehension and the process of logical re-construction, Septimus's perceptual paralysis seems to amplify the disproportion between his mental processes and phenomenal perception. In this character it is not mental activity in itself which appears to be paralyzed, but rather the subject's capacity to establish a connection between his internal reality and the external world, and the ability to root mental elaboration in the perception of the surrounding reality. As already noted in the preceding chapters, the subject's relation to language acts as fundamental in that process of spreading doubt which suspends any definitive signification of experience. In *To the Lighthouse*, this temporary inability to bestow a meaning on reality ignites in Lily a process which, by moving from the awareness of how ordinary language is unable fully to convey experience, stimulates the character to turn to the different and more significant semantic system offered by art. In *Mrs Dalloway* in contrast, Septimus experiences a profound alienation from ordinary language which allows him to plunge into the more significant dimension of literary language ("He could read Dante . . . quite easily"[35]), but which also implements his more and more definitive separation from reality. In *To the Lighthouse*, the painting accomplished by Lily embodies the completion of a process of breaking up and questioning of reality which culminates in the reconstruction of a *different* design, in which new and significant relations crystallize the moment of revelation. In the 1927 novel the character of Lily moves from her perception of loss of control of reality and absence of meaning to the achievement of a work of art which temporarily re-organizes her chaotic perception. The painting thus embodies both the subject's potential to crystallize significant instants and her awareness of how moments of revelation escape any fixed and definitive interpretation.

The character of Septimus is instead portrayed as unable to access this stage of re-composition in perception and his experience of a suspension in the linear proceeding of time produces in him a vision of eternity which takes the form of endless suffering and solitude. Woolf's characterization of Septimus insists repeatedly on the character's inability to communicate his vision ("communication is health"[36]) and in this seems to reside the more profound origin of his sense of isolation ("the eternal loneliness"[37]). Septimus's alteration activates a process of internal breaking up which involves not only the subject's phenomenal perception but also his employment and apprehension of language. Furthermore, the character's turning to a hypersignificant perception of language is not transformed here, as in *To the Lighthouse*, into a fundamental stage in the process which leads the subject to translate his experience into the language of art, but functions instead as an *obstacle* which amplifies the subject's impossibility to communicate. In the diagnosis of Septimus's illness, Doctor Bradshaw interprets the character's loss of proportion ("he called it not having a sense of proportion"[38]), and the excess of meanings which Septimus perceives in language as revealing symptoms of his altered state of mind ("He was attaching meanings to words of a symbolical kind. A very serious symptom to be noted on the card"[39]).

The character of the doctor appears crucial both in defining the most subtle implications of Septimus's alteration and in illuminating Woolf's complex position on the issue of mental illness. As Ricoeur underlines, Doctor Bradshaw embodies in the novel a "figure of authority"[40] which, the opposite of his patient, adheres perfectly to the beating of chronological time. Doctor Bradshaw's insistence on the loss of proportion as a main symptom of mental illness is in fact diametrically opposed to the emphasis which he places on his own ability to master reality: "they watched him go through, for their benefit, a curious exercise with the arms, which he shot out, brought sharply back to his hip, to prove (if the patient was obstinate) that Sir William was master of his own actions, which the patient was not."[41] This boasted capacity of mental control is immediately connected by Woolf to the character's non-problematic coinciding with the conventional measure of time: "Shredding and slicing, dividing and subdividing, the clocks of Harley Street nibbled at the June day, counselled submission, unhelped authority, and pointed out in chorus the supreme advantage of a sense of proportion."[42] This ironical exaltation of the scientific method of subdivision and measure of time is also closely connected in *Mrs Dalloway* with a harsh criticism of the examination of the mind carried out by doctors. Woolf's skeptical attitude, though obviously deriving from her personal experience[43], is certainly not only to be interpreted as a subjective and circumscribed recrimination, but involves rather the writer's approach to the analysis of human consciousness. Beyond the specific field of mental disorders, Woolf's sarcastic portrayal of Doctor Bradshaw in fact raises the question of to what extent and by what means states of mind are intelligible and classifiable. In this sense, as I will show, Woolf's employment of interior monologue techniques works precisely by emphasizing the impossibility of completely comprehending mental experience, both scientifically and linguistically. What from Doctor Bradshaw's point of view appears a rigid distinction between *sane* and *insane* is in fact re-questioned by Woolf in her double-sided portrayal of mental alteration. Septimus's loss of proportion, which is interpreted by the doctor as the main symptom of the character's illness, acts also as the key element for his access to a different and more meaningful dimension.

The suspension in meaning operated by Septimus, his process of breaking up language into its single phonic components and his sensitiveness to the supra-semantic and symbolic aspects of words, do not however open the way to the utterly other communication inherent in art, but instead mark the character's increasing separation from reality. While in *To the Lighthouse* and *Orlando* the characters' sensitivity to the hidden potentialities of language is expressed by their profound love for and understanding of poetry, in *Mrs Dalloway* this takes the more radical form of a dramatically altered perception. Septimus's acoustic hallucinations in fact implement the character's separation from reality and ingress into an utterly other dimension. The character's impression of hearing birds singing in Greek does not only draw on Woolf's personal experience[44], but also implies an opening to the lost and impersonal world of ancient literature which Woolf deeply admired.[45] This world, in being irremediably far and separate from the subject's real existence, does not provide an inspiration for Septimus's re-elaboration of his perception, but rather increases his alienation from the phenomenal world. The character's hallucinatory point of view does not culminate in the fertile translation of experience into the work of art, but imprisons him rather within a different dimension, from which any attempt at communication seems to fail. Shortly before his suicide, Septimus asks his wife Rezia to burn his writings, which in his judgment are only unrelated fragments and do not convey a coherent act of communication.[46] Unable to access the second creative phase of re-construction of broken-up reality, Septimus thus appears incapable of any verbalization of his state of mind.

It is the peculiar quality of Septimus's "stammering"[47] self which provides me with the elements to transpose the analysis from thematic and stylistic levels to a structural examination of Woolf's work. According to Ricoeur, the character of Septimus can be considered a key example of how the experience of time is re-configured in narrative[48]; furthermore, this character also proves to function as a fundamental element in analyzing Woolf's employment of the *stream of consciousness* techniques. As Daniel Ferrer underlines, in *Mrs Dalloway* the character of Septimus embodies an altered point of view which is able to shed light on Woolf's conception and employment of her tunneling process:

> There are signs which refer to nothing, which stop referring, or rather which suddenly and ostentatiously start referring in the void. In a fictional text, there is a doubling of the void, but this doubling, this step too far towards the void, corrodes the whole system of referencing, and with it the system of enunciation constructed, symmetrically, upstream of the discourse.[49]

Ferrer envisages in Septimus a role in the establishment of an *empty reference* which simultaneously builds and de-constructs the basis of representation. Septimus's determining position in the novel's representation of consciousness seems to derive from Woolf's particular disposition and deployment of the various narrative voices present in this work. As Dorrit Cohn[50] notes, *Mrs Dalloway* is structured on the continuous and often imperceptible shift from one narrative technique to another. This results in a blending of voices which seems to reproduce both the indefinite nature of consciousness and the role of connection exerted by the narrator.[51] Furthermore, Woolf seems here not only to mix the three techniques of representation of consciousness indicated by Cohn[52], but also to operate an increase of ambiguity in their employment. This is particularly evident in Woolf's use of narrated monologue[53], in which the already fluctuating borders of this technique are rendered even less determined by the fading of the narrator's voice into those of the characters. The entire novel is structured on this indeterminacy of voices, which is particularly evident in the scene already mentioned of the motorcar engine's explosion.[54] In this scene the distinction between the narrator's and the character's voice appears blurred and not clearly defined: the shift from the external description carried out by the narrator to Septimus's free indirect speech takes place in an almost invisible way. The considerations which are situated between the clearly signaled third person voice and the character's voice remain in an ambiguous position, starting from the sentence "the world has raised its whip; where will it descend?"[55] which, though probably marking the passage to free indirect speech, does not present any grammatical change underlining any such shift. The two following images which convey both a sense of immobility ("Everything had come to a standstill") and pulsation, seem again to belong to the narrator's voice, as Ferrer[56] notes by underlining the change of tense from "has raised" to "had come"; on the other hand, the peculiar sensations described in the passage, such as the sense of the increasing heat of the sun, can not be attributed to an impersonal voice, but seem rather to pertain to Septimus's altered perception. Finally, the passage to Septimus's point of view is marked by the sentence "Septimus thought," which follows a series of descriptions operated by the narrator's voice ("Everyone looked . . . Septimus looked . . . Boys on bicycles . . . traffic accumulated"). Also in this case, the shift from one voice to another appears imperceptible, giving the reader the impression that narrator and character have metaphorically merged in the formulation of a set of "intermediate" sentences which could be attributed to either voice ("And there the motorcar stood . . . the world wavered and quivered").

As Auerbach remarked in his famous comment on the opening of *To the Lighthouse*[57], Woolf's ambiguous employment of the narrated monologue technique is not limited to the blurring of the boundaries dividing the different voices, but also involves an enigmatic characterization of the narrator's voice, which appears in her works as different from that of the traditional omniscient narrator. Woolf's employment of the narrator's voice in fact seems to emphasize the *intermediate* position of this narrative role, which in her novels proves to hold both an all-encompassing position able to penetrate the characters' interior lives, and simultaneously, a limited point of view which confesses the impossibility to explore human consciousness fully. In this sense, Auerbach defines the narrator's presence in Woolf as a *not entirely human* voice, which seems to belong to kinds of disembodied souls, able to penetrate but not entirely to understand human consciousness.[58]

The emergence of a perspective which transcends subjectivity both in the characters' and in the narrator's voice leads the discourse again to examination of the simultaneous presence of personal and impersonal components in Woolf's writing. Her particular employment of narrated monologue acts as a fundamental part of the writer's process of distancing from the "damned egotistical self"[59] and of her quest for a narrative point of view which is non-embodied, one able to raise the question (which will be central in *To the Lighthouse*) of how the world can be perceived *in absence* of the subject. The process of distancing from the "I" takes in Woolf the form, in the first instance, of an attempt to achieve a collective representation, in which the author gives voice to the "we" able to express the constellation of single voices composing a community[60]:

A centre. All lit.[erature] discussed in connection with real little incongruous living humour; & anything that comes into my head; but "I" rejected: "We" "We."... composed of many different things.[61]

Furthermore, the end point of the Woolfian process of purification from the "I" also coincides with emphasis on the *autonomous* aspects of language, leading the writer to overcome the most subjective and personal elements in writing:

> But has any writer, who is not a typewriter, succeeded in being wholly impersonal? . . . Only after the writer is dead do his words to some extent become disinfected, purified of the accident of the living body.[62]

It is nevertheless important to note how the passage quoted contains a process of reversal which is typical of Woolf's theorization, and which indicates how concepts in Woolf always require to be further analyzed and re-examined. While stating the necessity of and desire for a distancing from subjectivity, Woolf also denies in these lines that the act of writing can (and maybe also should) be *completely* impersonal. As I have shown in the previous chapters, in Woolf the relation between subject and words is not simply resolved in the idea that the writer should let himself be guided by a transcendental automatism in writing, but involves instead a constant and active tension between passivity and activity, and between subjectivity and impersonality. In a similar way, as Ferrer underlines, the presence of the narrator in Woolf's novels is not structured on a technique of complete disappearance, but rather on a process of "radical decentering"[63] of voices.

This technique leads to the previously mentioned lack of distinction and *distance* between narrator's and characters' voices, thus establishing according to Ferrer the "joint responsibility" of the two in the sentences of narration. In the light of these narrative features, Septimus's presence in *Mrs Dalloway* does not only introduce the *theme* of perceptual alteration, but functions also as a determining element in the novel's structure. Septimus's simultaneous perception of two different and opposing realities, as well as the process of fracturing in his language, become elements which activate both a process of deciphering, and the opposite, a radical internal de-construction of the text. On one hand Septimus acts in the novel as the character who, like the narrator, is able to establish connections between separate characters and scenes and to unveil the secret pattern on which the narrative is built[64]; on the other, Septimus's inability to re-access the communicative level of language and to convey objective reality insinuates doubt into any structured discourse on consciousness. As Ferrer underlines, Woolf's experimental employment of the narrator's voice leads in this novel to the unveiling of the fictive nature of any act of representation of consciousness.[65]

Woolf's attempt to shift the focus of narration from external reality to the representation of consciousness clearly seems to be centered on a process of reconfiguration which aims at avoiding any fixed crystallization of thoughts into a superimposed rational structure, and which seeks instead to convey the dynamic nature of the "thousand disagreeables"[66] composing consciousness. In this sense, Woolf appears to focus less on the logical result of the process of verbalization, but rather on the stages in which sense and language converge. The elements so far underlined in Woolf's representation of consciousness, the peculiar role of the narrator's voice, the attention on the unconscious[67] stages of formation of thoughts, the rejection of hierarchy in the characterization of the narrative voice, all seem to emphasize the overtly fictitious nature of any attempt to represent consciousness. In this sense, Woolf avoids any mystifying belief in the potentiality of language fully to convey and structure the formless and inexplicable processes of mind, and works instead on the fertile point of connection between the subject's passivity and activity:

> It is within language (in every aspect of language, including its ellipses, and not just in a series of "specific forms") that the subject comes to be, and in a form necessarily divided through being inserted into a pre-existing order of signification. It is this division which it is the function of the given subject defined by the formal apparatus of enunciation to sew up, to suture. . . . Enunciation is both this fixing point and what Roland Barthes describes as "this gulf opened up at every word, this madness of language which in scientific terms, we call enunciation"—and the two features cannot be separated.[68]

Woolf's writing focuses on these instances in which the subject acquires existence *through* language, thus reproducing the forces which allow the act of writing to function as an attempt to master experience and simultaneously as the opening of an abyss of non-communication. This in fact adheres to Woolf's double-sided conception of language, which, as I have shown in Chapter Five, involves both the belief in the possibility of reaching an extraordinary communication and the awareness of the limits of the effable. The necessity stated by Woolf that words should preserve their "sunken meanings"[69] confirms the author's emphasis on the empty spaces of the inexpressible which can only be alluded to in language. In *Mrs Dalloway*, Clarissa's reaction to Septimus's death ratifies the close connection linking profound communication and death, and confirms how the ineffable finds expression in silent communion rather than in verbalization.[70]

In this sense, Woolf's techniques of representation of consciousness underline the double-sided potentiality of novel to act both as the place where consciousness can find expression and as the overtly fictitious result of this impossible attempt of representation:

Represented consciousness is not a "realistic reproduction" of the mind at work; it does not create "transparent minds." The mind is never transparent, not even to "omniscient narrators." Its contents are hypothetically reconstructed and represented in a language sensitive to its various modes.[71]

There is something essential to fiction in its representation of consciousness. The linguistic cotemporality of past and now and the coreference of SELF and the third person supply a language for representing what can only be imagined or surmised—the thought of others. By separating SELF and the SPEAKER, this style reveals the essential fictionality of any representation of consciousness, of any approximation of words to thought, even of our own.[72]

The novel can be considered as the only narrative genre which enables "unspeakable sentences" to be expressed, thanks to its potential to convey the thoughts of other than the writing subject; at the same time the narrative features which allow the novel to enact such a representation (the separation of the "self" from the "speaker" and the co-temporality of "past" and "now") also reveal the fictitious nature of this representation and the essential un-representability of consciousness.[73]

Woolf's writing seems to work on an implement of this double potentiality of the novel, through the blending of techniques which, instead of re-composing the fracture between language and experience, seem to underline the limits of verbalization. The non-omniscient character of the narrator's voice, the preference for the "represented thought" technique in place of direct enunciation, thus are elements which reveal Woolf's awareness of how the mind is never entirely circumscribable and language can only partially convey it.[74]

In this sense, Woolf's representation of consciousness appears to focus on the attempt to give voice to what Banfield has defined as "intermediate states of consciousness"[75], through an act of re-configuration which does not coincide with description but rather with the reproduction of the process through which sensorial knowledge "by being converted into language, becomes another kind of knowledge."[76] Thus the act of representation of consciousness in Woolf attempts to reproduce the processes of exit from habitual lines of perception and communication and the establishment of new and meaningful connections. This is not conveyed by Woolf as crystallized into a fixed system of representation, but rather as re-created in its dynamic nature. The continuous shift from one voice to the other and the tension between opposing forces act in Woolf's novels as elements able to suggest how the novel holds the potential to allude to what can not be entirely grasped by language. By refusing the simplifications of superimposed forms and the untenable belief in a total intelligibility of consciousness, Woolf's works mirror a complex and multi-leveled notion of consciousness. Human mind is in fact conveyed by Woolf not as an or-

ganic and unified datum, but rather as a streaked and vertiginous phenomenon which escapes complete representability.[77]

Notes

1. I follow here Robert Humphrey's definition of the *stream of consciousness*
which relates more to the content than to the technique of narration and thus underlines
how this technique differs from the other forms of narration since "concerned with
those levels of consciousness that are more inchoate than rational verbalization—
those levels on the margin of attention," Robert Humphrey, *Stream of Consciousness
in the Modern Novel* (Berkeley: University of California Press, 1959), 2-3. According
to Humphrey it is possible to individuate four different techniques of representation of
the *stream of consciousness*: direct and indirect interior monologue, omniscient narration and soliloquy. In this sense, the *stream of consciousness* is conceived as a literary
genre, and interior monologue as one of the possible techniques which can be employed for conveying it. In this chapter I will consider Woolf's employment of different techniques of representation of consciousness which will question the traditional
interpretation of Woolf as exclusively engaged with interior monologue. If we consider Genette's definition of this technique as an uninterrupted report of the character's
immediate and direct thought, Woolf does not appear to fall into this category, but
rather to explore the hybrid possibilities of the indirect speech techniques; see Gerald
Genette, *Figures of Literary Discourse*, translated by A. Sheridan (Oxford: Blackwell,
1982). See also on this problem Naremore, who analyses Woolf's representation of
consciousness proposing a similar distinction between *stream of consciousness* and interior monologue; James Naremore. *The World Without a Self: Virginia Woolf and the
Novel* (New Haven & London: Yale University Press, 1973), 60-76.

2. As I have explained in the Introduction, my analysis does not follow the chronological order of Woolf's publications, but rather establishes among the three novels
examined connections as they arise in the development of my discourse. It is useful to
remark that *Mrs Dalloway*, the novel focused on in this chapter, was published in 1925,
before *To the Lighthouse* (1927) and *Orlando* (1928).

3. The whole novel is structured on the coincidences and connections linking the
characters of Clarissa and Septimus, and this system of relations culminates in the final scene of Clarissa's party, in which the news of the suicide of the unknown
Septimus reaches the hostess. At the beginning of the novel Clarissa and Septimus participate together yet separately in two scenes: the one in which a crowd of people is
collected around the explosion of a motorcar engine and the following scene in which

an airplane traces some words in the sky. Later in the novel, Peter Walsh leaves Clarissa's house and enters Regent's Park, where he notices a couple (Septimus and his wife Rezia) and misunderstands the discussion that they are having. Peter and Rezia also share the meeting with an old tramp at the exit of the tube, and this event stimulates in both characters several reflections. Finally, while Peter is on the way to Clarissa's party, he hears the sound of the ambulance which is driving to assist Septimus, who has jumped out of the window. Apart from the several events and places where the characters converge, the strongest point of connection between Clarissa and Septimus is represented by the recurrent resounding in their minds of the same lines: "Fear no more the heat of the sun." These words, taken from *Cymbeline* by Shakespeare, signal how the mental experiences of the two characters, though very different, hold aspects of profound coincidence and this proves, as I will show, how Clarissa and Septimus can be perceived as two different manifestations of the same experience of a-linearity.

4. Virginia Woolf, "Introduction to *Mrs Dalloway*" in Andrew McNeillie, ed., *The Essays of Virginia Woolf* (Washington: Harvest Books, 1994) vol. 4, 550.

5. "Yet there is no independent evidence of any such "first version," and she later commented that "her character of Septimus in *Mrs Dalloway* was invented to complete the character of Mrs Dalloway" (which looks nearer the mark). There is certainly no suggestion of Clarissa's death in "Mrs Dalloway in Bond Street," where it is the young men who die, and are survived by mourning older woman." Julia Briggs, *Virginia Woolf: An Inner Life* (London: Allen Lane, Penguin Books, 2005), 141.

6. Virginia Woolf, *The Diary of Virginia Woolf*, Anne Olivier Bell and Andrew McNeillie, eds. (London: The Hogarth Press, 1977-84), vol. 2, 207.

7. "Clarissa's "plunge" into the city is not Woolf's, and the celebratory force of plunging is later qualified by Septimus's plunge through an open window, but, nevertheless, throughout Woolf's work the city is associated with life and love: the rhyme and alliteration reshape the city's shower of atoms into a rhythmical form"; Michael Whitworth, "Virginia Woolf and Modernism," in *The Cambridge Companion to Virginia Woolf* (Cambridge: Cambridge University Press, 2000), 153.

8. Virginia Woolf, *Mrs Dalloway* (London: Penguin, 1992), 6.

9. The allusion to the fact that Clarissa's perception may have been affected by influenza anticipates the theme of the perceptual alteration involved in illness which Woolf will develop in *To the Lighthouse* and in the essay "On Being Ill," as I have shown in Chapter Five.

10. Virginia Woolf, *To the Lighthouse* (London: Penguin, 1993), 26-29.

11. Woolf, *Mrs Dalloway*, 10-11.

12. Woolf, *To the Lighthouse*, 236.

13. Woolf, *Mrs Dalloway*, 36.

14. Woolf, *To the Lighthouse*, 236.

15. Crocus: "a small low-growing plant with a single purple, yellow, or white flower which opens in early spring," *Longman's Dictionary of Contemporary English* (Edinburgh: Longman, 1987).

16. Woolf, *Mrs Dalloway*, 17-18.

17. The term "apprehension" is often employed by Woolf to convey the alteration

of the subject's relation with external reality. The word suggests a deformation and acceleration of time which is opposed to the sense of expansion and deceleration which characterizes *moments of being*. The word is also recurrent in Woolf's descriptions of her psychological suffering: "She frequently uses the word "apprehension" to describe her states of mind—saying that her mother's death and subsequent events states "had formed my mind and made it apprehensive" . . . The word is a crucial one: the awful fear which accompanied her breakdowns and the possibility of their recurrence can never be underestimated." Hermione Lee, *Virginia Woolf* (London: Vintage, 1997), 175.

18. Woolf, *Mrs Dalloway*, 25.

19. Woolf, *Mrs Dalloway*, 25-26.

20. Woolf, *To the Lighthouse*, 178.

21. Septimus's experience of the moving backward and forward of images and of their transformation anticipates Woolf's allusion to the pre-cinematic device of the *phantasmagoria* in *Orlando*. Furthermore, the sky-writing technique is employed here by Woolf as a "cinematic linking device"; see Elaine Showalter, "Introduction," *Mrs Dalloway* (London: Penguin Books, 1992), XXIII-IV.

22. Woolf, *Mrs Dalloway*, 26.

23. See Daniel Ferrer's analysis of the different narrative implications in the dream section of the "solitary traveller" and in the passages conveying Septimus's hallucinatory perception; Daniel Ferrer, *Virginia Woolf and the Madness of Language* (London and New York: Routledge, 1990), 31-34.

24. Woolf, *Mrs Dalloway*, 26.

25. See Lucio Ruotolo, *The Interrupted Moment: a View of Virginia Woolf's Novels* (Stanford: Stanford University Press, 1986).

26. Virginia Woolf, *Orlando* (London: Penguin, 1993), 113.

27. Woolf, *Mrs Dalloway*, 29.

28. Paul Ricoeur, *Time and Narrative* (Chicago: The University of Chicago Press, 1984), vol. 1, 30.

29. Ricoeur, *Time and Narrative*, vol. 2, 101-112.

30. Woolf, *Mrs Dalloway*, 202.

31. Woolf, *Mrs Dalloway*, 77-78.

32. The same image of a shell cracking will be employed by Woolf in the essay "Street Haunting: A London Adventure" (1927) to convey how consciousness is exposed to the stimuli of the city: "The shell-like covering which our souls have excreted to house themselves, to make for themselves a shape distinct from others, is broken, and there is left of all these wrinkles and roughnesses a central oyster of perceptiveness, an enormous eye." Virginia Woolf, "Street Haunting: A London Adventure" in *The Crowded Dance of Modern Life* (London: Penguin, 1993), vol. 2, 71.

33. Ricoeur, *Time and Narrative*, vol. 2, 101-112.

34. Woolf, *Mrs Dalloway*, 96-98.

35. See on this idea Woolf's recollection of her sudden and profound understanding of poetic words while affected mentally by the death of her mother; Virginia Woolf, "A Sketch of the Past" in *Moments of Being: Unpublished Autobiographical Writings* (London: The Hogarth Press, 1978), 93.

36. Woolf, *Mrs Dalloway*, 103-104.
37. Woolf, *Mrs Dalloway*, 29.
38. Woolf, *Mrs Dalloway*, 107.
39. Woolf, *Mrs Dalloway*, 106.
40. Ricoeur, *Time and Narrative*, vol. 2, 108.
41. Woolf, *Mrs Dalloway*, 112.
42. Woolf, *Mrs Dalloway*, 113.
43. See the chapter "Madness" in Lee, *Virginia Woolf*, 175-203.
44. On Woolf's experience of acoustic hallucinations, see again Hermione Lee, "Madness" in *Virginia Woolf*, 175-203.
45. Woolf, "On not Knowing Greek" in *Collected Essays* (London: The Hogarth Press, 1966), vol. 1, I-13.
46. Woolf, *Mrs Dalloway*, 162.
47. Woolf, *Mrs Dalloway*, 109.
48. Ricoeur, *Time and Narrative*, vol. 2, 101.
49. Ferrer, *Virginia Woolf and the Madness of Language*, 37-38.
50. In *Transparent Minds* Dorrit Cohn proposed a redefinition and classification of the interior monologue techniques which derives from an analysis combining literary and linguistic elements. The three techniques resulting from this division are: 1) *psycho-narration*; 2) *quoted monologue*; 3) *narrated monologue*. Cohn's theorization takes into account and re-discusses most of the previous texts which analyze interior monologue. Among these I mention as fundamental: Marguerite Lips, *Le Style Indirect Libre* (Paris: Payot, 1926); Edouard Dujardin, "Le Monologue Intérieur" in *Les Lauriers sont coupés* (Paris: Bibliothèque 10/18, 1968); Robert Humphrey, *Stream of Consciousness in the Modern Novel* (Berkeley: University of California Press, 1959); Melvin Friedman, *Stream of Consciousness: A Study in Literary Method* (New Haven: Yale University Press, 1955); Kate Hamburger, *Die Logik der Dichtung* (Stuttgart: Ernst Klett, 1957); Harald Weinrich, *Tempus* (Stuttgart: Metzler, 1964); Gérard Genette, *Figures III* (Paris: Seuil, 1972).
51. "The narrated monologue also enables a narrator to weave in and out of several characters' minds. Virginia Woolf is the master-weaver of such multi-figural novels. From Clarissa to Peter, from Rezia to Septimus, from Mrs. to Mr. Ramsay, narrated monologue pass from hers to his and back again, often without any intervening narrative sentence." Dorrit Cohn, *Transparent Minds*, 118.
52. Cohn underlines how *Mrs Dalloway*, though mainly based on the employment of the narrated monologue technique, also presents the insertion of passages of psycho-narration and quoted monologue. Furthermore, according to Cohn Woolf appears to use a writing largely based on "psycho-analogies": "Many modern novels are interlaced with psycho-analogies. We find them most frequently in works where the narrated monologue is the prevailing method for rendering consciousness, but at moments when an author is for some reason unwilling to entrust the presentation of the inner life to the character's own verbal competence. . . . Virginia Woolf *is* the stream-of-consciousness novelist who employs psycho-analogies most copiously. . . . Woolf often uses her imagistic excursion to convey the "moments of vision" that are a hallmark of her novels." Cohn, *Transparent Minds*, 44-45. On the ambiguity characteriz-

ing the *free indirect speech* technique, Benvenuto Terracini's analysis is also fundamental in showing how in Luigi Pirandello's work the narrator's and characters' voices
overlap; Benvenuto Terracini, *Analisi stilistica Teoria, storia, problemi* (Milano:
Feltrinelli Editore, 1966).

53. "In its meaning and function, as in its grammar, the narrated monologue holds a
mid-position between quoted monologue and psycho-narration, rendering the content
of a figural mind more obliquely than the former, more directly than the latter." Cohn,
Transparent Minds, 105-106.

54. Woolf, *Mrs Dalloway*, 17-18.

55. Woolf, *Mrs Dalloway*, 17.

56. See Daniel Ferrer's analysis of this passage from *Mrs Dalloway* in *Virginia
Woolf and the Madness of Language*, 22-23.

57. Erich Auerbach, "The Brown Stocking" in *Mimesis: The Representation of Reality in Western Literature* (Princeton: Princeton University Press, 2003), 525-554.

58. Auerbach, *Mimesis*, 525-554.

59. "Suppose one thing should open out of another . . . only not for 10 pages but 200
or so—doesn't that give the looseness & lightness I want: doesn't that get closer & yet
keep form & speed, & enclose everything, everything . . . I suppose the danger is the
damned egotistical self, which ruins Joyce & [Dorothy] Richardson to my mind: is one
pliant & rich enough to provide a wall for the book from oneself without its becoming,
as in Joyce & Richardson, narrowing & restricting?" Virginia Woolf, *The Diary*, vol. 2,
13-14. On Woolf's impersonality in writing, see also James Naramore, who analyses
how Woolf achieved a form of interior representation which did not focus on individual consciousness, but rather on a "different sort of watery world where the "common
element" sometimes dissolves all sense of individuality." Naremore, *The World without a Self: Virginia Woolf and the Novel*, 76.

60. Gillian Beer notes how *Mrs Dalloway* represents Woolf's first attempt to give
voice to a community and how this does not involve the writer's depersonalization and
homology of single consciousnesses: "We" is an elastic pronoun, stretching in num-
bers and through time. Its population ranges from the exclusive pair of lovers, now, to
the whole past of human history. It can welcome or rebuff the hearer. It can also colo-
nise. Virginia Woolf saw clearly that "we" may be coercive and treacherous. It invites
in the individual the subset, the excluded, who once inside may find themselves vanished within an alien group claiming on their behalf things of no benefit or relevance
for them. Virginia Woolf was chary of the "we" of patriotism, and of the self-gratifying
claims of male writers to speak in universals which cover (in many senses) the experience also of women. Her reaction in writing to social communities was skeptical and
wary; she needed to find ways of maintaining difference as well as constellation."
Gillian Beer, *Virginia Woolf: The Common Ground* (Edinburgh: Edinburgh University
Press, 1996), 50.

61. Virginia Woolf, *The Diary*, vol. 5, 135.

62. Woolf, "Craftsmanship" in *The Crowded Dance of Modern Life*, 140.

63. Ferrer, *Virginia Woolf and the Madness of Language*, 6.

64. "When Septimus, leaping over the linear connection of events and ignoring the
ordinary laws of causation, establishes unexpected relations between two points in the

text by setting up a link between widely separated signifiers, he obliges us to do the same and deepen our research into the networks that traverse the novel." Ferrer, *Virginia Woolf and the Madness of Language*, 29.

65. Ferrer, *Virginia Woolf and the Madness of Language*, 35.

66. Woolf, *Orlando*, 4.

67. Woolf's attention to the supra-semantic and pre-rational aspects of language is conveyed in her novel by the emphasis on rhythm. This in fact largely structures Woolf's works, both on the stylistic and on the structural levels. On the presence of rhythm in Woolf's novels, see Stella McNichol, *Virginia Woolf and the Poetry of Fiction* (London and New York: Routledge, 1990). The book focuses on the formal aspects of Woolf's writing which show an overlapping of poetry and prose, with the intent to go beyond a traditional interpretation of Woolf's works as psychological novels. My analysis does not however completely agree with McNichol's thesis that the poetic elements are employed by Woolf to convey a sense of "wholeness" and a process of harmonic re-composition of consciousness. In my opinion, and as I have so far illustrated, it is important to take into account the temporary quality of the moments of re-composition as portrayed and linguistically conveyed in Woolf.

68. Ferrer, *Virginia Woolf and the Madness of Language*, 5. See also two Lacanian readings of Woolf's work: Emily Dalgarno, *Virginia Woolf and the Visible World* (Cambridge: Cambridge University Press, 2001) and Elizabeth Abel, *Virginia Woolf and the Fictions of Psychoanalysis* (Chicago: Chicago University Press, 1989).

69. Woolf, "Craftsmanship" in *The Crowded Dance of Modern Life*, 140.

70. Woolf, *Mrs Dalloway*, 202-203.

71. Ann Banfield, *Unspeakable Sentences: Narration and Representation in the Language of Fiction* (Boston: Routledge & Kegan Paul, 1982), 211.

72. Banfield, *Unspeakable Sentences*, 260.

73. See Dorrit Cohn, who draws for her thesis on Hamburger's *Die logik der Dichtung*, which she quotes in the introduction of her book: "For Hamburger the representation of characters' inner lives is the touchstone that simultaneously sets fiction apart from reality and builds the semblance (*Schein*) of another, non-real reality. She argues this thesis and explores its causes and results in two successive stages: 1) starting out from Aristotelian mimesis (understood as representation, not as imitation) she arrives at a theoretical differentiation between the language of fiction and the statement-language of reality; and 2) starting out from textual observations, she demonstrates that certain language patterns are unique to fiction, and dependent on the presence of fictional minds within the text. These language patterns are primarily the conveyors or signals of mental activity: verbs of consciousness, interior and narrated monologues, temporal and spatial adverbs referring to the characters' here and now." Cohn, *Transparent Minds*, 7-8.

74. See also Deleuze and Guattari's considerations on the communicative implications in *free indirect speech:* "The "first" language, or rather the first determination of language, is not the trope or metaphor but *indirect discourse*. The importance some have accorded metaphor and metonymy proves disastrous for the study of language. Metaphors and metonymies are merely effects; they are a part of language only when they presuppose indirect discourse. There are many passions in a passion, all manner

of voice in a voice, murmurings, speaking in tongues: that is why all discourse is indirect, and the translative movement proper to language is that of indirect discourse." Gilles Deleuze and Félix Guattari, *A Thousand Plateaus, Capitalism and Schizophrenia*, translation and foreword by Brian Massumi (London: Continuum Books, 2004), 85. From the linguistic point of view, Banfield underlines how the separation between SELF and SPEAKER present in *free indirect speech* determines precisely this double effect of *expression* and *non-communication:* "Represented though is the linguistic style which captures the direct (non-interpreted) expression of the "stream of consciousness" without suggesting that this latter is communication. The SELF, who is not necessarily the first person, is addressing no one. Through represented speech and thought, the subject of consciousness emerges free from the speaking subject. Represented speech is thus defined positively as expression, and negatively as non-communication. In this latter sense it qualifies as a "literary style." Ann Banfield, "Where Epistemology, Style, and Grammar meet Literary History," *New Literary History*, Volume IX, no. 3 (Spring 1978): 415-454.

75. Banfield, *Unspeakable Sentences*, 197. This particular form of knowledge can be interpreted in Woolf as coinciding with the revelation inherent in *moments of being*, which, as I have underlined in the first part of my analysis, involves a combination of senses and mind and a transcendence of phenomenal perception.

76. Banfield, *Unspeakable Sentences*, 199.

77. See again Terracini's analysis of Pirandello, which underlines how the Italian writer's employment of *free indirect speech* is not limited to a simple description, but rather conveys the tumult of consciousness while in the process of being de-constructed. Terracini, *Analisi stilistica*, 365.

Mrs. Dalloway:
Portrait of the Artist as a Middle-Aged Woman

Jacob Littleton

If the nature of the artist is to transmute personal experience and feeling into a public act, Clarissa Dalloway is certainly an artist, and Virginia Woolf's novel a portrait of the artist as a woman in middle age. The fundamental action of *Mrs. Dalloway* is to elucidate the mechanisms of Clarissa's thoughts and actions and to chart the ways in which her existence profoundly controverts the ideology and power relations of her cultural sphere.

Critical appraisals of the novel have recognized Clarissa's identity as an artist, but usually in the context of another interpretation. Suzette Henke, for instance, notes that Clarissa's "gatherings serve as . . . creative acts of social artistry" (127), but centers her analysis on the religious models Woolf uses. David Daiches writes, "There is a suggestion throughout that the experiences of individuals combine to form a single indeterminate whole" (73), a suggestion central to Dalloway's aesthetics. Deborah Guth reveals Clarissa's modes of self-invention, glancing at the importance of her parties to the character's self-definition.

Clarissa's artistry is the essential key to understanding her character, and the depiction of that character is the novel's key event. Woolf is concerned, before anything else, with the absolutely private mental world of a woman who, according to the patriarchal ideology of the day as well as her own figure in the world, was not imagined to have any artistic feeling at all. Woolf criticizes conceptions of character bound by the exterior forms of life: the whole complex (job, family, assets) that fixes every person firmly in the world of business and power relationships. Against this system Woolf places a world of private significance whose meaning is wholly irreducible to facts of the external world. By conceiving of personality as a private fact, apparently alienated from "public, political culture" and "its imperialistic and death-dealing ways" (Rosenman 77), Woolf shows Clarissa's "actual" existence to be an unrecognized but fundamental contradiction of traditional assumptions about gender.

Maria DiBattista points out "the novel's vague but universal sense of malaise, of spiritual incapacity, of frustrated expectations" (24). This malaise arises from each character's perception of an inadequacy in her or his world view to encompass a world that increasingly seems unexplainable. The Europe of the early twentieth century was characterized by a breakdown of traditional models, as Woolf emphasized throughout her work. Clarissa is "modernist" in outlook, fundamentally a nonbeliever. With her "horror of psychological engulfment" (Henke 139), she rejects society's common props against the void: Walsh's passion, Kilman's religion, Bradshaw's Proportion, the simplistic patriotism of her husband and Lady Bruton. As a result, she must face disordered reality without accepted props and create her own meaning for it. This process is central to *Mrs. Dalloway.*

Perhaps the most fundamental fact of Clarissa's psyche is the pleasure she takes in physical, sensual existence. She bursts onto the street to buy flowers and appreciates everything; "carriages, motorcars, omnibuses, vans, sandwich men shuffling and singing" (*Mrs. Dalloway* 4). She neither condemns what seems like an altogether noisy and irritating urban scene (her London is not a Waste Land), nor approves it with the air of a connoisseur; her appreciation depends only on experience. In fact, her delight is free of self-interest or discrimination. She does not appreciate the scene for *what* it is, but simply *because* it is. Her world view is suffused with the sense of the solemnity and wonder of existence, but most of all by the wonder of living; she takes life very seriously. Being is a self-sufficient value without reference to other values, rational thought, or emotion; indeed, she sees the worth of being as directly opposed, and superior, to those other values. She uses the non-hierarchical joy-in-life to counter her emotions and desires, conceived of as threatening to her dignity and autonomy. After her hatred for Miss Kilman first flares up, she is soothed by the experience of the florist's shop, "as if this beauty, this scent, this colour . . . were a wave which she let flow over her and surmount that hatred, that monster, surmount it all; and it lifted her up and up" (13). Because she loves life without judgment, Clarissa neither categorizes or coerces; "Had she ever tried to convert anyone herself? Did she not wish everyone merely to be themselves?" (126). This flight from forms into existence is irreducibly opposed to the Edwardian world view as exemplified by Bradshaw's Proportion and Conversion, whose "interpersonal imperialism dehumanizes and objectifies the Other to block out any disturbing sympathy or sense of likeness which might impede conquest" (Rosenman 78). Whereas Clarissa's nonjudgmental interest and love "subvert the masculine grammar of subject and object, unifying and protecting both in a single field" (Rosenman 78), dominant men of Clarissa's society seek only to inscribe their own characters on all "deviants," however slight in itself the deviation—a desire that is ultimately an urge for power. While Woolf labels judgment and hierarchy generally as masculine, and love and acceptance as principally feminine, her novel uses them as potential traits for either gender. J. Hillis Miller writes, "the same images of unity, of reconciliation, of communion well up spontaneously from the deep levels of the minds of all the major characters" (13). Lady Bruton after her luncheon, Peter dozing in the park, Richard on his walk home all sense the same wholeness, a contentment in the mere experience of daily life.

Clarissa passes the rest of the characters by turning love of existence into an existential starting point. Ellen Rosenman notes that Clarissa's thought is centered on the moment: "The moment is not, strictly speaking, an epiphany, a sudden illumination which takes one out of time. It is, literally, a 'movement in time', stretching the boundaries of an hour to achieve more commodious proportions" (80). This "movement" occurs in the mind of one who experiences life at the moment; it is a sudden awareness of/union with the miraculous fact of being itself, a melting away of conscious thought, a reverie. As Lucio Ruotolo writes,

"The important consideration about Being is not 'what' or 'how' it is, but rather 'that' it is" (29); Clarissa's moments of being share this outlook, even though she is only half-aware of it: "But every one remembered; what she loved was this, here, now, in front of her; the fat lady in the cab" (*Mrs. Dalloway* 9). In the moment, then, the boundaries of conscious selfhood dissolve into awareness of basic physical existence.

Clarissa creates a faith based on this unit of heightened awareness of existence. Her belief converts the hour of "more commodious proportions" into an immortal, everlasting existence. Dalloway has a preternaturally vivid awareness and fear of the termination of the existence she loves so much; Peter notes her "horror of death." She is capable of imagining, minutely, her own progression toward death (and is in poor physical health); she links her isolated attic bedroom with her loneliness and death. Her bed, no longer the marriage bed symbolizing fertility, is symbolized by her fertile mind as shrinking into her coffin and burial shroud (31). Against this graphic intimation of death, Clarissa has intimations of immortality. Peter recalls her philosophy as she expressed it in their youth: "Since our apparitions, the part of us which appears, are so momentary compared with the other, the unseen part of us, which spreads wide, the unseen might survive, be recovered somehow attached to this person or that, or even haunting certain places after death" (153). "The unseen part of us" simply means the memory of a moment which survives in the memories of those who experienced that moment. Although the moment's actual Being ends, it lives in the memory, an existence which Dalloway does not denigrate for its intangibility. The answer to individual death is the immortality of collective experience. This immortality springs from the common sensual world in which people experience each other. The common region is the Existence central to Clarissa Dalloway's understanding. Ruotolo states, "the I can meet the Thou only because *There* is—i.e., can meet only within some encompassing region of Being. After all, I have to meet thee *somewhere*, in relation to something and in some context" (16).

Remembrance of shared experience is an underpinning of the novel, the summer at Bourton the most prominent example. That summer is so vivid in Clarissa and Peter's memory that, as Miller notices, Woolf's language obfuscates the passage from "living" present to "dead" past. The past at Bourton remains so vivid that it remains "present" for Clarissa even though she has changed so much that one of the central emotions of that time—her love of Sally—seems dead to her. But the principle lines of force in her life are the rites of memory established at Bourton: her marriage, her love/antagonism for Peter Walsh, her half-awareness of her love of women.

Human interaction and communication, then, form a network by which individuals merge into one another through experience, imagination, and memory. Miller explains, "No man or woman is limited to him or herself, but each is joined to the others by means of this tree, diffused like a mist among all the people and places he or she has encountered" (173). Throughout *Mrs. Dalloway* Woolf shows this network of communication as it is formed. Lady Bruton muses on how Hugh and Richard remain with her after they leave, "as if one's friends were attached to one's body, after lunching with them, by a thin thread, which . . . became hazy with the sound of bells, striking the hour" (112). On the walk home, Richard feels his link to Lady Bruton attenuate and snap, replaced by the sudden awareness of his bond with Clarissa.

Another significant instance is the experimental line established between Dalloway and Septimus Warren Smith. Clarissa never even glimpses the character whom Woolf called her double, and yet he plays the central role in her day. She hears of his death through Bradshaw; this news strikes a chord that reverberates with her mood at the party, and she withdraws to consider her party's deeper meaning for her. She imaginatively recreates Smith's suicide and clearly understands him, as her thoughts mirror his. But not only does his act catalyze an emotional change in her, her act of remembrance in turn insures that his life will survive in a sympathetic context, and not simply as a figure in Bradshaw's utilitarian world. A meeting is not necessary for their communion; to know what is essential in a person requires only a sort of sympathetic psychic awareness. And the two meet also, more tenuously, when Peter sees Septimus and Rezia; he speculates that Clarissa would have spoken to them had she been there. Peter is infinitesimally changed by seeing them (and carries this change to the party), and something of Clarissa enters into his experience of the couple.

The possible conquest of death is the wider significance of the sensory experience of life. Clarissa's self is diffused by the people who experience her, and she spreads the salves of those she experiences. A universal spirit fills the apparently empty space between people, which allows Clarissa and Peter to hold a silent conversation behind the spoken one when he visits her drawing room. It allows Clarissa to feel the physical impact of Smith's plunge. This void-filling force outlasts individual death, as Elizabeth experiences on her ramble through London:

> It was not conscious. There was no recognition in it of one fortune, or fate, and for that very reason even to those dazed with watching for the last shivers on the faces of the dying, consoling. Forgetfulness in people might wound, their ingratitude corrode, but this voice pouring endlessly, year in year out . . . this procession would wrap them all about and carry them on. (138)

An anonymity provided by shared experience relieves humans of the loneliness of individual existence. Woolf's characters struggle to find their way to some sort of shared experience, from the unexamined patriotism displayed in the incident of the car on Bond Street (14), even to the anti-social lunacy of Septimus Warren Smith.

The value of experiences is not individual but collective; in Clarissa's skeptical mind this collective experience takes the place of "love and religion," and other potential rocks against the void, in which she places no faith. According to Daiches, "The significance of the whole is not the sum of the significance of the different parts, but depends on the shape and disposition of the completed story" (61); this comment on the structure of Woolf's novel also holds true for the world view of her heroine. Clarissa finds an answer to the malaise of existence in this Existence; it is her faith. There is, no doubt, a minimal level of faith at which she no longer is certain, but doubt is a characteristic of all faiths, particularly in a cultural moment of conflicted ideologies and the crumbling of Victorian certitude. This faith explains and orders her world in a way that other outlooks available to her do not.

Perhaps most important, it grants her the sense of an urgent call to action. From her world view Clarissa progresses to a mode of existential behavior. For Clarissa's Being is not an invincible antidote to death. This collective Being, so dependent on a common fund of experience, disintegrates in the separation of people, just as memory (by which Being comes into existence) is challenged by forgetfulness. Miller claims, "Nothing could be less like the intermittencies and difficulties of memory in Wordsworth or in Proust than the spontaneity and ease of memory in *Mrs. Dalloway*" (176). But while in most respects Woolf does show memory as spontaneous, she too deals with intermittencies. There are instances of profound lapses of memory, as when Lady Bruton remembers Hugh's kindness, but not the occasion for it (*Mrs. Dalloway* 104). Insofar as metaphysical Being exists in human minds and not in the objective world, losing awareness of Being is tantamount to losing Being. For Clarissa, forgetfulness is not simply a prefiguration of death; it is itself a very real death. The procession of time leads to death, and time's passage leads also to the oblivion of forgetfulness. This condition of oblivion is inherent in the fractured, isolated conditions of life, in which people drift toward experiential isolation. Clarissa had a theory, "to explain the feeling they had of dissatisfaction; not knowing people, not being known. For how could they know each other? You met every day, then not for six months, or years. It was unsatisfactory . . . how little one knew people" (152). She thinks, "But what was this thing she called life? . . . Here was So-and-So in South Kensington; some one up in Bayswater; and somebody else, say, in Mayfair. And she felt quite continuously a sense of their existence; and she felt what a waste, and she felt what a pity" (122). She must act to end that separation. Referring to the above trio, "She felt if only they could be brought together; so she did it. And it was an offering; to combine, to create; but to whom? An offering for the sake of offering, perhaps" (122). She sees a way for her to act to strengthen collective being through her parties. Her parties are her art.

Clarissa creates and controls her event-art in ways similar to, and in certain ways significantly different from, the way art was traditionally understood to be generated. These points of similarity and contrast firmly establish Clarissa Dalloway as a real artist, but one whose modes of creation destabilize not only traditional boundaries of art, but boundaries of personhood fundamental to English culture.

In keeping with modernist aesthetics, in the development of which Woolf played a key role, a Dalloway party creates a mode of being seen as fundamentally separate from mundane life. It "creates a scene that wrenches her guests from the dullness of habitual activity and serves as a stage for moments of heightened consciousness" (Henke 142). Like a conventional drama, her party distorts the forms of everyday life to reveal a truth she believes to be more profound and important. Her art is both false and true; it is life, but life transformed. Clarissa muses, "Every time she gave a party she had this feeling . . . that everyone was unreal in one way, much more real in another" (*Mrs. Dalloway* 259). Critics have noted the religious connotations of this celebration of a higher, more profound reality. In light not only of Clarissa's characteristic distrust of religion, but of the decline of religious faith of Woolf's time, I feel it more appropriate to emphasize the urge of creation as the original impulse for this action. For Woolf, as for many artists of her time, the inevitable motion of human consciousness to impose order on a world without apparent meaning was itself the motive force of religion and philosophy. Artists, as knowing manipulators and expressors of consciousness, replaced priests and monarchs as actual creators of order and meaning. DiBattista says,

"Woolf's psychology . . . necessarily predicates that the form-engendering power of the mind naturally shapes the life of Monday or Tuesday into orders that are not adventitious, but truly expressive of the life apprehended from within" (4). As Peter Walsh muses, "If he can conceive of her, then in some sort she exists" (*Mrs. Dalloway* 57); the truths created by the mind are not false because they are, in crude terms, "made up." They are made true simply by being felt.

Both hostesses and artists must create a world that draws in the reader or guest and takes her or him out of the logic of the mundane. But if Clarissa's intent and effect correspond closely to the vision of art espoused by her creator, her methods are certainly quite different from those employed by writers of fiction. Even performed dramas of the day, followed a set script. Dance and music could be improvisational, even revolutionary in form, but like fiction they maintained a dichotomy between the subject (the viewer) and object (the work of art), or the subject (the transforming work of art) and object (the viewer whose feelings are to be worked upon). The party cannot be characterized this way. The party-goers are actors as well as viewers, including Clarissa herself, and the party's creator neither controls nor thinks of controlling the actions of her subjects/objects, even though her beliefs about life imbue every aspect of her gathering. Most important, the element of intentionality is absent. No one is consciously aware of her or his involvement in a work of art. Clarissa herself seems only imperfectly aware of what she is creating.

Nevertheless, it is also possible to overstate the extent to which the party is unreasoned, a product of unknown urges. Without some intentionality and control, Clarissa ceases to be an artist and is a hostess simply. But Clarissa does have control. First, she controls the party's physical aspect: when it is to occur (has she seen people as feeling isolated lately?), who will come (what combination will be successful?), what the scene will look like. Richard's intercession for Ellie Henderson piques Clarissa to make her central defense of her parties as meaningful events; she feels a *need* for control of the party which indicates how much of her personality is involved in it. Clarissa's control is in the physical scene of the party, from which arise the actions of the guests which constitute the beginnings of the hum of Life which is Clarissa's real goal. If she has judged the moment correctly, laid the scene correctly, she will be rewarded with what she wants from her guests without coercion or persuasion. In the end, this is not very different from the writer or painter, who must also succeed technically for the reader to comprehend his or her message.

Clarissa is minutely aware of how her party fares by her aesthetic standards. In the beginning, before the fire of companionship has been lit, she is terrified that her endeavor has failed: "Anything, any explosion, any horror was better than people wandering aimlessly, standing in a bunch at a corner" (168). As the evening progresses, she feels more optimistic; the hum of life, of communication and connection, has begun. At last she judges her party a success when a guest beats back a curtain while continuing to talk (170). Significantly Clarissa interprets physical signs. Not only does she know just what she wants, she also knows just what it looks and sounds like. Her material focus reinforces the sensual, physical locus of her pleasure. All her philosophy and ideas about life return to the primary fact of enjoyment of life. Her interest in the way her party appears also reveals what *isn't* important to her as a hostess: great names, prominent people, or the social ladder. The butler rattles off names of guests; for this Clarissa has no response. Everyone, Sally and Peter included, see in her only a status-minded hostess for whom the party is, first and last, an attempt at increasing social stature. While Clarissa does love the conventional symbols of her class, the significance they have for her is far from conventional. The complex of values embodied in Clarissa's beloved Lady Bexborough relate to her parties not practically, but obliquely; she creates parties not to advance herself or her husband's career in society, but to express society's values (filtered through Clarissa's consciousness) as part of the whole array of ideas brought to life by the party.

Finally, Clarissa senses herself to have a stake in her production that goes beyond that of the ordinary hostess: "She . . . couldn't help feeling that she had, anyhow, made this happen, that it marked a stage" (170). This feeling is insubstantial and fleeting, not surprisingly in that she has neither cultural not personal support for it. Yet the feeling cannot be wholly eradicated either. This suspicion of her power is symptomatic of Clarissa's philosophy and art generally; uncertainty enveloping an undeniable but mysterious presence.

The artist's role is to create and express the truths that she or he apprehends in the world; the artist is Woolf's high priest of consciousness. This is the role that Clarissa plays in her party. Her parties project the truth she sees onto a ritual physical structure freed in many ways from the forms and concerns of everyday life. This truth is expressed not through the use of power as Bradshaw or Kilman impose their own beliefs, by manipulating the power they have. Rather, the party establishes a zone of influence in which, far from having one's personal beliefs imposed upon or subjugated, one's beliefs are transformed by contact with the other system. Art's effect is not to force or even to persuade, but (once again) to "subvert the masculine grammar of subject and object, unifying and protecting both in a single field" (Rosenman 79). Woolf displays this opening of experience in the conversation of Peter and Sally. Dalloway's old friends have not been in close contact for years, perhaps since Bourton; nevertheless they fall quickly into confidence: Sally says, "Peter was an old friend, a dear friend—did absence matter? did distance matter?" (*Mrs. Dalloway* 189). Unconsciously, of course, she sees life on the terms that Clarissa gives it. Her philosophy is born in Sally; Sally will carry away not simply a memory of Peter and one of Clarissa, but also a sense of the significance of these friendships she might not have had, had she seen Peter on a street corner or Clarissa at the florist's. The party marks a place of special awareness of friendship and connection, for it is a celebration of these aspects of humanity in common culture as well as in Clarissa's more developed scheme of life.

When Ellie Henderson looks at the Prime Minister and thinks, "He looked so ordinary. You might have stood him behind a counter and bought biscuits—poor chap, all rigged up in gold lace" (172), she likewise seems to be under the influence of Clarissa's disregard of hierarchies and distinctions, made visible in the party where the minister's status is less important than his physical presence. From all such individual realizations, taken together, arises the Existence that Clarissa wishes to create or make visible. "The interaction of personalities in ritual gesture establishes a lasting, collective relationship crystallised in bonds of joyful affiliation," writes Henke (142). Clarissa's view is congruous with most analyses of the novel, which interpret her parties as an offering—fundamentally for other people and for the external force, not as acts with a principally private significance.

These aspects of the party challenge the notion of art accepted in that time. There is no room in Clarissa for the identity of the artist as master of every aspect of her creation. She does not see herself as part of a tradition, much less a centrally important one; although she has confused intimations of the significance of what she does, the disdain shown by society is more than enough to undercut thoroughly any self-esteem her creations give her. Clarissa's art controverts even what the modernists consciously understood about art. It is possibly more understandable to present-day readers, accustomed to forms of art which attempt to transform traditional dynamics of the relationship between performer and viewer. The endeavors of Woolf's character are so far beyond the art of England in 1923 that their participants, and even their facilitator, went into them with no artistic expectations. Clarissa's existence as an artist, the forms of her art, destabilize tradition far more completely than the most revolutionary form of art-as-art. It exists outside the forms of art while doing what art alone is supposed to be able to do: express life as viewed by a unique individual, and impress that view of life on the art's observers. Clarissa Dalloway, as a woman, is an outsider to the male-dominated realm of official art; therefore the art she does create, which she is compelled to create by her Self, cannot but be revolutionary in form.

But although the parties undeniably influence the collective psyche of those present, their primary importance for Clarissa remains personal. Paradoxically, her modes of art, built of collective interaction and unfolding as a communal experience, spring from Dalloway's sense of her own isolation as an individual. If communal experience is the focal point of Clarissa's universe, awareness of individual isolation, even alienation, from others is the key to her awareness of herself. As effective as she proves to be in managing the party, her actual human connections are clumsy and unsatisfying: "Certainly Clarissa's more metaphorical femininity, her 'woman's gift' and diffuse consciousness, overshadows her actual motherhood" (Rosenman 81). Although Clarissa's party art is fundamentally consistent with her milieu's vision of feminine nature as inherently nurturant of interpersonal connection, the kinship of art to social belief is purely ideological. Her unquestioned faith in the "angel in the house" is undercut by her own inability to function as an effective focal point for her family, at least by ordinary means. She fears her daughter's gravitation to Kilman will vitiate the filial bond, while she broods over having failed Richard at some past point, presumably in the role of politician's spouse (*Mrs. Dalloway* 31). But as fervidly as Clarissa admires Lady Bexborough and all she embodies, she just as tenaciously remains distanced from this world view, in which a woman is to the world little more than the sum of her relations with others, particularly men. She demands room for private development: "In marriage a little licence, a little independence there must be between people living together day in day out in the same house" (8). The less intense alliance with Richard allows Clarissa greater space to fulfill her submerged desires. Peter Walsh might have destroyed this aspect of her, not by mere closeness but by the incessant judgment of her secret beliefs about the world.

Others understand that Clarissa did not marry for standard romantic love, but misunderstand her actual motives. When Clarissa disappears from her party, "Sally supposed . . . that there were people of importance, politicians, whom neither of them knew unless by sight . . .

whom Clarissa had to be nice to, had to talk to" (186); in fact, the hostess has withdrawn from everyone to probe her feelings about the death of Septimus Smith. She imagines herself as isolated, alone. In the end Clarissa stands alone in that the "truth," what is essential about her life, remains unknown to all even as all partake of the field of that truth which she generates. To the extent that she could have made herself known through love, and Peter understands her more completely than anyone else, albeit still haltingly, Clarissa's expression of herself through art is a free choice. But to the extent that other options, such as a passionate relationship, require subjugation of her artistic urges, Clarissa is a victim of a regime which denied artistically inclined women the chance to express themselves, and she ended with the life she had, not because it best suited her, but because it most closely approached the minimum condition of her happiness: capacity to express herself in art. Her conscious agreement with the principles of her class ought not be slighted; her love of Peter does not stop her criticizing his marginality, passion, and instability. Clarissa is of the solid center. However, the use to which she puts the apparatus of her class profoundly destabilizes the center she ostensibly upholds.

Clarissa's complex position comprises external conformity, ideological affinity, and substantive subversion. This difficult spot is the source of Clarissa's world view in which isolation battles with connection. For Woolf does not merely portray the thought and art of her central character, she also paints a complex portrait of the artist's situation in the world. This portrait uncovers the way in which the artist's experience is transformed and recapitulated in art; more, it also reveals and critiques the society that gave rise to the artist.

Just as Clarissa's mind imposes a pattern of isolation and connection on existence, so the existence she must lead imposes a pattern of isolation and connection on Clarissa. But whereas the truth the woman creates for the world moves toward apolitical universality, the truth the novelist reveals in the life is specific and social. For it is the power of the patriarchy that imprisons Clarissa in loneliness, while an individual feminine power fundamentally opposed to the male-dominated social order is the source of her feelings of human affiliation.

Clarissa characterizes herself as virginal, in some way inept with people: "She could see what she lacked. It was not beauty; it was not mind. It was something central which permeated; something warm which broke up the surfaces and rippled the cold contact of man and woman, or of women together" (31). This coldness is the trait she associates with her attic bed and isolation; the reader can also see the source of her deep fear of isolation as the precursor of death. But Clarissa, just after the above reflection, sees in her life

> a sudden revelation, a tinge like a blush which one tried to check and then, as it spread, one yielded to its expansion, and rushed to the farthest verge and there quivered arid felt the world come closer, swollen with some astonishing significance, some pressure of rapture, which split its thin skin and gushed and poured with an extraordinary alleviation over the cracks and sores! Then, for that moment, she had seen an illumination, a match burning in a crocus, an inner meaning almost expressed. (32)

The source of this extraordinary feeling, described in overtly sexual terms, is pleasure in certain moments with women. This blush of woman love seems to provide Clarissa with a touch of "something central which permeated"; the specificity of these moments seems to correspond to Clarissa's delight in existence, while their social nature (conversation with women) points to the importance to her of human interaction. These moments of awareness, of connection (awakened in her when she met Sally Seton) in her actual life are the wellspring of Clarissa's highly developed beliefs about the nature and significance of existence. Likewise, "the bed and Baron Marbot and the candle half-burnt" (32), the isolation and awareness of death in her own life, generate her abhorrence of isolation and fear of death more generally. Deborah Guth points out that "the private, supposedly 'real' inner self that Clarissa explores during the day in fact duplicates rather than de-

---

nies the artificial, ceremonial quality of her public self" (35). Despite her alienated, isolated position in society, the private world of Clarissa's consciousness is fundamentally determined by her existential position.

Clarissa's isolation, the fact of death in her life, is caused by a social order which requires the subjugation of the private self, for Clarissa the real self, to the individual's social position. This imprisonment of the self is symbolized in Woolf's use of names (DiBattista 36). Woolf writes, "She had the oddest sense of being herself invisible, unseen . . . this being Mrs. Dalloway; not even Clarissa any more; this being Mrs. Richard Dalloway" (11). "Mrs. Dalloway" is that part of her fixed in a social position: her femininity, in a patrilineal culture, subsumed by her identity as Richard's wife. The novel begins with the words "Mrs. Dalloway." But the name used by everyone who thinks of her at all personally is her Christian name, the name not of social relationships but of emotional ones. The novel closes with a view of Peter Walsh: "What is this terror? what is this ecstasy? . . . What is it that fills me with extraordinary excitement? It is Clarissa, he said. For there she was" (194). It is significant that Septimus is the other character for whom Woolf brings up this dichotomy (84); Septimus replicates Clarissa's threatened position. They are threatened more than other characters because, more than any others, their private selves diverge from public expectations of them.

The social order of Britain in 1923 was resolutely inimical to the reality of actual life cherished by Clarissa and Septimus. It created standards that, far from allowing for free, individual expression, forced individuals into rigid roles with unfulfillable expectations. The regime's ideals are antithetical to life itself. No one measures up to these standards. Peter is a failure, and Richard has not gone as far as expected. The accomplished Lady Bruton, due to her putative nonrationality, feels she cannot write a letter. The Prime Minister would look more in place selling bread. Even Whitbread and Bradshaw, the enthusiastic enforcers of the ideal, are almost universally disliked. The regime works on ideals and ideal symbols relating to the glory of patriarchal society. Peter Walsh encounters a regiment of young soldiers marching past the "exalted statues" in Regent's Park; they tramp "as if one will worked arms and legs uniformly, and life, with all its varieties, its irreticencies, had been laid under a pavement of monuments and wreaths and drugged into a stiff yet staring corpse by discipline" (51). Undisciplined, aimless life must be forced to work for financial or political gain, for the advancement of Britain, for any number of reasons connected not only to "war, patriotism, and nationalistic ardour, but also to the auxiliary vices of force and possessiveness that bolster the dictatorial spirit" (Henke 129). This ideal-machine's agents cannot help desiring to fix things. Richard, presented benevolently by Woolf, still must ponder "the problem of the female vagrant" (116). Clarissa, by contrast, thinks, "the most dejected of miseries sitting on doorsteps (drink their downfall) . . . can't be dealt with, she felt positive, by Acts of Parliament for that very reason: they love life" (4). Not only is desire to change, even if the reasons are benevolent, necessarily linked to the desire to use power, but the ability to effect change is inevitably tied to the possession of power. Sir William Bradshaw seems to demonstrate this. His method of treatment is quite simply to cut off whatever sets his patients apart, makes them unique, living human beings, however idiosyncratic or unhappy, and reduce them to the human Proportion he prefers: "his, if they were men, Lady Bradshaw's if they were women" (99). The form of his Proportion is determined by traditional ideology: "family affection; honour; courage; and a brilliant career" (102). He enforces his will through traditional structures: the power of doctor over patient, "sane" over "insane," wealthy over poor. His personal aim is power as well; the end result of his labor is his colleagues' respect, his subordinates' respect, and the gratitude of the relatives of his patients (99).

The judgment regimes which discard life as it is lived naturally fail to find worth in that life. Socioeconomic regimes, like Bradshaw's, work principally to *change* life; thus his misperceptions are actually useful to him. But for "interpersonal imperialists" like Walsh and Kilman, misunderstanding only perpetuates divisive, alienating walls which destroy Existence as Clarissa conceives it. Walsh is described as sharp; he thinks, "The All-Judging, the All-Merciful might excuse— Peter Walsh had no mercy. Villains there must be" (173). Clarissa is his most frequent target. He continually judges her actions with words such as "annoying," "irritating," "too far." This judgment militates against his understanding her as thoroughly as she understands him. His occasional insights are ruined by complete misunderstandings grounded in his perceptions of what she should be. He understands her enjoyment of life, but blasts her parties: "She frittered her time away, lunching, dining, giving these incessant parties of hers, talking nonsense . . . losing her discrimination" (78). Clarissa accepts him even when she disapproves, and she understands him completely; at the party she senses the exact moment at which his disdain turns to approval. Like Peter, Kilman uses a critical viewpoint to overcome her fears: "Whenever the hot and painful feelings boiled within her . . . this grudge against the world, she thought of God. . . . Rage was succeeded by calm. A sweet savour filled her veins" (124). Like Bradshaw's Proportion, Doris's religious piety masks a desire for power. She thinks of Clarissa, "If only she could make her weep; could ruin her; humiliate her; bring her to her knees crying, You are right" (125). Doris is afflicted with a "grudge against life," an inability to accept or appreciate sensual existence.

The anti-existence judgment of Bradshaw, Walsh, and Kilman works to attain personal power over individuals. Septimus bemoans the dominance of Bradshaws, "who saw nothing clear, yet ruled, yet inflicted. 'Must' they said" (148). Clarissa calls Walsh's love and Kilman's love "the cruelest things in the world . . . clumsy, hot, domineering, hypocritical, eavesdropping, jealous, infinitely cruel and unscrupulous" (127). Both Walsh and Kilman condemn Clarissa for her social position. Walsh calls her "the perfect hostess" (62), while Kilman puts her in "the most worthless of all classes—the rich, with a smattering of culture" (123). Such judgments are like death for Clarissa; they are the forces that affix her permanently in isolation.

Clarissa's love of mere existence, the importance to her of the means she has to bolster the communal spirit of life, and her refusal to judge or force, alienate her from her milieu. This environment, in which people are separated by social role and position, is the Death she fears so much. She is kept alive by the fugitive communion she senses, particularly by her own ability to bolster communion. These life-giving feelings originate in passion for the presence of other women, a feeling that is ambiguously homosexual, as Emily Jensen notes (173), but is overtly opposed to the rigid and utilitarian social order. Thus Clarissa and Septimus each face threats from social forces to whom their rejection of useful labor (including a tendency to "nonproductive" homosexuality) and joyful embrace of sensual joy in turn pose a threat. Clarissa and Septimus threaten the utilitarian order merely by being passive, half-unconscious alternatives to it. But the differences between Septimus and Clarissa's experience of their own deviation also present a profound analysis of society's expectations about gender.

Septimus goes mad while Clarissa hides her difference and remains externally integrated with society because conformity was a practical necessity for women, particularly of Clarissa's class, imprisoned by centuries of male control of all wealth and almost all means to wealth, indeed, of practically every aspect of public life. As a man, Septimus could not avoid subjection to the most extreme dysfunctions of the social order: war and Bradshaw. His response is similarly extreme. The manifestations of his madness are guided by the tradition of male poetry: "Was he not like Keats?" Isabel Pole asks (85). His scraps of paper, laughed at by the maid, are in the tradition of men's poetry judged as insane by contemporaries and cherished by posterity. Most important, he has open access to the public world, even though this access is more curse than blessing to him, because along with comparative freedom of motion came the requirement of productive paid labor. But independent social position allowed men the freedom to throw away virtue, career, and social approbation, and eke out survival on the edges of respectability, as Peter Walsh does. Woolf wrote on the opportunities open to Tolstoy: "There was a young man living freely with this gypsy or that great lady; going to the wars; picking up unhindered and uncensored all that varied experience of life that was to serve him so splendidly later when he came to write his books (*A Room* 71). Merely being a man opened to Septimus vistas of life absolutely closed to an upper-class woman like Clarissa. She is denied experiences that could have profoundly transformed her, but she is also spared the worst extremes of patriarchal dysfunction by her very isolation.

Clarissa inherits not the opportunity to rove and write, but the elite woman's inheritance of social communication and parties. Her culture claimed women to be essentially nonrational, and Clarissa does not care about abstract knowledge as understood by England's intellectual apparatus. Defending her parties as an offering, she thinks, "She could not think, write, even play the piano. She muddled Armenians and Turks; loved success; hated discomfort; must be liked; talked oceans of nonsense; and to this day, ask her what the Equator was, and she did not know" (122). Clarissa does not externally contradict this self-analysis, which touches on the central points of the gender ideology of the time. But the significance of her actions to her private mental life could not be more at odds with the superficial hostess all assume her to be. While Mrs. Bradshaw is "balancing like a sea-lion on the edge of its tank, barking for invitations, Duchesses" (183), Clarissa worries not about the status-success her party brings, but about its mere physical success in the terms of her world view. Clarissa remains allied to society for two interlocking reasons. Respectability is essential to her first of all because, unlike Peter Walsh, she could not have remained in society with a faint aura of disrepute. As she would have to depend on a man to maintain her, virtue was in fact her greatest asset. But it should not be thought that Clarissa consciously felt trapped by this condition; in fact, she admires her class and culture just as much as Whitbread and the other characters. She loves the activities open to her without considering them secondary to or a substitute for pursuits more overtly intellectual. These activities constitute a separate female inheritance, and there was no Keats or Tolstoy in the female tradition. Woolf compares George Eliot to Tolstoy; she "escaped after much tribulation, but only to a secluded villa in St. John's Wood . . . for was she not living in sin with a married man and might not the sight of her damage the chastity of Mrs. Smith or whoever it was that chanced to call? One must submit to social convention" (*A Room* 70). Clarissa submits to social convention by subverting it in ways that express herself without destabilizing her own position.

To accomplish this she wholeheartedly embraces the very isolation that her personal beliefs suggest is to blame for all unhappiness. So secret is her pleasure that no one understands her. Clarissa embraces the more distanced marriage to Richard over the more passionate option of marrying Peter to maintain an autonomy which the latter man would certainly not have allowed: "There is a dignity in people; a solitude; even between husband and wife a gulf; and that one must respect" (120). As one critic put it, "Clarissa's frigidity is a response to that threat and not simply a character flaw. Clarissa denies her actual sexuality only to participate in it imaginatively" (Rosenman 83). And of course the apparatus of her class is essential to the fulfillment of Clarissa's artistic goals: "Behind it all was that network of visiting, leaving cards, being kind to people; running about with bunches of flowers, little presents" (*Mrs. Dalloway* 77). Clarissa makes subversive use of this network; although this subversion remains undetected, it subtly affects those who enter its sphere of influence, Clarissa's parties.

Woolf's presentation of Clarissa Dalloway is itself subversive on many levels. By creating a viable heroine with many intellectual attributes ascribed solely to men, Woolf destabilizes gender boundaries. Clarissa's talents derive, moreover, from her social femininity, presenting an alternative to male-identified utilitarian ideology. Perhaps most important, Woolf's novel attempts to uncover a female intellectual inheritance not preserved in rigid cultural vessels such as libraries and universities. Woolf, in her own way, is in search of her mother's garden. Just as Clarissa's intuitive completion of Septimus's suicide rescues that act from the oblivion to which it might otherwise have been consigned, so Woolf's creation rescues Clarissa, or someone like her, from the same oblivion, at the same time serving to erase the isolation felt by women artists excluded from the male intellectual tradition.

From *Twentieth Century Literature* 41.1 (Spring 1995): 36-53. Copyright © 1995 by *Twentieth Century Literature*. Reprinted with permission of *Twentieth Century Literature*.

Works Cited

Daiches, David. *Virginia Woolf*. New York: New Directions, 1963.

DiBattista, Maria. *Virginia Woolf's Major Novels: The Fables of Anon*. New Haven: Yale UP, 1980.

Guth, Deborah. "Rituals of Self-Deception: Clarissa Dalloway's Final Moment of Vision." *Twentieth Century Literature* (1990) 36.1: 34-43.

Henke, Suzette. "*Mrs. Dalloway:* The Communion of Saints." *New Feminist Essays on Virginia Woolf*. Ed. Jane Marcus. Lincoln: U of Nebraska P. 1981. 125-47.

Jensen, Emily. "Clarissa Dalloway's Respectable Suicide." *Virginia Wolf: A Feminist Slant*. Ed. Jane Marcus. Lincoln: U of Nebraska P, 1983.

Miller, J. Hillis. "Repetition as Raising the Dead." *Virginia Woolf*. Ed. Harold Bloom. New York: Chelsea, 1986.

Rosenman, Ellen Bayuk. *The Invisible Presence: Virginia Woolf and the Mother Daughter Relationship*. Baton Rouge: Louisiana State UP, 1986.

Ruotolo, Lucio P. *Six Existential Heroes: The Politics of Faith*. Cambridge: Harvard UP, 1973.

Woolf, Virginia. *Mrs. Dalloway*. New York: Harcourt, 1925.

_____. *A Room of One's Own*. New York: Harcourt, 1929.

"The sane & the insane, side by side":
The Object-Relations of Self-Management in *Mrs. Dalloway*_____

Thomas C. Caramagno

It has long been suspected that Virginia Woolf suffered from manic-depression (or bipolar disorder), ever since her husband, Leonard, diagnosed her symptoms in 1915. But how would genetically induced, biochemically produced mood swings affect our reading of her writing? I argue here that, in *Mrs. Dalloway*, Virginia Woolf represents not only the symptoms of manic-depression but also how she coped with it. She was very aware that her moods produced alterations in perspective, judgment, and self-esteem, as Leonard's observations attest:

> When Virginia was quite well, she would discuss her illness; she would recognize that she had been mad, that she had delusions, heard voices which did not exist, lived for weeks or months in a nightmare world of frenzy, despair, violence. When she was like that, she was obviously well and sane. (*Beginning Again* 79)

For Woolf, this problem of relatedness—the seeming disconnection between the "sane" Virginia and the "insane" Virginia—was crucial. She recognized her instability: "You know how cameleon I am in my changes—leopard one day, all violet spots; mouse today" (*Letters* 5: 209). Yet she also believed that "life is made up, superficially, of such moods; but they cross a solid substance . . ." (*Diary* 2: 221-22). Like other manic-depressives, she knew that, beneath the wave-like moods tossing her up and down, there was a core Self that persisted.

Woolf invites us to search for that core by complicating our reading of the novel. She eliminates the self-conscious narrator who conveniently raised questions of interpretation in her previous novels, and replaces it with a shifting and impersonal narration that verbalizes the thoughts of diverse characters in diverse moods but gives us no guidance about how to evaluate them. The descriptive style, highly ordered and rhythmic, does not change from one character to another, so the indirect interior monologues we hear from each of the characters sound curiously alike, paralleling and even blending thoughts—a provocative act since some of these thoughts are "insane" (Harper, "Mrs. Woolf"). The mixture can be disturbing to readers because it reveals common mechanisms at work in both psychotic and normal thinking. Despite this strange comingling, in the end Woolf offers us a vision of unity and discovers a greater sense of, and greater control over, her Self.

Writing *Mrs. Dalloway* was a process of open experimentation. In 1922, Woolf began a short story entitled, "Mrs. Dalloway in Bond Street," which quickly expanded beyond her original plans, as she noted in her diary: "Mrs Dalloway has branched into a book; & I adumbrate here a study of insanity & suicide: the world seen by the sane & the insane side by side—something like that" (*Diary* 2: 207). The phrase "something like that" is apt. Initially, she had planned the novel without the psychotic war veteran, Septimus Warren Smith, focusing exclusively on Clarissa Dalloway who dies—or commits suicide—at her own party. Second thoughts prompted her to separate sanity and insanity between the two characters, but she wanted to keep them closely related: "Septimus and Mrs Dalloway should be entirely dependent upon each other" (*Letters* 3: 189). Third thoughts led her to worry as to "whether the book would have been better without" Septimus and the mad scenes (*Diary* 2: 321). In the end Woolf anticipated reader confusion "owing to the lack of connection, visible, between the two themes" (*Diary* 3: 4) and predicted that "reviewers will say that it is disjointed because of the mad scenes not connecting with the Dalloway scenes." But, since, for her, such a disjunction was not "unreal" psychologically, was in fact the experience she wanted to create, she hoped her audience would somehow see a connection (*Diary* 2: 323).

Woolf was also hesitant about writing the mad scenes for personal reasons, for they were "a very intense & ticklish business" (*Diary* 2:

310): "It was a subject that I have kept cooling in my mind until I felt I could touch it without bursting into flame all over. You can't think what a raging furnace it is still to me—madness and doctors and being forced" (*Letters* 3: 180). Remembering involved plunging "deep in the richest strata of [her] mind" (*Diary* 2: 323), and she feared being too explicit about it, not only because readers might misunderstand or judge it self-indulgent and confessional, but also because her break-downs showed her just how transparent the dividing line between mad-ness and sanity could be: "Why is life so tragic; so like a little strip of pavement over an abyss. I look down; I feel giddy; I wonder how I am ever to walk to the end. . . . And with it all how happy I am—if it weren't for my feeling that its [sic] a strip of pavement over an abyss" *(Diary* 2: 72-73). Bipolars are often unaware when they do lose their balance because mood shifts exaggerate normal and habitual modes of perception, thinking and feeling, so the individual may fail to notice the subtle but growing discrepancies, losing their sense of the Self as distinct from their moods. Only when one is living on the narrow strip of "normality" can one see what the Self is or is not.

But how to describe this sense of living out three lives to readers who have felt only solid ground beneath them? "Health," intones Dr. Holmes, brushing aside Septimus' symptoms, "is largely a matter of our own control" (138). Holmes decides that there is "nothing what-ever seriously the matter with" Septimus (31), and Bradshaw agrees: "'we all have our moments of depression,' said Sir William" (148). The temptation to oversimplify mental illness is strong. Blatant, gib-bering madness is a popular stereotype and readily identifiable, *Dra-cula*'s Renfield or *Batman*'s Joker, but mild manic-depression swings can be indistinguishable from normal mood shifts, the Monday morn-ing blues or the Friday night highs (Goodwin and Jamison 3). Can one be explicit about such a profound sense of unreality so closely con-nected to normal life without losing all distinction between the two? Or is the difference between sanity and insanity too great to bridge with-out oversimplification? The paradoxical nature of manic-depression is that it is at times obvious, at times transparent, posing special formal problems for a fiction that purports to express it.

Although an omniscient narrator would seem an ideal device to make such connections visible, Woolf chose instead an impartial narrator who does not make interpretations about what is described or overheard, creating what Suzanne Ferguson calls an "ambiguity of perspective," which produces not only uncertainty but "multiplicity and mystery" (250, 245) for the reader to grapple with. Only broad brushstrokes paint these characters' pasts. Of Septimus' childhood we know only that his mother had "lied" (127). But what lie? Was it significant? Or was it one of Septimus' delusions? Woolf remains silent. All is hearsay. Septimus' "betrayal" carries equivalent weight with Clarissa's irretrievable past, Peter's bruised ego, or Miss Kilman's spiritual conversion. Truth is in the eye of each character. Such a technique muddles characterization, as Howard Harper has noted (*Language* 133-34), which explains Woolf's reminder to herself in her diary: "Characters are to be merely views: personality must be avoided at all costs" (2: 265). Although Peter Walsh's sexual affairs in India clearly differentiate his life from Doris Kilman's cramped and pernicious religiosity in a London working class slum, these circumstantial facts seem secondary to how the characters think and feel about themselves, reflections that sound alike in style and tone (Haring-Smith 145).

To avoid distinguishable "voices," Woolf seldom transcribes dialogue, preferring thoughts over conversations, and what little action does occur serves only as a spur to further reflection, as James Naremore points out:

Almost all of the characters' thoughts in *Mrs. Dalloway* are daydreams of one kind or another. Relatively little of the inner monologues are related to or determined by the actual circumstantial context. . . . Because so much of the novel is given over to the relatively uninterrupted flow of daydreams and meditations controlled by an authorial voice, the book has an almost seamless quality. (80-82)

Naremore makes a provocative point here. Daydreaming is stylized by mood. How we create and interact with our daydreams (which can become reassuring or terrifying, exciting or depressing) reveals how the underlying mood skews perception and self-esteem. We are perpetually engaged in a complex relationship with ourselves, managing our thoughts and emotions. As we think, we talk to ourselves, but we are both speaker and listener. Analyst Christopher Bollas uses his own experience as an illustration:

> As I have been planning this chapter, for example, I have thought from the second person pronoun objectifying myself to say: "You must include Winnicott and Khan because much of your thinking comes from their work." . . . Naturally this intrasubjective relationship will change according to the person's state of mind. (42)

This changing state of mind is what Woolf portrays in order to represent mood swings in fiction. Peter, for instance, casts himself in his daydreams as a second person. When following an anonymous woman across Trafalgar Square, he imagines that she silently calls to him, using "not Peter, but his private name which he called himself in his own thoughts. 'You,' she said, only 'you' . . . . (79). Peter is essentially flirting with himself when he feels romantic and adventurous; he need not involve the woman at all except as a transitional object embodying his own inflated desires. When they do deflate, he quickly abandons the hunt ("Well, I've had my fun"), which was only taking place in his mind anyway.

Daydreams are ideal barometers of mood. Variations of self-esteem, an essential feature of mood swings, can be detected in how we value, and are valued by, figures in our inner dramas. Mood itself is but a "view," as Woolf wrote. Shifting from daydream to daydream allows her to express the subtlest aspect of bipolar illness: its connections with normal mentality, the ups and downs of how one feels about oneself and others, changes that can obscure when one is no longer walking upright on the narrow strip of pavement Woolf called sanity. Each character participates in self-representation, comprising various aspects of Woolf's experience of mood swings: milder cycles of high and low self-esteem (Peter), severe psychotic delusions (Septimus), and the balanced, or euthymic, state (Clarissa) which successfully integrates the other two.

Peter Walsh's daydreams represent the normal range of mood swings. As a youth, he had quarreled with Clarissa so often that she married his opposite—the quiet but effective Richard Dalloway. Expelled from Oxford, he left England, hastily wedded a woman onboard ship, formed an adulterous liaison in India, and has now returned to London to arrange, half-heartedly, for a divorce. Fifty-three years old, he is unemployed and still obsessed with the one woman he has never been able to conquer. But in daydreams he entertains himself with romantic adventures and future successes, elated fantasies that leave him with little patience for Clarissa's real needs. Significantly, Peter's divided style of self-representation elicits divided responses from readers: some critics take the part of his own self-accusations and condemn him as an "awkward outsider," a "shadowy identity" (Harper, *Language* 124), a "passive, ineffectual, and self-defeating" man who resorts to self-humiliation and childishness in order to attract motherly concern from Clarissa, exploiting his own worthlessness (Leaska 96; Poresky 115). All these are Peter's own worst fears, which he feels intensely when in a depressed mood. But is that all there is to Peter? Other critics are caught up in his flights of inflated masculinity and charisma, and so they admonish his carnal passion (Kelley 95) and the sexual threat he presents to Clarissa's psychic autonomy (Rosenthal 97; Apter 62; Spilka 66). Both critical views replicate the ways Peter deals with/ imagines himself in different moods, feeling alternately powerful and degraded.

But, like the narrator, we must resist taking sides to see the larger picture. Bipolar disorder varies enormously in intensity, from mild mood shifts to severe, shading into normal moodiness imperceptibly.

Peter illustrates mild shifts when he creates idealized objects and expectations that are repeatedly destroyed. On a walk about town, he extols London as a "splendid achievement," unknown butlers as "admirable"; motorcars arrive "accurately, punctually, noiselessly, there, precisely at the right instant" (82). Because of "these alternations of mood; good days, bad days, for no reason whatever," he finds chance women he meets are all "blooming, elegant" (107)—and life itself seems "absorbing, mysterious, of infinite richness" (248). Captivated, "as if inside his brain by another hand strings were pulled, shutters moved, and he, having nothing to do with it," Peter feels so "utterly free" that he pursues a young woman,

> a stranger, who, as she passed Gordon's statue, seemed, Peter Walsh thought (susceptible as he was), to shed veil after veil, until she became the very woman he had always had in mind; young, but stately; merry, but discreet; black [exotic], but enchanting. (78-79)

Once he reassures himself that "she was not worldly, like Clarissa; not rich, like Clarissa," he can fancy himself "a romantic buccaneer." Losing sight of her, he ends his fantasy abruptly: "Well, I've had my fun . . . . this escapade with the girl; made up, as one makes up the better part of life, he thought—*making oneself up*" (81, my italics).

What has Peter made up, and how is it fun? He attributes exaggerated value to all the objects he sees, including himself; desire and self-confidence are dilated by "moments of extraordinary exaltation" (85)—as long as the stranger does not resemble Clarissa. But if the woman knew him as Clarissa does, as he really is, the bubble would burst. If he actually caught up with the woman, she would know that "his whole life had been a failure" (11). What Peter wants is someone with no identity, who mirrors back whatever he projects, which is what mania does.

Clarissa refuses to serve as glorifying mirror to Peter's illusions (Squier 280), and so she becomes his scapegoat. Although he finds

Daisy's indiscriminating adoration a bit of a bore, it is what he expects of a woman; he accuses Clarissa of coldness, of withholding the "woman's gift" that might have saved him from himself. When sitting together in Clarissa's parlor, she and Peter engage in a duel of unvoiced accusations that nevertheless get communicated:

> For Heaven's sake, leave your knife alone! she cried to herself in irre-pressible irritation; it was his silly unconventionality, his weakness; his lack of the ghost of a notion what any one else was feeling that annoyed her, had always annoyed her; and now at his age, how silly!
> I know all that, Peter thought; I know what I'm up against. . . ." (69)

Although his first impulse is to deny what he sees in Clarissa's look, Peter loses control of his pose as a martyr for love:

> I know all that, Peter thought; I know what I'm up against, he thought, running his finger along the blade of his knife, Clarissa and Dalloway and all the rest of them; but I'll show Clarissa—and then to his utter surprise, suddenly thrown by those uncontrollable forces thrown through the air, he burst into tears; wept; wept *without the least shame*, sitting on the sofa, the tears running down his cheeks.
> And Clarissa had leant forward, taken his hand, drawn him to her, kissed him,—actually had felt his face on hers . . . holding his hand, patting his knee . . . . (69, my italics)

For many critics this is a difficult scene because the knife invites Freudian readings of phallic symbolism and fantasized rape, while Clarissa's refusal to respond is regarded as evidence of her frigidity and his impotence. But why Peter cries is connected to what he does with his knife. It is not necessarily a symbol of his childish insecurity or her "masculinity" (Schlack 50; Leaska 98). Critics who see the knife as a sexual symbol will subsequently interpret Peter's tears as a defeat, as if we were watching a scene of symbolic emasculation rather than realization. What Peter loses is an illusion about himself that requires the cooperation of an object: a woman, a daydream, a knife. When Clarissa interrupts Peter's self-generated illusions, he sees himself in her eyes as she sees him. He does not desire her as a sexual partner but as a perceptual partner. His elaborate egotistical illusions about civilization and manly adventurism end in disillusionment because he has severed the connection between self and world, which is what manic-depression does too.

As Alan McLaurin has already noted, the novel's frequent use of the word "cut" suggests a deep concern for "divisive activities," for disconnections (41). Clarissa's mirroring forces Peter momentarily to reintegrate what had been split; her motherliness reassures him that integration is not equivalent to self-destruction; it is only a safer form of *dis*-illusionment. She tries to heal the cut of his knife. Peter realizes that even painful and depressive emotions are endurable if faced. As long as moods are non-psychotic, the individual still possesses the capacity to make self-corrections based on a mirroring relationship with the external world.

But while Peter's cut is self-indulgent and treatable, Septimus' injury is psychotic and involuntary. Septimus creates illusions, endowing certain objects with value, but, without Peter's self-consciousness, Septimus is unaware that he is manipulating objects. He cannot have "fun" because his fictions look devastatingly real. Septimus experiences intense despair not as an emotion but as a hostile world. Woolf knew by experience that psychotic depression is not just Peter's self-loathing but seems, to the sufferer, to be an active, corrosive agent loose in the world. Literally self-estranged, Septimus is haunted by split-off pieces of himself that appear, inexplicable and strange, in trees, in dogs, in aeroplanes. Thus, the birds communicate a revelatory message aimed at him alone, but their songs are sung in Greek, which he does not understand; the message originates in himself, but it cannot be reincorporated because it cannot even be read. "Knowledge comes through suffering, said Mr. Whittaker" (196), Miss Kilman's minister, but this is true only if the pain can be made intelligible, can be "owned" by the Self that feels it. No tears, no realization can heal Septimus' lacerated mind. For him, *integration is equivalent to self-destruction* because it would require identifying himself with estranged elements of Self he cannot recognize or understand.

Woolf's insight here is that psychotic belief shares some disturbing similarities with "normal" convictions, as modern psychology now shows. Harvard University's Brendan A. Maher argues persuasively that deluded patients are like normal people in at least one respect: they form theories to explain their experiences (Oltmanns and Maher 15-33). Ordinary events (e.g. stubbing your toe, hearing music in a park) can be explained by reasonable theories ("the uneven pavement must have tripped me," we suppose, or "someone's playing a portable tape recorder"). Anomalous experiences (feeling that your body is out of your control, hearing voices inside your head) elicit explanations too (you are fatigued, or you may be manifesting the first signs of multiple sclerosis). Even hearing voices can be explained as radio transmissions picked up by fillings in your teeth. These are interpretations made with intact reality testing: the radio station and multiple sclerosis are real things. But if you are psychotic, and your biochemically altered brain mishandles perception, even bizarre explanations may seem believable to you because they fit bizarre experiences. Woolf herself relates such an episode: "One night I lay awake horrified hearing, as I imagined, an obscene old man gasping and croaking and muttering senile indecencies—it was a cat, I was told afterwards; a cat's anguished love making" (*Moments* 123). Woolf's explanation supplies an intelligible meaning to non-linguistic sounds, while still preserving the cat's actual message. In *Mrs. Dalloway*, when a nursemaid spells out a sky writing advertisement, Septimus experiences isolated letters as if they were already full of profundity:

> "K . . . R . . ." said the nursemaid, and Septimus heard her say "Kay Arr" close to his ear, deeply, softly, like a mellow organ, but with a roughness in

her voice like a grasshopper's, which rasped his spine deliciously and sent running up into his brain waves of sound which, concussing, broke. A marvelous discovery indeed—that the human voice in certain atmospheric conditions (for one must be scientific, above all scientific) can quicken trees into life! (32)

Intensified sensations suggest that meaning lies not in the semantic codes of language but in the sensations themselves.

Intensified perceptions are typical of mania, and they may be positive or negative (since in mixed states, an individual may experience both mania and depression simultaneously). This is why Septimus' daydreams have become nightmares. In normal thinking we may talk to ourselves without speaking, using an implied "you" to mark the split in our subjectivity. A thought in psychosis can take on an existence and a voice of its own: thinking is perceived as an exterior event, as a real voice. Bollas' note to himself, "You must include Winnicott and Khan" could then be perceived as a divine command ("thou shalt include Winnicott and Khan") in mania or a verbal attack of hellish proportion ("include Winnicott and Khan, or you will suffer eternal damnation") in depression. Mood is no longer experienced as an inner state but as an outer reality. What's worse, Septimus' world has coincidentally colluded with his paranoia, objectified by military authorities (who can force one to kill others) and by Drs. Bradshaw and Holmes (who can force one to kill one's Self through "conversion"). The First World War was a psychotic dream come true. Because of this confabulation between inner and outer horrors, Septimus' vividly distorted perceptions of ordinary urban life persecute him with the same power as images of bloody conflict would assault us. The fact that he never daydreams of the war in violent terms (instead, civilian life takes on all the terror of battle) dramatizes the split in his thinking: he cannot even connect his suffering to his own personal history: "But what was his crime? He could not remember it" (148). Septimus is *guilty of having suffered*—a common depressive belief, one that makes sense when despair comes out of nowhere (Oltmanns and Maher 179). Septimus reads his own despair in the objects he sees—a situation that creates even more unmeaning, confusion, and terror. Horror on a battlefield is understandable; horror in Regent's Park is inexplicable and so doubly frightening. The individual who hallucinates while "tripping" on LSD may also see beatific or nightmarish visions, but he is not judged insane because he understands their source. To see flames beneath the pavement and say, "That is really the fear I deny myself; it belongs to me; it is really inside of me," is *still* sanity. Septimus cannot make the connection. In psychosis, the old saying, "seeing is believing," is just as true as "believing is seeing."

Some Freudian critics attribute Septimus' despair to unconscious conflicts, for instance, that he is repulsed by repressed homosexual feelings for Evans which he displaces onto symbolic objects (Henke; Leaska 108; Bazin; Schlack, 52-53). But his guilt is too severe to be merely neurotic. Septimus is introduced to us as one whose eyes have "that look of apprehension in them which makes complete strangers apprehensive too" (20), a reaction he is incapable of analyzing, and so the fear he sees in others' eyes only serves to reinforce his terrible suspicion that something outside of himself is terribly wrong. Faced with a traffic jam, he is terrified that some horror has come almost to the surface and is about to burst into flames:

> The world wavered and quivered and threatened to burst into flames. It is I who am blocking the way, he thought. Was he not being looked at and pointed at; was he not weighted there, rooted to the pavement, for a purpose? But for what purpose? (21)

The world quivers, but it is he who is shaking. The street threatens to burst into flames, but the unintelligible horror exists inside him.

When self and object are confused, mood-disordered patients see the world in terms of their internal states. Objects and events gain uncanny significance. Depressives often make derogatory statements about objects which are really displaced self-accusations—not through neurotic displacement (to avoid recognition) but because it is difficult for these patients to see themselves *as depressed*, to step outside of the mood and perceive the discrepancies in their judgment. Instead they tend to focus on the negative aspects of external objects ("Life is pointless," "people dislike me," or "this food is poison"). Septimus too feels that the world is worthless and degraded, that it cries out for redemption; he hears the cry for help but cannot trace it back to its origin. His suicidal impulses are cut off from their source, creating a vicious circle: he feels he must die because he is depressed, but he thinks he is depressed because the world is murderously insane and wants him to die. Since objects embody his suicidal ideas, Septimus is often afraid to look too closely at them, for "real things were too exciting. He must be cautious. He would not go mad" (215). When he fears madness, he shuts his eyes (32), as if insanity too were an external state imposed upon self: "it must be the fault of the world then—that he could not feel . . . . it might be possible that the world itself is without meaning" (133).

Septimus attempts to deal with his despair by deciphering its meaning, but interpretation is problematical for an isolated mind that projects its moods upon everything it sees. Ordinary events assume profound, though inexpressible, significance:

> "It is time," said Rezia.
> The word "time" split its husk; poured its riches over him; and from his lips fell like shells, like shavings from a plane, without his making them, hard, white, imperishable words, and flew to attach themselves to their places in an ode to Time; an immortal ode to Time. (105)

What the word "time" means, Woolf does not say; she focuses our attention on language as object, not signifier. It is Septimus' *relation* to language (and to himself), not his intended or unintended meaning, that illustrates her insights into how manic-depression alters perception. For instance, Septimus examines skywriting for an advertisement, believing that an important message for him has been sent, and finds a beauty implying some transcendent meaning: "So, thought Septimus, looking up, they are signalling to me. Not indeed in actual words; that is, he could not read the language yet; but it was plain enough, this beauty, this exquisite beauty . . ."(31). Because he cannot read the message, he imposes significance indiscriminately, desperately when he is depressed, eagerly when he is manic—in a mixed state, both simultaneously (Jamison and Goodwin, 262-64). Manic-depressives often connect their moods together in this way. The onset of sudden, manic fulfillment in the midst of emptying despair in a mixed state can be "explained" as their having been given a "mission," an exalted purpose to oppose the hellish abyss that has opened up inside them. The structure of mood swings becomes their meaning. For Septimus, manic dilation complements depressive hollowness: he concludes that he must be the Savior who fills the empty world—this must be why he feels he must die even though he also loves life. This is a truly "bipolar" explanation.

Septimus' role as Savior collapses the space between Self and daydream. The communication and the communicator are now one. His messianic delusion reverses his earlier relationship with the world. No longer does he feel passive, selfless, weak, a "relic straying on the edge of the world . . . who lay, like a drowned sailor, on the shore of the world" (140). As a messiah, he feels "excited" and powerful: "he knew the truth! He knew everything!" (212) Being re-created by his exalted identity makes sense of his earlier "revelations": "Men must not cut down trees. There is a God . . . Change the world. No one kills from hatred" (35). What these statements say is not the point. They are assertions of a Self against meaninglessness.

Since there is no evidence of actual impairment of reasoning ability in delusional patients, they do not readily abandon bizarre or unlikely explanations that do, in fact, seem to explain anomalous experiences they're having. In neither stage of his illness does Septimus ever gain insight into his perceptual problems. Even in a relatively calm passage, he accepts both objective and subjective readings side by side, as if the contradictions between the two did not exist:

> He lay back in his chair, exhausted but upheld. He lay resting, waiting, before he again interpreted, with effort, with agony, to mankind. He lay very high, on the back of the world. The earth thrilled beneath him. Red flowers grew through his flesh; their stiff leaves rustled by his head. Music began clanging against the rocks up here. It is a motor horn down in the street, he muttered; but up here it cannoned from rock to rock, divided, met in shocks of sound which rose in smooth columns (that music should be visible was a discovery) and became an anthem, an anthem twined round now by a shepherd boy's piping (That's an old man playing a penny whistle by the public-house, he muttered) . . . . Now he withdraws up into the snows, and roses hang about him—the thick red roses which grow on my bedroom wall, he reminded himself. The music stopped. He has his penny, he reasoned it out, and has gone on to the next public-house. (103)

This is divergent thinking carried to an extreme, splitting his attention into two. Septimus is aware of both kinds of knowledge—what he is perceiving objectively and what the perception means to him subjectively—but he is unable to connect or integrate them and so feel unified himself. Only briefly can he question the basis of his delusions:

> Why then rage and prophesy? Why fly scourged and outcast? Why be made to tremble and sob by the clouds? Why seek truths and deliver messages . . . ? (216)

But he finds no way to bridge these two interpretations of experience and so feels fragmented himself, an unidentifiable thing, a transparency through which even flowers can grow. With no corrective image of itself mirrored back, the mind cannot discern what role it plays in perception. Thus, as Howard Harper has already pointed out, when

Septimus agrees to see Sir William Bradshaw for treatment, he does so with a "melodramatic gesture" and a "complete consciousness" of its "insincerity": he does not want to be cured because he cannot see that he is ill ("Mrs. Woolf" 229).

Clarissa illustrates how to cultivate good mental health. Like Peter, she treasures all the "bits and pieces" of existence—June, leaves in St. James's Park, Peter, flowers, "the fat lady in the cab" (12), the unadorned features of daily life, but, unlike Peter, she can let them go. She occupies an object-relational space between Peter's defensiveness against chaos and Septimus' helpless surrender to it. We first meet her exulting in party preparations ("what a morning—fresh as if issued to children on a beach"); she plunges into delightful memories of the past and the young Peter; but, reminded of her bitter estrangement from him, "she stiffened a little on the kerb" (4). Big Ben strikes a "warning" that the "irrevocable" hour is passing, creating a heart-rending sense of "suspense." Feeling momentarily isolated and empty, she wonders why people love life since it "dissolves" so quickly, but she admits her love for it too, "with an absurd and faithful passion, being part of it" (6).

Most trying is the intense hatred Doris Kilman inspires in Clarissa—Kilman, who "was never in the room five minutes without making you feel her superiority, your inferiority," whose "soul rusted" with bitterness (16). Clarissa's initial reaction is like Peter's against her—defensive—but self-analysis reveals that her hatred "undoubtedly had gathered in to itself a great deal that was not Miss Kilman; and become one of those spectres with which one battles in the night . . . dominators and tyrants" (16-17)—not Kilman alone, but oneself. Clarissa discovers that there is a connection between the way she feels about Kilman and the way she feels about herself:

It rasped her, though, to have stirring about in her this brutal monster! . . . . this hatred, which, especially since her illness, had the power to make her feel scraped, hurt in her spine; gave her physical pain, and made all pleasure in beauty, in friendship, in being well, in being loved and making her home delightful rock, quiver, and bend as if indeed there were a monster grubbing at the roots, as if the whole panoply of content were nothing but self love! this hatred!

Nonsense, nonsense! she cried to herself, pushing through the swing doors of Mulberry's the florists. (17)

Like Septimus, Clarissa visualizes her hatred as a horrible monster lurking beneath normality, but, unlike him, she detects its source. Upon Kilman is visited the denial of self-love transformed into object-hate—actually, an insightful reaction because Kilman does despise "women like Clarissa" who like themselves too much. In Doris' own daydream, she wants to attack Clarissa, "overcome," "humiliate," and "unmask" her, subdue her "soul and its mockery" (189). Clarissa responds, first by hating Kilman, then by hating herself, which she can then dismiss as "nonsense!" Her ability to examine mood and question its source and its meaning diffuses the attack. She need not fear fear itself, as Septimus does, for she realizes that it cannot destroy the self. Self, for Clarissa, is more real than transitory emotions.

The novel charts her progress in strengthening her self-image. Clarissa learns to tie together the goodness of life with the goodness of self: organizing parties; reviewing and reaffirming her decision not to marry Peter; finding peace when alone in her attic room. There she thinks of herself as a nun, child, or virgin (45-46), undefined by the role of wife or mother or friend, to protect a vital central core hidden beneath the cosmetic personality one presents to others. This deep core is too vulnerable to be exposed, anonymous because unknown and private, chaste because it is the untouched center of Self undistorted by mood swings. Unadorned, she achieves a state of purity that Woolf herself said she learned from her illness: "We do not know our own souls, let alone the souls of others. . . . There is a virgin forest in each; a snowfield where even the print of birds' feet is unknown. Here we go alone, and like it better so" (*Moment* 14). Both Woolf and Clarissa sink deep enough into themselves to escape the waves of mood swings. It is significant, then, that when Peter barges into her private room shortly thereafter and criticizes Clarissa, she does not retreat. If his knife stands for the ability to believe in himself, she finds her own standard to bear against his assault—her needle—and takes him on:

> What an extraordinary habit that was, Clarissa thought; always playing with a knife. Always making one feel, too, frivolous; empty-minded; a mere silly chatterbox, as he used. But I too, she thought, and, taking up her needle, summoned . . . to her help the things she did; the things she liked; her husband; Elizabeth; her self, in short, which Peter hardly knew now, all to come about her and beat off the enemy.
>
> "Well, and what's happened to you?" she said. So before a battle begins, the horses paw the ground. . . . So Peter Walsh and Clarissa, sitting side by side on the blue sofa, challenged each other. (65-66)

Clarissa does not flatter Peter by becoming frivolous, empty-headed; in this sense, she has failed him too—failed to give what he expects of a woman.

Independence helps Clarissa face the novel's climax: Septimus' suicide. She imagines his point of view and calmly considers what it could mean:

> A thing there was that mattered; a thing, wreathed about with chatter, defaced, obscured in her own life, let drop every day in corruption, lies, chatter. This he had preserved. Death was defiance. Death was an attempt to communicate; people feeling the impossibility of reaching the centre which, mystically, evaded them; closeness drew apart; rapture faded, one was alone. There was an embrace in death. (280-81)

Acting on his beliefs (whether they are delusional or not), Septimus throws his life away, but not necessarily his sense of Self. As George Ella Lyon argues, Septimus faces a loss of autonomy in the hands of

Bradshaw and Holmes: "His state again is Clarissa's, is woman's; he becomes an object; his body is not his own. As Dr. Bradshaw approaches, Septimus literally has no room, so he hurls himself out the window to reality." His death affirms Clarissa's "sense of herself as *subject*," not object (119). Self must be real if it can decide to die.

The form of *Mrs. Dalloway* invites the reader to experience the frustration of the manic-depressive, the one person who seems to be three but is not three. A bipolar identity is periodically deconstructed because he or she possesses three sets of beliefs and affects. Woolf reasoned that the surface "personality" camouflages one's true identity, just as her manic-depressive swings did. Who would she be without her moods? Undoubtedly, psychotic behavior can be dangerous and self-destructive. Still, it bothers some patients to put blinkers on and dismiss the inconvenient but vivid perspectives that mood swings impose. However much Woolf felt terrorized by her hellish nightmares of persecution or her ecstatic hallucinations, she valued these unusual experiences as insights. As she wrote in her diary:

> I have a great & astonishing sense . . . . of my own strangeness . . . . Who am I, what am I, & so on: these questions are always floating about in me; & then I bump against some exact fact—a letter, a person, & come to them again with a great sense of freshness. (3: 62-63)

Clarissa experiences the same kind of rhythmic withdrawal and emergence. Having sunk into "the depths of her heart" (281) in empathy for Septimus' suicide, she resurfaces, thrilling at an ordinary sight, the sky above Westminster: "It held, foolish as the idea was, something of her own in it, this country sky, this sky above Westminster . . . . It was new to her" (282-83). Self and world are rhythmically connected and disconnected again and again. The novel ends with a return to her party, her secret joy inside her. Peter momentarily becomes aware of irreducible, inexplicable feelings ("What is this terror? What is this ecstasy?" [296]), but characteristically attributes them to Clarissa's "womanly" magic (an essential feature of <u>his</u> identity theme) and so gains no insight. Even the novel's narration seems to draw our attention away from Clarissa's vision by concluding, "For there she was," as if to undercut the majesty of Peter's adoration with a deliberately subdued declarative sentence, one as unquestionable as it is unremarkable. Like the Westminster sky, Clarissa *is* there, but what makes her so special cannot be shared with anyone else because it cannot be formulized or said "straight out." Language cannot go into that secret, untrammeled wood of self that lies beyond ego. Manic-depressives find no words that can reliably formulate their shifts of mood. One must learn to question all moods and ideas, tolerate chaos, and hope that some wordless unity exists somewhere to embrace all that one is, senseless or sensible.

"'The sane & the insane, side by side': The Object-Relations of Self-Management in *Mrs. Dalloway*" by Thomas C. Caramagno. From *The Flight of the Mind: Virginia Woolf's Art and Manic-Depressive Illness* (1992) by Thomas C. Caramagno. Copyright © 1992 by the Regents of the University of California. Published by the University of California Press. Reprinted with permission of the University of California Press.

Works Cited

Apter, T. E. *Virginia Woolf: A Study of Her Novels*. New York: New York UP, 1979.

Bazin, Nancy Topping. *Virginia Woolf and the Androgynous Vision*. New Brunswick: Rutgers UP, 1973.

Bollas, Christopher. *The Shadow of the Object: Psychoanalysis of the Unthought Known*. New York: Columbia UP, 1987.

Ferguson, Suzanne. "The Face in the Mirror: Authorial Presence in the Multiple Vision of Third-Person Impressionist Narrative." *Criticism* 21 (1979): 230-50.

Goodwin, Frederick K., and Kay Redfield Jamison. *Manic-Depressive Illness*. New York: Oxford UP, 1990.

Haring-Smith, Tori. "Private and Public Consciousness in *Mrs. Dalloway* and *To the Lighthouse*." *Virginia Woolf: Centennial Essays*. Elaine K. Ginsberg and Laura Moss Gottlieb, eds. Troy, New York: Whitson, 1983. 143-67.

Harper, Howard M. *Between Language and Silence: The Novels of Virginia Woolf*. Baton Rouge: Louisiana State UP, 1982.

_____. "Mrs. Woolf and Mrs. Dalloway." *The Classic British Novel.* Ed. Howard M. Harper and Charles Edge. Athens, GA: U of Georgia P, 1972. 220-39.

Henke, Suzette A. "Virginia Woolf's Septimus Smith: An Analysis of 'Paraphrenia' and the Schizophrenic Use of Language." *Literature and Psychology* 31(4) (1985): 13-23.

Kelley, Alice van Buren. *The Novels of Virginia Woolf: Fact and Vision.* Chicago: U of Chicago P, 1973.

Leaska, Mitchell A. *The Novels of Virginia Woolf: From Beginning to End.* New York: John Jay, 1977.

Lyon, George Ella. "Virginia Woolf and the Problem of the Body." *Centennial Essays.* 111-26.

McLaurin, Allen. *Virginia Woolf: The Echoes Enslaved.* Cambridge: UP, 1973.

Naremore, James. *The World Without a Self: Virginia Woolf and the Novel.* New Haven: Yale UP, 1973.

Oltmanns, Thomas F., and Brendan A. Maher. *Delusional Beliefs.* New York: John Wiley and Sons, 1988.

Rosenthal, Michael. *Virginia Woolf.* New York: Columbia UP, 1979.

Schlack, Beverly Ann. "A Freudian Look at Mrs. Dalloway." *Literature and Psychology* 23 (1973): 49-58.

Spilka, Mark. *Virginia Woolf's Quarrel With Grieving.* Lincoln: U of Nebraska P, 1980.

Woolf, Leonard. *Beginning Again: An Autobiography of the Years 1911 to 1918.* New York: Harcourt, 1964.

_____. *The Diary of Virginia Woolf.* Eds. Anne Olivier Bell and Andrew McNeillie. 5 vols. New York: Harcourt, 1976-84.

_____. *The Letters of Virginia Woolf.* Eds. Nigel Nicolson and Joanne Trautmann. 6 vols. New York: Harcourt, 1975-80.

Woolf, Virginia. *"The Moment" and Other Essays.* New York: Harcourt, 1948.

_____. *Moments of Being: Unpublished Autobiographical Writings.* 2nd ed. Ed. Jeanne Schulkind. New York: Harcourt, 1985.

_____. *Mrs. Dalloway.* New York: Harcourt, 1953.

RESOURCES

Chronology of Virginia Woolf's Life_____

1882	On January 25 Virginia Woolf is born at 22 Hyde Park Gate in London, England, the second daughter and third child of Leslie and Julia Stephen.
1895	Woolf's mother, Julia Stephen, dies. Woolf experiences her first breakdown.
1904	Woolf's father, Sir Leslie Stephen, man of letters, dies. In October, Woolf moves with her brothers and sister to 46 Gordon Square, London. Here she and her older sister Vanessa host "Thursday Evenings," a gathering of writers, critics, and artists who will comprise the Bloomsbury Group. Woolf publishes her first review in *The Guardian*.
1905	Woolf accepts a part-time job teaching composition at Morley College.
1906	Woolf travels on holiday to Greece with her sister and two brothers. Upon their return to England, her brother Thoby dies of illness contracted abroad.
1907	Vanessa marries art critic Clive Bell and moves to Fitzroy Square, London, the new site for "Thursday Evenings."
1909	Writer Lytton Strachey proposes marriage. Initially Woolf accepts, but has a change of heart the following day to their shared relief.
1911	Woolf relocates to 38 Brunswick Square, London. Her roommates include her brother Adrian, economist Maynard Keynes, artist Duncan Grant, and writer Leonard Woolf, soon to be her suitor.
1912	Woolf marries Leonard on August 10; they set up residence at 13 Clifford's Inn, a building that dates back to medieval London.
1915	Woolf's first novel, *The Voyage Out*, is published. She experiences a severe depression and is placed temporarily in a nursing home.

1916	Vanessa Bell moves to Charleston, a rural cottage, where artists David Garnett and Duncan Grant share her residence. Woolf and Leonard are frequent visitors.
1917	The Woolfs establish the Hogarth Press. They will publish works by emerging modernists including Katherine Mansfield and T. S. Eliot.
1919	Woolf's second novel, *Night and Day*, is published.
1922	Woolf's third novel, *Jacob's Room*, is published.
1924	Woolf and Leonard establish a new residence at 52 Tavistock Square, London.
1925	Woolf's fourth novel, *Mrs. Dalloway*, is published. Woolf begins an intimate relationship with writer Vita Sackville-West.
1927	Woolf's fifth novel, *To the Lighthouse*, is published.
1928	Woolf's sixth novel, *Orlando*, is published. *To the Lighthouse* receives the Femina-Vie Heureuse prize for literature. At Cambridge University, Woolf delivers two lectures on women and literature, ideas that will find further development in *A Room of One's Own*.
1929	*A Room of One's Own*, Woolf's feminist treatise, is published.
1931	Woolf's seventh novel, *The Waves*, is published.
1933	*Flush: A Biography*, an account of poet Elizabeth Barrett Browning's cocker spaniel, is published.
1937	Woolf's eighth novel, *The Years*, is published.
1938	*Three Guineas*, Woolf's anti-war manifesto, is published.
1939	Woolf and Leonard move to 37 Mecklenburg Square, London.
1941	Woolf drowns herself in the River Ouse on March 28. Her ninth and final novel, *Between the Acts*, is published in July.

Long Fiction

Melymbrosia, wr. 1912, pb. 1982, revised pb. 2002 (early version of *The Voyage Out*;
    Louise DeSalvo, editor)
The Voyage Out, 1915
Night and Day, 1919
Jacob's Room, 1922
Mrs. Dalloway, 1925
To the Lighthouse, 1927
Orlando: A Biography, 1928
The Waves, 1931
Flush: A Biography, 1933
The Years, 1937
Between the Acts, 1941

Short Fiction

Two Stories, 1917 (one by Leonard Woolf)
The Mark on the Wall, 1919
Kew Gardens, 1919
Monday or Tuesday, 1921
A Haunted House, and Other Short Stories, 1943
Mrs. Dalloway's Party, 1973 (Stella McNichol, editor)
The Complete Shorter Fiction of Virginia Woolf, 1985

Nonfiction

The Common Reader: First Series, 1925
A Room of One's Own, 1929
The Common Reader: Second Series, 1932
Three Guineas, 1938
Roger Fry: A Biography, 1940
The Death of the Moth, and Other Essays, 1942
The Moment, and Other Essays, 1947
The Captain's Death Bed, and Other Essays, 1950
A Writer's Diary, 1953
Letters: Virginia Woolf and Lytton Strachey, 1956
Granite and Rainbow, 1958
Contemporary Writers, 1965

Collected Essays, Volumes 1-2, 1966

Collected Essays, Volumes 3-4, 1967

The London Scene: Five Essays, 1975

The Flight of the Mind: The Letters of Virginia Woolf, Vol. I, 1888-1912, 1975 (pb. in U.S. as *The Letters of Virginia Woolf, Vol. I: 1888-1912*, 1975; Nigel Nicolson, editor)

The Question of Things Happening: The Letters of Virginia Woolf, Vol. II, 1912-1922, 1976 (pb. in U.S. as *The Letters of Virginia Woolf, Vol. II: 1912-1922*, 1976; Nigel Nicolson, editor)

Moments of Being, 1976 (Jeanne Schulkind, editor)

Books and Portraits, 1977

A Change of Perspective: The Letters of Virginia Woolf, Vol. III, 1923-1928, 1977 (pb. in U.S. as *The Letters of Virginia Woolf, Vol. III: 1923-1928*, 1978; Nigel Nicolson, editor)

The Diary of Virginia Woolf, 1977-1984 (5 volumes; Anne Olivier Bell, editor)

A Reflection of the Other Person: The Letters of Virginia Woolf, Vol. IV, 1929-1931, 1978 (pb. in U.S. as *The Letters of Virginia Woolf, Vol. IV: 1929-1931*, 1979; Nigel Nicolson, editor)

The Sickle Side of the Moon: The Letters of Virginia Woolf, Vol. V, 1932-1935, 1979 (pb. in U.S. as *The Letters of Virginia Woolf, Vol. V: 1932-1935*, 1979; Nigel Nicolson, editor)

Leave the Letters Til We're Dead: The Letters of Virginia Woolf, Vol. VI, 1936-1941, 1980 (Nigel Nicolson, editor)

The Essays of Virginia Woolf, 1987-1994 (4 volumes)

Carlyle's House, and Other Sketches, 2003 (David Bradshaw, editor)

Bibliography

Allen, James Sloan. "*Mrs. Dalloway* and the Ethics of Civility." *Sewanee Review* 107 (1999): 586-94.

Bagley, Melissa. "Nature and Nation in *Mrs. Dalloway*." *Woolf Studies Annual* 14 (2008): 35-52.

Barnett, Claudia. "*Mrs. Dalloway* and Performance Theory." *English Language Notes* 40.2 (2002): 57-68.

Barrett, Eileen, ed. *Approaches to Teaching Mrs. Dalloway*. New York: MLA, 2009.

Bell, Vereen. "Misreading *Mrs. Dalloway*." *Sewanee Review* 114.1 (Winter 2006): 93-111.

Bloom, Harold, ed. *Major Literary Characters: Clarissa Dalloway*. New York: Chelsea House, 1990.

Briggs, Julia. "'What a Lark! What a Plunge!': *Mrs Dalloway*." *Virginia Woolf: An Inner Life*. Edinburgh, UK: Edinburgh University Press, 2005. 130-59.

Childs, Donald J. "*Mrs. Dalloway*'s Unexpected Guests: Virginia Woolf, T. S. Eliot, and Matthew Arnold." *Modern Language Quarterly* 58 (1997): 62-82.

Collett, Anne. "Sex and the City: T. S. Eliot's and Woolf's Visions of Post-WW1 London." *Virginia Woolf Miscellany* 75 (Spring-Summer 2009): 10-13.

Crater, Theresa L. "Septimus Smith and Charles Watkins: The Phallic Suppression of Masculine Subjectivity." *Journal of Evolutionary Psychology* 21.3-4 (2000): 191-202.

Curd, Patricia Kenig. "Aristotelian Visions of Moral Character in Virginia Woolf's *Mrs. Dalloway*." *English Language Notes* 33.1 (1995): 40-57.

de Gay, Jane. "Literature and Survival: *Jacob's Room* and *Mrs. Dalloway*." *Virginia Woolf's Novels and the Literary Past*. Edinburgh, UK: Edinburgh University Press, 2006. 67-95.

DeMeester, Karen. "Trauma and Recovery in Virginia Woolf's *Mrs. Dalloway*." *Modern Fiction Studies* 44 (1998): 649-73.

Dick, Susan. "Literary Realism in *Mrs. Dalloway, To the Lighthouse, Orlando* and *The Waves*." *The Cambridge Companion to Virginia Woolf*. Eds. Sue Roe and Susan Sellers. New York: Cambridge University Press, 2000. 50-71.

Dodd, Elizabeth. "'On the floor of the mind': Sentence Shape and Rhythm in *Mrs. Dalloway*." *Midwest Quarterly* 36 (1995): 275-88.

Falcetta, Jennie-Rebecca. "Geometries of Time and Space: The Cubist London of *Mrs. Dalloway*." *Woolf Studies Annual* 13 (2007): 111-36.

Froula, Christine. "*Mrs. Dalloway*'s Postwar Elegy: Women, War, and the Art of Mourning." *Virginia Woolf and the Bloomsbury Avant-Garde*. New York: Columbia University Press, 2005. 87-126.

Furman, Yelena. "Translating Dostoevsky, Writing a Novel of One's Own: The Place of 'Stavrogin's Confession' in the Creation of *Mrs. Dalloway*." *Modern Language Review* 104.4 (Oct. 2009): 1082-97.

Garvey, Johanna X. K. "Difference and Continuity: The Voices of *Mrs. Dalloway*." *College English* 53.1 (Jan. 1991): 59-76.

Gualtieri-Reed, Elizabeth J. "*Mrs. Dalloway*: Revising Religion." *Centennial Review* 43 (1999): 205-25.

Hagen, Benjamin D. "A Car, a Plane, and a Tower: Interrogating Public Images in *Mrs. Dalloway*." *Modernism/Modernity* 16.3 (September 2009): 537-51.

Hoff, Molly. "The Midday Topos in *Mrs. Dalloway*." *Twentieth Century Literature* 36 (1990): 449-63.

_____. *Mrs. Dalloway: Invisible Presences*. SC: Clemson University Digital Press, 2009.

Howard, Douglas L. "*Mrs. Dalloway*: Virginia Woolf's Redemptive Cycle." *Literature & Theology* 12.2 (1998): 149-58.

Hussey, Mark. "*Mrs. Dalloway*." *Virginia Woolf: A-Z*. New York: Oxford University Press, 1995. 169-79.

Jones, Gloria G. "Free Indirect Style in *Mrs. Dalloway*." *Postscript* 14 (1997): 69-80.

Joyes, Kaley. "Failed Witnessing in Virginia Woolf's *Mrs. Dalloway*." *Woolf Studies Annual* 14 (2008): 69-90.

Kennard, Jean E. "Power and Sexual Ambiguity: The Dreadnought Hoax, *The Voyage Out*, *Mrs. Dalloway*, and *Orlando*." *Journal of Modern Literature* 20.2 (Winter 1996): 149-64.

Kitsi-Mitakou, Katerina K. "Clarissa Dalloway's Body: Transformation of Christian Concepts of Femininity and Maternity in Virginia Woolf's Mrs. Dalloway." *Gramma: Journal of Theory and Criticism* 1 (1993): 96-104.

Kostkowska, Justyna. "'Scissors and Silks,' 'Flowers and Trees,' and 'Geraniums Ruined by the War': Virginia Woolf's Ecological Critique of Science in *Mrs. Dalloway*." *Women's Studies: An Interdisciplinary Journal* 33.2 (2004): 183-99.

Krouse, Tanya. "Sexual Deviancy in *Mrs. Dalloway*: The Case of Septimus Warren Smith." *Virginia Woolf Miscellany* 70 (Fall 2006): 15-17.

Kuhlken, Pam Fox. "Clarissa and Cléo (En)durée Suicidal Time in Virginia Woolf's *Mrs. Dalloway* and Agnès Varda's *Cléo de 5 à 7*." *Comparative Literature Studies* 45.3 (2008): 341-69.

Lee, Hermione. *Virginia Woolf*. New York: Alfred A. Knopf, 1997.

Lilienfeld, Jane. "'Success in Circuit Lies': Editing the War in *Mrs. Dalloway*." *Woolf Studies Annual* 15 (2009): 113-34.

Lorentzen, Eric G. "Foucault's Normalizing Judgment, Deviancy, and Woolf's *Mrs. Dalloway*." *Virginia Woolf Miscellany* 70 (Fall 2006): 11-12.

McPherson, Karen S. "Speaking Madness: *Mrs. Dalloway*." *Incriminations: Guilty Women/Telling Stories*. Princeton: Princeton University Press, 1994. 130-57.

Matson, Patricia. "The Terror and the Ecstasy: The Textual Politics of Virginia

Woolf's *Mrs. Dalloway.*" *Ambiguous Discourse: Feminist Narratology & British Women Writers.* Ed. Kathy Mezei. Chapel Hill: University of North Carolina Press, 1996. 162-86.

Maze, John. "Mrs. Dalloway: A Questionable Sanity." *Virginia Woolf: Feminism, Creativity, and the Unconscious.* Westport, CT: Greenwood Press, 1997. 61-85.

Mendelson, Edward. "Love: *Mrs. Dalloway.*" *The Things That Matter: What Seven Classic Novels Have to Say About the Stages of Life.* New York: Pantheon, 2006. 160-203.

Mezei, Kathy. "Free Indirect Discourse, Gender, and Authority in *Emma, Howards End,* and *Mrs. Dalloway.*" *Ambiguous Discourse: Feminist Narratology and British Women Writers.* Ed. Kathy Mezei. Chapel Hill: University of North Carolina Press, 1996. 66-92.

Monte, Steven. "Ancients and Moderns in *Mrs. Dalloway.*" *Modern Language Quarterly* 61 (2000): 587-616.

Peele, Thomas. "Queering *Mrs. Dalloway.*" *Literature and Homosexuality.* Ed. Michael J. Meyer. Amsterdam: Rodopi, 2000. 205-21.

Primamore, Elizabeth. "A Don, Virginia Woolf, the Masses, and the Case of Miss Kilman." *Literature Interpretation Theory* 9 (1998): 121-37.

Reed, Donna K. "Merging Voices: *Mrs. Dalloway* and *No Place on Earth.*" *Comparative Literature* 47.2 (1995): 118-35.

Rosenfeld, Natania. "Links into Fences: The Subtext of Class Division in *Mrs. Dalloway.*" *Literature Interpretation Theory* 9 (1998): 139-60.

Schiff, James. "Rewriting *Mrs. Dalloway*: Homage, Sexual Identity, and the Single-Day Novel by Cunningham, Lippincott, and Lanchester." *Critique* 45.4 (Summer 2004): 363-82.

Schröder, Leena Kore. "*Mrs. Dalloway* and the Female Vagrant." *Essays in Criticism* 45 (1995): 324-46.

_____. "The Politics of Englishness in *Mrs. Dalloway.*" *English Review* 6.3 (1996): 28-31.

Shaffer, Brian W. "Civilization in Bloomsbury: Woolf's *Mrs. Dalloway* and Bell's 'Theory of Civilization.'" *Journal of Modern Literature* 19 (1994): 73-87.

Simpson, Kathryn. "Queering the Market: 'Mrs Dalloway in Bond Street', *Mrs Dalloway,* and 'The Hours'." *Gifts, Markets, and Economies of Desire in Virginia Woolf.* New York: Palgrave, 2010.

Tate, Trudi. "*Mrs. Dalloway* and the Armenian Question." *Textual Practice* 8 (1994): 467-86.

Taylor, Nancy. "Erasure of Definition: Androgyny in *Mrs. Dalloway.*" *Women's Studies* 18 (1991): 367-77.

Usui, Masami. "The Female Victims of the War in *Mrs. Dalloway.*" *Virginia Woolf and War: Fiction, Reality, and Myth.* Ed. Mark Hussey. Syracuse, NY: Syracuse University Press, 1991: 151-63.

Wachman, Gay. "Pink Icing and a Narrow Bed: *Mrs. Dalloway* and Lesbian History." *Virginia Woolf and the Arts: Selected Papers from the Sixth Annual Conference on Virginia Woolf*. New York: Pace University Press, 1997. 344-50.

Webb, Caroline. "Life after Death: The Allegorical Progress of *Mrs. Dalloway*." *Modern Fiction Studies* 40 (1994): 279-98.

Wicke, Jennifer. "Mrs. Dalloway Goes to Market: Woolf, Keynes, and Modern Markets." *Novel* 28 (1994): 6-23.

Wood, Andelys. "Walking the Web in the Lost London of *Mrs. Dalloway*." *Mosaic* 36.2 (2003): 19-32.

CRITICAL INSIGHTS

About the Editor

Dorothy Dodge Robbins earned degrees in English at the University of Nebraska-Lincoln (Ph.D.), the University of South Dakota (M.A.), and Oklahoma City University (B.A.). Additionally, she holds the M.A. in Communication from the University of Oklahoma. Robbins is an associate professor and the Charlotte Lewis Endowed Professor of English at Louisiana Tech University. She teaches both undergraduate and graduate courses in twentieth-century British literature, including seminars on Virginia Woolf's novels and Woolf and the Bloomsbury Group, the latter offered in the Bloomsbury district of London in conjunction with the Tech-London Study Abroad Program. At Tech she has received the F. Jay Taylor Undergraduate Teaching Award and the Virgil Orr Undergraduate Junior Faculty Award. Her research interests include modernism, British and American; regional literatures, midwestern and southern; and onomastics, the study of names and naming practices. Her essays on Virginia Woolf have appeared in *Names, A Journal of Onomastics*, *The Centennial Review*, *The Southern Gazette*, and *Masterplots*. Additional articles and reviews have appeared in *Critique*, *The Southern Quarterly*, *The Midwest Quarterly*, and *Ecumenica*, among others. Robbins has written extensively for various Salem Press publications. With husband and colleague Ken Robbins, she is coeditor of four literary anthologies: *Christmas Stories from Louisiana* (University Press of Mississippi, 2003), *Christmas on the Great Plains* (University Press of Iowa, 2004), *Christmas Stories from Georgia* (University Press of Mississippi, 2005) and *Christmas Stories from Ohio* (Kent State University Press, 2010), recipient of the *USA Book News* Best Book Award 2010 for Literature Anthology. She lives with her husband and four cats in the piney hills of Ruston, Louisiana.

About *The Paris Review*

The Paris Review is America's preeminent literary quarterly, dedicated to discovering and publishing the best new voices in fiction, nonfiction, and poetry. The magazine was founded in Paris in 1953 by the young American writers Peter Matthiessen and Doc Humes, and edited there and in New York for its first fifty years by George Plimpton. Over the decades, the *Review* has introduced readers to the earliest writings of Jack Kerouac, Philip Roth, T. C. Boyle, V. S. Naipaul, Ha Jin, Ann Patchett, Jay McInerney, Mona Simpson, and Edward P. Jones, and published numerous now-classic works, including Roth's *Goodbye, Columbus*, Donald Barthelme's *Alice*, Jim Carroll's *Basketball Diaries*, and selections from Samuel Beckett's *Molloy* (his first publication in English). The first chapter of Jeffrey Eugenides's *The Virgin Suicides* appeared in the *Review*'s pages, as have stories by Rick Moody, David Foster Wallace, Denis Johnson, Jim Crace, Lorrie Moore, and Jeanette Winterson.

The Paris Review's renowned Writers at Work series of interviews, whose early installments include legendary conversations with E. M. Forster, William Faulkner, and Ernest Hemingway, is one of the landmarks of world literature. The interviews received a George Polk Award and were nominated for a Pulitzer Prize. Among the more than three hundred interviewees are Robert Frost, Marianne Moore, W. H. Auden, Elizabeth Bishop, Susan Sontag, and Toni Morrison. Recent issues feature conversations with Jonathan Franzen, Norman Rush, Louise Erdrich, Joan Didion, Norman Mailer, R. Crumb, Michel Houellebecq, Marilynne Robinson, David Mitchell, Annie Proulx, and Gay Talese. In November 2009, Picador published the final volume of a four-volume series of anthologies of *Paris Review* interviews. *The New York Times* called the Writers at Work series "the most remarkable and extensive interviewing project we possess."

The Paris Review is edited by Lorin Stein, who was named to the post in 2010. The editorial team has published fiction by Lydia Davis, André Aciman, Sam Lipsyte, Damon Galgut, Mohsin Hamid, Uzodinma Iweala, James Lasdun, Padgett Powell, Richard Price, and Sam Shepard. Recent poetry selections include work by Frederick Seidel, Carol Muske-Dukes, John Ashbery, Kay Ryan, Mary Jo Bang, Sharon Olds, Charles Wright, and Mary Karr. Writing published in the magazine has been anthologized in *Best American Short Stories* (2006, 2007, and 2008), *Best American Poetry*, *Best Creative Non-Fiction*, the Pushcart Prize anthology, and *O. Henry Prize Stories*.

The magazine presents three annual awards. The Hadada Award for lifelong contribution to literature has recently been given to Joan Didion, Norman Mailer, Peter Matthiessen, John Ashbery, and, in 2010, Philip Roth. The Plimpton Prize for Fiction, awarded to a debut or emerging writer brought to national attention in the pages of *The Paris Review*, was presented in 2007 to Benjamin Percy, to Jesse Ball in 2008, and to Alistair Morgan in 2009. In 2011, the magazine inaugurated the Terry Southern Prize for Humor.

The Paris Review was a finalist for the 2008 and 2009 National Magazine Awards in fiction and won the 2007 National Magazine Award in photojournalism. *The Los Angeles Times* recently called *The Paris Review* "an American treasure with true international reach," and *The New York Times* designated it "a thing of sober beauty."

Since 1999 *The Paris Review* has been published by The Paris Review Foundation, Inc., a not-for-profit 501(c)(3) organization.

The Paris Review is available in digital form to libraries worldwide in selected academic databases exclusively from EBSCO Publishing. Libraries can contact EBSCO at 1-800-653-2726 for details. For more information on *The Paris Review* or to subscribe, please visit: www.theparisreview.org.

Contributors

Dorothy Dodge Robbins is an Associate Professor and the Charlotte Lewis Endowed Professor of English at Louisiana Tech University, where she teaches undergraduate and graduate courses in twentieth-century British literature, including seminars on Virginia Woolf's novels and Woolf and the Bloomsbury Group. Her essays on Woolf have appeared in *Names, A Journal of Onomastics*; *The Centennial Review, The Southern Gazette*, and *Masterplots*. With her husband and colleague Ken Robbins she is coeditor of four literary anthologies, most recently *Christmas Stories from Ohio* (2010).

Thomas C. Caramagno is Associate Professor of English at Folsom Lake College, California. He received his Ph.D. in English from the University of California, Los Angeles, and his M.A. in clinical psychology from the Professional School of Psychology in Sacramento. He is the author of *The Flight of the Mind: Virginia Woolf's Art and Manic-Depressive Illness* (1992), *Irreconcilable Differences? Intellectual Stalemate in the Gay Rights Debate* (2002), and a novel, *Visible Love* (2002).

Thessaly La Force lives in New York City. She is an editor at *The Paris Review*.

Justyna Kostkowska is Professor of English at Middle Tennessee State University, Murfreesboro, and the author of *Virginia Woolf's Experiment in Genre and Politics 1926-1931: Visioning and Versioning "The Waves"* (Edwin Mellen Press, 2005). She teaches and publishes in modern British literature and twentieth-century women writers, especially Virginia Woolf, Jeanette Winterson, and Wisława Szymborska. In cooperation with W. D. and Kathleen Snodgrass, she has published numerous translations of contemporary Polish poets. Her translations of the poems of the Nobel Prize-winning Polish poet Szymborska have appeared in *The New Yorker, Mid-American Review, Pleiades*, and *The American Poetry Review*.

Vereen M. Bell is Professor of English and Associate Chair at Vanderbilt University, where he teaches modern British and American literature. He has published books on Robert Lowell, Cormac McCarthy, and W. B. Yeats and articles on Yeats, McCarthy, Virginia Woolf, T. S. Eliot, E. M. Forster, and others. He is currently at work on a project that examines the attitudes of British writers and intellectuals toward democracy in the 1920s and 1930s.

Yelena Furman is a Lecturer in the Humanities Language Learning Program at the University of California, Irvine, and in the Slavic Department at the University of California, Los Angeles. Her areas of interest include contemporary Russian literature, feminist theory, and comparative literature. She has published on Virginia Woolf's collaboration with S. S. Koteliansky on the translation of Dostoevsky's *Stavrogin's Confession*, as well as on writing the body in Russian literature and film. Her current research focuses on Russian-American fiction.

Pam Fox Kuhlken, Ph.D., teaches the Bible as literature and world literature in the

Department of English and world religions and religion and film in the Department of Religious Studies at San Diego State University. She has edited literary and religious manuscripts for Eerdmans, Doubleday, and Oxford University Press. Her essays have appeared in *Modernism/Modernity* and *Comparative Literature*. She is the author of *A Poetics of Time* (Northwestern University Press, forthcoming), a phenomenological treatment of time and eternity in four modern stream-of-consciousness novels, including *Mrs. Dalloway* and *Ulysses*, and *God's Wife* (Rowman & Littlefield, forthcoming), an exploration of the *Shekinah* or goddess in monotheism.

Molly Hoff is the author of *Virginia Woolf's "Mrs. Dalloway": Invisible Presences* (Clemson University Press, 2009), a work that examines cultural, historical, literary, and biographical references in Woolf's novel. She has published broadly in Woolf studies with articles appearing in *Twentieth Century Literature*, *Woolf Studies Annual*, *Explicator*, and *Virginia Woolf Miscellany*. She resides in San Antonio, Texas.

Lorie Watkins Fulton is Assistant Professor of English at William Carey University in Hattiesburg, Mississippi. Her research interests include southern literature, African American literature, and American modernism. She is the author of *William Faulkner, Gavin Stevens, and the Cavalier Myth* and has published essays in *The Faulkner Journal*, *The Hemingway Review*, *African American Review*, *The Mississippi Quarterly*, *The Southern Literary Journal*, and *Modern Philology*, among others.

Susan Bennett Smith received her Ph.D. from Stanford University. Her dissertation, "Virginia Woolf and Death: A Feminist Cultural History, 1880-1940," examines Woolf's ideas about death in the context of contemporary attitudes and practices.

Kathryn Stelmach Artuso received her Ph.D. from the University of California, Los Angeles. She is Assistant Professor of English at Westmont College in Santa Barbara, California. Her research traces the transatlantic and diasporic intersections among the Irish, Harlem, and Southern Renaissances. Her articles have appeared in *Studies in the Novel*, *Celtic Studies Association of North America Yearbook*, *Comitatus*, and *Christianity and Literature*.

Christopher Herbert (Ph.D. Yale University) is Chester D. Tripp Professor in the Humanities at Northwestern University. His research focuses chiefly on the literary, cultural, and intellectual history of England in the nineteenth century. He is the author of *Trollope and Comic Pleasure* (1987), *Culture and Anomie: Ethnographic Imagination in the Nineteenth Century* (1991), and *Victorian Relativity: Radical Thought and Scientific Discovery* (2001), as well as articles on Charles Dickens, George Eliot, Anthony Trollope, Henry Mayhew, Bram Stoker, and Virginia Woolf. His most recent publication is *War of No Pity: The Indian Mutiny and Victorian Trauma* (2009).

George A. Panichas (1930-2010) is best known for his stewardship of *Modern Age*; from 1984 through 2004 he served as the journal's editor. Panichas was Professor of English and comparative literature at the University of Maryland in College Park for thirty years, retiring in 1992. He penned twenty-five books, including *Growing Wings to Overcome Gravity* (1998), *The Critical Legacy of Irving Babbitt* (1999),

Dostoevsky's Spiritual Art (2004), and *Joseph Conrad: His Moral Vision* (2005). As a scholar and critic, Panichas was interested in the relationship between Western literature and other branches of the humanities.

Nathalia Wright (1913-2004) was a native of Athens, Georgia. She earned her B.A. from Maryville College (1933) and her M.A. (1938) and Ph.D. (1949) from Yale University. From 1949 through 1982, she taught at the University of Tennessee. A distinguished scholar in the field of letters, she was named a Guggenheim Fellow and an American Association of University Women Fellow. "*Mrs. Dalloway*: A Study in Composition" (1944) was among her earliest scholarship. Additional publications include *Melville's Use of the Bible* (1949), *American Novelists in Italy* (1965), and a collection of poetry, *Other Rooms, Other Voices* (1992).

Teresa Prudente is a Research Fellow in English and comparative literature at the University of Turin, Italy. She is the author of *A Specially Tender Piece of Time: Virginia Woolf and the Experience of Time* (2009), an honorable mention for the 2010 ESSE Book Award, and the coeditor, with Dr. Federico Sabatini, of *Cinematic Strategies in Twentieth-Century Narratives and Beyond* (2011). She is at work on a monograph on Woolf and Joyce, tentatively titled *Speaking from the Void: Modernism and Impersonality*.

Jacob Littleton earned his doctorate in English from the University of California, Los Angeles. His research interests include British and Irish literature. In addition to his Woolf scholarship, Littleton has published on English Renaissance drama and Samuel Richardson's *Pamela*.

Acknowledgments _____

"The *Paris Review* Perspective" by Thessaly La Force. Copyright © 2012 by Thessaly La Force. Special appreciation goes to Christopher Cox, Nathaniel Rich, and David Wallace-Wells, editors at *The Paris Review.*

"The Pseudo-Homeric World of Mrs. Dalloway" by Molly Hoff. From *Twentieth Century Literature* 45.2 (Summer 1999): 186-209. Copyright © 1999 by *Twentieth Century Literature*. Reprinted with permission of *Twentieth Century Literature.*

"A Direction of One's Own": Alienation in *Mrs. Dalloway* and *Sula*" by Lorie Watkins Fulton. From *African American Review* 40.1 (Spring 2006): 67-77. Copyright © 2006 by *African American Review*. Reprinted with permission of *African American Review.*

"Reinventing Grief Work: Virginia Woolf's Feminist Representations of Mourning in *Mrs. Dalloway* and *To the Lighthouse*" by Susan Bennett Smith. From *Twentieth Century Literature* 41.4 (Winter 1995): 310-327. Copyright © 1995 by *Twentieth Century Literature*. Reprinted with permission of *Twentieth Century Literature.*

"From Text to Tableau: Ekphrastic Enchantment in *Mrs. Dalloway* and *To the Lighthouse*" by Kathryn Stelmach Artuso. From *Studies in the Novel* 38.3 (Fall 2006): 304-326. Copyright © 2006 by the University of North Texas. Reprinted with permission of the University of North Texas.

"Mrs. Dalloway, the Dictator, and the Relativity Paradox" by Christopher Herbert. From *NOVEL: A Forum on Fiction* 35.1 (Autumn 2001): 104-124. Copyright © 2001 by Duke University Press. All rights reserved. Reprinted with permission of Duke University Press.

"Virginia Woolf's *Mrs. Dalloway*: 'A Well of Tears'" by George A. Panichas. From *Modern Age* 46.3 (Summer 2004): 234-245. Copyright © 2004 by Intercollegiate Studies Institute. Reprinted with permission of Intercollegiate Studies Institute.

"*Mrs. Dalloway*: A Study in Composition" by Nathalia Wright. From *College English* 5.7 (April 1944): 351-358. Copyright © 1944 by the National Council of Teachers of English. Reprinted with permission of the National Council of Teachers of English.

"A-linear Time and Stream of Consciousness" by Teresa Prudente. From *A Specially Tender Piece of Eternity: Virginia Woolf and the Experience of Time* (2009) by Teresa Prudente. Copyright © 2009 by Lexington Books. Reprinted with permission of Lexington Books.

"*Mrs. Dalloway*: Portrait of the Artist as a Middle-Aged Woman" by Jacob Littleton. From *Twentieth Century Literature* 41.1 (Spring 1995): 36-53. Copyright © 1995 by *Twentieth Century Literature*. Reprinted with permission of *Twentieth Century Literature.*

"'The sane & the insane, side by side': The Object-Relations of Self-Management in *Mrs. Dalloway*" by Thomas C. Caramagno. From *The Flight of the Mind: Virginia Woolf's Art and Manic-Depressive Illness* (1992) by Thomas C. Caramagno. Copyright © 1992 by the Regents of the University of California. Published by the University of California Press. Reprinted with permission of the University of California Press.

Index

Themes and motifs; alienation, 8, 39, 125, 135, 174, 222, 239, 274, 297, 303-304, 311; androgyny, 86; appetite, 101; art, 37, 68, 158, 166, 170-171, 179, 189, 274, 291, 298, 301, 304; color, 170, 195, 256, 260; death, 4, 56, 79, 106, 110, 128, 139, 144, 150, 158, 174, 188, 245, 252, 271, 294, 296, 305; doubles, 4, 7, 24, 47, 61-62, 106, 128, 148, 152, 159, 192, 234, 249, 262, 295, 306, 314; friendhip, 40, 133, 140, 151, 295, 301; friendship, 132, 137, 142; gender roles, 19-20, 47, 71, 85-86, 144-145, 147, 154, 157, 169, 186, 193, 293, 302, 309, 320, 329; grief and mourning, 55, 144-145, 147, 149, 151, 153, 155, 157, 159, 161, 163, 204, 228, 232, 321, 323; homosexuality, 8, 17, 49-50, 56, 64, 88, 152, 324; insanity, 10, 49, 66, 144, 147, 235, 266, 269, 275, 314, 321; juxtaposition, 6, 9, 78, 203, 273, 304; love, 64, 81, 182, 186, 293, 304, 320; marriage and divorce, 45, 98, 110, 135, 151, 318; memory, 3, 23, 63, 82, 126, 152, 158, 167, 170, 183, 191, 204, 251, 255, 294, 297; social class, 44, 79, 155, 304, 306, 308; sound, 35-36, 263, 268, 322; suicide, 4, 10, 24, 56, 66, 68, 130, 203, 244, 249, 252, 314, 330; time, 6, 35, 84-85, 98, 126, 140, 159, 168, 178, 185, 187, 233, 254, 261, 263, 270, 275; unity, 19, 29, 31, 34, 61, 83, 175, 179, 185, 190, 214, 294, 296, 302, 309, 314; violence, 202, 205; vision and perception, 34, 36, 39, 68, 84, 109, 167, 177, 183, 185, 193, 209, 212, 265-266, 269, 276, 317, 331; war, 66, 128, 130, 189, 231; water, 7-8, 53, 102, 106, 110, 113, 159, 180

Three Guineas (Woolf), 205, 209

Time, 6, 35, 84-85, 98, 126, 140, 159, 168, 178, 185, 187, 233, 254, 261, 263, 270, 275

To the Lighthouse (Woolf), 3, 19, 179, 264; and art, 274; form and style, 188, 278; grief and mourning in, 144; writing of, 154

Ulysses (Joyce), 53, 77, 80-81, 95

Unity, 19, 29, 31, 34, 61, 83, 175, 179, 185, 190, 214, 294, 296, 302, 309, 314

Vaughan, Clarissa (*The Hours*), 59, 64; and artistry, 69

Violence, 202, 205

Vision and perception, 34, 36, 39, 68, 84, 109, 167, 177, 183, 185, 193, 209, 212, 265-266, 269, 276, 317, 331

Voyage Out, The (Woolf), 4-5, 18, 171

Walsh, Peter (*Mrs. Dalloway*), 9, 103, 205, 316-317; as a dictator, 308; and Clarissa Dalloway, 23, 45, 64, 248, 330; as Odysseus, 100, 104, 106-107, 109, 115

Warren Smith, Rezia (*Mrs. Dalloway*), 10, 235, 243

Warren Smith, Septimus (*Mrs. Dalloway*), 8, 24, 66, 128, 174, 203; and Clarissa Dalloway, 61-62, 249, 262, 306; in earlier works, 4; and Evans, 50, 109, 151-152, 237; insanity, 148, 150, 233, 235, 243, 266, 268, 274, 309, 314, 321, 324; and social class, 49; and unity, 31; and World War I, 49, 101, 235